si numero:y despues q̃ los veyā llegar fuyan a no aguardar padre a hijo: y estance por que nin
guno se aya hecho mal antes a todo cabo adōde yo aya estado y podido
do de todo loque tenia asi paño como otras cosas muchas si recebir por
so asi temerosos sin remedio: verdad es que despues que aseguran y pierdē este miedo ellos son
tanto si engaño y tan liberales delo q̃ tienē que no locreerian sino el q̃lo viese:ellos de cosa que
tēgan pidiēdogela iamas dizē deno antes cōuidan lapsona cō ello y muestran tāto amor que
darian los corazones y quierē sea cosa deualor quien sea depoco precio luego por qual quiē
ra cosica de qual quiera manera que sea q̃ sele deporello sea cōtentos:yo defendi q̃ noseles dē
sen cosas tan siuiles como pedazos de escudillas rotas y pedazos de vidrio roto y cabos dagu
getas:haū que quā do ellos esto podia llegar los parecia hauer lamedor ioya del mūdo. que
se acerto hauer vn marinero por vna agugeta de oro depesode dos castellanos y medio:yotros
de otras cosas q̃ muy marcs valiā mucho mas ya por blācas nueuas dauan por ellas todo
quanto tenian haū que fueē dos ni tres castellanos de oro o vna arzoua o dos de algodō fila
do fasta los pedazos delos arcos rotós delas pipas tomauan ydauan loq̃ tenian como besti
as asi que me parecio mal:yo lo defēdi ydaua yo graciosas mil cosas buenas q̃ yo leuaua por
que tomen amor y allēda desto se farā cristianos quē seclinan al amor eceruicio de sus altezas
y de toda la naciō castellana: e procurā de aiūtar de nos dar delas cosas que tenē en abundā
cia que nos sō necessarias y no conocian niguna seta ni idolatria saluo que todos creen q̃ las
fuercas yelbiē es enilcielo y creian muy firme que yo cōstosnauios ygenteuenia del cielo yental
catamiento me recebian entodo cabo despues dehauer poido elmiedo y esto no procede porq̃
sean ignorantes saluo demuy sotil igenio y ōbres que nauegan todas aquellas mares que es
marauilla labuena cuenta quellos dan de todo saluo porquenūca vierō gēte vestida nisemeian
tes nauios yluego que legue alas sias ēla primera isla q̃ halle tome pforza algunos dellos pa
ra que deprēdiesen yme diese noticia delo que auia enaquellas partes casi fue que luego ētendirō
y nos aellos quando por lengua oseñas:yestos ban aprouechado mucho oy enbia los traigo
q̃ siēpre estā deproposito q̃ vēgo del cielo por mucha cōuersasiō q̃ ayan hauido cōmigo y estos
eran los primeros apronunciarlo adonde yo llegaua y los otros andauan corriendo decasa ē
casa:yalas villas cercanas cō bozes altas venit :venit auer lagente del cielo asi todos hōbres
como mugers despues dehauer elcorazō seguro de nos venia q̃ nō cadauā grande nipequeño
ytodos trayaan algu decomer ydebeuer quedaūan cō vn amor marauilloso ellos tienē todas
las yslas muy muchas canoas amanera defustes dereino dellas maiores dellas menores yal
gunas :ymuchas sō mayores que bña fusta dediez cochō bācos :nosō tan auchas porque sō
dehun solo madero mas buna fusta notern̄a tō ellas alremo porque van queno es cosa decre
er y cō estas nauegan todas aquellas islas q̃ sō inunerables:ytraté sus mecaderias:alguas
destas canoas he visto cō lxx ylxxx ōbres enella y cada vno cō su remo ēntodas estas islas no
vide mucha diuersidad dela fechura dela gente ni en las costumbres ni enla lengua:saluo que
todos se entienden q̃ es cosa muy sigular para lo que espero q̃ determinaran sus altezas para la
cōuersaciō dellos de nuestra santa fe ala qual sō muydispnestos :ya dire como yohauia andado
c.vii leguas porla costa dela mar por laderecha liña ē sidcte aoriente por la isla iuana segū el
qual camino puedo desir que esta isla ēmaior que inglaterra yescocia iuntas por que allēde des
tas c vii.leguas me queda dela parte deponiente dos prouinias que yo nōbe andado:lavna de
las q̃les llaman auau:adōde nasē lagēte cōcola las q̃les prouinias nopueden tener enlōgura
menos de.l.o lx.leguas segun puede entender destos idios qu yo traigo los q̃les saben todo s
las yslas esta otra española ercierco tiene mas que la españa toda desde colunya por costa de
mar fasta fuēte rauia en uiscaya pues en vna quadra andoue clxxviii grandos leguas por rec
ta linia de occidenta oriente este es para deficar:e es para nunca dexar enla qual puesto
nas tenga tomada possessiō por sus altezas ytodas sean mas abastadas delo querio
todas las tengo por sus altezas que dellas pudiesen disponer así como delos reinos

This book is dedicated to all those,
past or present, whose writings or researches
have taught me practically all
I know about Columbus.

COLUMBUS

The story of Don Cristóbal Colón

Admiral of the Ocean

and his four voyages westward to the Indies

according to contemporary sources

retold and illustrated by

Björn Landström

ALLEN & UNWIN

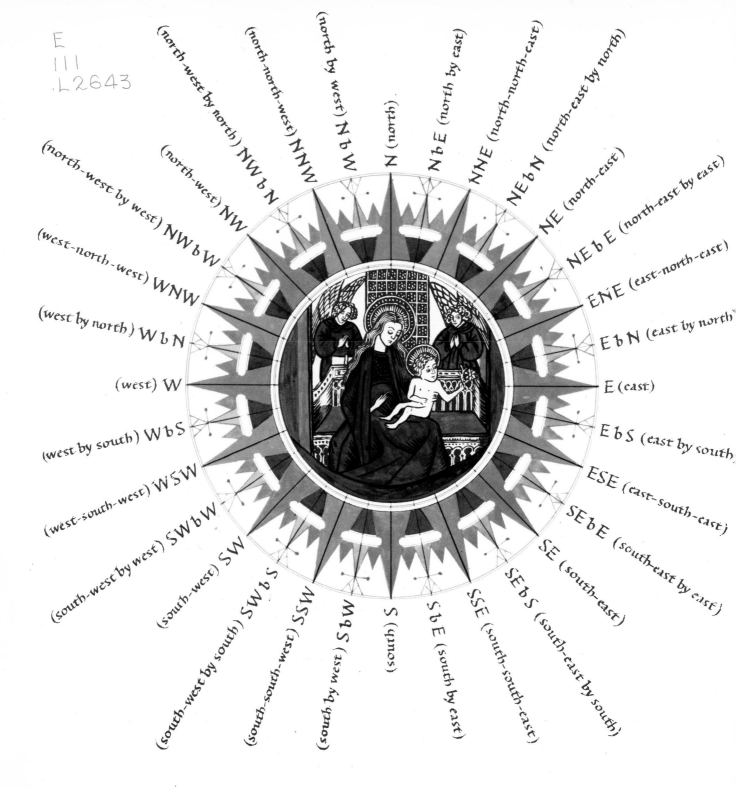

(north) N
(north by west) N b W
(north-north-west) NNW
(north-west by north) NW b N
(north-west) NW
(north-west by west) NW b W
(west-north-west) WNW
(west by north) W b N
(west) W
(west by south) W b S
(west-south-west) WSW
(south-west by west) SW b W
(south-west) SW
(south-west by south) SW b S
(south-south-west) SSW
(south by west) S b W
(south) S
(south by east) S b E
(south-south-east) SSE
(south-east by south) SE b S
(south-east) SE
(south-east by east) SE b E
(east-south-east) ESE
(east by south) E b S
(east) E
(east by north) E b N
(east-north-east) ENE
(north-east by east) NE b E
(north-east) NE
(north-east by north) NE b N
(north-north-east) NNE
(north by east) N b E

Spanish weights, measures, and money in the reign of Ferdinand and Isabella

1 Spanish mile = 8 stadia = 1,000 double paces = 1,619 yards

4 Spanish miles = 1 league = 6,476 yards = 3.2 nautical miles

1 Arabian mile = 2,363 yards

1 tonelada of wine = 2 bottes = 60 arrobas = 290 U.S. gallons

1 quintal = 4 arrobas = 101 pounds

Currency consisted of gold coins, measured by weight. One mark (Sp. *marco*) contained 230 grams of gold

1 excellente = 1/25 mark = 870 maravedis = 9.1 grams

1 castellano = 1/50 mark = 435 maravedis = 4.55 grams

1 ducat = 1/65 mark = 375 maravedis = 3.48 grams

Maravedis were no longer coined, but the word remained in use as a unit of value, and there was a small copper coin called a blanca, equivalent to half a maravedi.

Contents

Endpapers: a facsimile of the first printing of Columbus' letter about his discovery, printed at Barcelona in 1493.
From the unique copy in the New York Public Library.

Preface

The texts on which this book is based are drawn almost exclusively from the numerous and very full sources which deal with the life and voyages of Christopher Columbus. Many of the original letters and documents are extant; others are contemporary or near-contemporary copies, in manuscript or print. Facsimile reproductions of these records are now quite easily available, and they have been translated, with full commentaries, into most European languages. I have no idea how many books and papers have been written about Columbus and the problems associated with him, but the number must run into thousands. My bibliography contains only the most important of them, together with other material which I have found helpful. I will often be quoting the earliest sources, and I would like to mention the most important ones here.

The essential primary source is *El Libro de la Primera Navegación*. This is the journal Columbus kept on his first voyage, as retold, and partly copied verbatim, by Bishop Bartolomé de las Casas, who possessed a copy of the original. He also wrote a description of Columbus' third voyage; this is an abridgment of the original journal for that journey, and his manuscript is still extant. Las Casas probably sailed to Española in 1502; there he became the leading—perhaps the only—champion of the rights of the native inhabitants. Between 1527 and 1561, he wrote his *Historia de las Indias*, which includes also material from Columbus' journals.

Columbus' second son, Fernando, wrote a biography of his father, probably between 1537 and 1539. He too had copies of the journals, but in addition he actually accompanied his father on the fourth voyage, and his book is therefore one of our most valuable sources. The original Spanish text has disappeared (it could not be printed in Spain for political reasons), but an Italian translation was printed in Venice in 1571. Its title, a very long one, can be found in the bibliography.

At least thirty-two letters written by Columbus are extant, but those which deal with the voyages are known to us only from contemporary copies and reprints. A letter that Columbus wrote to Luis de Santángel about the first voyage was in print within a month of his return to Spain, and its contents gradually came to be known all over Europe. Concerning the third voyage, we have Las Casas' copy of Columbus' letter to Ferdinand and Isa-

bella, as well as several contemporary copies of his letter to Doña Juana de Torres. From the fourth voyage we have the *Lettera rarissima*. It was dispatched from Jamaica in 1503, and an Italian version was printed in 1505. On returning from his third voyage, Columbus had at least four copies made of each document which concerned his titles, privileges, and other royal concessions; these copies are still in existence. From about the same date we have the *Libro de las Profecías*, in the original manuscript. We also have a transcript of Toscanelli's letter that Columbus himself wrote on the last pages of his volume of Aeneas Sylvius' *Historia rerum ubique gestarum;* and the copious notes that he made in the back of his volume of Pierre d'Ailly's *Imago Mundi* do much to help us understand his ideas about geography.

Andrés Bernáldez, the chronicler, knew Columbus personally, and when he was writing Chapters 123 to 131 of his *Historia de los Reyes Católicos* he had access to the journal and other papers dealing with the second voyage. Dr. Diego Alvares Chanca, who sailed on the second voyage, wrote a letter describing it to the Council of Seville in 1494; a mid-16th-century copy of this letter is extant. Michele de Cuneo, a friend of Columbus, also described the second voyage in a letter to a compatriot, Hieronymo Annari of Savona, in 1495, and we have a copy of this letter made in 1511. For the fourth voyage, the main sources, apart from those already mentioned, are the original list of Diego de Porras' crew, and a copy of Diego Mendez' will.

There is only one living scholar whose name I shall mention, and his work has been of inestimable value in our knowledge of Columbus, and in my own researches; and that is Professor Samuel Eliot Morison of Harvard University. He has made voyages of his own in the Caribbean, and these have enabled him to make a convincing reconstruction of Columbus' passages through the islands; he has identified nearly all the anchorages and ports of call. I have been able to check some of his conclusions during my own cruises; where I have not been able to check them in person, I have used Professor Morison's findings as a guide throughout this book.

The illustrations in this book are taken chiefly from sketches made on cruises to Spain and the West Indies, and on visits to museums. I have also included a number of contemporary, or near-contemporary, woodcuts and maps to show how Columbus' discoveries were made known to the world at large. The three portraits of Columbus are not only the oldest we know but also agree most closely with the descriptions we have of him. Where the illustrations are reproductions or copies, the originals are enumerated in the Sources of Illustrations on page 201.

I have been collecting material on Columbus for fifteen years, and I am only too well aware that I have forgotten the names of many whose advice and stimulating discussion have helped me. I hope that this rather formal expression of gratitude may reach them. Of the names I have not forgotten, the foremost is Rear Admiral Julio F. Guillén y Tato, the director of the Museo Naval in Madrid, who has been of invaluable assistance to me for many years; among other things, he has placed at my disposal the material for his researches into Juan de la Cosa's World Map of 1500. Alexander O. Vietor, the curator of maps at Yale Univesity, has made it possible for me to study Martellus' World Map of 1490 in close detail, and he has had the great kindness to let me have a large number of photographs. Don José de la Peña, the director of the Archivo de las Indias in Seville, has helped me on several occasions with advice and material. I have had many valuable discussions with Dr. R. C. Anderson of Fordingbridge, and with Captain José M Martínez-Hidalgo of Barcelona about the details of Columbus' flagship, the *Santa María,* and they have both allowed me to study their drawings and reconstructions. Edmond Mangones of Port-au-Prince has presented me with a unique collection of photographs of pre-Columbian art, Dr. Nils Ambolt of Djursholm has given me valuable information about compass errors during the 16th century, and Gunnar Pipping of the Saltsjöbaden Observatory, in this country, has greatly increased my knowledge of medieval astronomy. H. W. Stubbs of Exeter University has most carefully checked and revised this translation of the original Swedish text. To each of these gentlemen, my wholehearted thanks.

And finally, a word of thanks to my ever optimistic publisher, Adam Helms, and to the producer of this book, Bengt Stenström, both of whom have given me so much encouragement in so many ways for so many years.

Saltsjöbaden, Sweden, September, 1966
Björn Landström

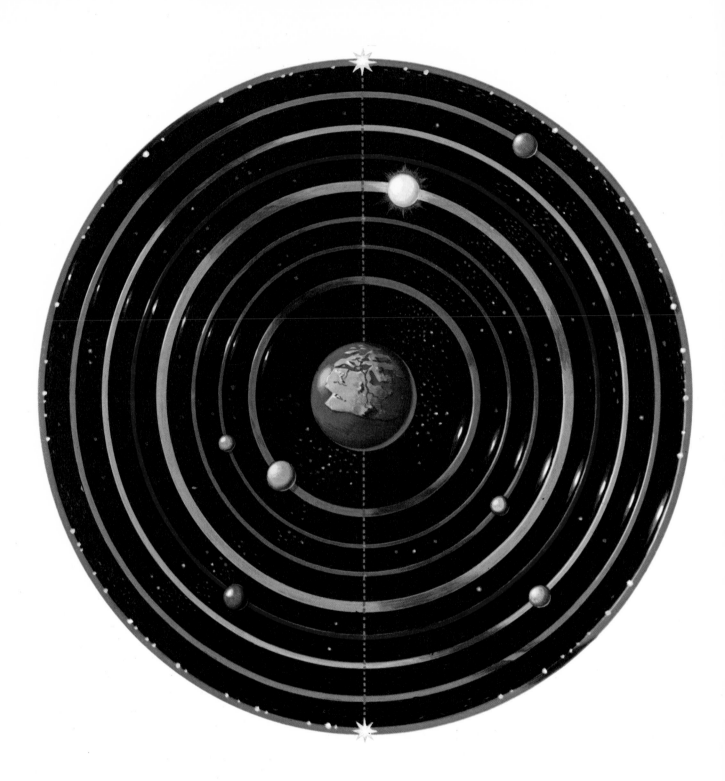

This is a simplified representation of the geocentric universe, as the Greeks saw it. The earth is suspended in the center, with eight crystal spheres envisaged as surrounding it. From the center outward, we see the spheres of the moon, Mercury, Venus, the sun, Mars, Jupiter, Saturn, and the firmament of the fixed stars. This, the outermost sphere, turns on an imaginary axis which runs from the polestar in the north to an imaginary south polestar in the south.

The world picture

It all began when people decided that the world was round.

For hundreds, indeed for thousands, of years, the people of the Mediterranean coasts had noticed that the starry firmament moved round slowly in the night, and that one star in the north stood still in the black sky, while the constellations swept slowly round it in vast circles. Seafarers who sailed south, from Greece to Crete and Egypt, for instance, saw completely new stars rising from the sea in the south, and it looked as if the entire firmament were slipping gradually away in the north. The fixed north star itself dropped toward the northern horizon, and as the Great Bear swung low in its arc, some of its stars disappeared into the sea. As the seafarers sailed back to the north, the polestar rose again in the night sky, and with it, the whole revolving firmament. Back in Greece, the Great Bear in its entirety could be seen during the whole course of its journey round the polestar.

Other seafarers and travelers in other parts of the world had presumably noticed the same sort of thing, but as far as we know, the Greeks were the first to draw the right conclusions about the apparent motion of the stars from north to south. The great Pythagoras of Samos is believed to have been the first to suggest that the world was round. During the 6th century B.C. he founded a school of mystical philosophy at Croton in southern Italy, and it is within this secret brotherhood that he is said to have taught that the earth, the sun, and the planets were spherical.

A few decades after this, a pupil of his, Parmenides of Elea, wrote a didactic poem called *Nature,* which contained a geocentric picture of a universe with the earth hanging suspended in the center. He also explained that the earth possessed five climatic zones: a hot zone about the equator, a temperate zone on either side of it, and two cold zones round the poles. The Greeks had long believed that the inhabited world consisted of three divisions: Europe, Asia, and Libya (Africa). Aristotle, who lived during the 4th century B.C., thought that there might be four inhabited continents on the earth, separated from one another by the sea. But he was equally ready to believe that the earth was very small and, consequently, that it was not very far across the ocean from the west coast of Africa to the east coast of Asia.

A hundred years later, Eratosthenes measured the circumference of the earth and found it to be 250,000 stadia, or 27,750 miles. The true circumference is about 25,000 miles. According to Strabo, the geographer, who flourished at about the beginning of the Christian era, Eratosthenes had said: "If the Atlantic Ocean were not so extremely large, we could sail from Iberia [Spain] to India along the same latitude on the other side of the earth. Our inhabited world accounts for about one-third of the circumference of the earth. Along the parallel of Athens, for instance, the entire circumference is about 200,000 stadia. Of these, our inhabited world accounts for about 70,000 [7,700 miles], all the way from Iberia in the west to the remotest Indies in the east. What remains to be traveled by sea in the opposite direction, therefore, is 130,000 stadia [14,400 miles]."

Strabo embraced and developed Aristotle's idea of several continents in the ocean. Apart from a Terra Australis, a southern continent, he believed, there existed a Terra Occidentalis, a new continent to the west. He wrote: "It may be that in this same temperate zone there are in fact two inhabited worlds, or even more, especially along the latitude of Athens, if the parallel is produced into the Atlantic."

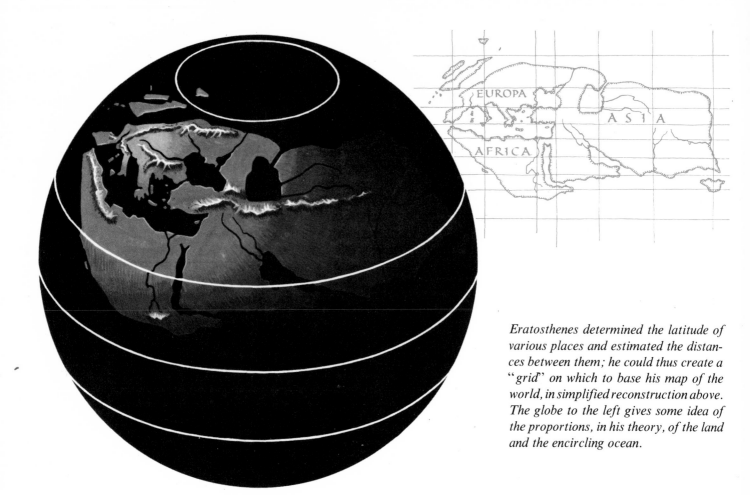

Eratosthenes determined the latitude of various places and estimated the distances between them; he could thus create a "grid" on which to base his map of the world, in simplified reconstruction above. The globe to the left gives some idea of the proportions, in his theory, of the land and the encircling ocean.

Written at about the same period were these often-quoted lines by the Roman dramatist Seneca in his play *Medea:*

> . . . venient annis
> Secula seris, quibus Oceanus
> Vincula rerum laxet, et ingens
> Pateat tellus Tiphysque novos
> Detegat orbes nec sit terris
> Ultima Thule.

Columbus himself made a free translation of these lines in his *Libro de las Profecías* (Book of Prophecies): "There will come a time after many years when the Ocean will loose the chains that fetter things, and the great world will lie revealed, and a new mariner, like unto him who was Jason's pilot, called Tiphys, will reveal a new world, and then Thule will not be the most extreme of all lands."

Not everyone believed Eratosthenes' calculations of the size of the earth and the smallness of the inhabited world, and Strabo, who himself was among the doubters, quotes Poseidonius, who thought that the continent reached halfway round the earth. Regarding the possibility of making a sea journey to India by way of the Atlantic, Poseidonius said: "It is true that the distance is great, but it could be done with a good east wind following."

As time passed, people gradually learned more about the lands behind the coasts of Asia, and they found completely new countries, or heard tell of them. On their maps, the continent grew larger; in about A.D. 120. Marinus of Tyre drew a map on which the continent occupied 225 of the 360 degress which composed the whole circumference. He had accepted Poseidonius' correction of Eratosthenes and proceeded from the supposition that the circumference of the earth was no more than 180,000 stadia. By his calculations, the width of the continent at the equator was 112,500 stadia. The great geographer Ptolemy was highly critical of Marinus, believing that the continent was hardly more than 90,000 stadia across, but he accepted Poseidonius' and Marinus' calculations of the circumference of the earth, 180,000 stadia (20,000 miles). Eratosthenes had been nearest the truth.

During the Dark Ages, many of the ancient pagan teachings about the shape of the earth and the known world were openly rejected and then forgotten. There were some

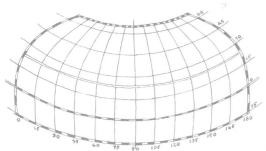

Ptolemy might never have drawn a map himself, but he worked out a system for other geographers and map makers. He constructed several projections to serve as a framework; the projection above was still used, with modifications, by cartographers until the Renaissance. To the right is an early 14th-century relief by Giotto and Andrea Pisano. Ptolemy is measuring the altitude of the stars with a quadrant. The globe is technically known as an armillary sphere.

who tried to create an entirely new picture of the world with the Bible as their only guide, and to them the earth became a rectangular slab with the sky covering it like the canopy of a tabernacle. But this solution was not accepted by everyone. By no means all classical authors had admitted that the earth was a sphere. Authorities such as Cicero and Pliny the Elder saw it as a disc hanging in space, although for the sake of balance they added that the lower side of the disc was also inhabited—by antipodeans, people who walked with their feet toward us. Other classical authors accepted the idea of the disc but did not recognize the existence of antipodeans; such authors were supported by the leaders of the Church.

St. Augustine of Hippo did not think it out of the question that the earth might in fact be a sphere, but he was unable to believe that there were inhabited continents in the lower half. When God created the earth, He had commanded all the water beneath heaven to gather together in one place, and that place to St. Augustine was the southern hemisphere. The leaders of the Church found it completely incompatible with Christian doctrine that men who were not descended from Adam should exist on another continent, isolated from any hope of Christian salvation.

In the 5th century A.D., however, the Roman philosopher Macrobius wrote a book that was widely read all through the Middle Ages. It contained maps of the world on the classical pattern—with climatic zones and a southern continent. Bishop Isidore of Seville, who was later canonized, very likely had Macrobius in mind when he wrote two hundred years later: "Over and above the three continents of the world, there is yet a fourth beyond the Ocean, which, by reason of the heat of the sun, has remained unknown to us, and whose regions are only able to support mythical Antipodeans." He seems, then, by calling them mythical, to have been unwilling to commit himself on the subject. Goblins and monsters, yes—but not real human beings.

In the 8th century, St. Virgilius of Salzburg was denounced as a heretic by Pope Zacharias for insisting that there were such creatures as antipodes—human antipodeans, presumably. We may assume that he was not alone in this belief, but it is likely that most people who held heretical views about the shape of the world, and its

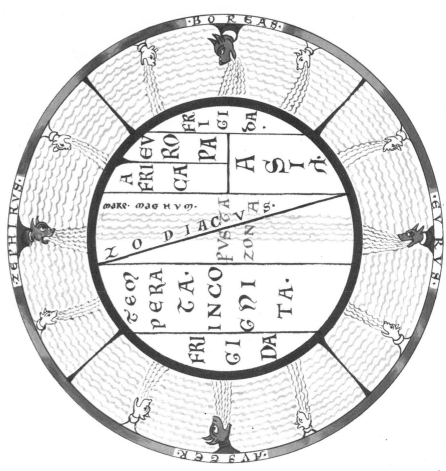

A mid-13th-century miniature showing the Emperor Augustus, enthroned with an orb and a sword of state. The orb is an "O–T" map, and the picture shows that the world was regarded as a sphere. To the right is a map by Macrobius, with the climatic zones and the Mare Magnum, the Great Ocean which was thought to separate the inhabited world from an unknown continent in the south.

inhabitants, preferred to keep quiet about it in the presence of Church leaders.

A hundred years later, a French theologian named Rabanus Maurus was a little more cautious when he openly described the earth as a sphere: "In the centre of the upper hemisphere lies Jerusalem. An unendurably hot zone separates the three continents of the upper hemisphere from the opposite world of the lower hemisphere, which is incorrectly said to be inhabited by people called *Antipodes*."

The upper half of the globe as Rabanus Maurus described it in his lectures is reproduced on the "O–T" maps of the 9th and 10th centuries. We may see the broad circular line as the great Ocean separating the continents of the two hemispheres. The vertical column of the "T" is the Mediterranean, separating Europe from Africa, and the horizontal bar above it the Don and the Nile, beyond which is the continent of Asia. The T shape also represents the Cross, with Jerusalem at the point of intersection. It is possible and even probable that the "O–T" maps originally portrayed a flat earth disc, but those who believed in a

spherical earth were no less able to accept them as a reasonable picture of what they believed in.

Albert of Bollstädt, a German count and Dominican friar who lived during the 13th century and was given the honorary name of Albertus Magnus, rejected the assertion that the hot zone was uninhabitable. He maintained that the same types of climate which existed in the northern hemisphere must also exist in the southern, and he was quite convinced that there were antipodes. It was not the heat, he thought, that separated the people of the north from the people of the south, but the great distance across the ocean sea. He believed that the stretch of water between Spain and easternmost India was small.

His contemporary, Roger Bacon, the Oxford philosopher and scientist, held similar views, and in his *Opus Majus* he invoked the classical authorities: "Aristotle says that only a small sea separates the outermost coast of Spain from farthest India in the east. He holds that more than one-fourth of the earth's surface is habitable. Averroës confirms this." Averroës is the European form of Ibn Roshd, an Arab philosopher and physician who

Above, an "O – T" map from the mid-11th century. To the right, an armillary sphere representing the universe, with the earth in the center and the sphere of the fixed stars outside. The Zodiac moves between the Tropic of Cancer and the Tropic of Capricorn. The armillary sphere enabled astrologers to see the position of the zodiacal signs at any time of the day or year.

lived in the 12th century in Spain and Morocco. He was a great admirer of Aristotle, and it was probably through his writings and those of others that Bacon had come into contact with the works of Aristotle and other great classical authors.

Bacon continued: "Seneca says that this sea can be sailed in a few days if the wind is favourable. Pliny says that men have in fact sailed from the Arabian Gulf [the Red Sea] to Cadiz. Since the Arabian Gulf is an entire year's journey from the Indian Sea [the sea off the coast of east Asia], it is clear that easternmost Asia cannot be far from us. The sea between Spain and Asia can in no wise cover three-quarters of the surface of the earth. Moreover, it is written in the fourth book of Esdras [in the Apocrypha] that six parts of the earth are habitable, while the seventh is covered with water. . . . Therefore, even though Ptolemy may say that the inhabited world is contained within one-quarter of the surface of the earth, I assert that a greater part of this surface is habitable. Aristotle had greater knowledge of these matters than other men, for by the favour of Alexander he was able to

send two thousand men to study these things. And so it was with Seneca. The Emperor Nero dispatched men to explore the world in the same way. All this shows that the inhabited part of the world must be extensive, and that the part covered with water is small in comparison."

It appears from this passage that Bacon was familiar, to a certain extent at least, with the geographical ideas of Ptolemy. There is no doubt that he came to learn of them through Arab sources, and he was probably acquainted with Ptolemaic ideas long before most other scholars in medieval Europe. When the Arabs overran Egypt in the 7th century, they found, in the academy and library at Alexandria, the cream of classical scientific writings. Ptolemy's *Geographike Hyphegesis* was translated to Arabic as early as the 9th century. It contained lists of over 8,000 places, together with their locations, directions for map making, and various map projections. But it was only in the 15th century that this work was translated to Latin and made generally available in Europe. Ptolemy's projection for a world map actually covers about a fourth part of a sphere, but in his notes he informs us that the

13

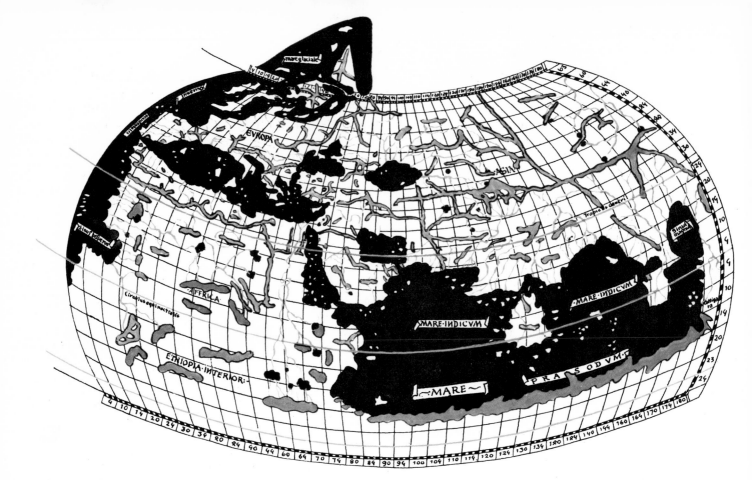

Ptolemy's world projection covers 180° of longitude — half the circumference of the earth — over 60° of latitude north of the equator, and only 25° south of it. Above is a simplification of a map printed at Ulm in 1486, shown here only to indicate the projection, with the shape and distribution of the continents. Note that Ptolemy joined Africa and Asia to the south of the Indian Ocean, which thus became an inland sea. Below right is the Earthly Paradise, from Hanns Rüst's map of the world; late 15th century.

area of land may continue off the map in the east and the south, and to a certain extent in the north as well. It is not likely that Bacon ever had a map drawn according to Ptolemy's instructions.

About 1300, Raimundus Lullus, a Spaniard, wrote about the causes of tides, arriving at, among other things, the conclusion that there must be another continent beyond the great Ocean: "As on our side there is a portion of the world that we see and know, so must there also be on the other side, the western, a continent that we neither see nor know."

The Church was unable to suppress belief in the antipodes, and it seems that Church spokesmen soon began to use and develop the solution proposed by Isidore of Seville. They populated the countries beyond the reach of salvation and the Church with imaginary beasts and fabulous monsters. There were men without heads, with their faces on their chests; there were men with the heads of dogs, one-legged men with one gigantic foot apiece; there were giants and dwarfs, harpies and dragons. These monsters, which were naturally regarded as the offspring of the Devil and excluded by their very appearance from the grace vouchsafed only to those who were created in the image of God, were described in wildly imaginative travelers' tales and shown on maps as living on islands outside the known world.

In 1316, Pietro d'Albano, an Italian physician, was accused of black magic and heresy because he said that he believed in the antipodes. He died from natural causes while his case was being tried, but an effigy of him was burned at the stake. Cecco d'Ascoli, a contemporary of his, who also held the same belief, was less fortunate; he died in the flames at the ripe age of seventy. But that is the last we hear of the death sentence for belief in antipodes. Only a few years later, one Guillaume Adam, a Dominican friar, wrote in a report to Philip IV of France of his travels in East Africa that belief in the antipodes was neither a crime nor a heresy and that not a tenth or even a twentieth part of the world's inhabitants were true Christians.

By the middle of the 15th century it was common practice for Jerusalem to be placed in the center of the world maps. Far to the east, on the coast of the continent, lay the Paradisus Terrestris, the Earthly Paradise. Sometimes it was shown as a lake with the four Rivers of Paradise flowing to the west, at other times as a fortress with towers and parapets. In the 8th century, John of Damascus wrote of Adam as a king and ruler of the earth: "And so God made for man a sort of royal citadel, where he could dwell and live in happiness. . . . This haven of peace and joy lies towards the rising sun, higher than the rest of the earth."

Sir John Mandeville, the most popular writer on geography in the Middle Ages, also described Paradise: "This Earthly Paradise is surrounded by a wall, which seems to be covered with moss, so that people shall not see whether it is made of stone or other material. And in the centre of Paradise, at its highest spot, there is a spring, which is the source of the four rivers that flow through divers countries. The first is called the Pison or Ganges, and flows through India. In this river there are many precious stones and aloes and gold dust. The second is called the Gihon or Nile, and flows through Ethiopia and Egypt. The third is called the Tigris, and flows through Assyria and Greater Armenia. The fourth is called the Euphrates, and flows through Armenia and Persia. And it is said that all the sweet fresh water in the world comes from these rivers. . . . And you shall know that no living person can walk to Paradise, for in one's way are the wild beasts of the desert, and mountains and rocks that no one can pass. Nor is it possible to reach this place by the rivers, for they rush along at such a speed and with such great waves that no ship can sail against them. . . . No one can reach this place except by the especial grace of God. And of this place I can tell you no more."

Apart from this, Mandeville's book consisted mainly of passages describing the countries and the peoples of the Near East, Africa, Amazonia, India, and China, all of which he claimed to have visited in person. But many of his descriptions are taken from earlier works, and the very great popularity of the book can be ascribed only to the numbers of monsters and fabulous creatures he describes as living in the outskirts of the world. There was no such person as Sir John Mandeville; the name is a pseudonym for Jean de Bourgogne, a physician of Liége, who wrote the book in the middle of the 14th century. Copies were made by hand and circulated in manuscript until it was first printed in 1470. For the times, some of Mandeville's opinions were rather advanced. He says: "Ordinary people will not believe that it is possible to walk on the under side of the earth without falling into space." And speaking of the islands off the coast of Asia, he wrote: "These islands belong to the country of Prester John and lie directly beneath us. And there are further islands, and he who wishes to reach them must, with the help of God, travel round the earth in order to complete the journey. He might reach those countries whence he comes and where he belongs, round the earth. But since this takes so much time and there are so many dangers to be overcome, there are few men who attempt to do this."

A less imaginative and less popular geographer than Mandeville was Pierre d'Ailly, a French cardinal who wrote his great work, the *Imago Mundi,* in 1410. As the title indicates, it purported to be a description of the entire known world, but it was based not on the personal experiences or observations of the author or his contemporaries but on an anthology which in its turn was derived from older authorities. By all accounts, d'Ailly had never read the story of Marco Polo's travels. He made much use of Roger Bacon's *Opus Majus*, which he often repeated directly, and it is probable that Bacon's idea of the world would have remained unknown to most people in medieval Europe if it had not been served up under d'Ailly's name. As far as we know, *Imago Mundi* was first printed in 1480.

We shall have reason to return to this book later, but there is one short passage I should like to quote here: "The Earthly Paradise is an Elysian spot situated in a certain region in the east, far distant from our inhabited world both by land and sea. It rises so high in the sky that it touches the path of the moon, and the waters of the Flood were unable to reach it."

The map of the world shown above was made about 1489 by Henricus Martellus Germanus, a German cartographer living in Italy. It measures approximately 4 by 6 feet and was probably intended as a model for Francesco Roselli, a Florentine wood engraver. An inventory of the possessions left by Roselli on his death shows that he had several wood blocks of maps of the world, but none of these maps have been discovered. Martellus began with Ptolemy's projection, but he wanted to include all the known world and increased its extent to 280°. He also went as far as 80° north and 40° south of the equator, but the southern extremity of Africa is not included; the official reports, which were deliberately misleading, represented the Cape of Good Hope as lying 45° south. This map, discovered only in 1961, is now in the Yale University library.

A comparison with Ptolemy's map (page 14) will show that Martellus slavishly followed his ancient model as far as concerned the coasts of East Africa, Arabia, and India, up to Ptolemy's eastern limit at Cattigara; but he knew from Portuguese sources that Africa could be circumnavigated, and in consequence he allowed Ptolemy's landlocked Indian Sea to become part of the great ocean. In the east, his continent extends 60° beyond the limits of Ptolemy's world.

Twenty degrees further east, beyond the easternmost point of Asia, he shows Marco Polo's Cipangu, or Japan as we know it.

If we give the earth its full circumference by adding 80° to Martellus' 280°, we find that the distance between Portugal and Cipangu, or the east coast of Asia, is in perfect agreement with Toscanelli's estimate (see pages 19—21); hence I believe that the new coastlines and the eastern islands on Martellus' map were copied from a map by Toscanelli. Martin Behaim's well-known globe, made in 1492, agrees in almost every detail with Martellus' map; Behaim must have either used Martellus' source or copied directly from him.

In four and a half centuries the colors of this map have grown dark, and a small-scale reproduction could not do it full justice. Accordingly, I have redrawn the right-hand half (right) in colors which should approximate those of the original, and superimposed a graticule so that it can be reproduced on different projections. The picture below right shows a globe with the continents distributed as on Martellus' map. It will be shown later that this was the picture Columbus had of the world before he set out on his first voyage.

West to the East

There has been much speculation and many books have been written about pre-Columbian discoveries of America. Some people have tried to prove a direct connection between the pyramids of Egypt and the pyramids of Mexico, and it has been suggested that the Phoenicians, who could sail to the Canary Islands, might just as well have been able to sail across the Atlantic with the trade winds. This is possible. The Egyptians and, even more so, the Phoenicians were good mariners, and their ships were seaworthy enough to have taken them over the seas with the trade winds. But even if they actually did cross the ocean, there is no record that any of them returned to tell the tale, and as long as we have no written records or other forms of evidence, that possibility has no place in the history of exploration.

There are many Irishmen who think that St. Brendan was the first to discover America, and in Scandinavia such wishful thinking is directed toward Leif Ericson. It is not unlikely that Irishmen had drifted over and settled at some spot on the North American continent several hundred years before the Norsemen, just as they were in the Faeroes and Iceland before the Norsemen were. The "evidence" supporting the Scandinavian claim consists of references in the Icelandic sagas. These sagas tell us a great deal about the voyages of Leif Ericson and others, and today it is generally taken as established that a Norse Colony, although a small one, existed in Newfoundland about A.D. 1000. However, these early northern voyagers had no idea that they had reached a new world. To them, Great Ireland, Markland, and Vinland were only islands in the sea south of Greenland, and their discoveries did not lead to further discovery.

It has been said that the Norse voyages across the Atlantic had been entirely forgotten by the end of the Middle Ages, but on a recently discovered map from about 1440, Vinland is shown as an island to the southwest of Greenland, and when the Danes sent an expedition across the north Atlantic in 1476 and rediscovered Labrador—the Norse Helluland or Markland—it was hardly a voyage into the unknown. The Portuguese mariner João Vaz Corte-Real probably took part in this voyage, but these "islands" in the northwest, which in wintertime were covered with snow and in summertime were surrounded by icebergs, had nothing in common with the rich and coveted Indies, and they did not attract any further searches in that area. The quest for India was still on.

After the capture of Ceuta in 1415, Prince Enrique of Portugal—known to history as Henry the Navigator—began to send out expeditions in order to reach the golden land of Guinea, lying somewhere in southwest Africa, by sea, and to try to find islands or a continent in the great ocean sea round his world. Diogo Gomes, the chronicler, wrote explicitly: "When Prince Henry wanted to obtain information about the more distant parts of the western Ocean, in order to find out whether *islands or a continent* were to be found outside the world described by Ptolemy, he dispatched caravels at a certain time to discover land." We presume that the continent in the prince's thoughts was the imaginary western continent mentioned by Strabo and Raimundus Lullus.

Islands were indeed found, but no continent. The islands of Madeira and Porto Santo, already known, were now colonized; the Azores were explored; and eventually the Cape Verde Islands were reached. There are some who believe that Henry the Navigator's men also discovered the West Indies. Far out in the Atlantic on a map drawn in 1424 by Zuane Pizzigano, a Venetian, lie the islands of Braxil, Ventura, Saya, Satanazes, Antilla, and Ymana. Satanazes and Antilla are large and rectangular, and this is the first time that the imaginary island of Antilla appears on a map. Some see this as evidence that Portuguese caravels had sailed to the Caribbean islands even before the Azores had been discovered, and managed to return home to report their findings. Antilla and the other islands are therefore supposed to be those that were later called the Antilles. But there is still the question of how an Italian cartographer could have come to know of such a great discovery when not a single Portuguese chronicler of the times ever mentioned it, for at that period, reports of Portuguese discoveries could still be communicated to the general public. It was not until the death of Henry the Navigator, in 1460, that they were kept a state secret by the authorities. Pizzigano's map is neither the first nor the last to include islands that have never actually been found.

Prince Henry's African objective had been to reach the gold of Guinea and try to make contact with Prester John, who was identified with the Emperor of Abyssinia. Only after the death of the prince do we hear that the Portuguese under Afonso V deliberately sought to reach India by circumnavigating Africa. When Cape Palmas had been rounded and the coastline began to stretch mile after mile to the east, it was imagined that the southernmost cape of Africa had been reached and that the goal was close at hand. But at the Cameroons the coastline again swung round to the south.

That was when Toscanelli was approached.

Paolo dal Pozzo Toscanelli was a Florentine physician and, like other scientists of the age, a jack of many trades.

He had written treatises on perspective and meteorology, he had calculated architectural stresses, and he had studied geography. In Florence with his friend Fernão Martinez de Roriz, a Portuguese canon, he had discussed the size of the earth and the area of the inhabited world, and as he obviously based his ideas on Pierre d'Ailly's *Imago Mundi,* and consequently on the classical authors and Bacon, he thought that the western route to India across the ocean must be a short one.

Fernão Martinez de Roriz became Afonso V's confessor and adviser, and when the king grew pessimistic about the reports from Africa, the canon told him of Toscanelli's ideas. The king then told the canon to write a letter to Toscanelli, asking him to elaborate on his theory of a western route. Toscanelli sent a long letter in reply, enclosing a map of the sea between Europe and India. The letter runs:

"To Fernam Martins, Canon of Lisbon, Paulus the Physician sends greetings.

"It pleased me to hear of your intimacy and friendship with your great and powerful King. Often before have I spoken of a sea route from here to India, the land of spices; a route which is shorter than that by way of Guinea. You tell me that His Highness wishes me to explain this in greater detail so that it will be easier to understand and to take this route. Although I could show this on a globe representing the earth, I have decided to do it more simply and clearly by demonstrating the way on a nautical chart. I therefore send His Majesty a chart, drawn by my own hand, on which I have indicated the western coastline from Ireland in the north to the end of Guinea, and the islands which lie along this path. Opposite them, directly to the west, I have indicated the beginning of India, together with the islands and places you will come to; how far you will have to keep from the Arctic Pole and the Equator; and how many leagues you must cover before you come to these places, which are most rich in all kinds of spices, gems, and precious stones. And be not amazed when I say that spices grow in lands to the west, even though we usually say the east; for he who sails west will always find these lands in the west, and he who travels east by land will always find the same lands in the east.

"The upright lines on this chart show the distance from east to west, whereas the cross lines show the distance from north to south. The chart also indicates various places in India which may be reached if one meets with a storm, a head wind, or any other misfortune.

"That you may know as much about these places as possible, you should know that the only people living on any of these islands are merchants who trade there. There are said to be as many ships, mariners, and goods there as in the rest of the world put together, especially in the principal port called Zaiton, where they load and unload

Paolo dal Pozzo Toscanelli, copied from a detail in a mural by Giorgio Vasari in the Palazzo Vecchio at Florence

a hundred great ships of pepper every year, not to mention many other ships with other spices. That country has many inhabitants, provinces, kingdoms, and innumerable cities, all of which are ruled by a great prince known as the Grand Khan, which in our language means 'The King of Kings,' who resides chiefly in the province of Cathay. His forefathers greatly desired to make contact with the Christian world, and some two hundred years ago they sent ambassadors to the Pope, asking him to send them many learned men who could instruct them in our faith; but these ambassadors met with difficulties on the way, and had to turn back without reaching Rome. In the days of Pope Eugenius, there came to him an ambassador who told him of their great feelings of friendship for the Christians, and I had a long conversation with the ambassador about many things: about the vast size of the royal buildings, about the amazing length and breadth of their rivers, and about the great number of cities on their banks—so great a number that along one river there were two hundred cities with very long, wide bridges of marble which were adorned with many pillars. This country is richer than any other yet discovered, and not only could it

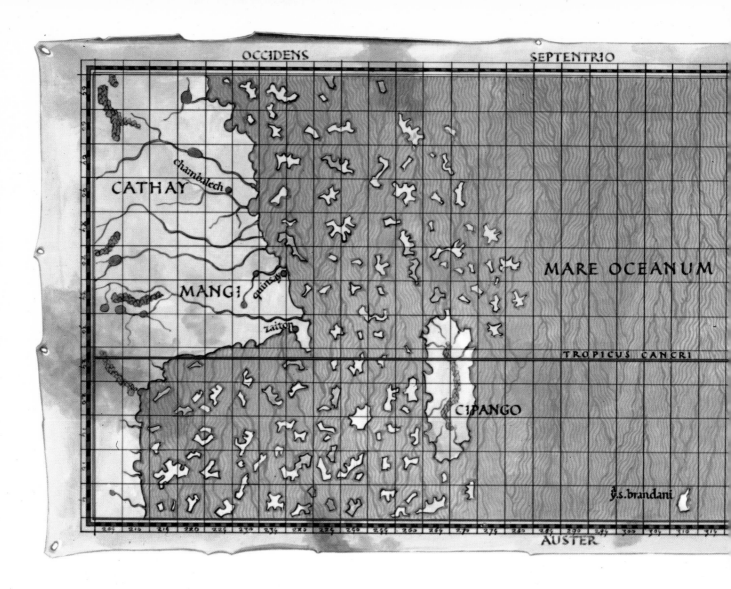

provide great profit and many valuable things, but it also possesses gold and silver and precious stones and all kinds of spices in large quantities—things which do not reach our countries at present. And there are also many scholars, philosophers, astronomers, and other men skilled in the natural sciences, who govern that great kingdom and conduct its wars.

"From the city of Lisbon to the west, the chart shows twenty-six sections, of two hundred and fifty miles each—altogether, nearly one-third of the earth's circumference—before reaching the very large and magnificent city of Quinsay [Hangchow]. This city is approximately one hundred miles in circumference, possesses ten marble bridges, and its name means 'The Heavenly City' in our language. Amazing things have been related about its vast buildings, its artistic treasures, and its revenues. It lies in the province of Mangi, near the province of Cathay, where the king chiefly resides. And from the island of Antilia, which you call the Island of the Seven Cities, to the very famous island of Cipangu are ten sections, that is, 2,500 miles. That island is very rich in gold, pearls, and

precious stones, and its temples and palaces are covered in gold. But since the route to this place is not yet known, all these things remain hidden and secret; and yet one may go there in great safety.

"I could still tell of many other things, but as I have already told you of them in person, and as you are a man of good judgement, I will dilate no further on the subject. I have tried to answer your questions as well as the lack of time and my work have permitted me, but I am always prepared to serve His Highness and answer his questions at greater length should he so wish.

"Written in Florence on the 25th of June, 1474."

It is quite clear that Toscanelli's chief source of information on India was Marco Polo. The provinces of Cathay and Mangi are parts of what we know as China, and the descriptions of their riches and the magnificence of their cities are not exaggerated. Cipangu is Japan; there is no record that any Europeans had ever set foot there, and Marco Polo's description of its opulence had probably come from some imaginative Chinese. Toscanelli's

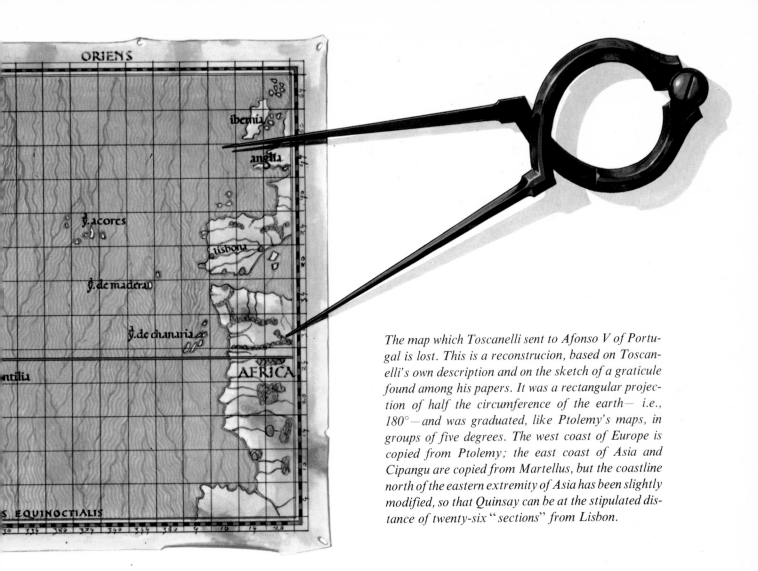

ORIENS

ibernia

angria

y. açores

lisbona

y. de madera

y. de chanaria

antilia

AFRICA

S EQUINOCTIALIS

The map which Toscanelli sent to Afonso V of Portugal is lost. This is a reconstrucion, based on Toscanelli's own description and on the sketch of a graticule found among his papers. It was a rectangular projection of half the circumference of the earth— i.e., 180°—and was graduated, like Ptolemy's maps, in groups of five degrees. The west coast of Europe is copied from Ptolemy; the east coast of Asia and Cipangu are copied from Martellus, but the coastline north of the eastern extremity of Asia has been slightly modified, so that Quinsay can be at the stipulated distance of twenty-six "sections" from Lisbon.

estimate of the size of the earth, of the extent of the Eurasian land mass, and hence of the relative narrowness of the ocean between Europe and Asia, was probably based on the *Imago Mundi,* on Ptolemy, and on Marco Polo.

We do not know how Toscanelli's letter, and his maps, were received in Lisbon. The likeliest answer is that they were scrutinized by the Junta de Mathemáticos, a royal commission of scholars, and that the Junta found that it could not accept his conclusions or recommend the idea of sailing west to reach India. Arab science was greatly respected in Portugal, and as early as the 9th century an astronomer called al-Farghani had worked out that one degree of latitude equalled $56\frac{2}{3}$ Arabian miles, and hence that the circumference of the earth was 360 times $56\frac{2}{3}$ Arabian miles ($20,397\frac{2}{3}$ Arabian miles, or 27,585 English miles, which is slightly more accurate than Eratosthenes' result). Even if Ptolemy's 180 degrees for the Eurasian land mass was admitted to be an underestimate, that still left far too wide an ocean to be crossed. Such might have been the arguments of the Junta; alternatively, it might have accepted Toscanelli's ideas in principle but found his 6,500 miles across the ocean an insuperable objection.

There are written records of other minor attempts at finding new islands in the western ocean, but these were made by private enterprise and merchant adventurers with the royal assent. King Afonso had little time to interest himself in exploration, for between 1475 and 1479 he was wholly occupied by his war with Castile. He died in 1481 and was succeeded by his son, John II, who in the very first year of his reign sent out an expedition under Diogo de Azambuja with the object of building a fortress to protect trade. Diogo Cão sailed further south with two caravels, discovered the Congo River, and reached a latitude of 13° 16′ south. On his return to Lisbon, Cão was richly rewarded by the king, who must nevertheless have been bitterly disappointed to find that his quest for India was still obstructed by the vast unknown continent of Africa.

It was at that time, in 1483 or 1484, that a Genoese mariner named Cristoforo Colombo sought audience with John II.

21

Cristoforo Colombo of Genoa

There is not much that we can say for certain about the life of Columbus before he was presented to the King of Portugal. He preferred to keep quiet about his background, and later in life he seems to have told some flat lies about himself: that he came from a distinguished family, that he had studied at the University of Pavia, and

that he was not the first member of his family to have been an Admiral.

Most of these dubious assertions, and some others, are found in his biography, written long after his death by his son, Fernando Colón. Many people think it was edited and substantially modified before it was published, in an Italian translation, in 1541; in any case, it is in these doubtful passages that we can most clearly detect the pretentious tones of this overeducated son. Fernando Colón was an outrageous snob. He refused to admit any origins except on his father's side; the book does not contain a single reference to the woman who had openly lived with Columbus in Spain; still less is there any admission that Fernando himself was the fruit of that union. He had seen how the Spanish Court had treated his father in his latter years, and we can easily understand that when at last he sat down to write the biography of his father he

There are many portraits of Columbus, but it is not likely that any of them were painted during his lifetime. The oldest datable is a woodcut made in the late 16th century by a Swiss artist named Tobias Stimmer, who copied the collection of portraits of distinguished people by Paolo Giovio of Florence. The picture agrees with Fernando Colón's description: "The Admiral was a well-built man of more than average height. His face was long, with rather high cheekbones; his person neither fat nor thin. His nose was aquiline, his eyes light; his complexion was also light, with a ruddy tinge. In his youth his hair was fair, but it turned white in his thirties." Las Casas gave a similar description, saying that Columbus' eyes were bright blue and his beard and hair red in his youth, "but anxiety had turned them white at an early age." Oviedo, the historian, added that Columbus was freckled.

wanted to gild the dim origins which the father had wished to forget as much as had the son.

If it could be proved that the beginning of the biography was deliberately falsified by Fernando or by someone else, Columbus himself would no longer bear the onus for the various untrue and incredible stories for which he has been held responsible. Even if we assume that Fernando heard the evidence from Columbus' lips, we should remember that he obtained his information from a dying man, whose mind was probably impaired. Moreover, Fernando was only seventeen when his father died, and he did not write the biography until many years later.

A considerable number of books have been written about Columbus' origins. Apparently depending on the nationality and preference of the writer, he has been represented as a citizen of Genoa or of any of sixteen other Italian cities, as a Portuguese, as a Catalan, a Catalonian Jew, a Majorcan Jew, a Galician, an Andalusian, a Swiss, an Armenian, a Greek, and heaven knows what else. Yet there can hardly be any doubt that he was Genoese, nearly all contemporary chroniclers and authors described him as Genoese, and a great many other documents point quite unmistakably in the same direction.

Cristoforo Colombo was born in Genoa, between August 25 and October 31, 1451. His father was Domenico Colombo, a woolweaver; his grandfather Giovanni Colombo was also a woolweaver. His mother, Suzanna, was the daughter of a weaver, one Giacomo Fontanarossa. Cristoforo was the eldest of five children. His brother Bartolomeo, who remained his closest friend throughout life, was probably a few years younger. His second brother, Giovanni Pellegrino, died young; his sister, Bianchinetta, married a cheesemonger. His youngest brother, Giacomo, was seventeen years his junior.

We do not know whether the Colombo children learned to read and write. If they did, it must have been in Latin. The Genoese dialect never rose to the status of a literary language and as far as we know it was not used for writing. Cristoforo is not included in the rolls of students at the University of Pavia, and reliable witnesses from his later life say that he was a man of much intelligence but little learning.

The two eldest brothers went to sea at an early age. Antonio Gallo, who was the official chronicler of Genoa from 1477 until his death, writes of Cristoforo and Bartolomeo that they sometimes worked as woolcarders, that they had received little education, and that they had spent much of their youth in seafaring, as was the common local practice. Since Cristoforo later proved himself a good seaman and an exceptionally skilled navigator, we must presume that he had learned the trade thoroughly, by much experience.

It is probable that the whole Colombo family moved to Savona, west of Genoa, in 1470; it is certain that Cristoforo lived there in 1472, and he went back to Genoa in the following year with his brother Giovanni Pellegrino in order to sell his father's house. Bartolomeo might have been living in Lisbon by that time; he is known to have earned his living there later as a mapmaker.

If we are to believe Fernando Colón, Columbus was at this time one of the main characters in a very tall story. In a letter he is said to have written to Ferdinand and Isabella in 1495, he describes how, in the service of Duke René of Anjou, he had been sent to capture a galleass in the harbor of Tunis. But his crew lost their nerve and wanted to go back to Marseille for reinforcements. Therefore he hit on the idea of manipulating the compass so that in the dark the ship sailed south instead of north without the crew's knowledge. We are not told the rest of the story.

In the same chapter of the Life occurs the following passage, which is presented as a statement by Columbus: "In the month of February, 1477, I sailed one hundred leagues beyond the island of Thule [Iceland], the north part of which lies at a latitude of 73 degrees north, and not 63 degrees as some affirm. Nor does it lie on the

meridian where Ptolemy says the West begins, but much further west. And to this island, which is as large as England, the English come with their wares, from Bristol in particular. When I was there, the sea was not frozen, but the tides were so great that in some places the water rose twenty-six fathoms, and fell to the same extent."

If these are Columbus' own words, he was a liar. He cannot possibly have been "beyond Thule" in February. In those days no one sailed to Iceland in the depths of winter. If he really told that story, he could only have been repeating what he heard, and believed, from mariners in Bristol. Just as the Phoenicians, the Portuguese, and the Spaniards kept their trade routes secret and gave the wrong positions for their overseas discoveries, so too did the English have reason to keep southerners away from the ports that they regarded as theirs. The tide in the Bristol Channel was the worst known at that time, and it must have given Mediterranean-born sailors a good deal of trouble. A coast where the tide was said to rise 26 fathoms, or five times as much as at Bristol, would therefore have been a real deterrent.

Fernando Colón also said that his father reached Portugal after a dramatic sea fight and shipwreck off Cape St. Vincent, but that tale is so patently false that there is no need for us to look into it. We do not know

The shrewd policy of the Portuguese kings had made Lisbon one of the most important trading cities in Europe. Its excellent and capacious harbor was frequented by ships from Britain, Flanders, France, Aragon, and the Italian trading republics.

what first took Columbus to Portugal. He might have sailed there on a Genoese merchantman and then been persuaded by his brother Bartolomeo to settle in Lisbon, where greater things seemed to be in the offing than at home in the quarrelsome upheavals of Genoa. Gallo, the chronicler, writes that it was the mapmaker Bartolomeo who directed Cristoforo's attention to the possibility of there being land to the west. Perhaps Columbus set out for Lisbon in the service of the Genoese trading house of Centurione; he might have sailed on Genoese trading galleys to Bristol during the summers; he might himself have commanded some smaller trading vessels. All we know of that period with certainty is that he sailed from Lisbon in July, 1478, to buy sugar for Centurione in Madeira. He went back to Genoa in the following year, probably for the last time.

Cristovão Colom in Lisbon

During the war between Portugal and Castile, Queen Isabella encouraged Andalusian trading houses to send ships to Guinea and promised them warships for escort. A fleet of thirty-five caravels sailed from Seville in 1487 to trade along the Gold Coast, and there seem to have been plans for a purely military expedition to drive the Portuguese from the coveted coasts of Africa. But the war came to an end, and at Alcaçovas in 1479 it was agreed that Portugal was to retain the sole right to trade with and sail to Guinea and the countries beyond.

It might have been in this year that Columbus married Felipa Moniz de Perestrello, a Portuguese lady of the lesser nobility, at the same time obtaining Portuguese citizenship. She was the daughter of Bartolomeu Perestrello, former governor of the island of Porto Santo, by his second wife. While in Portugal, Columbus spent some of his time in Lisbon, some at the home of his mother-in-law in Porto Santo, and some in nearby Madeira, going to sea in the intervals. We know that he, like his brother, made a livelihood by mapmaking, but the work could not have brought in much money, for as time passed he

seems to have fallen into considerable debt. The brothers' mapmaking must mean that they were employed by some privileged cartographer. This was a profession surrounded by much secrecy in the Portugal of those days, at least as regards the maps of the west coast of Africa. We know that the masters of ships sailing on the Guinea route had to hand over all their maps to a royal commission as soon as they returned to Portugal.

During Columbus' stay in Portugal, and here I also include the time he spent in Porto Santo and Madeira or on Portuguese ships, his plans matured. Books on Columbus provide many different accounts of how his idea was born. Fernando's version is that he was inspired by some notes and a chart which had belonged to his father-in-law, who had been a mariner and an explorer. According to Fernando, Columbus was shown them by the widow. But Perestrello had been neither a mariner nor an explorer.

Fernando continues thus: "He obtained information about other journeys and the voyages that the Portuguese were making to Mina [the Gold Coast] and down the coast of Guinea at that time, and he found great satisfaction in conversing with the men who sailed in those regions. To tell the truth, I do not know if it was during this marriage that the Admiral sailed to Mina and Gui-

25

nea, but it seems reasonable to assume that he did so. Be that as it may, one thing led to another and gave life to many thoughts, so that the Admiral, while in Portugal, began to think that, if the Portuguese could sail so far to the south, it should be possible to sail equally far to the west, and that it was logical to expect to find land in that direction. To obtain confirmation on this point, he returned to those writers on geography with whose work he was already familiar, and began to consider the astronomical arguments that might support his design, at the same time noting down all pieces of information given to him by mariners and others."

This is an explanation that is commonly accepted, at least in its general terms, even though there are authors who think that Columbus only appropriated the ideas of others, or that when in England or Iceland he had come to hear of the Norse voyages and therefore knew that there was land not far off to the west. He might possibly have heard of Markland and Vinland, and he could hardly have failed to hear of the Danish expedition which Corte-Real had led to Labrador only a few years earlier. But, as we have already seen, neither he nor anyone else in Portugal at that time felt any interest in a few "bare" northwestern islands which gave no indication of any continent farther west and seemed simply to be extensions of that singular unattractive island, Greenland.

Voyages of discovery were in the air of Lisbon of those days, and it was fashionable to dream of a governorship of a hitherto unknown island in the Atlantic. And with the king's permission a number of private adventurers did sail off to discover some island that they might have thought they had seen, that others had thought they had seen, or those that were marked on the maps, like Antilla, Satanazes, and the others. Every year, the people of the Canary Islands, Porto Santo, and the other Azores thought they saw misty blue islands on the western horizon; these enchanted lands, which appeared and vanished before anyone could come near them, soon became a legend, and a very long-lived one.

It was only natural for a young and ambitious man like Columbus to dream such dreams, or even bolder ones. He might have found some fascinating charts in the Perestrello house. He must certainly have listened to mariner's tales of elusive islands, of bodies washed ashore that belonged to people of a different race, of enormous treetrunks of unknown varieties thrown up on the beaches of the Azores during westerly storms, of pieces of wood carved into outlandish shapes. In his copy of Aeneas Sylvius' *Historia Rerum*, Columbus himself wrote: "Men from Cathay, which lies towards the east, have arrived here. We have seen many remarkable things, above all in Galway in Ireland, a man and a woman of outlandish appearance, in two drifting boats."

But what gave him most support in his theories, or rather, what made him give his intentions clear expression, was undoubtedly Pierre d'Ailly's *Imago Mundi*. It was probably first printed in 1480, as already mentioned, and Columbus' own well-thumbed copy is still to be seen at the Biblioteca Columbina in Seville. Nearly every page has marginal notes by Columbus himself, and there are also some by his brother Bartolomeo, who must have shared in his plans from the very beginning and who—if Antonio Gallo is to be believed—might have been the first to draw his brother's attention to the possible existence of a western route.

A large number of the notes are simply abridgments of d'Ailly's text, often of such a character that we can hardly help thinking that the *Imago Mundi* was the first textbook from which Columbus learned geography. A few of his notes: "Each country has its own west and its own east in relation to its own horizon.... A man travelling from east to west will reach a new meridian.... Mount Olympus, where the comets come from.... The earth is round and spherical.... Sea and land combine to form a round body.... Aristotle: Between the end of Spain and the beginning of India lies a narrow sea that can be sailed in a few days.... Esdras: Six parts of the earth are habitable, and the seventh is covered with water.... N.B., the blessed Ambrose and St. Augustine, with many others, thought that Esdras was prophet and approved his

The reconstruction to the right is of a late 15th-century compass. An iron needle was fitted over a brass cap. Over the needle was placed a compass rose, divided into 32 points. The bowl was usually made of a single block of wood. The needle and the compass rose were supported by a brass pin. When Columbus was in Duke René's service, he doctored the compass to make it point south instead of north; he did this by turning the compass rose halfway round. It seems likely, though I have found no evidence to support the suggestion, that on long ocean voyages the compass was regularly adjusted to local deviations; these could easily be determined by taking bearings on the polestar, and the compass rose could be adjusted accordingly.

book....A part of our inhabited world ends in an unknown country, towards the rising sun....To the south, an unknown country....Where the sun sets, an unknown country....Note that the Kingdom of Tarshish lies at the end of the Orient, at the end of Cathay. It was to that kingdom, to a place called Ophir, that

Solomon and Jehoshaphat sent ships which returned with gold, silver and ivory."

Columbus was fascinated by d'Ailly's descriptions of the riches of the world, repeating them in the margins: "In Germany there are crystals and other precious stones ....Pactolus, the river that carries gold dust.... Where the Phoenix was born....In Taprobane [Ceylon] there are elephants and precious stones. In India there are many desirable things, including aromatic spices, a superfluity of precious stones, and mountains of gold."

Columbus' copy of Marco Polo's travels has also been preserved. Here he has underlined the points that were of the most importance to him: *pearls, precious stones, brocades, ivory, or pepper, nuts, nutmeg, cloves and an abundance of other spices.*

So he wrote to Toscanelli. It was natural that he or Bartolomeo, as mapmakers in Lisbon, should have heard of Toscanelli's important map, and, as it seemed to fit in with the picture that was gradually becoming clearer in his mind, Columbus decided to approach the Florentine scientist directly and ask for his opinion. His letter, together with a small globe to illustrate his theory, was delivered to Toscanelli by a Florentine named Lorenzo Girardi. Toscanelli's answer ran:

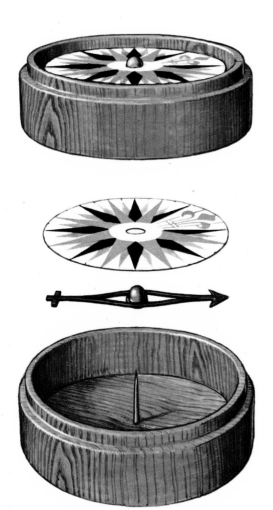

"To Christopher Columbus, Paulus the Physician sends greetings.

"I understand your noble and grand desire to go to the regions where the spices grow, and in reply to your letter I send you a copy of another letter which I sent some time ago to a friend of mine, a gentleman in the service of the most serene King of Portugal, before the wars with Castile, in reply to another which he had written to me on this subject by command of His Highness. And I send you a sea chart, like the one I sent him, that your wishes may be satisfied."

It is probable that Toscanelli, now an old man, forgot to send the chart and enclosed only a copy of the letter to Fernão Martinez de Roriz; for Columbus received another letter, which ran:

"To Christopher Columbus, Paulus the Physician sends greetings.

"I have received your letters together with the things you sent me. They have been of great use to me, and I applaud your noble and grand desire to sail to the regions of the east by those of the west as indicated on the map I send you, though the route would be better indicated on a globe. I shall be very pleased if it is understood correctly, for the voyage is not only possible to make, but sure and certain, and will bring inestimable gain and the utmost recognition among Christians.

"But these things you will not fully understand without experience, which I have had in abundance, or without good and true information from learned men who have come from those said regions to the Court in Rome, and also from merchants who have travelled for long periods in those countries, people with great authority. So that when the said voyage is made, it will be to powerful kingdoms and cities and provinces, very noble, very rich in all kinds of products, abundant, of great importance to us; rich in all manner of spices, with precious stones in abundance. Furthermore, it will be very welcome to some of their kings and princes as are very eager, more eager than we are, to meet Christians from our countries, for many of them are Christians themselves. Likewise will it be pleasing for them to meet and speak with men of talent and learning from these our countries, both about religion and about all other branches of learning, by reason of the fame of these our Empires and Kingdoms. For these reasons and many others that might be mentioned, I am not amazed to see that you, a man of bold heart, as well as the whole of the Portuguese nation, which has always bred courageous men for great enterprises, are now aflame with zeal to undertake this voyage."

Toscanelli was eighty-four when he wrote this letter and was already imagining the opportunities Columbus would have of conversing with Eastern scholars. A year later, he was dead. The map that he sent with the letter

27

was probably rather simpler than the one he made for King Afonso.

At that time, about 1481, Columbus' son Diego was born in Porto Santo, and it seems that the mother died in childbirth, or shortly after, for we no longer hear anything about her. We learn from Diego's will that she was buried in the Moniz family chapel at the Carmelite abbey in Lisbon.

Columbus' own notes inform us that he made several voyages to Guinea. He might have taken part in the large expedition which sailed under Diogo de Azambuja down to the Gold Coast in 1482, when the fortress of São Jorge da Mina was established. He might also have sailed in the following year on one of the many ships which the energetic João II sent to fetch slaves and gold. And he might have accompanied them as cartographer, to check and supplement the maps already made. His exceptional skill as a cartographer can be seen in a small sketch map, still extant, which he made off the north coast of Española in 1492 (see page 95).

On one of the margins in the *Imago Mundi* he wrote: "Africa is half the size of Europe, and though there is a desert in its centre, many parts of it are nevertheless inhabited. Innumerable people live in the northern and southern parts, in spite of the great heat. And under the equator, where the days are 12 hours long, lies the fortress of the Most Serene King of Portugal, which I visited. And I found that the place was temperate."

In the same work, beside the chapter which deals with the circumference of the earth, we find: "Note that often when sailing from Lisbon south to Guinea I made careful study of the course we followed, as pilots and mariners do. And later I took the altitude of the sun with quadrants and other instruments many times, and I found them to agree with Alfraganus [Latinized form of al-Farghani], which is to say that each degree was equivalent to $56\frac{2}{3}$ miles, and so this measurement is to be trusted. We may therefore say that the circumference of the earth at the equator is 20,400 miles, and likewise that Master Yosepius, the physician and astrologer, found it to be the same, as did many others who were sent out for this purpose by the Most Serene King of Portugal."

There is a short note on the same page: "One degree corresponds to $56\frac{2}{3}$ miles, and the circumference of the the earth is 5,100 leagues. That is the truth."

And that was Columbus' fateful mistake.

From this time on he became almost fanatical in his belief that the sea between Spain and India was very narrow, and of criticism he would hear nothing. Where he found no evidence he made it up. The Master Yosepius he mentions was the astronomer José Vicinho, and it seems likely that this man once sailed on a caravel to Guinea to find out for the king whether al-Farghani's measurements had been correct. Columbus might have been on the same ship, or at any rate in the same squadron, and heard José Vicinho say that al-Farghani's measurements suited the facts.

He goes on to write that the circumference of the earth at the equator is 5,100 leagues (we must understand here that a league equals four Roman, not Arabian, miles). He accepted al-Farghani's calculation of $56\frac{2}{3}$ miles for one degree at the equator and believed that both José Vicinho and he himself had verified this measurement. And he also seemed to be the only person in the world who believed that al-Farghani was counting in Roman, not Arabian, miles!

One Roman mile is 1,616 yards, and so Columbus' equatorial circumference of 20,400 Roman miles would then be about 18,750 of our miles, or something like 6,300 miles too short. European geographers of that time made their calculations on the assumption that one degree of longitude at the equator equalled $61\frac{1}{2}$ Roman miles, which made the circumference of the earth 360 times $62\frac{1}{2}$ or 22,500 Roman miles, or 20,650 of our miles. This was still 4,400 miles short. It is almost certain that Toscanelli proceeded from this estimate. In his letter to Fernão Martinez de Roriz, he wrote: "From the city of Lisbon to the west, the chart shows twenty-six sections, of two hundred and fifty miles each [i.e. nearly one-third of the earth's circumference in all] before reaching the very large and magnificent city of Quinsay." Each "section" on his map comprised five degrees. Thus each degree of longitude on the parallel of Lisbon would be equivalent to 50 Roman miles. But if it is assumed that each degree at the equator equals $62\frac{1}{2}$ Roman miles, then the degrees along the parallel of Lisbon would be only 48 Roman miles wide. Only a little further south, just beyond Cape St. Vincent, at the latitude of $36\frac{1}{2}°$ N, does Toscanelli's degree of longitude measure 50 Roman miles precisely. He might have thought that Cape St. Vincent lay exactly on the latitude of $36\frac{1}{2}°$ N and made his measurements from that point, as had been the usual practice ever since classical times. In any case, he chose 50 Roman miles as a round number, since his calculations also involved the distance from Lisbon to Antilla and Cipangu, which were farther south than Quinsay.

Toscanelli might have been the first man to draw a map on which the Eurasian landmass extended farther than the 180 degrees of longitude which Ptolemy allowed for the world as known to the ancients. If so, he must have made use of the information brought back by Marco Polo and other travelers, and added 60 degrees to the earlier 180 degrees, so that the extent of the inhabited world from Cape St. Vincent (really from the Canary Islands) to the remotest Indies now became 240 degrees.

To show the size of the earth, and the distance from Europe to Cipangu, as Columbus saw them, I have reproduced Martellus' map on an extended Ptolemaic projection which covers 360°, or the whole circumference of the earth.

Columbus had been a professional mapmaker in Lisbon, and he had been to Guinea in person; he must, therefore, have known more about the West African coastline than Martellus did. I have accordingly copied that part of the coastline from Portuguese maps, and placed São Jorge da Mina immediately south of the equator.

To show the difference between Columbus' impressions and the reality, a true map of the world on the same scale and projection is given also. America is shaded in on the ocean. The only clue that Columbus might have had about America consisted of the discovery of land southwest of Greenland, and no one could have guessed that that land was part of a large and fertile continent.

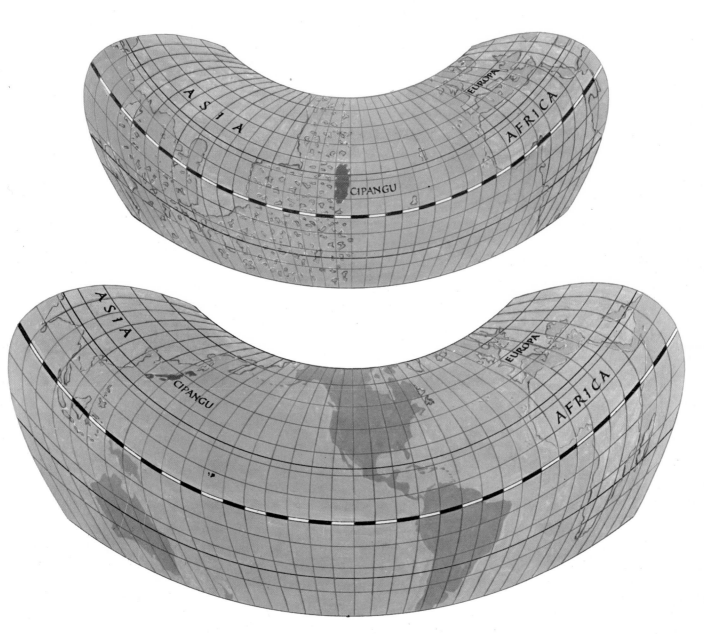

On both of these maps the arcs and the meridians are 10° apart. One degree at the equator is equivalent, on the upper map, to 52½ miles, and on the lower to 69½.

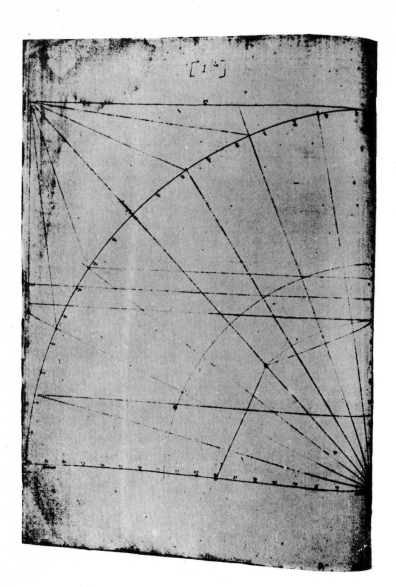

and Cipangu and the other islands came nearer. On a little map that has been ascribed to Bartolomeo Colombo, though it was probably the work of Alessandro Zorzi, we find the following note: "Secodo Marino e Colo da c. sa Vicetio a Cathicara g. 225, sia hore 15. Secodo Ptol. in fino a Cattigara g. 180, che sia hore 12," which probably means, "According to Marinus [of Tyre] and Columbus, the distance from Cape St. Vincent to Cattigara is 225 degrees, which equals 15 hours. According to Ptolemy, the distance to the uttermost limits [of the known world] at Cattigara is 180 degrees, which equals 12 hours."

If Columbus had accepted Marinus' 225 degrees and, like Toscanelli and other geographers, had added 60 degrees for newly discovered land, his continent would

Facsimile of a page in Pierre d'Ailly's Imago Mundi, *with a graduated sector drawn by Columbus. The book is kept at the Biblioteca Columbina, Seville.*

have become 285 degrees in extent. The western ocean would then have been 75 degrees wide, and the distance to Cipangu about 50 degrees—or, measured along the 28th parallel, 625 leagues. But Columbus' figure for this distance was 750 leagues.

I do not believe that he began from Marinus. I think that, by this time at least, he had come to accept Toscanelli's suggestion about the number of degrees covered by the Eurasian land mass. His 750 leagues sprang from a momentous miscalculation. On a blank page in his *Imago Mundi* he draw a map projection, a 90 degrees sector. Both the arc and the radii are graduated from 0 to 90, and the picture may be seen either as a map projection of a quarter of the northern hemisphere or as a diagrammatic aid for Columbus while calculating the distance from Europe to Cipangu. He draw a parallel arc at 50 degrees and another at $36\frac{1}{2}$ degrees; the latter is the one along which Toscanelli's degrees measure 50 Roman miles. If we now measure this arc in relation to the arc which represents the equator and proceed from Columbus' $56\frac{2}{3}$ Roman miles to one degree at the equator, the result is 3,022 Roman miles, or 755.6 leagues, which is not so very far off Columbus' 750.

If this was the method of reckoning that Columbus actually used—and I am unable to find any other explanation for this arc at $36\frac{1}{2}$ degrees—it was obviously incorrect. Such a map projection does not present a true picture, even though Ptolemy made use of the principle for small areas, and several famous cartographers were to apply it well into the 16th century. At any rate, the

This distance was to be accepted by all cartographers for the next hundred years. A graduated map of the world which Henricus Martellus made in 1490 is, except for the shape of Africa, a copy of Ptolemy's map, plus the 60 degrees of new land east of Cattigara.

On Martellus' map as well as on Behaim's globe, the distance from the zero meridian, off the coast of Africa, to Cipangu is 90 degrees. If this distance is measured along the 28th parallel—the approximate latitude of the Canaries—it should, by Columbus' reckoning, be about 4,500 Roman miles, or 1,125 leagues. But Fernando Colón says that his father expected to find land 750 leagues from the Canaries and also that Cipangu would be found in the same area.

This statement is generally taken to mean that Columbus made the continent even larger than did Toscanelli, and that in so doing his sea grew correspondingly narrower results of his calculations should have satisfied Columbus, for thereby the much-coveted Cipangu fell within comfortable reach. His 750 leagues were equivalent to 2,760 miles. The true distance due west from Portugal to Cipangu (Japan) is roughly 12,200 miles.

We know nothing of the way in which Columbus presented his plans to John II or anything about what he may have asked for in return, if such a stage was ever reached. Even so, it seems that his main objective was Cipangu, and we may feel sure that he used Marco Polo's description of its riches as an argument. "They have the greatest abundance of gold, for the sources of it are without end . . . . The entire roof of the palace is covered with plates of gold. . . . The ceilings of the rooms are made of the same precious metal. Many of the rooms have tables of massive thick gold, and the windows are also decorated with gold. . . . Also to be found on this island are great numbers of pearls, which are slightly reddish in colour, round, and very large; of the same value as white pearls, or even more valuable. . . . There are also quantities of precious stones."

According to Fernando Colón, John II showed little interest in the project, since the expeditions to Guinea had already cost so much trouble and money and had given nothing in return. The Portuguese chronicler Barros, who felt no sympathy for Columbus, wrote: "He came to the conclusion that it was possible to sail across the western Ocean to the island of Cipangu and other unknown lands. For since the time of Prince Henry, when the Azores were discovered, it was held that there must be other islands and lands to the west, for Nature could not have set things on earth so out of proportion that there should be more water than land, which was intended for life and the creation of souls. With these fantastic ideas that he had obtained on his continual voyages, and from talks with men who were versed in such matters and in this kingdom had great knowledge ,of past discoveries, he came to King John II, asking him for ships that he might sail away and discover the island of Cipangu in the western Ocean. . . . When the King found that this Cristovão Colom was very proud and boastful in presenting his talents, and more fanciful and full of imagination than accurate when speaking of his

island of Cipangu, he had little faith in him. But as he would not be put off, the King sent him to Dom Diogo Ortiz, the Bishop of Ceuta, and to Master Rodrigo and Master Josepe, who dealt with such questions of cosmography and discoveries; and all of them found that Cristovão Colom's words were empty, for they were based on fantasy, or on such things as Marco Polo's island of Cipangu."

The royal commission that studied Columbus' plan was composed entirely of learned men. The Bishop of Ceuta, like many of those in the service of the Church, was a scientist; Rodrigo was an astronomer and the king's physician; and Josepe was José Vicinho, the well-known cosmographer and astronomer, whom Columbus mentions in his notes as Yosepius. Columbus could not have asked for, or been granted, a more learned body of men in the whole of Europe, but their decision was inevitable: the route to Cipangu, if there really was any such island, was much too long. The earth was far larger and the ocean far wider than Colom imagined. Al-Farghani was right, but his miles were Arabian and not Roman ones. The king was not encouraged to place any faith in the theories of this man Colom.

It has been said that João II wanted to rob Columbus of his plan and that he dispatched Fernam Dulmo in 1486 with the purpose of doing so. It is true that a Fernam Dulmo applied that year for permission to sail to "a large island, or many islands, or a mainland, which I consider to be the Island of the Seven Cities, at my own cost and risk." He was, then, one of the many private adventurers of those days. The idea was that the expedition should set out from Terçeira, one of the Azores; but if it ever took place, then Dulmo and his followers must soon have tired of the hopeless battle against unremitting westerly winds.

Columbus had asked the king for ships, but there were none available for so uncertain an undertaking, for Guinea had the first claim on all resources. Columbus himself was deeply in debt at the time, and it is said that he left the country in secret to escape his creditors. This may be true, but he had not allowed the Portuguese scholars to argue him out of his convictions. At the end of 1484, he and his son Diego left the country, openly or in secret, to try their luck in Castile.

Ferdinand the Catholic, after a portrait by an unknown artist in Windsor Castle

Ferdinand and Isabella

The royal couple who were destined to unite Spain and build the country up into a great power had come to the throne thanks to a series of unusual events. By his first marriage, John II of Castile and León had a son, Henry, and by his second he had a daughter, Isabella, and another son, Alfonso. Henry, who was to become the fourth monarch of that name, succeeded to the throne in 1454 and continued to misgovern the kingdom which had already been misgoverned for many generations. Of his marriage with Joanna of Portugal, a sister of Afonso V, a daughter was born; she was also called Joanna, but since it was generally held that the queen's lover, Beltran de la Cueva, was her true father, she was often referred to as Joanna Beltraneja.

Powerful opposition in the country refused to accept the new-born princess as heir to the throne and demanded that Henry IV should recognize his half-brother Alfonso in her stead. This the king refused to do, and his refusal led to a minor civil war on the question of the succession until 1468, when Alfonso suddenly died. The opposition then transferred its sympathies to Isabella.

She was very religious, and it is said that she detested the profligate life at court, where she had been forced to live ever since the birth of the Princess Joanna. In order to exclude Isabella from the succession, her half-brother, the king, planned to marry her off to one of his knights. The opposition immediately wanted to dethrone King Henry and proclaim Isabella as queen regnant, but she did not want to disrupt a kingdom which was sufficiently disturbed already, and would only agree to be proclaimed heir to the throne. The king accepted this arrangement, and she was proclaimed by the Cortes, the Castilian parliament, as the lawful successor. But later the king revoked his decision and threatened Isabella with imprisonment, and Joanna was once again put forward as his successor.

Meanwhile, Isabella's followers had been secretly negotiating for a marriage between her and Prince Ferdinand of Aragon. Both parties agreed and signed a contract of marriage, which stipulated that Ferdinand should not be allowed to come to any decisions of civil or military nature in Castile without hearing her opinion and obtaining her permission, that he was to continue the war against the Moors in Granada, and that he would not demand a return of the regions in Castile which had once belonged to his father, the King of Aragon. Neither Ferdinand nor Isabella had any funds, and in order to

Isabella the Catholic, after a portrait by Bartolomé Bermejo in the Museo del Prado, Madrid

have a wedding in keeping with their station they had to borrow the means. The marriage took place in October, 1469, when Ferdinand was eighteen years old and Isabella nineteen. The ceremony was performed without the knowledge of King Henry, and when he heard the news, he and his queen swore a solemn oath that Princess Joanna was their legitimate child.

There followed a period of almost complete anarchy in the kingdom. Rival factions of knights came to blows with one another, and in the south, in Andalusia, the families of Guzmán and Ponce de León fought regular pitched battles. But the most disturbing thing of all was the drop in the value of money. Previously, the kingdom had had five privileged royal mints. During the reign of Henry IV, the nobles on their small domains began to mint money themselves, and it is estimated that there were finally something like one hundred and fifty mints in Castile. The price of the most ordinary consumer goods rose 500 or 600 per cent. Ultimately, all faith in the currency was lost, and trade was reduced to the elementary form of barter. Henry IV died in December, 1474.

Isabella was accepted as queen regnant in most of Castile, but the aged Afonso V of Portugal, with some justification, asserted that his niece, Joanna, was the only true heir to the throne, and she was therefore the true Queen

of Castile. In order to create a more direct Portuguese interest in Castile, Afonso obtained from the Pope a dispensation to betroth himself to the twelve-year-old Joanna.

Early in May, 1475, Afonso V entered Castile with a large army. He was welcomed by the princess and her supporters, and ordered an announcement to be sent round various parts of the country asserting that he and Joanna were its rulers. This intrusion on the part of their hereditary enemy united the Castilians once and for all. While Afonso was waiting in vain for King Henry's old supporters to join him and his troops, Castilian units crossed into Portugal to harass the almost undefended country. This gave Ferdinand and Isabella breathing space in which to assemble an army, and, in 1476, this army won a great victory over Afonso at Toro.

In 1479, after three years of skirmishing and diplomatic intrigue, the Spanish war of succession at last came to an end, and Isabella was recognized by all parties as Queen of Castile. Ferdinand's father died in the same year, and thenceforward the royal couple reigned over both Castile and Aragon. Poor Joanna, who by her mere existence had been the cause of so much disquiet, withdrew to a convent in Portugal. King Afonso, her betrothed, had already decided to abdicate and was about to do so when he died suddenly in 1481.

Ferdinand and Isabella would have had little chance

33

of success in their attempt to calm the incessantly rebellious factions if they had not had the support of the people and of the Cortes, which was composed of representatives of the Church, the nobility, the gentry, and the towns. All Ferdinand and Isabella's most important acts—the withdrawal of the pensions and annuities which had been far too readily granted, the banning of noblemen's private armies, the prohibition of castle-building, private warfare, and dueling—were ratified by the Cortes.

Inflation had almost completely disrupted trade and industry, but the monetary reform that was now introduced gave them new lease on life. Only five royal mints were authorized, and all other coining was liable to the severest penalties. Laws were introduced to encourage domestic industries and to protect both home and overseas trade, and special license was given to the import of foreign books, on the ground that "they brought to the kingdom both honour and gain, in that they made it possible for the citizens to become learned men." The several legal codes current in different parts of the country were collected and standardized, so that one and the same law came to apply throughout the land.

It may be questioned whether this royal couple, who received from the Pope the honorary title of "Their Catholic Majesties" were so unbelievably perfect in all they did that not a foot was set wrong. They were obviously a very well-matched couple. It seems that Isabella was an unusually wise and courageous woman, but her decisions were often influenced by a consuming religious passion which had a touch of bigotry and fanaticism. It is said that Ferdinand was heartless and cunning and very brave, qualities that were certainly necessary in the royal couple's difficult task. But the opinions of chroniclers were nearly always one-sided, colored by their own likes and dislikes; when rulers have long been dead, we can only judge their characters by their actions. Ferdinand and Isabella certainly did a great deal that we can regard as good, but they also did bad things. Unwise and bad things.

Ever since Moorish times, Castile had harbored a great many Jews, who, like the Christians, had enjoyed complete religious liberty. Most men of learning in the kingdom, its physicians, teachers, and astronomers, were of Jewish origin; much of the kingdom's banking and most of its commerce and skilled handicrafts, were under Jewish management. There were also thousands of Jews in every section of the community.

Early in the 15th century they had undergone severe persecution at Christian hands, and many of them had become Christians. It is probable that a great many of these *Marannos,* as they were called, were only nominal Christians and privately continued to keep the Sabbath and other Jewish customs. The clergy were disturbed by the suspicion, and perhaps the certainty, that such things were going on, and some of the leaders of the Spanish Church, headed by the queen's confessor, Tomas de Torquemada, succeeded in persuading Isabella to appeal to the Pope for the reintroduction of the Holy Inquisition.

It was the task of the Inquisition to detect these false Christians, to expose them, and then to hand them over to the temporal courts. It urged all citizens to denounce heretics, and all information, even if anonymous, was carefully studied. Tomas de Torquemada himself became the Grand Inquisitor, and during his term of office 10,220 heretics, real or alleged, were burned at the stake. There were 6,860 heretics who had died, or escaped, and were burned in effigy, and 97,321 lesser or penitent offenders were condemned to minor penalties.

In Castile, and later in Aragon, the Inquisition was bitterly opposed by the people, but the Church exploited an age-old hatred of the Jews, and its proceedings were allowed to continue.

The quarrelsome knights, who had had to surrender some of their estates and privileges, were compensated by magnificent titles that cost the Crown nothing and found an outlet for their surplus energies in the war against the Moors in Granada, which for the next ten years was to cost the Crown nearly the whole of its revenue. The war began in 1481, and the Moors themselves gave a welcome pretext for it by attacking and destroying the small fortress-town of Zahara, which had been wrested from them by Ferdinand's grandfather.

The fortunes of war wavered during the first years, and the Spaniards often held public thanksgiving for their victories, only to experience crushing defeat soon afterward. The Pope proclaimed the war against Granada a crusade, and many foreign knights came to fight for God, for everlasting glory, and for the forgiveness of their sins. The war consisted mainly of skirmishes and raids, in which villages were destroyed and crops burned. During one such operation in 1483, the young King Boabdil of Granada fell into the hands of the Spaniards, but the contemporary code of chivalry allowed him to buy himself free. This cost him an annual payment of 12,000 doubloons, the release of four hundred Christian prisoners, and in addition the maintenance and safe-conduct through his dominions for the Spanish troops operating in the part of Granada which belonged to his father. In return, he was promised a two years' armistice.

As it was generally agreed that the fortress of Granada could never be taken without a powerful artillery, Ferdinand and Isabella brought cannon makers and other experts from Germany and Italy. They thought that they were facing their greatest and most historic task, and their state coffers were almost empty. It was only to be expected, then, that they should have had little time for such an insignificant person as Cristoforo Colombo.

Cristóbal Colón in Castile

It is probable—the words "perhaps," "probable," and "possible" must inevitably recur in any biography of Columbus—that it was in the spring or summer of 1484 that Columbus left Portugal for Castile; we do not know whether he went by land or by sea. Presumably he went first of all to the little town of Huelva, where his wife's sister was living with her husband, Miguel Molyart, and left his son Diego under their protection. Diego could hardly have been more than three years old at the time.

After this, the data are obscure and contradictory. We can say with certainty only that he visited Luis de la Cerda, then Count and later Duke of Medina Celi. This nobleman later wrote a letter to the Grand Cardinal of Spain, containing the words: "I do not know whether Your Grace is aware that Cristóbal Colombo stayed at my house for a time. He had come from Portugal, and was disposed to make his way to the King of France to obtain his support for a voyage to the Indies. I was greatly inclined to arrange matters myself and dispatch him from my harbour, for I had three or four caravels, and more he did not require. But when it occurred to me that this might be a matter for the Queen, our Mistress, I wrote to Her Majesty on the subject from Rota; and her reply was that I should send him to her." Later on in the letter he says that Columbus had stayed with him for two years.

This period can probably be reduced to eighteen months, for Columbus himself says that he was attached to Queen Isabella's court from January 20, 1486. It might have been on that very day that he arrived at the house of the royal treasurer, Alfonso de Quintanilla, in Cordova, where he might have signed a receipt for a small donation from the royal coffers. In any case, Ferdinand and Isabella were not in Cordova during the winter and did not

return to, that city before April. Meanwhile, Columbus was forced to earn his living, and as there could hardly have been any call for a mapmaker of his caliber in the middle of Andalusia, we must suppose that this was the time when he became a bookseller. The chronicler Bernaldes, who knew him well, writes: "He was an itinerant seller of printed books, and pursued his trade in Andalusia."

It might have been during this winter in Castile that he met Beatriz Enriques de Harana, an ordinary woman in straitened circumstances, of whom we know little more than that she gave birth to Columbus' second son, Fernando, in the autumn of 1488. In his Will, Columbus entreats his son Diego to provide for Beatriz Enriques, Fernando's mother, "so that she may be able to live honorably, for she is someone to whom I owe a great deal. And this shall be done so that I may satisfy my conscience, for the matter weighs heavily on my soul. This is not the place to give the reasons." The reasons were doubtless that he had never made her his wife and that she was left in the shade when he had won his place in the sun. Bastardy was by no means uncommon in those days, and neither kings nor church dignitaries were

ashamed to recognize their illegitimate children; but for Columbus, who was a very religious man, it must have been a heavy burden to have lived in sin with the woman who should have been his wife. She was good enough for the penniless bookseller in Andalusia, but she could scarcely fit in with his increasingly ambitious fantasies of Cipangu and the golden Indies.

No chronicler describes Columbus' first meeting with Ferdinand and Isabella. He might well have been an insignificant figure in a long line of petitioners. He might have had to present his case in the intervals between far more important meetings on the government of the kingdom and the preparations for war. Yet his proposal to lead Castilian ships to the Indies by sailing due west must surely have awakened the royal interest from the very beginning. By the Treaty of Alcaçovas, the route to the Indies by way of the southern cape of Africa was a Portuguese preserve, but if the Genoese mariner was right, then the western route was both shorter and better, as well as being available. But the royal couple did not know enough about cosmography to be able to form an opinion of their own, and the whole question was referred to a commission of experts.

It is not known when the commission was set up, but some years were to pass before it reached a decision and could give its recommendations. At that time, Castile had no permanent body for such questions and those who were to advise the Sovereigns on the route to the Indies must have had many other more pressing matters to deal with during the long years of the war.

But this impoverished Genoese mariner must have made a favorable impression. We know that he continued to receive some small gratuities from the depleted Treasury for several years longer, so that he could keep himself and his plans alive. But the years of waiting caused him much suffering, and in his letters and other writings he refers time and time again to these bitter years when everyone mocked him, to these long years when no one would believe him. But both he and his biographers must have been unjust in their complaints. If everyone really mocked him, he must have given them reason for doing so, by broadcasting his assertions about Cipangu and about sailing west to reach the east. It is probable that in the eyes of the Spaniards, as in those of Barros, the Portuguese historian, he was a conceited boaster. If one is poor, and a foreigner, such characteristics are unpopular.

Meanwhile, he could not remain idle. Presumably, he had heard from Bartolomeo in Lisbon that Diogo Cão in the course of his second long voyage had never reached the end of Africa but had only seen a long coastline stretching interminably to the south. Columbus then wrote to João II, again asking him to consider his theory of a western route to the Indies, and it may well be that he also assured

him that he, Cristóbal Colón, was the only man who knew that route. The king's reply has been preserved, and it runs thus:

"To Cristovam Colon, our especial friend, in Seville.

"Cristoval Colon: We, Don João by the Grace of God, King of Portugal and Algarve within and beyond the Sea of Africa, Lord of Guinea, send you good greetings. We have seen the letter which you wrote to Us, and we thank you heartily for the good will and enthusiasm you show to serve Us. We desire you to come to Us, both because you yourself have indicated such a wish, as well as for other reasons; for your industry and great talent will be useful to Us. Regarding the things that worry you, matters will be arranged as you wish. And since you may have fear of Our justice because of certain debts, we assure you by this Our letter that neither on your way hither nor during your stay with Us, nor on your return, will you be arrested, detained, accused, charged, or prosecuted in any suit, civil or criminal, of any kind whatever; and by this same letter We commend all Our judges to comply with this order. We therefore urge and instruct you to come at once and without fear. We shall be grateful to you and consider that you have served Us well.

Written at Avis, March 20, 1488
The King"

It is this letter which tells us that Columbus had fled from Lisbon, from the hands of his creditors, to avoid being thrown into the debtors' prison. We do not know whether he accepted the royal invitation and went to Portugal. Perhaps the journey was never really necessary, for at the end of that year Bartolomeo Diaz sailed into Lisbon with the news that he had reached the southernmost cape of Africa and that the route to the Indies now lay open.

Columbus was named after St. Christopher, the Bearer of Christ. This name was one of the reasons which made him regard his enterprise as a sacred mission.

Bartolomeo Colombo witnessed the arrival of Diaz and made a note of it in the margin of the *Imago Mundi*.

As it seemed that there was nothing more to be done in Portugal, Columbus persuaded his brother to go to England and try to negotiate with Henry VII. After a series of adventures, Bartolomeo arrived in that country and was given audience with the king. He presented the project and handed over a map of the world that he had drawn, perhaps a copy of Toscanelli's map. According to Fernando Colón, King Henry showed great interest in the idea. According to the chronicler Oviedo, the king

The city of Granada, with the fortress of the Alhambra, was the most powerful Moorish stronghold in Spain. In the background, the Sierra Nevada.

thought Bartolomeo was a fool and regarded his ideas as madness.

In Spain, Cristoforo Colombo had begun to call himself Cristóbal Colón. It seems as if he also referred to himself as Colom while in Portugal and during his early days in Spain. We do not know why he altered his name. Bishop Bartolomé de Las Casas writes in his *Historia de las Indias:* "He was baptized Cristóbal, that is Christum Ferens, which means the bringer or bearer of Christ. And thus it was he often signed his name, for he was verily the first to open the gates of the Ocean and to carry our Saviour, Jesus Christ, to these distant lands and kingdoms. . . . His surname was Colón, which means repopulator, a name fitting the man who by his works, and by his teaching of the Gospel, has repopulated the glorious city of Heaven with so many souls."

Columbus might already have begun to regard his project as a sacred mission, and he might also have had a long-standing ambition to emulate the saint whose name he had been given. St. Christopher was a giant who carried people across a swift-flowing river that had no bridge. One day, as he was carrying a little child, he felt that his burden was almost unbearably heavy and that his legs were beginning to give way; then he discovered that he was carrying the Creator of All Things upon his shoulders.

The war with Granada had begun. The Christians had already celebrated great victories, and in 1489 their forces were gathered outside Baza. But Columbus was not forgotten in the delirium of war. He received a letter calling him to the Court, which was encamped in tents outside the beleaguered city; the letter also enjoined all local authorities to see that he received food and lodging on the road. He might have been summoned to Court in this way a number of times, for other such injunctions might have gone completely unrecorded. He might have written an impatient letter to one of his patrons, threatening to leave the country. Perhaps someone remembered that the Genoese mariner had received no support from the Treasury for a year. We do not know how long he stayed at Court, whether he took part in the siege, or whether he was there when the city fell in December, 1489.

At last, a year after Baza, the commission that was to deal with his project met. One of the queen's confessors, Hernando de Talavera, presided over it, and one of its members was named Rodriguez de Maldonado; we know nothing of the others. The commission's recommendation was negative.

Fernando Colón writes: "As there were not so many geographers then as now, the members of the commission were not so well informed as the business required. Nor did the Admiral wish to reveal all the details of his plan, for fear that it might be stolen from him in Castile as it had been in Portugal." Fernando is thus one of those who assert that João II stole Columbus' idea. But I am convinced that Columbus did not disclose all the details of his plan in Lisbon either. Had he done so, then Fernam Dulmo, if the king really sent him, would never have tried to sail west from Terçeira. For Columbus had a secret, a trump card that he had not yet played, and would not play until the very last moment. If it should prove necessary. But that moment had not yet come.

38

Fernando continues about the commission: "Some argued in this way: During the thousands of years that have passed since God created the world, those lands had remained unknown to innumerable scholars and experts in navigation; and it was most unlikely that the Admiral should know more than all other men, living and dead. [Fernando always speaks of his father as the Admiral.] Others, who based their opinions on geography, claimed that the world was so large that it would take more than three years to reach the end of India, whither the Admiral wished to sail. In support of this, they cited Seneca, who discusses the question in one of his books, saying that many scholars disagreed as to whether the Ocean was infinite or not, and doubted that men could ever sail across it; and even if this could be done, they questioned whether habitable lands existed on the other side. . . . Others argued, as some Portuguese had done, about the sea-route to Guinea, asserting that if a voyage was made due west, as the Admiral proposed, it would be impossible to return to Spain, because the earth was round. These men were convinced that men who left the hemisphere known to Ptolemy would be going downhill, and so could not return; for that would be like sailing a ship to the top of a mountain: a thing that ships could not do even in the most powerful of winds."

It is possible that Fernando exaggerates the inadequacy of the commission. But regardless of the course the discussion took, the commission had come to the same conclusion as their Portuguese counterpart, and it was explained to the Sovereigns that it would be beneath their dignity to have anything to do with a project that was based on such weak and uncertain foundations. And yet it seems that Ferdinand and Isabella were not completely convinced by the findings of the scholars. Las Casas says that they assured Columbus that his business could be taken up at a more opportune time, when the war against Granada had been brought to a successful conclusion.

The spring of 1490 opened with great celebrations of the betrothal of Doña Isabel, the daughter of Ferdinand and Isabella, and Afonso, the Crown Prince of Portugal. At the same time, a great effort was made to take the fortress of Granada. Boabdil was urged to surrender, but the weak, young king replied that he was no longer master of his city and his kingdom, which were crowded with refugees still determined to resist the Christians. This year passed with nothing more than skirmishings and crop burnings.

Fighting on a larger scale was resumed the next year, and it had been decided in the meantime that there would be no withdrawal until Granada had capitulated. After a summer of indecisive skirmishes the Christians began to build a complete city, called Santa Fé, on the plain below the fortress to make it clear to everyone that they had come to stay.

Bartolomeo Colombo had failed in his mission to England and therefore tried to deal with Charles VIII of France. He might have sent a hopeful report to his brother in Andalusia at the beginning of 1491, but in any case Columbus was preparing to leave for the French court that year.

His son Diego, who was now about ten years old, had probably been living with him in Cordova during these last years, and now they set out together and came to the monastery of La Rábida on the Atlantic coast at the mouth of the Rio Tinto, near Palos and Huelva. The prior of the monastery, Juan Pérez, succeeded in persuading Columbus to postpone his journey to France. It might have been Juan Pérez who introduced Columbus to Martín Alonso Pinzón and his brothers in Palos, and it might have been on this occasion that they all reviewed the project together, and the prior was so impressed that he wrote a letter about it to the queen. It is said that he was another of the queen's confessors; he must in any case have been on fairly close terms with her, for she replied to his letter almost immediately. She thanked him for his intervention, asked him to give her assurances to Columbus and to present himself at court immediately.

We are told that he left his monastery in secret at night to ride to his Sovereign Lady. After they had discussed the matter, she sent 20,000 *maravedis* to Diego Prieto, the mayor of Palos, and asked him to give the money to Columbus so that he might buy some suitable clothes and a horse and ride immediately to join her at Santa Fé, the city of the Holy Ghost, on the battlefield below the infidel fortress.

He might have taken part in the last petty skirmishes of the siege, in his new clothes and on his new horse. Negotiations for surrender were already being made, but in the greatest secrecy. Boabdil and Ferdinand and Isabella signed the terms of surrender at the end of November. Formal surrender, and the cession of Granada to the Spaniards, took place on January 2, 1492, and soon the entire Christian world was celebrating the magnificent victory over the last infidel kingdom in the Iberian Peninsula.

Ferdinand and Isabella at last had time to turn their attentions to Columbus and his project. A new commission was set up, and it is probable that it had already accepted the plan of our Genoese mariner when the question of payment began to be discussed. This came as a shock. This poor foreigner, who could afford neither to dress himself properly nor to keep his own horse, now demanded in return for his services not only one-tenth of all the riches that might be found in the Indies, but also the title of Don Cristóbal Colón and the rank of Admiral of the Ocean and Viceroy and Governor of the Indies. The commission and the Sovereigns were astonished. Columbus was given a flat refusal.

It was presumably at this stage that he played his trump card. During talks with Luis de Santángel, the king's treasurer, who had very probably been Columbus' friend and spokesman for a long time, Columbus explained *how* to sail to the Indies.

41

He had sailed both to the Azores and to Britain, perhaps many times, and had observed that the winds were nearly always westerly in the northern part of the ocean. He had sailed south to Guinea and seen that the prevailing winds became northeasterly at the Canary Islands and remained in this quarter all the way down to Cape Verde. On the way back from Guinea, the Portuguese used to beat to the northwest and north in the ever reliable northeasterly winds. Once out of this region, after the Canaries, they had to force their way north in weak variable winds as far as the Azores, where they came into the area of good westerly winds that carried them all the way to Lisbon. Columbus had noticed this and discussed it with other mariners. All of them had noticed the same thing, but Columbus alone had understood that the northeast winds must blow as far as the Indies and that the west winds must blow from the Indies to Portugal.

Portuguese mariners had actually set out with the intention of discovering islands or a continent in the west, but they had tried to sail straight into the west wind, instead of taking the northeast wind out and the west wind on the way home. Poseidonius had said that it was possible to cross the ocean with a favorable east wind, and Seneca had said the same. But Cristóbal Colón was the only one who had found this wind, because God had so willed it, because Columbus was a chosen man.

I have no proof that Columbus really kept this knowledge to the end as a trump card. But Fernando Colón says that Columbus did not want to disclose all the details of his plan, and this was the only new feature of the enterprise as it was presented, apart from the fact that Columbus' earth and, consequently, his ocean were even smaller than Toscanelli's. That he did in fact have this knowledge is shown most clearly by the fact that on all his voyages to the West Indies he sailed out with the northeast trades and came back by the belt of westerly winds, and that these were the routes which continued to be taken as long as ships sailed between Spain and the West Indies. It is understandable that he kept his secret as long as possible.

But we are running ahead of events. The commission had refused his conditions, and Columbus left Santa Fé and rode off in the direction of Cordova. But he had got no farther than the bridge at Pinos when he was overtaken by a horseman who commanded him to return in the name of the queen.

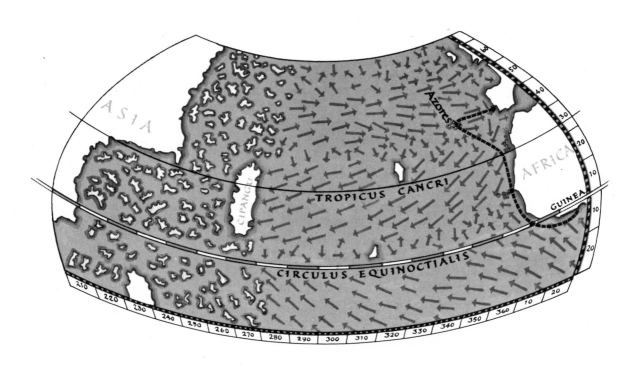

This is approximately how Columbus envisaged the direction and extent of the prevailing Atlantic winds. The broken line shows the route of the Portuguese caravels from São Jorge da Mina to Lisbon.

The Agreement

The monogram of Ferdinand and Isabella. The Y stands for the Spanish form, Ysabel.

Fernando Colón says that it was Luis de Santángel who took immediate steps to persuade the Spanish sovereigns to reverse their decision. We are told that he visited the queen and expressed his surprise that she, who had never hesitated to decide for herself on questions of great importance, should now turn away from an enterprise that involved so little risk and yet at the same time might bring everlasting glory to God and His Church, to say nothing of what it might bring to herself and to her kingdom. Moreover, the project was of such a nature that if it was realized in the name of some other ruler, it would damage her own kingdom and give cause for justifiable reproaches from her friends and complaint from her enemies. Yet since everything seemed so carefully planned, and since the Genoese mariner seemed to be a skilled and intelligent man who wanted rewards in proportion to his discoveries and was prepared not only to jeopardize his own life but also to risk some of his own money toward the cost of his project, Her Highness could not say that the plan was impossible, as certain experts had maintained. As for the foolish assertion that it would harm the queen if she supported an enterprise that might fail, then he, Santángel, was of the opinion that Their Majesties would sooner be regarded as generous and farsighted rulers who had done what they could to unravel the secrets of the universe.

The queen thanked Santángel for his services and said that she would gladly accept the proposals of the Genoese mariner if she was given a little time to recover from the exertions of the siege of Granada; she also added that she was prepared to pledge her jewelry to help to pay for the expedition. But Santángel assured her that this would not be necessary, saying that he himself would be only too happy to obtain the necessary money on her behalf. And thus it was that Isabella sent a messenger along the road to Cordova to bring Cristóbal Colón back to Santa Fé.

This account is perhaps somewhat simplified and dramatized, yet Luis de Santángel was undoubtedly one of the men best in a position to make Ferdinand and Isabella reverse the decision they had already made. In later years Columbus mentioned two members of the clergy, Diego de Deza and Antonio de Marchena, who had done more than anyone else to support his project, but their efforts might have been made at an earlier stage. Preliminary agreement was now reached, and it is possible that Colum-

bus heard at the same time about the plans for the deportation of the Jews, for he later wrote, incorrectly, that the Sovereigns reached their decisions for his voyage and for the expulsion of the Jews in the same month. Many Jews were employed at the court, and Santángel himself and the treasurer-general, Gabriel Sánchez, were both *Marannos,* converts from Judaism. They were never threatened with expulsion, it is true, but they must have been horrified that such things were discussed. Both had relatives who were burned at the stake, and Santángel himself had been sentenced to a degrading penance some years earlier.

Columbus was still a poor man, but his position was now completely changed, and his rich friends and patrons—perhaps Santángel and Gabriel Sánchez, perhaps Medina Celi—lent him the money that was to be his own investment in the enterprise. It must have been a happy and exhilarating time, full of plans that were no longer dreams, and of work for a goal that now seemed really attainable. Even though he was certainly obsessed by his plan, Columbus must nevertheless have doubted and despaired many times during the years that had passed, for otherwise the great bitterness that never left him would not have made so deep an imprint.

He then, apparently, went to La Rábida and Palos, with Juan Pérez, who thenceforward acted as his representative at the Court. To quote a deposition made about twenty years later: "What he knows is that Don Cristóbal Colón, before he set off to negotiate with Their Catholic Majesties about his expedition, came to the town of Palos to seek support for this said expedition. And he sojourned at the monastery of La Rábida, and went from there many times to Palos and spoke with one Pero Vasquez de la Frontera, a man very skilled in the art of sailing the ocean, who had once set out himself to make the same expedition with the Infante of Portugal. And this Pero Vasquez de la Frontera gave advice to the said Colón and to Martín Alonso Pinzón, and encouraged the people and said publicly that they would all be allowed to take part in this voyage and that they would discover a very rich land."

This deposition, which was given some time after Columbus' death, during the protracted lawsuit between his heirs and the Crown, has often been taken to mean that Pero Vasquez was the first man to give Columbus the idea of land to the west. It has also been regarded as evidence that the Portuguese had been there before Columbus. We know that that cannot be true. It is quite possible, however, that Columbus was in Palos in the spring of 1492, trying to interest its sailor citizens in his expedition. Most of his dealings were probably with the Pinzón brothers and their spokesman, Martín Alonso. Since many were sceptical, he would have profited by the old seamen's stories of the opulent country on the other side of the ocean. Pero Vasquez was one of the many who had sailed with Henry the Navigator's captains in search of "islands or a continent," and he had not been the first or the last to see imaginary blue islands on the horizon. And it is always the islands on the horizon that are the most promising and attractive.

On the whole, the men of Palos were not enthusiastic about the project. We learn from depositions that there were many who would have no part of it, not from any lack of courage but because they did not believe in this man from Genoa and his theories. A Portuguese who was on Columbus' second voyage, though not on his first, explained that he thought Columbus would be sailing in vain and find no land, since the King of Portugal had made the same attempt several times with no success.

On March 30, the axe fell on the Jewish community. All unbaptized Jews, regardless of age, sex, or social standing, were ordered to leave the country within three months, never to return on pain of death. They were allowed to take with them all the portable goods they possessed — except their gold, silver, and currency.

Ferdinand and Isabella signed the agreement with Columbus on April 17. The document runs:

"The things humbly sought, and which Your Highnesses give and grant Don Cristoval de Colón, in some return for what he has discovered in the Ocean, and for the voyage which with the help of God he is now about to make in the service of Your Highnesses, are the following:

"First, that Your Highnesses, as true Sovereigns of the said Ocean, henceforth appoint the said Cristoval Colón, in all those islands and mainlands which by his labour and industry shall be discovered or acquired in the said Ocean, Admiral during his life, and after his death his heirs and successors, from one to the other perpetually, with all the rights and privileges belonging to that office, in the same manner as the High Admiral of Castile in the said office held it in his jurisdictions.

"*It so pleases Their Highnesses. Juan de Coloma.*

"Further, that Your Highnesses appoint the said Don Cristoval Colón Their Viceroy and Governor-General in all the said islands and mainlands which, as has been said, he may discover or acquire in the said Ocean, and that for the government of each and every one of them he may propose three persons for each office and that Your Highnesses may take and choose the one most suitable to Your service, so that the lands which Our Lord allows him to discover and acquire in the service of Your Highnesses may best be governed.

"*It so pleases Their Highnesses. Juan de Coloma.*

"Item, that of all merchandise, whether pearls, precious stones, gold, silver, spices, or other things of whatever kind, name, or description they may be, which may be bought, bartered, found, acquired, or obtained within the bounds of the said Admiralty, Your Highnesses will and decree that the said Don Cristoval Colón shall take and keep for himself one tenth part of the whole, after all expenses have been deducted, so that of all that remains he may take the tenth part for himself and dispose of it as he pleases, the other nine parts to belong to Your Highnesses.

"*It so pleases Their Highnesses. Juan de Coloma.*

"Further, that if, on account of the goods that he brings from the said islands and mainlands, which, as has been said, he may acquire or discover, or on account of things obtained in exchange for these from other merchants here, any suit shall arise in the place where the said trade shall occur, and if, by the authority of his office of Admiral it appertains to him to take jurisdiction over such a suit, it may please Your Highnesses that he or his deputy, and no other magistrate, take jurisdiction of the said suit, and so it shall be done henceforth,

"*It so pleases Their Highnesses, in so far as the same privileges appertain to the said office of Admiral as the said Admiral Don Alonso Enriques and his predecessors held it. Juan de Coloma.*

"Further, that the said Don Cristoval Colón may, if he wish, pay and contribute one eighth part of the total cost of the equipment on all the vessels which shall be dispatched on the said trade and traffic, on each and every occasion, whenever and as often as this may occur; and likewise that he may take and retain an eighth part of

44

such profits as may accrue from this traffic.

"*It so pleases Their Highnesses. Juan de Coloma.*

"This is drawn up and given the approval of Their Highnesses, at the end of each article, in the city of Santa Fé de la Vega de Granada, on the seventeenth day of April, in the year of Our Saviour Jesus Christ, one thousand four hundred and ninety-two.

I the King   I the Queen
By order of the King and Queen
Juan de Coloma."

Juan de Coloma was the State Secretary of Aragon. Eighteen days earlier he had countersigned the order for the deportation of the Jews. His own mother was of Jewish origin.

Juan Pérez and Juan de Coloma had drawn up this contract together. Many people have been puzzled by the preamble, with its promise of recompense "for what he has discovered in the Ocean." It has been maintained that he had already crossed the Atlantic and found land and that his only motive in making this new "voyage of discovery" was to provide a legal basis for his claims. It has also been suggested that the preamble was added considerably later, immediately before Columbus' second voyage. But the whole phraseology is clumsy, and this may simply be a piece of official writing, meaning nothing but "for what he has discovered about the size of the earth and the extent of the ocean," or perhaps, "for what he has discovered about the ocean crossing." But this is, of course, pure speculation.

Some people have been surprised by the words "islands and mainlands." There is no mention of Cipangu, Cathay, or the Indies. Columbus' objective was clearly defined. That is evident from his Journal. Nor had any pearls, gold, or spices been found on any of the Atlantic islands so far discovered. The phrase was presumably a safety precaution, because there were political reasons against mentioning a voyage to India at this moment. And after all, much the same words—*islands or a mainland*—had been used by Henry the Navigator and João II, and an equally vague expression was used when Henry VII of England signed his agreement with John Cabot.

On April 30, Ferdinand and Isabella signed a long list of documents about Columbus and his expedition. The longest of them was a formal acknowledgment of his titles and privileges. He was to receive full powers of jurisdiction in the lands he discovered and acquired, and his titles and offices were to pass to his heirs for all time. He was furnished with letters of introduction to be presented to the rulers of the countries he discovered, as well as a sort of passport, to be shown if necessary. An order was drawn up instructing the people of Palos to place two caravels at his disposal. Another decree offered a free par-

don to any criminals who agreed to sail with him. All the authorities, and indeed all the inhabitants along the coast of Andalusia, were instructed to place labor and materials at his disposal, without delay. And, finally, there was a document exempting the expedition from export duty on the provisions and other goods that would be taken out of the kingdom.

Columbus left Granada on May 12, traveling to Palos in the company of Juan Pérez. On May 23, the mayor of Palos, his aldermen, and other leading citizens were summoned to the church of San Jorge, where the notary public of the town, in the presence of Columbus and Juan Pérez, read out a Royal Command. In consequence of certain offences against the Sovereigns, the town had been commanded to keep two caravels ready for the use of the Crown for the period of one year. The people of Palos were now ordered to provision and equip these ships within ten days, so that they could leave with Cristóbal Colón for the place to which the Sovereigns had commanded him to sail. The Crown was to pay the crews four months' wages in advance, at the rate of pay laid down for service on the high seas. The ships were to follow the course set by Cristóbal Colón in the name of the Sovereigns, and neither he nor those who sailed with him were allowed to sail to Guinea or to concern themselves with Portuguese trade in Africa. These orders were to be obeyed under pain of the Sovereigns' displeasure, and every breach of them would be subject to a fine of 10,000 *maravedis.*

Columbus' coat of arms before he was ennobled

45

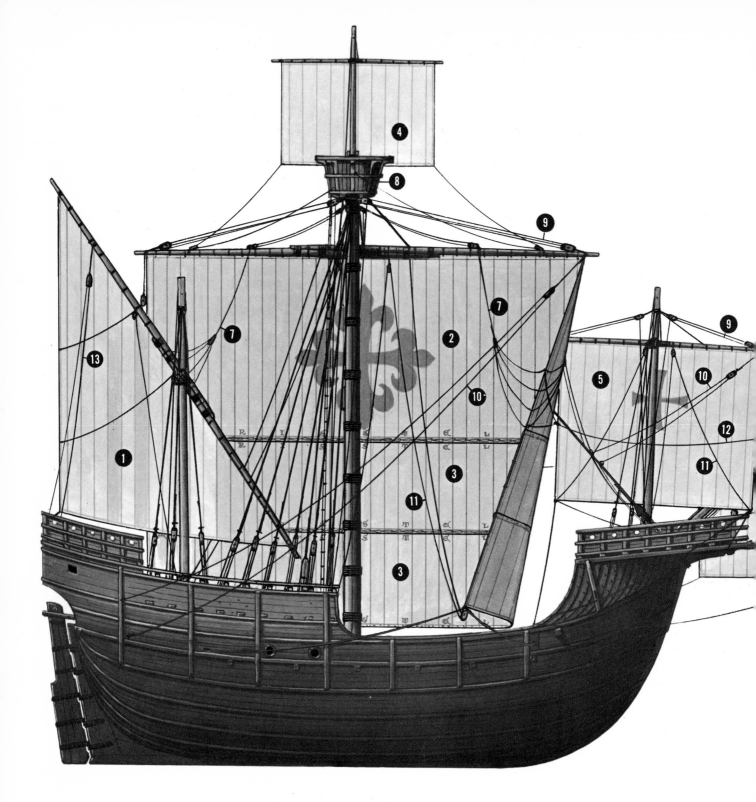

For the past seventy-five years people have been trying to reconstruct the Santa María, *the flagship of Columbus' first voyage. In fact, no such attempt can hope to be successful; none of the models or "replicas" we have seen in museums or at international exhibitions can claim to represent anything but, at best, a ship of approximately the same kind and* the same size as the celebrated original. We simply do not know what the Santa María *looked like.*

We do know that, unlike the Pinta *and the* Niña, *she was a* nao, *a small round-bellied vessel, and we know what sails she carried; but beyond this the field is open for speculation. To get a more accurate picture, we would have to analyze* and compare all pictures and descriptions of ships of that period; but there is relatively little contemporary source material, and many questions must still remain unanswered. The second half of the 15th century saw many changes in ships, especially in the rigging. We do not know whether the Santa María belonged to the northern type, which among other things had the main shrouds attached with deadeyes and lanyards, and had ratlines in the shrouds, or to the southern type, with tackles to attach the shrouds, and a ladder running to the top.

I have chosen the latter type for my reconstruction. I assume that she was between 80 and 100 tons, since it is known that the Niña was assessed at 60 tons, and Las Casas says that the Santa María was only "slightly" larger. This means that she could be loaded with between 80 and 100 "tuns" of wine. A Spanish tonelada of wine was equivalent to 213 imperial gallons, almost a ton in weight. By comparing measurements in a mid-15th-century Italian shipbuilder's manuscript, I have arrived at these approximate dimensions: keel 56 feet, over-all length 82 feet, beam 28 feet.

Key to the reconstruction: 1. Mizzen. 2. Mainsail. It is generally assumed that the Santa María had crosses painted on the sails, but there is no evidence to support this view. The cross shown on the mainsail here is the fleur-de-lis cross of the Spanish Order of St. James, but another type of cross is just as likely. 3. Bonnets, to increase or decrease the area of sail. 4. Topsail. 5. Foresail. 6. Spritsail. 7. Martnets, to draw the sail together while the yard is lowered. 8. Top. 9. Topping lifts. 10. Braces. 11. Clewlines. 12. Bowlines. 13. Braces. 14. Captain's cabin. 15. Poop deck. 16. Quarterdeck. There may have been cubicles or small cabins below the quarterdeck for the officers. 17. Main deck. 18. Orlop. 19. Forecastle, and beneath, a platform. 20. Knight, with sheave holes. 21. Beam or catena; the anchor cable may have been made fast to this. 22. A metal box with sand, used for cooking. 23. Windlass, used to raise the anchor; alternatively, the anchor may have been raised by a capstan, which would probably have been mounted under the quarterdeck. 24. Hatch. 25. Pumps. 26. Compass in binnacle, in front of the helmsman.

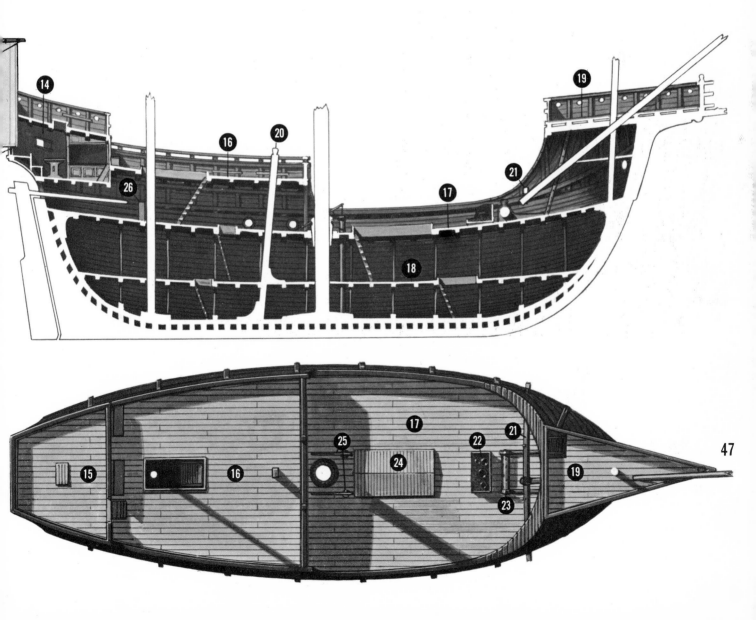

48

Crews and equipment

Neither the rulers nor Columbus imagined that the people of Palos could possibly fit out and provision two caravels for an ocean voyage in ten days. In fact, ten long weeks were to pass before all was ready for departure.

The town of Palos hired the two caravels that were to atone for their offences against the Crown. One belonged to Cristóbal Quintero of Palos and for some unknown reason was called the *Pinta*. The other belonged to Juan Niño of the nearby town of Moguer and was officially called the *Santa Clara,* though she was usually known as the *Niña,* after her owner. At that time, ships commonly had an official name, the name of a saint or a word of religious significance, and a pet name given by the crew. This was often a feminine form of the owner's name, as this ship was called the *Niña* after Niño; sometimes it was taken from the town or district in which the ship had been built, or its place of origin. Columbus' flagship, the *Santa María,* which had been hired by the Crown, belonged to Juan de la Cosa of Santoña, near Santander in the province of Guipúzcoa, but she had been built in Galicia and was accordingly known as *La Gallega.*

It was probably with much reluctance that Columbus accepted the *Santa María.* He had wanted a caravel, but the *Santa María* was only a *nao,* a small round ship of a type used mainly in the Mediterranean, though it had a large hold and was therefore sometimes used in Atlantic waters. The caravel, probably a development from the fishing boat, was more lightly built, with a narrower beam, and made better speed; and it was in caravels that the Portuguese had explored the whole west coast of Africa. Later on, Columbus wrote in his Journal that the *Santa María* was very unwieldy and unsuitable for voyages of discovery, and he blames the people of Palos for not keeping their promise to provide ships that were really suitable for his expedition. But by the terms of the Royal Command, the people of Palos were obliged only to place two caravels at the disposal of the Crown, and Columbus' chief grievance seems to be against those townsmen of Palos who owned caravels but would not let him hire them, so that in the end he had to be content with the heavy and unwieldy *Santa María.*

The three ships were all small ones. The *Niña* and the *Pinta* have been estimated at about 60 tons each; that is, they could carry 60 tuns of wine. They were 70 to 80 feet long; as the *Pinta* was the faster of the two, she might well have been a little longer. They were 20 to 30 feet in the beam and had a draught of 6 to 7 feet. The *Santa María* might have been of 90 to 100 tons, perhaps even smaller. She was not much longer than the caravels, perhaps 3 feet broader in the beam, perhaps with a draught of a little more than 7 feet. But this is all conjecture, based on comparisons with other contemporary ships and on the vague information contained or suggested in contemporary sources.

No documents dealing with the fitting and provisioning of the ships have come down to us, but no complaints are recorded, and we may assume that everything was in satisfactory order. Both Columbus and the seamen of Palos had some experience of long voyages, and a standard pattern was presumably adhered to. The list that follows is not complete, but it will give an idea of the equipment and provisions usually carried by an ocean-going ship in the 15th century.

Planks, spars, bolts, nails
Tools for carpentry, ropes, and metalwork
Pitch, tar, whale oil, fat, sulphur
Sailcloth, leather, yarn, wax, ropes
Tackle, blocks, deadeyes
Anchors, drags, anchor chains, buoys
Flags, pennants

Lombards, falconets, muskets
Powder, stone balls, scrap metal, wadding matches
Crossbows, arrows, helmets, shields, swords, lances

Ship's biscuit, beans, peas
Wine, vinegar, olive oil, honey, syrup
Water
Dried fish, salt meat, salt pork
Pigs, hens (to be killed at sea)
Salt, flour, rice, cheese, figs, almonds
Medicines

Copper cauldrons, three-legged cooking pots
Knives, ladles, measuring vessels, bowls
Candles, lamps, oil, wicks, snuffers
Steel, flint, tinder, lanterns
Firewood
Manacles and leg irons
Boathooks, sweeps, buckets, mats, baskets
Fishhooks, lines, sinkers, nets, harpoons

Notebooks and account books
Nautical almanacs, tables, journals
Quills, ink, sealing wax, wax
Charts, paper, parchment
Compasses, compass needles, magnets
Half-hour glasses, dividers, rulers

Astrolabes, quadrants
Plumbs, plumb lines, tallow

Drums, tambourines
Glass beads, hawk bells, brass rings, knitted caps
  (for trading)
Gold, silver, pearls, spices, etc. (in small quantities
  as samples)

There are different opinions of the role of the Pinzón brothers in the preparations for the voyage and on the voyage itself. They are sometimes given the whole credit for the fact that the voyage ever took place; this view is based chiefly on the testimony of witnesses in the suit between Columbus' heirs and the Crown, when Counsel for the Crown tried to give particular weight to the part played by Martín Alonso Pinzón, and to minimize the part played by Columbus.

At the hearings in 1515, the Crown Fiscal put the following two questions, among others, to the people of Palos: "Do you know that when the Admiral set out to discover these regions, Martín Alonso Pinzón of Palos was in readiness to go in search of them at his own cost, with two vessels of his own; and that he had certain knowledge of the said land, and writings concerning it, which he had seen at Rome, in the library of Pope Innocent XIII in the year in which he left Rome, and had begun to speak of discovering it, and had encouraged him?... Do you know that the said Martín Alonso Pinzón informed the said Admiral Don Cristóbal Colón of this land and discussed with him the said writings, in which it was stated that, in the reign of King Solomon, it was believed that the Queen of Sheba had sailed through the Mediterranean to the furthest bounds of Spain, and that he [Columbus] would find, at 95 degrees to the west, after an easy voyage, between north and south, the land of Sypanso [Cipangu], which is fertile and rich, and in size exceeds Africa and Europe?"

It was from Martín Alonso's son, Arias Pérez Pinzón, that the fiscal had heard about some important documents and a chart, which Martín Alonso allegedly had seen in Rome in 1491. The fiscal's questions to the witnesses were leading ones, to say the least, but of the twenty-two people examined, only four were able to say that they knew anything of the matter.

Martín Alonso Pinzón might quite possibly have seen a map at Rome, perhaps a map drawn by Martellus, which showed Cipangu as lying 95 degrees west of the Iberian peninsula. If we take the trouble to work out the missing longitudes, we find that Martellus' 1490 map shows Cipangu at exactly 95 degrees west of Spain. The story about the Queen of Sheba cannot be traced.

We know that Pinzón could not have brought Columbus any new geographical knowledge. After all, Columbus had been in Lisbon presenting his plans for a voyage to Cipangu eight years before Pinzón had gone to Rome. But if, as is quite possible, Martín Alonso saw the map in Rome, and thus had "private" knowledge of Cipangu, this would explain why he and his brothers had reacted so favorably to Columbus' plans from the outset. We can also believe that the Pinzón brothers did much to persuade the seamen of Palos and Moguer to sign on for this

Cross section of the Santa María *reconstruction just aft of the mainmast. 1. Poop deck. 2. Quarterdeck. 3. Main deck. 4. Orlop. 5. Falconets, light iron swivel guns. 6. Lombards, heavier guns on a carriage.*

journey into the unknown. Garcia Fernández, the steward of the *Pinta,* declared at the hearings: "Martín Alonso was a very brave man and very confident, and I know that if he had not given the two vessels to the Admiral, the Admiral would not have been able to reach the places he did, and he would not have been able to persuade men to go with him; for no one knew the Admiral, and it was thanks to the said Martín Alonso and to the ships he gave him that the said Admiral could make the said voyage." All we can say about this is that by 1515 the said Garcia Fernández seemed to have forgotten that the two caravels for the voyage had been supplied not by Martín Alonso but by the town of Palos, and that the flagship had been hired by the Crown.

Another witness said that Pinzón had lent money to Columbus before his first visit to Ferdinand and Isabella, and that after the agreement with the Sovereigns was signed, Columbus had promised Pinzón half his profits and half of all his privileges. But no one in the Pinzón family ever asked Columbus to make good such a promise, and this testimony is certainly false.

All these statements have thrown a shadow over the excellent relations that must have existed between Columbus and the Pinzón brothers. It is an exaggeration to say that the voyage could never have been made without their help. A royal decree could not be ignored, and we may be sure that Columbus would have been able to obtain ships and crews without the help of the Pinzóns. But their assistance enabled him to set out with skilled and trustworthy crews. The royal pardon for convicted criminals was invoked only four times, and we may add that there were mitigating circumstances in all four cases. One Bartolomé de Torres had accidentally killed a man in a fight and had been sentenced to death for manslaughter. Three of his friends had tried to help him escape from prison, but they were discovered and, in accordance with the law of the time, they too had the sentence of death

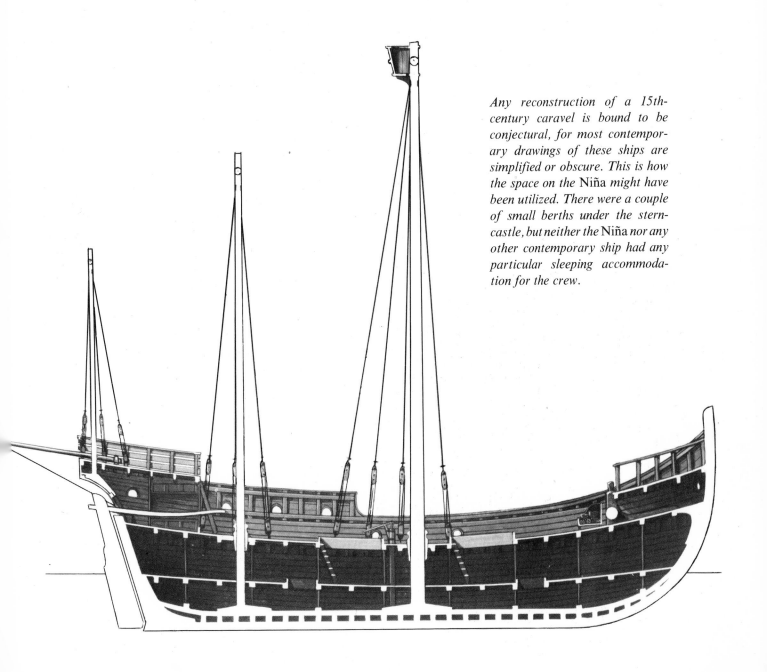

Any reconstruction of a 15th-century caravel is bound to be conjectural, for most contemporary drawings of these ships are simplified or obscure. This is how the space on the Niña *might have been utilized. There were a couple of small berths under the sterncastle, but neither the* Niña *nor any other contemporary ship had any particular sleeping accommodation for the crew.*

pronounced on them. All four saved their necks by sailing with the ships, and all received full pardon when they came home. Later, of their own free will, two of them accompanied Columbus on his second voyage.

Ninety men sailed in the three ships. The list that follows contains the names of the officers and the other more important persons on board.

The Santa María, flagship

    Cristóbal Colón, captain-general
    Juan de la Cosa of Santoña, master and
      owner of the ship
    Peralonso Niño of Moguer, pilot
    Chachu, boatswain
    Rodrigo Sánchez of Segovia, royal inspector
    Pedro Gutiérrez, officer of the royal household
      (perhaps the inspector's assistant)
    Diego de Harana of Cordova, marshal
    Juan Sánchez of Cordova, surgeon
    Rodrigo de Escobedo, secretary
    Luis de Torres, interpreter
    Pedro de Terreros, steward
    Also a further 30 or so: a carpenter, a caulker,
    a cooper, a master gunner, seamen, ship's boys,
    servants, etc.

The Pinta, caravel

    Martín Alonso Pinzón of Palos, captain
    Francisco Martín Pinzón of Palos, master
    Cristóbal Garcia Xalmiento, pilot
    Juan Quintero of Palos, boatswain
    Master Diego, surgeon
    Garcia Fernández of Palos, steward
    Cristóbal Quintero of Palos, seaman, owner of
      the ship
    Also some 20 seamen, etc.

The Niña, caravel

    Vicente Yáñez Pinzón of Palos, captain
    Juan Niño of Moguer, master, owner of the ship
    Sancho Ruiz de Gama, pilot
    Master Alonso of Moguer, surgeon
    Also some 20 seamen, etc.

Apart from Columbus himself, only four were not of Spanish blood: one Portuguese, one Genoese, one Venetian, and one Calabrian. Luis de Torres, the interpreter, was a Christianized Jew who knew Hebrew, Aramaic, and Arabic, and it was thought that Arabic would be understood at Cipangu and in farthermost India. Diego de Harana, the marshal, was a cousin of Beatriz Enriques de Harana, whom we have already met as Columbus' mistress in Cordova. The total wages of the crews probably amounted to something like 250,000 *maravedis* a month. Only a part of this was paid out in advance. The captains were given 2,500 *maravedis* a month, masters and pilots 2,000, seamen 1,000, and ship's boys 666. At that time a cow cost 2,000 *maravedis,* a pig 400 *maravedis,* and a *fanega* of wheat (about $1\frac{1}{2}$ bushels) 73 *maravedis.*

We do not know exactly how much the expedition cost Castile. Luis de Santángel, who was treasurer to the Santa Hermandad, borrowed 1,000,000 *maravedis* from its funds, but he might have borrowed further sums from other quarters. Columbus is said to have contributed an eighth part of the total cost of the expedition—with borrowed money, as already mentioned. What must also be included in the seven-eighths contributed by Castile is the sum paid by the town of Palos for the two caravels, which might have come to about 150,000 *maravedis.* But each calculated sum is based on so much guesswork and so many unknown factors that we must satisfy ourselves by saying that the enterprise cost something between 1,200,000 and 2,000,000 *maravedis.*

A circumstance that doubtless delayed preparations and put off the day of departure was the great exodus of Jews from Spain. Originally, it was decided that all unbaptized Jews would be expelled from the country by June 30, but when the authorities saw that this plan would never hold, the final day was set at August 2. The richest Jews hired ships in all the Spanish ports, and these were then loaded to the full with people and their belongings. Perhaps the ship owners of Palos and Moguer thought that they might get better money at considerably less risk from the hard-pressed Jewish deportees, and were unwilling to hire out their caravels to Columbus; this would explain why he had to be content with the *Santa María.*

It is not definitely known how many Jews left Spain in 1492. Some sources say 160,000, others 800,000. The first figure is probably nearer the truth. To the very last moment, the throngs of deportees were dogged by priests urging them to become Christians, and many of them must have accepted baptism so that they could remain in the country where their ancestors had lived for 700 years. But the majority, their convictions reinforced by the rabbis, remained loyal to their religion and preferred to leave the country. The sea crossing had its dangers. Wind and weather were on their side, but off the coasts pirate ships lay in wait for them, and many of the emigrant ships were boarded and pillaged. Many of them crossed to North Africa, where the people were more tolerant than the Spaniards. Others went to Italy, France, Turkey, or Britain. Many, too, crossed the land frontier into Portugal, where João II gave them temporary shelter.

Columbus waited for the last announcement concerning the date of their expulsion and then fixed his own departure for August 3.

Southwest by south

During their last few days ashore, everyone had made his confession and taken the communion, and on the evening of August 2 the crews were called aboard. Early the next morning, Columbus took the communion and was rowed out to his ship before dawn. Then, in the name of Jesus, he gave the order to set the sails and weigh anchor. There was half an hour to go before sunrise, and the cocks of Palos were not yet crowing. On the River Saltés, in which the Rio Tinto and the Rio Odiel joined for a few miles before flowing out into the sea, one last shipload of Jews was still waiting for the turn of the tide. Then, in company with the *Santa María,* the *Pinta,* and the *Niña,* their vessel sailed out in a freshening west-south-westerly wind. After some hours, the Jews turned to the southeast and ran with the wind towards the Mediterranean, while the three other ships continued to press their way south.

Columbus' own journal of the voyage is lost, but Bishop Bartolomé de Las Casas had a copy from which he wrote a version for himself, perhaps an abridged one, and this version is still in existence. Las Casas often complains that the copy was inaccurate, and to judge by his own version (which I shall refer to as the Journal), the copyist had made his worst mistakes over directions and distances. He was often confused between *oeste* (west) and *leste* (east) and confused leagues and miles. Modern critics have pointed out his mistakes, and in any quotations I shall be making from the Journal, I will be using words which are considered to correspond to those in the original document. I do not think that Las Casas' version can differ greatly from the original; Fernando Colón also had access to a copy of the journal while he was writing his father's biography, and his direct quotations often agree almost word for word with Las Casas' version. Las Casas may have been intending to do no more than correct Columbus' bad Spanish; when he makes a direct quotation, it is easy to see that the style is weak in vocabulary and shades of meaning.

The Journal opens with a long dedication to Ferdinand and Isabella:

"In the Name of Our Lord Jesus Christ.

Most Christian, most high, most excellent and most mighty princes, King and Queen of the Spains and of the isles of the sea, our Sovereigns: whereas in this present year of 1492, when Your Highnesses had put an end to the war with the Moors who ruled in Europe, and had concluded that war in the great city of Granada, where, on the second day of January in this same year, I saw the royal banners of Your Highnesses placed by force of arms on the towers of the Alhambra, which is the citadel of that city, and I saw the Moorish king come out of the gates of the city and kiss the royal hands of Your Highnesses and of my Lord the Prince; and straightway in that same month, on the ground of information which I had given to Your Highnesses about the lands of India, and about a prince who is called Grand Khan, which is to say in our Romance tongue 'King of Kings' [i.e., the Great Khan of the Mongols, who in Marco Polo's time had resided at Cambalu, the modern Peking], how many times he and his forebears had sent to Rome to entreat for men learned in our holy Faith, to instruct him therein, and how the Holy Father had never granted this request, whereby so many people had been lost, by falling into idolatries and following doctrines which led to perdition;

"Wherefore Your Highnesses, as Catholic Christians and as princes who ever loved the holy Christian Faith and promoted it, and as enemies of the sect of Mahomet and of all idolatries and heresies, determined to send me, Cristóbal Colón, to the said parts of India, to see those said princes and peoples and lands, and to discover their character, and to find the means that might serve to convert them to our holy Faith, and ordered that I should not go by land to the East, as the custom was, but by way of the West, by a course which no man, to our certain knowledge, has taken until this day;

"For which reason, after having expelled all the Jews from your lands and dominions, in the said month of January, Your Highnesses commanded me to go with a sufficient fleet to the said parts of India; and did for this purpose confer great favours upon me, entitling me thenceforward to call myself Don, and to be High Admiral of the Ocean, and Viceroy and Governor in perpetuity of all islands and continents which I should discover and gain, and which might hereafter be discovered and gained in the Ocean, and that my eldest son should succeed me, and so on from generation to generation for all time.

"Therefore I departed from the city of Granada on Saturday, the twelfth day of the month of May, in the said year of 1492, and came to the town of Palos, which is a seaport, and there I made ready three ships, well suited for such an enterprise, and I set out from the said seaport, well furnished with suitable supplies and with many seamen, on Friday, the third day of the month of August in the said year, half an hour before sunrise, and I made my course towards the Canary Islands of Your Highnesses, thence to set my course and sail until I should arrive at the Indies, and deliver the message of Your Highnesses to those princes, and accomplish all that you had commanded me to do.

"For which purpose, I have it in mind to write down on this journey with great care from day to day all that I may do and see and experience, as will hereafter be seen. Also, my Sovereign Princes, in addition to writing down every night what has occurred during the day, and every day how I have sailed in the night, I intend to draw a chart of all the seas and lands of the Ocean, in their true places and according to their bearings; and moreover to compose a book and to illustrate everything in a true picture, by

latitude from the equinoctial line and by longitude from the West. And above all it is necessary that I should forget my sleep and pay great attention to my navigation, since that is essential; and this will be a great labour."

They had to sail south until sunset, by which time they reckoned that they had covered 60 Roman miles or 15 leagues from Saltés. Then the wind gradually swung round to the northwest and north so that a course could be set toward the Canary Islands, to the southwest, by south. They lit lanterns and hung them astern so that they would not lose one another in the dark. They sang the "Salve Regina," the hymn sung by sailors before retiring for the night at sea. The youngest member of the watch kept an eye on the half-hour glass, turned it when the sand ran out, and called out the hours as they passed slowly in the darkness.

It was noticed from the very first day that the *Santa María* was the slowest ship, while the *Niña,* with her lateen sail, kept well up in the wind. But when the wind freshened and became variable on the second and third days, it was found that the tall lateen sail of the Niña was harder to control than the square rigs of the other ships. On the fourth day out the *Pinta's* rudder sprang out of its sockets, and the ships hove to in the heavy sea while the rudder was temporarily made fast with ropes. Columbus was unable to give any assistance to the Pinta, but he writes that he relied on Martín Alonso Pinzón, "a brave and intelligent man." They were able to resume the old course after a few hours, but on that day they covered only 29 leagues, compared to the previous day's 40.

The *Pinta's* rudder held for only one day. On August 7 the wind increased, and the strain on the ropes which held the rudder was too great. In addition to this, Pinzón reported that she was leaking more than usual. So the three ships hove to again, and more repairs were made. But it was whispered that Cristóbal Quintero, the owner of the *Pinta,* had damaged the rudder on purpose because he did not want to make the voyage, and because the *Pinta* had been requisitioned against his will. The distance covered on that day, in spite of the favorable wind, was only 25 leagues, and it was suggested that before going any farther the fleet put in at Lanzarote, which was the nearest of the Canaries. The long halts and interruptions had upset the pilots' calculations, and they could not agree about the position of the fleet, but Columbus writes that his own estimate turned out to be nearest the truth.

On August 8 he decided that they would sail to Grand Canary to see if the *Pinta* could be replaced by a better ship. They sighted the island the very next day, but the wind died, and they lay becalmed or in light head winds off Grand Canary for several days without being able to

The Niña, *the* Santa María, *and the* Pinta *becalmed. To give steerageway, the men are rowing with the long oars, technically known as sweeps.*

get any nearer. Columbus then left Martín Alonso Pinzón with orders to try to put in to the port of Gando and to negotiate there for another caravel, while he himself continued with the *Santa María* and the *Niña* to the island of Gomera for the same purpose.

It seems that even at this early stage there was some disagreement between Columbus and Pinzón. Only once in the Journal does Columbus praise him, and that is in the already-quoted passage in which Pinzón directs the repairing of the *Pinta's* rudder. It would have been natural to leave the *Niña* off Grand Canary as well, so that she could assist the semidisabled *Pinta* if necessary, but Martín Alonso's brother, Vicente Yáñez, was the captain

of the *Niña*, and by all accounts Columbus does not seem to have placed much reliance on the loyalty of these two brothers.

On August 12 the *Santa María* and the *Niña* reached the port of San Sebastian on Gomera, and they found that there was not a single vessel to be had on the entire island. However, the authorities said that Doña Beatriz de Peraza y Bobadilla, the governor of the island, was on

her way home from Grand Canary in a ship of 40 tons which belonged to a man from Seville, and that it might be possible to hire this vessel.

Columbus decided to wait, and two days later, when he was told that a small ship was leaving for Grand Canary, he sent one of his best men with it to help Pinzón and to tell him where the *Santa María* and the *Niña* lay. The calm continued, and since he heard nothing from Beatriz de Peraza or Pinzón, Columbus eventually decided, on August 24, to sail back to Grand Canary. To increase their speed, they probably rowed with the sweeps, and they soon caught up with the small boat carrying the messenger to Pinzón, which had spent ten days becalmed

between Gomera and Tenerife. They took the messenger aboard and continued their journey. During the night they passed Tenerife, which was erupting flames from its summit. The crews were terrified, but Columbus, who had seen active volcanoes in the Mediterranean, explained the phenomenon to them. Most were reassured, but some still said that it was a bad omen. They reached Grand Canary on the following afternoon and found Pinzón there; he had made port on the previous day after great difficulties. Columbus also discovered that Beatriz de Peraza had left five days earlier.

There were no vessels of any value to be had at Gando either, and after all these days of inactivity and wasted

1

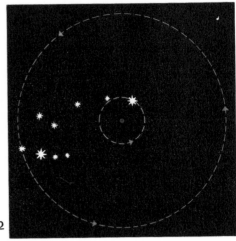

2

time, great energy was now put into repairing the *Pinta*. Much of her cargo was taken ashore, the ballast was retrimmed so that her stern was lifted higher out of the water, and the leaks were caulked; a new rudder was made, and new sockets for it were hammered out. The opportunity was taken also to rerig the *Niña*. Her aftermost mast was moved into the bow to serve as a foremast. She was given a bowsprit, her yards were shortened to a suitable length, and her sails were cut and resewn so that when all was done she was square-rigged, like the other two ships. Columbus presumed that his fleet would henceforward be sailing with the wind behind it.

In six days everything was ready, and the ships set sail on September 1. Next day they anchored at Gomera, and at last Columbus met Beatriz de Peraza. Whether he had met her before or not—and he may well have done so at the Spanish Court— he seems to have been anxious to meet her now, and one witness from his second voyage says that Columbus was in love with the lady. She had been one of the most beautiful ladies at the Court, but she had proved only too attractive to Ferdinand, and Isabella had married her off to Hernán Peraza, the Governor of Gomera. Some years later, Peraza was killed in a local uprising which allegedly he himself had provoked by seducing a Guanche girl. Beatriz de Peraza was not yet thirty years old—Columbus was forty-one—and she ruled the island with a rod of iron until her son came of age.

We know nothing of what she might have felt for Columbus, and this is the only evidence we have of Columbus' infatuation—apart, that is, from the fact that he had spent twelve days waiting in vain for her at San Sebastian while Martín Alonso Pinzón limped his way to Grand Canary with a damaged rudder.

No more time was wasted on Gomera. Fresh provisions, firewood, and water were taken aboard. At the house of Beatriz de Peraza, Columbus met people from Ferro, the westernmost of the Canaries, who were willing to declare on oath that every year, they saw land to the west in the ocean, and people of Gomera said the same. Columbus could tell them that men in the Azores had seen similar islands to the west, and that a man from Madeira had come to the King of Portugal to ask for a caravel so that he could sail to the land he had seen on the horizon.

The crews now made their confessions and took the Sacrament in the church of San Sebastian. On September 8, after Columbus had taken his leave of the beautiful widow and was ready to sail, a caravel arrived from Ferro with the news that three Portuguese caravels were close at hand with orders to take Columbus prisoner. Columbus was undismayed, and on the same morning the *Santa María,* the *Pinta,* and the *Niña* weighed anchor. But the wind died down, and for the whole of that day and the next the ships rode listlessly on the waters between Gomera and Tenerife.

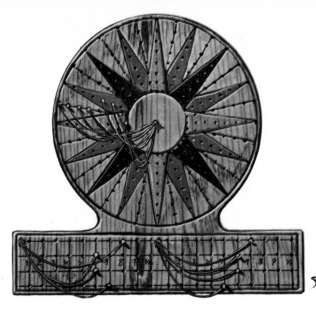

Ocean navigation in Columbus' time was chiefly a matter of compass courses and distances covered; it was only under very favorable circumstances that one could hope to make a fairly accurate reckoning by taking the height of the polestar above the horizon with an astrolabe or quadrant, and thus determine one's latitude.

The steering compass (fig. 1) was suspended on gimbals in a box in front of the helmsman. At the end of the 15th century, the compass had an easterly deviation all over Europe, and probably also in the African waters known to the Portuguese. Columbus seems to have been the first to notice a westerly deviation. At regular intervals pilots used to check the ships' compasses against the polestar, which at that time rotated round the true pole with a radius of 3° 27'. The astronomers had worked out a key to help sailors find out when the polestar was due north, and when its altitude was the same as that of the true pole, by checking the position of the polestar against the other stars in the Little Bear (fig. 2). They made a diagram of a man with his elbows at his sides and his hands stretched out sideways (fig. 3). The polestar was his navel, and the two outermost stars of the constellation, then known as the Guards, were said to be at his head, at his left shoulder, at his left hand, at the line below his left arm, at his feet, etc., according to their position in the sky. As the position of the Guards at midnight was recorded in the almanacs for every night in the year, they could be used on clear nights as a reliable chronometer.

Watches at sea lasted four hours, usually kept with a half-hour glass (fig. 4). The youngest man on every watch kept his eye on the glass; when the sand ran out he turned it, and called out the half-hour.

The direction and the strength of the wind might alter during a watch, and this would affect the speed and the course of the ship. Not all the crew were sufficiently literate to write these things down, and they used a traverse board, a wooden "wind-rose," with eight holes bored along each point of the compass (fig. 5). From the center outward, each hole stood for one half-hour of the watch. If the course for the first half-hour was due west, a peg was put into the first hole west of the center. If the course had to be changed to west by north during the next half-hour, a peg would be put into the second hole on the west-by-north line, and so on. Below the rose were eight horizontal grooves, with, e.g., ten holes in each; each hole represented one Roman mile per hour. No mechanical speed indicators existed, and nothing but experience could have enabled the sailors to make a rough estimate of their rate of progress. If they thought they had been making 6 Roman miles an hour during the first half-hour, they would put a peg into the sixth hole of the first groove; if they thought they had been making 4 Roman miles an hour in the second half-hour, they would put a peg into the fourth hole of the second groove, and so on. When the watch was over, the ship's pilot could see from the traverse board what the course and the rate of progress had been during the past four hours and make the necessary calculations for the next stage of the journey.

On the high seas, out of sight of land, everyone made as direct a course as possible to his destination. But a ship might often be blown off course, in which case the pilot had to estimate his position by what is known as "dead reckoning." There were rules and tables to help him, but dead reckoning necessitated some knowledge of elementary mathematics, and a great deal was left to individual judgment. Hence on a long expedition the pilots on different ships might have different opinions about the position of the fleet.

59

Crossing the Ocean

Columbus' Journal, September 8 – October 12, 1492, as retold by Bartolomé de Las Casas.

Saturday, September 8

"Three hours after midnight, on the Saturday, a northeast wind rose, and he altered his course to the west. He shipped much sea over the bows, which delayed his progress. That day and night he made 9 leagues. [Probably the *Santa María* was badly loaded, so that her bow was too deep. Since this trouble is not mentioned again, we must presume that she was immediately retrimmed.]

Sunday, September 9

"He made 15 leagues that day, and decided to reckon less than he made, so that the crews should not lose heart or be alarmed if the voyage grew long. That night he made 120 Roman miles at 10 Roman miles an hour, 30 leagues in all. The sailors steered badly, letting her fall off to west by north and even to west-north-west, for which the Admiral rebuked them many times.

Monday, September 10

"That day and night he made 60 leagues at 10 Roman miles, or 2½ leagues, an hour. But to avoid alarming the crew if the voyage were long, he only reckoned 48 leagues. [Ten Roman miles an hour is equivalent to 8 knots. It is known that Columbus overestimated speeds, and even his reduced estimates for the distances covered daily are rather too long].

Tuesday, September 11

"That day they sailed on their proper course, which was to the west, and they made 20 leagues and more. They saw a large piece of mast belonging to a 120-ton ship, but they could not secure it. During the night they made about 20 leagues, but he only reckoned 16, for the reason aforesaid.

Wednesday, September 12

"That day they continued on their course, and made in the night and day 33 leagues, and reckoned less for the reason aforesaid.

Thursday, September 13

"That day and night they followed their course, which was west, and covered 33 leagues; he reckoned 3 or 4 less. The currents were against them. On this day at nightfall, the compass-needles turned north-west, and in the morning they turned a little to the north-east. [Columbus checked his compass by the polestar, which at that time rotated with a radius of 3° 27′ round the true north; the present radius is about 1°.]

Friday, September 14

"That day and night they kept their course to the west, and covered 20 leagues. He recorded a slightly smaller figure. Those in the caravel *Niña* said that they had seen

a tern and a tropic bird; and these birds never go more than 25 leagues from land. [Columbus presumably thought that they were close to some as yet undiscovered island.]

Saturday, September 15

"He sailed that day and night 27 leagues, and rather more on his westerly course. And early that night, they saw a singular jet of flame fall from the sky into the sea some 4 or 5 leagues distant from them. [Presumably a meteor; Las Casas writes in his *Historia de las Indias* that the occurrence alarmed the seamen, who said it was a sign that they were sailing on an ill-starred course.]

Sunday, September 16

"He continued that day and night on his course to the west. They must have made 39 leagues, but he reckoned only 36. That day it was slightly cloudy, with a little rain. Here the Admiral says that on that day and all succeeding days they met with very mild breezes, and the mornings were very sweet, with naught lacking save the song of the nightingales. He adds: 'And the weather was like April in Andalusia.' Here they began to see many tufts of bright green seaweed, which seemed to have been lately torn from land; this made them all think that they must be near some island, though not in the Admiral's opinion to the mainland: since he said: 'I hold that the mainland is still far off.' [The ships were now sailing in the Sargasso Sea, and the seaweed was gulfweed or sargassum. Las Casas writes in his *Historia:* "Most of the weed was yellowish, and since they found the voyage to be long, and they were far from any harbour, they began to murmur

On September 16 the vessels entered the Sargasso Sea.

about the enterprise and about him who had led them out to that place; and when they saw the great congestion of seaweed ahead, they began to fear that there were rocks or flooded land . . . but when they saw that the ships could pass through the beds of weed they were relieved, though not completely so."]

Monday, September 17

"He sailed on along his westerly course, and they must have covered 50 leagues and more in that day and night, though he only reckoned 47. The current helped them. They saw much fine seaweed, and it was weed from rocks; and it came from the west. They concluded that they were near land. The pilots took a bearing on the Pole Star, and they found that the compass-needles declined a full point north-west; and the sailors took fright and were dejected, and they did not say why. But the Admiral knew the reason for this, and gave orders that they should take another bearing at dawn, and then they found that the needles were true. The reason for this is that it was the star, and not the needles, that appeared to move. During the morning of that Monday, they saw much more seaweed, which looked like riverweed, and in this they found a live crab, which the Admiral kept. And he says that this was a sure sign of land, because crabs are not found more than 80 leagues from land. The water of the sea was now less salt than it had been since they left the Canaries, and the

61

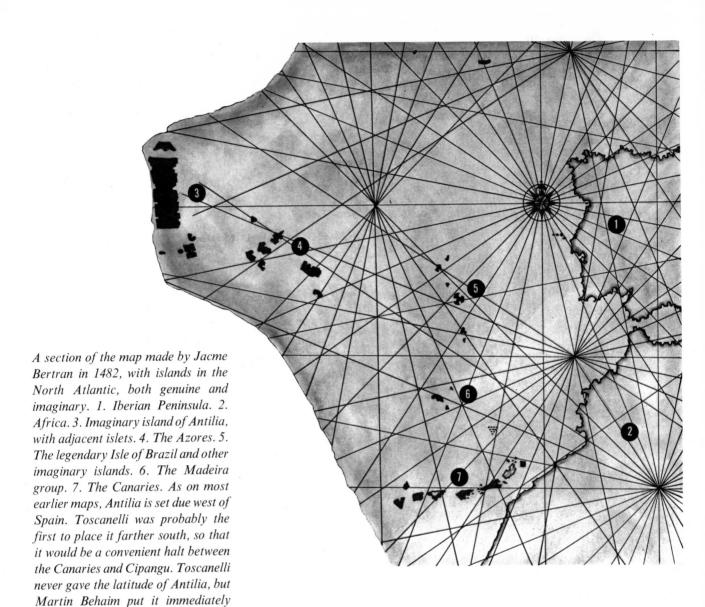

A section of the map made by Jacme Bertran in 1482, with islands in the North Atlantic, both genuine and imaginary. 1. Iberian Peninsula. 2. Africa. 3. Imaginary island of Antilia, with adjacent islets. 4. The Azores. 5. The legendary Isle of Brazil and other imaginary islands. 6. The Madeira group. 7. The Canaries. As on most earlier maps, Antilia is set due west of Spain. Toscanelli was probably the first to place it farther south, so that it would be a convenient halt between the Canaries and Cipangu. Toscanelli never gave the latitude of Antilia, but Martin Behaim put it immediately south of the Tropic of Cancer on his globe, and Toscanelli probably gave him the idea.

breezes ever gentler. All were much gladdened at this, and whichever ship was speediest forged on ahead, in the hope of sighting land before the others. They saw many tunnies, and the crew of the *Niña* killed one. The Admiral says here that these signs of land came from the west: 'Wherefore I hope that God on High, in Whose hands are all victories, will very soon bring us to land.' On that morning he says that he saw a white bird called a tropic bird, which does not usually sleep on the sea. [There is no difference in salinity anywhere in the open sea, and the "discovery" that the water here was less salt was pure imagination, aided, perhaps, by wishful thinking.]

Tuesday, September 18

"He sailed that day and night and they must have made more than 55 leagues, but he did not enter more than 48. The sea was very smooth on all these days, like the river at Seville. On this day, Martín Alonso in the *Pinta*, which was a fast sailer, did not wait. He called to the Admiral that he had seen from his caravel a great flock of birds flying west, and that he hoped to sight land that night, for which reason he was making such speed. A great bank of dark clouds appeared to the north, which is a sign of land.

Wednesday, September 19

"He continued along his course, but in that day and night he covered only 25 leagues, since it was calm. He entered 22. That day, at ten o'clock, a booby came to the ship, and in the evening they saw another, and it is not their habit to go more than 20 leagues from land. A drizzle came, without wind, which is a sure sign of land. The Admiral did not wish to be delayed by beating to windward in order to see whether there was land in that direction, but he was certain that there were some islands to the north and to the south, as indeed there were, and he passed through the midst of them, because he wanted to go straight on to the Indies. 'And the weather is favourable: so, God willing, let us see everything on the return voyage.' These are his words. Here the pilots calculated their position. The pilot of the *Niña* found them 440 leagues from the Canaries; the pilot of the *Pinta*, 420; the pilot of the flagship, exactly 400. [They presumably thought they were near Antilia, Satanazes, Ymana, and Saya. The distance they had covered corresponded approximately to Toscanelli's estimate for the distance to Antilia.]

Thursday, September 20

"On this day he sailed west by north, and west-north-west because, in the prevailing calm, the winds were very variable. They must have made some 7 or 8 leagues. Two boobies came to the ship, and later a third, which was a sign that they were near land; and they saw much seaweed, although they had seen none on the previous day. They caught by hand a bird which was like a tern; it was a river bird, not a sea bird, and it had feet like a gull. At dawn, two or three land birds came to the ship; singing, they disappeared before the sun rose. Later, a booby came; it came from the west-north-west and went south-east, which indicated that there was land to the west-north-west; for these birds sleep on land, and go out to sea in the morning in search of food, and never fly more than 20 leagues from land. [All these estimates of the distance birds can fly from land are incorrect. But up till then ships had seldom ventured more than 20 leagues from land; Columbus had as yet little experience in these matters, and he allowed himself to indulge in some wishful thinking.]

Friday, September 21

"Most of that day was calm, with a little wind toward evening. That day and night they must have covered some 13 leagues, including the distance off-course. At dawn, they found so much seaweed that the water appeared to be choked with it, and it came from the west. They saw a booby; the sea was as smooth as a river, and the air the best in the world. They saw a whale, which is a sign that land was near, since whales always keep close to it.

Saturday, September 22

"He sailed west-north-west, more or less, steering to one side and the other. They must have covered 30 leagues; they saw hardly any seaweed, but they did see some petrels and another bird. Here the Admiral says: 'This head-wind was very useful to me, for my men had been afraid that there were never any winds in these waters that would carry them back to Spain.' There was no seaweed for some part of the day, but afterwards it was abundant.

Sunday, September 23

"He sailed to the north-west, sometimes north-west by north, sometimes on his true course due west, and made about 22 leagues. They saw a dove, a booby, a small river bird, and some white birds. There was much seaweed; they found some crabs in it. And the sea grew calm and smooth, and the men murmured among themselves, saying that as there was no great sea there would never be wind enough to carry them back to Spain. But afterwards, without any wind, the sea rose greatly, and this amazed them, and the Admiral writes: 'So this high sea was very useful to me, for such a thing had not been seen since the time of the Jews, when they came up out of Egypt and murmured against Moses, who had led them out of bondage.'

Monday, September 24

"He sailed on his course to the west that day and night, and they made 14½ leagues; he entered 12. A booby came to the ship, and they saw many petrels. [Las Casas and Fernando Colón both say that during these days and nights the men were very unruly and kept grumbling, some even suggesting that they should throw Columbus into the sea and sail home with the story that he had fallen overboard while taking his bearings from the stars. But Columbus made jokes with his men and reassured them, and Las Casas says that he laughed with them though his heart was weeping. We should not take this to mean that the men threatened Columbus to his face. He might have overheard the more unruly members of the crew talking, or one of his close friends on board might have told him what they were saying.]

Tuesday, September 25

"This day was very calm, though there was wind later on, and they continued on their course to the west until nightfall. The Admiral talked with Martín Alonso Pinzón, captain of the caravel *Pinta*, about a chart which he had sent to the caravel three days earlier. On it the Admiral had shown certain islands in that sea, and Martín Alonso said that they were now near them. The Admiral replied that he agreed with him, but since they had not yet reached them, the reason must be that the currents had carried the ships north-east; nor could they have gone as far as the pilot said. The Admiral then asked him to return the chart. When it had been sent across on a

A frigate bird attacking a tropic bird

line, the Admiral began to fix his position on it, with his pilot and the crew. At sunset, Martín Alonso mounted the poop of his ship and with great joy called to the Admiral, claiming a reward because he had sighted land. The Admiral says that when he heard this so confidently asserted, he fell on his knees to render thanks to the Lord, and Martín Alonso said the *Gloria in Excelsis Deo* with his men; the Admiral's men did the same, and the men of the *Niña* all climbed the mast and the rigging, and they all declared that they saw land. The Admiral thought the same, and estimated it as 25 leagues distant. They all continued to say that it was land, until nightfall. The Admiral ordered that their course, hitherto due west, should be altered to the south-west, where they had seen land. During that day they sailed 4½ leagues to the west, and in the night 17 to the south-west, 21 in all, but he told the men that it was 13, since he always told the crew that they had sailed a short distance, so that the voyage should not seem too long; thus he kept two reckonings on that voyage, a short one which was false and a long one which was true. The sea was very smooth, and many sailors went swimming. They saw many dolphins and other fish.

Wednesday, September 26

"He continued on his course to the west until the afternoon; then they went south-west, until he found that what they had taken for land was only a cloud. They covered 31 leagues during the day and night, but the men

were told that it was 24. The sea was like a river, and the air sweet and very soft. [The record of this day's course is rather bewildering, unless we take it to mean that in the morning, when he did not see land, he returned to the original course, but later, at the entreaties of his crew, changed course again to the south-west. Fernando Colón says: 'The Admiral showed sympathy with their demands until nightfall, and since he wished to put them at their ease, so that they should not refuse to continue with the voyage, he complied with their wishes and kept to that course for a great part of the night. But next morning they realized that what they had taken for land was only a storm-cloud, which often looks like land. To the sorrow and disquiet of most of his people, they again sailed west, just as they had done since they had left Spain, saving only when the winds were against them.']

Thursday, September 27

"He continued on his course to the west. During that day and night he covered 24 leagues, and reckoned 20 for his crew. They saw many dolphins, and killed one; they saw one tropic bird.

Friday, September 28

"He kept on his course to the west. That day and night, because of calms, they only made 14 leagues; he reckoned 13. They saw a little seaweed; they caught two dolphins and in the other ships they caught more.

Saturday, September 29

"He kept on his course to the west. They went 24 leagues; he reckoned 21 to his men. Owing to the calms, they covered little distance either by day or by night. They saw a bird called the frigate bird, which makes the boobies disgorge what they have swallowed; this it eats itself, and lives on no other food. It is a sea bird, but it does not settle on the sea, and never flies more than 20 leagues from land; these birds are common on the Cape Verde Islands. Later, they saw two boobies. The air was very sweet and refreshing, so that he said that the only thing lacking was the song of the nightingale; the sea was as calm as a river. Later, on three occasions, three boobies and a frigate bird came in sight. They saw much seaweed.

Sunday, September 30

"He kept his course due west. By reason of the calms, he covered no more than 14 leagues in that day and night; he reckoned 11. Four tropic birds came to the ship; this is a sure sign of land, since so many birds together cannot be flying astray. Twice they saw four boobies, and there was much seaweed. Note, that the stars called the Guards are near the arm on the west side at nightfall, and at dawn they are on the line below the arm to the north-east; so it seems that in the whole night they only move three lines, which is to say nine [astronomical] hours, and this is the same every night. This the Admiral says here. Moreover, at nightfall the needles decline a point north-west, and at daybreak they are right on the star [the polestar], from which it appears that the star moves as the other stars, and that the needles always point truly. [Fernando Colón expresses this more clearly: 'He also noted that in the evening the needles varied a whole point, while at dawn they pointed directly towards the Pole Star. This fact greatly disquieted and bewildered the pilots, until he told them that its cause was the rotation of the Pole Star about the true Pole. This explanation partly allayed their fears, for on a voyage into such strange and distant regions these variations made them very apprehensive.']

Monday, October 1

"He kept his course due west. They made 25 leagues, and he reckoned 20 for his crew. Heavy rain. At dawn on this day, the Admiral's pilot reckoned that hitherto they had sailed 578 leagues west from Ferro. The smaller reckoning, which the Admiral showed to the crew, was 584, but the true distance, which the Admiral had arrived at and which he kept to himself, was 707. [Either Colum-

bus had added up wrong, or Las Casas had been giving the wrong distances earlier; the daily distances covered from September 7 add up to 652 leagues. In any case, the pilot, Peralonso Niño, had made a considerably better calculation; according to modern reckoning, he must have been almost completely correct.]

Tuesday, October 2

"He kept on his course, night and day, for 39 leagues, to the west; he reckoned for the men some 30 leagues. The sea was always smooth and calm. 'To God great praise be given,' the Admiral says here. Seaweed was floating from east to west, contrary to that which was generally the case. They saw many fish, and killed one. They saw a white bird which seemed to be a gull.

Wednesday, October 3

"He followed his regular course; they went 47 leagues; he reckoned 40 leagues for the men. They saw much seaweed, some much faded and some very fresh and bearing what seemed like fruit. They did not see any birds, and the Admiral believed that they had left behind the islands which he had depicted on his chart. The Admiral says here that he had not wished to spend the past week beating to windward on the days when he saw so many indications of land, although he had information of certain islands in that region. His object was to reach the Indies, and it would have been foolish, he says, to linger on the way. [Las Casas and Fernando Colón both say that the crews had wanted to search for the islands that seemed to be so near.]

Thursday, October 4

"He kept on his course to the west; they made, day and night together, 63 leagues; he reckoned 46 to his men. There came to the ship more than 40 petrels together, and with them two boobies. A boy in the caravel hit one with a stone. A frigate bird came to the ship, and a white bird like a gull.

Friday, October 5

"He kept on his course; they made 11 Roman miles an hour and in the night and day they went 57 leagues, since during the night the wind abated somewhat. He reckoned 45 for his men. The sea was calm and smooth. 'To God,' he says, 'great praise be given.' The air was very sweet and temperate; there was no vegetation; birds, many petrels. Many flying-fish flew into the ship.

Saturday, October 6

"He kept on his course westwards; they covered 40 leagues in that day and night; he reckoned 33 for his men. On that night Martín Alonso said that it would be well to steer south-west by west, and the Admiral thought that Martín Alonso meant that this was [the course] for the island of Cipangu; and the Admiral saw that, if they missed it, they would not be able to reach land so soon, and that it was better to go straight to the mainland and then to the islands. [As this important statement is not very clear, I quote the corresponding passage from Las Casas' *Historia*: 'Martín Alonso said on this night that they should sail south-west by west to the island of Cipangu, according to the chart that Cristóbal Colón had shown him. . . .']

Sunday, October 7

"He kept on his course to the west; they made 12 Roman miles an hour for two hours, and afterwards 8 Roman miles an hour; and up to an hour before sunset he went 23 leagues. He reckoned 18 for the men. On this day, at sunrise, the caravel *Niña*, which had gone ahead as she was a fast sailer—and they all went as quickly as they could in order to be the first to sight land and to secure the reward which Their Majesties had promised to the first man who should sight it—hoisted a standard at the mast-head and fired a lombard, as a sign that they saw land; for so the Admiral had ordered. He had also ordered that, at sunrise and at sunset, all the ships should join him, since these are the two periods when it is possible to see for the greatest distance, since the mists are then dispersed. In the evening they saw no land where those in the caravel *Niña* thought they had seen it. A great flock of birds passed from the north to the south-west, and it seemed that they were going to sleep on land or were, perhaps, flying from the winter which was coming to the lands whence they came. The Admiral knew that most of the islands which the Portuguese held had been discovered through the flight of birds, and therefore decided to abandon his westward course and to steer west-south-west, with the intention to proceed in that direction for two days. He began to do so one hour before sunset. They made in the whole night a matter of 5 leagues and 23 in the day; in the night and day together, they went in all 28 leagues. [Fernando Colón writes of this day: 'He reminded the men that he had often told them they must not expect to strike land until they had sailed seven hundred and fifty leagues west of the Canaries.' He also writes that 'In order to prevent men from crying "land, land!" at every moment and causing unjustified feelings of joy, the Admiral had ordered that anyone who claimed to have seen land and did not make good his claim in the space of three days would lose the reward even if afterwards he should actually see it.' Columbus' order that the ships should come together at sunrise and sunset was not very magnanimous; if they were all close together, the *Santa*

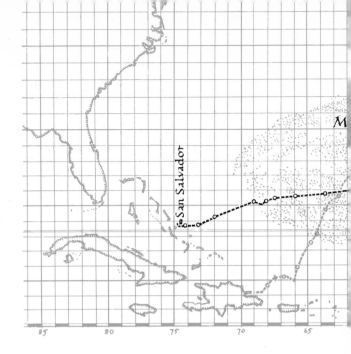

María, which had the highest mast, would inevitably be the ship from which land was first sighted.]

Monday, October 8

"He sailed west-south-west, and day and night together they went about 11½ or 12 leagues, and it seems that at times in the night they made 15 Roman miles an hour, if the journal is to be trusted. They had a sea like the river in Seville. 'Thanks be to God,' says the Admiral, 'the breezes were softer than in April at Seville, and it is a pleasure to be in them: they smell so sweetly.' They saw some fresh green seaweed, and many land birds, of which they caught one—they were flying south-west—terns and ducks and a booby.

Tuesday, October 9

"He sailed south-west; he made 5 leagues. The wind changed and he ran west by north, and made 4 leagues. Afterwards, in all, he made 11 leagues in the day and 20½ leagues in the night; he reckoned 17 leagues for the men. All night they heard birds passing.

Wednesday, October 10

"He sailed west-south-west; they made 10 Roman miles an hour and at times 12 and sometimes 7, and in that day and night together they made 59 leagues; he reckoned for the men 44 leagues, no more. Here the men could now endure it no longer; they complained of the long voyage. But the Admiral reassured them as best he could, holding out to them bright hopes of the gains which they could make, and he added that it was useless to complain, since he was going to the Indies and must pursue his course until, with the help of the Lord, he found them. [This was one of the greatest distances covered

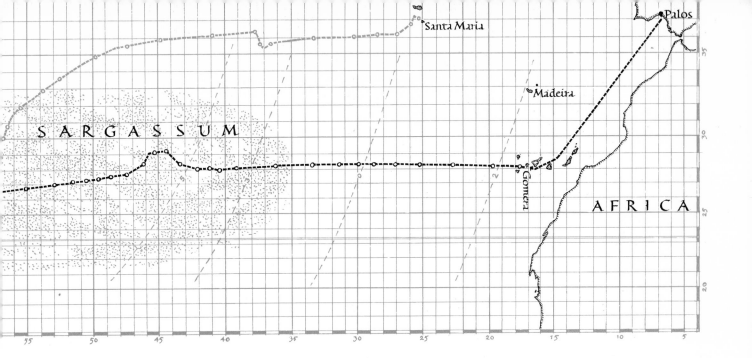

SARGASSUM

Santa Maria

Madeira

Gomera

AFRICA

Palos

in one day during the whole voyage, and the men were alarmed at their rapidly increasing distance from Spain with no sight of land ahead. This is also the only occasion on which the Journal records any direct protest from the crew to Columbus.]

Thursday—Friday, October 11—12
"He sailed west-south-west; they had a rougher sea than they had experienced during the whole voyage. They saw petrels and green seaweed near the ship. Those in the caravel *Pinta* saw a reed and a stick, and secured another small stick, which seemed to have been carved with a knife, and a piece of reed, and another plant which grows on land, and a small plank. The men in the *Niña* saw other signs of land, including a small twig with roses on it. At these signs, all breathed again and were happy. On this day, up to sunset, they made 27 leagues. After sunset, he steered his former course to the west; they made 12 Roman miles an hour, and up to two hours before midnight they had made 90 Roman miles, which is to say 22½ leagues. And since the caravel *Pinta* was swifter and went ahead of the Admiral, she found land and gave the signals which the Admiral had commanded. This land was first sighted by a sailor called Rodrigo de Triana, although the Admiral, at 10 o'clock in the night, saw a light as he stood on the sterncastle. But it was so dim that he would not affirm that it was land, but called Pedro Gutiérrez, one of the King's servants, and told him that there seemed to be a light, and that he should watch for it. He did so, and saw it. He also called to Rodrigo Sánchez of Segovia, whom the King and Queen had sent in the fleet as inspector, and he could see nothing, since he was not standing in the right place. After the Admiral had so spoken, it was seen once or

The broken black line is Columbus' approximate route across the Atlantic. The red line shows the return voyage as far as Santa Maria. The magnitude and direction of compass variations in the Atlantic at the end of the 15th century can only be conjectured. The broken red line immediately west of the Canaries indicates the 2° easterly isogon. Columbus passed the zero isogon at a longitude of about 30° west. On September 17, when a further 8° west, he noted that the compass deviated by about 3° to the west. This deviation may have increased to 7° or 8°, and then decreased again before he reached San Salvador.

twice more, and it was like a small wax candle being raised and lowered. Few thought that this was an indication of land, but the Admiral was certain that they were near land. Accordingly, they recited the *Salve*, which all sailors are accustomed to recite and sing after their manner, and when they had all been gathered together, the Admiral urged them to keep a good lookout from the forecastle and to watch carefully for land, and he promised to give a silk doublet immediately to the first man to cry out that he could see land, apart from the other rewards promised by Their Majesties, which were 10,000 *maravedis* annually to him who first sighted it. Two hours after midnight land appeared, at a distance of about two leagues from them. They took in all sail except the *treo,* which is the mainsail without bonnets, and lay by, waiting for day."

Guanahani, Island of the Saviour

They could just make out pale cliffs in the moonlight, and a dark line of trees beyond. The ships glided in toward the southern tip of the island during the few hours left before sunrise, and when the sun began to gild the sails and cliffs and foaming breakers, they set more sail, hoisted flags and pennants, and hung shields over the sides of the castles. Then they rounded the island to the south and turned north along the leeward coast. It was a low-lying, green island, and wonderful scents came out to them on the breeze. But a seething swell was breaking on the offshore reefs, and they had to sail nearly two leagues farther north before the lookouts on the yards and in the tops could see an opening wide enough for the ships to sail into and find anchorage.

Columbus then put on a scarlet doublet, and his officers changed into their best clothes. The boats were lowered, and the landing party armed themselves with swords, crossbows, and lances. It was a long, shallow beach, and they had to wade ashore. Columbus went first, with the royal standard in his hand, and after him came the two captains, Martín Alonso and Vicente Yáñez Pinzón, each carrying a banner with a green cross and the crowned initials of the Sovereigns. The land trembled under their feet. Through their tears they saw some naked men coming apprehensively toward them out of the trees. Lowering the standard and banners, they fell on their knees and kissed the ground. Then Columbus called upon the two captains and the secretary, Rodrigo de Escobedo, and the royal inspector, Rodrigo Sánchez, to witness that he took possession of this island in the name of the King and Queen, their liege Lord and Lady. He read out the majestic words prescribed for the occasion, and then they all solemnly knelt down once more as he spoke a prayer: "O Lord, Almighty and Everlasting God, by Thy holy Word Thou hast created the heaven, and the earth, and the sea; blessed and glorified be Thy Name, and praised be Thy Majesty, Which hath deigned to use us, Thy humble servants, that Thy holy Name may be known and proclaimed in this second part of the earth."

So Cristoforo Colombo had become Christoferens, the Bearer of Christ. He also realized that all the titles he had been promised were now his; he was now Grand Admiral of the Ocean, and Viceroy of the island, and Governor. Those who were with him on the beach saluted him in that capacity.

He describes his meeting with the people of this island, which the natives called Guanahaní and to which he himself gave the name San Salvador, Holy Saviour.

"So that they might be well disposed towards us, for I knew that they were a people to be delivered and converted to our holy Faith rather by love than by force, I gave to some red caps and to others glass beads, which they hung round their necks, and many other things of little value. At this they were greatly pleased and became so entirely our friends that it was a wonder to see. Afterwards they came swimming to the ships' boats, where we were, and brought us parrots and cotton thread in balls, and spears and many other things, and we exchanged for them other things, such as small glass beads and hawks' bells, which we gave to them. In fact, they took all and gave all, such as they had, with good will, but it seemed to me that they were a people very deficient in everything.

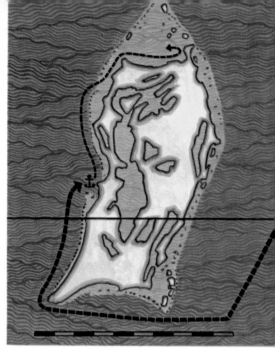

San Salvador in the early hours, just before sunrise. The pale limestone cliff belongs to one of the small islands off the southeast cape of the island. Nowadays it is called High Cay. The broad dotted line on the map to the right shows the route taken by the three ships before they found a suitable anchorage. The narrow line is the approximate path of Columbus' expedition to the north part of the island. It was on the peninsula farthest to the northeast that he planned to build a fortress. Each section on the scale along the lower edge of the map is equivalent to 1 nautical mile.

"They all go naked as their mothers bore them, and the women also, although I saw only one very young girl. All those whom I did see were youths, and I did not see one who was over the age of 30; they were very well built, with very handsome bodies and fine faces. Their hair is coarse, almost like the hair of a horse's tail, and short. They wear their hair down over their eyebrows, except for a few strands behind, which they wear long and never cut. Some of them are painted black—and they are the colour of the people of the Canaries, neither black nor white—and some of them are painted white, and some red, and some in any colour that they find. Some of them paint their faces, some their whole bodies, some only the eyes, and some only the nose. They do not bear arms or know of them; for I showed them swords, and they took them by the blade and cut themselves through ignorance. They have no iron. Their spears are certain reeds, without iron, and some of these have a fish tooth at the end, while others are pointed in various ways.

They are all generally fairly tall, good looking and well proportioned. I saw some who had scars on their bodies, and I asked them by signs what these were, and they indicated to me that people came from neighbouring islands to capture them, and they defended themselves. And I believed and still believe that they come here from the mainland to take them for slaves. They should make good servants of quick intelligence, since I see that they very soon repeat all that is said to them; and I believe that they would easily be made Christians, for it seemed to me that they had no religion of their own. Our Lord willing, when I depart I shall bring back six of them to Your Highnesses, that they may learn to talk [our language]. I saw no beast of any kind in this island, except parrots."

The Admiral wrote this during the evening of the first day on San Salvador. The following evening, Saturday, October 13, he continued: "At daybreak, many of these people came to the shore; all were young and well-proportioned, as I have said. Their hair is not curly, but straight and coarse as the hair of a horse. They have very broad foreheads and heads, more so than any people that I have seen hitherto. Their eyes are very lovely and not small. They are not at all black, but the colour of the people in the Canaries; and nothing else could be expected, since this is on the same parallel as the island of Ferro in the Canaries."

In fact, San Salvador lies 3° 41′ farther south than Ferro, but Columbus had read in the *Imago Mundi* of Aristotle's theory that people and objects on identical latitudes resembled each other.

Columbus' description continues: "Their legs are very straight, all alike; they have no great bellies but are well-shaped. They came to the ship in boats, which are made of treetrunks like long boats, all of one piece. They are very wonderfully carved, according to the resources of the country, and large, so that 40 or 50 men came in some of them; others are smaller, so that in some only a single man came. They propel them with a paddle, like a baker's shovel, and they travel wonderfully fast. If one capsizes,

A West-Indian canoe, from a woodcut made in 1563

all at once begin to swim and right it, bailing it out with calabashes which they carry with them.

"They brought balls of spun cotton and parrots and spears and other trifles, which it would be tiresome to write down, and they give all for anything that is given to them. I was vigilant and endeavoured to find out if they had gold, and I saw that some of them wore a small piece hanging from holes in their noses, and from signs I was able to understand that in the south there was a king who had large vessels of gold and possessed much of it. I endeavoured to make them take me there, but later I saw that they had no desire for the journey. I resolved to wait until the afternoon of the following day, and after that to leave for the south-west, for many of them indicated to me that there was land to the south and to the south-west and to the north-west, and that those of the north-west often came to attack them. So I resolved to go to the

south-west, to search for gold and jewels.

"This island is very large and very flat; the trees are bright green and there is much water. In the centre of it, there is a very large lake; there are no hills. Everything is so green that it is a pleasure to gaze upon it, and the people are also very quick-witted. Since they long to possess something of ours and fear that nothing will be given to them unless they give something in return, those who have nothing take what they can and immediately hurl themselves into the water and swim away. But all that they do possess, they give for anything which is given to them, so that they give things in exchange even for pieces of broken glass or crockery. I even saw one give sixteen balls of cotton for three *ceotis* of Portugal, which make one Castilian *blanca,* and in these balls there was more than an *arroba* of spun cotton. [A *blanca* was half a *maravedi.* An *arroba* was equivalent to about 25 pounds.] I should have forbidden this and should not have allowed anything to be taken, unless I had commandeered all upon Your Highnesses' account, if the quantity should prove large enough. It grows here in this island, but owing to lack of time, I can give no definite account [of how much is cultivated]; and here is also produced that gold which they wear hanging from their noses. But, in order not to lose time, I wish to go and see if I can find the island of Cipangu. Now, as it is night, they have all returned to land in their boats."

On Sunday, October 14, Columbus wrote: "At dawn I ordered the ship's boat and the boats of the caravels to be made ready, and I went along the island in a north-north-easterly direction, to see what was in the other part, which lay to the east, and also to see the villages. And I soon saw two or three, and the people all came to the shore, calling, and giving thanks to God. Some brought us water, others various foodstuffs; others, seeing that I was not inclined to land, threw themselves into the water and swam up to us, and we understood that they asked us if we had come from heaven. One old man got into the boat, and several shouted to the rest, both men and women. 'Come and see the men who have come from heaven; bring them food and drink.' Many came, numbers of women among them, and each brought something, giving thanks to God, throwing themselves on the ground and raising their hands to the sky, and then calling to us that we should land. But I was afraid to do so, for I saw a great reef of rocks which encircled the whole of that island, with deep water within it, and a harbour large enough for all the ships in Christendom; but its entrance is very narrow. It is true that inside the reef are many shallow places, but the sea is no more disturbed than the water in a well.

"In order to see all this, I was on the move all this morning, so that I might be able to give an account of all to

Your Highnesses, and also see where a fort could be built. I saw a piece of land, which is formed like an island although it is not one, on which there were six houses; it could be converted into an island in two days. [Columbus often found it difficult to express himself in Spanish. What he intended to say here was that he saw a peninsula, connected to San Salvador by a very narrow neck of land, through which a canal could easily be dug, so that the peninsula would be made an island.] But I do not see that it is necessary to do so, for these people are very unskilled in the use of arms, as Your Highnesses will see, for I caused seven of them to be taken away to learn our language and then return home, unless Your Highnesses command that they shall all be carried off to Castile or held captive in the island itself, since with 50 men they could be kept in subjection and forced to do whatever may be wished. Near the said islet, moreover, there are the loveliest groups of trees that I have ever seen, all green and with leaves like those of Castile in the month of April and May, and much water."

These days at San Salvador, when dreams seemed to come true and nothing happened to disturb them, were perhaps the happiest in Columbus' whole life. He had found land where he had said that land would be found. By his secret reckoning, they had actually sailed 1,090 leagues instead of 750, but all the men were aware that they had passed many islands before reaching this one. The feeling now was that they were so much nearer the mainland, the Outermost Indies and the province of Mangi. Marco Polo had said that there were 7,440 islands in this sea. And they had already seen gold on this primitive island.

And yet it seems that, for a moment, Columbus believed more in this solid reality under his feet and before his eyes than in all the legendary riches of India. Perhaps he had had to wait too long; perhaps doubts had had time to take root in his heart. Be that as it may, he was now prepared to fortify this insignificant island and enslave this petty body of people if the Sovereigns commanded him to do so.

From the first, the most popular objects of barter in the West Indies were the small brass bells which falconers in Europe tied to the legs of their hunting birds.

The quest for gold

The Admiral returned from his reconnaissance of the north point of the island before noon and gave orders to set the sails and weigh anchor. The beach behind the ships lay deserted; the inhabitants of the Saviour's Island were hiding among the trees in fear of the men from heaven, who had taken seven of their people with them by force. The foresails billowed out and swung the ships round from land, the great sails filled, and a course was set to the southwest. When they had covered a few leagues, a long chain of islands began to rise out of the sea along the horizon, and they decided to steer toward the largest of them. As they approached, however, they found that the chain of islands was in fact a single island, low and wooded like San Salvador. Darkness was, upon them

before they had time to reach the shore, and the Admiral signaled to the caravels to heave to for the night.

All sails were set with the dawn, and the ships sailed along the east and south coast of the island. Meanwhile, the Admiral amused himself by showing the captive Indians gold and asking them by signs if they knew where the metal could be found. All of them pointed excitedly toward the new island, and by their words and signs they seemed to want to explain that gold was to be had in great quantities there, that its inhabitants not only wore small gold ornaments in their noses but also large gold bracelets on their arms and legs. At least, this was what the Admiral understood by their signs, and indeed he was convinced that this was so, for Marco Polo had written that there was gold in undreamed of quantities on the islands in the Sea of Chin. And now they were actually sailing in this sea, and Columbus' joy was unbounded.

But the swell broke savagely on the reefs to the south of the new island, and the sun had set before they had left the breakers behind them and were able to anchor in a sheltered spot off the west point of the island. That night one of the Indian prisoners jumped overboard and swam ashore.

The Admiral began to suspect that the men of San Salvador had made up the story about the gold, simply to induce him to sail to the island so that they could escape. However, he had determined to anchor there in any case so that he might find out for himself, and take formal possession of the island for Castile, even though he knew that once he had taken possession of one island in that sea, he had taken possession of them all. So with the dawn he went ashore with his captains and repeated the San Salvador ceremonies, calling the island Santa María de la Concepción, St. Mary of the (Immaculate) Conception.

The inhabitants of this island were just as naked and impoverished as those of San Salvador, and there was not the slightest evidence of the promised wealth of the Indies. Moreover, the wind began to increase in strength and blow from the southeast, so they rowed back out to the ships and prepared to move on. One of the Indians, who was on the *Niña,* managed to throw himself overboard and swim to a native canoe, which picked him up. Men from the *Niña* immediately took to the boat and tried to catch them, but the canoe was too fast and reached the shore before they did. The natives and the man from San Salvador disappeared among the trees, and the men from the *Niña* gave up the chase and returned to the ship. Some time later, a lone native came paddling to the caravel from another direction. He held up a ball of cotton, and the men on the *Niña* showed him a string of glass beads and tried to entice him aboard. When he hesitated, several seamen jumped into the water and took him aboard by force, but the Admiral, who had seen everything from the poop deck, gave orders that the man should be brought to him.

The frightened native was then given a red woolen cap, a string of glass beads, and hawk's bells for earrings. Then he was set free. He paddled ashore and was met by astonished natives. The Admiral writes: "He was quite sure that we were good people and that the one who had run away must have done us some wrong, and been taken off for that reason. It was for this purpose that I had so acted with him, ordering him to be set free and giving him the aforesaid presents, so that we may be held in their esteem, and when Your Highnesses again send [men] here, they may not be unfriendly. All that I gave them was not worth four *maravedis.*"

Another island could just be discerned in the far west, and, sailing closer, they found that it was considerably larger than the two they had visited. The men from San Salvador again seemed to want to say that the people who lived there had gold in abundance, crying "Samaot, samaot!" and gesticulating so that the Admiral thought that "Samaot" was the name of an island or perhaps a city where there was plenty of gold to be found.

When they had covered about half the distance to the large island, which was low and green like the others, they saw a lone man paddling a small canoe. They sailed up to him and took him and his canoe aboard the flagship. In the canoe was a piece of bread, a calabash of water, a lump of brown mud kneaded together, and a few dry leaves. The Admiral was aware that the natives valued these leaves highly, for the men of San Salvador had given him some as a present, but he did not know why. They also found a little basket, which the man was reluctant to part with. In it he had a string of small glass beads and two Spanish coins of small value. This made it clear to them that he had paddled all the way from San Salvador, and by his signs they understood that he was bound for the large island ahead. They gave him food and treated him well, so that he would tell others that they were good people.

They did not find an anchorage before sunset on that day either, so they lay by for the night off the coast, which stretched as far as they could see to the southeast. When daylight came, they sailed closer and found that there was no reef barring their way to the shore of this island. They anchored just off a village and sent ashore the man they had picked up in the canoe. It was not long before the villagers themselves came out in their canoes, bringing calabashes of water, cotton, and other things to trade with.

The Admiral, as was now the custom, took formal possession of the island and called it Fernandina, after the name of the King. Men were sent inland for water, and the natives were only too willing to carry the filled casks back to the boats. But these people had no gold to speak of either. They were asked about "Samaot," and they repeated the word and talked among themselves and made signs, and the Admiral thought that they meant it was a city of gold. Martín Alonso Pinzón, who had some of the captives on the *Pinta,* said that one of them had explained that the best way of reaching "Samaot" was by rounding Fernandina to the north. This Columbus decided to try, so they rowed back to the ships, hoisted the sails, and then coursed slowly up toward the north point of the island in a light breeze.

On the way, the Admiral wrote in the journal: "These people are better disposed and the women wear in front of their bodies a small piece of cotton, which scarcely hides their secret parts. This island is very green and flat and very fertile, and I have no doubt that all the year they sow and reap panizo, and equally other things. [*Panizo* or panicum is a kind of grass. Columbus probably meant Indian corn, which was grown on these islands.

It was unknown in Europe at the time.] I saw many trees, very unlike ours, and many of them had branches of different kinds, which all came from one root. . . . For example: one branch has leaves like those of a reed and another leaves like those of a mastic bush, and thus, on a single tree, there are five or six different kinds all so different from each other. They are not grafted; it can be said that the grafting occurs of itself, for the trees grow wild in the forest, and the people do not tend them.

"I cannot find that they have any religion, and I believe that they would be speedily converted to Christianity, for they have a very good understanding. There are fish here so different from ours that it is a marvel. Some are shaped like dories, of the finest colours in the world, blue, yellow, red, and of all the colours of the rainbow; others are painted in a thousand ways, and the colours are so fine that no

man would not wonder at them or take great delight in seeing them. There are also whales. I have seen no land animals of any kind, except parrots and lizards. A boy told me that he had seen a large snake. I have not seen any sheep or goats or other animals, but I have been here a very short while, only half a day."

They came across a large bay, which seemed to be an excellent harbor, not far from the north cape of Fernandina. They anchored outside and sent the boats to reconnoiter, but found that it was too shallow. They took the opportunity to fill some casks with water, and the men who returned with the casks said that they had seen a man whose nose was decorated with a piece of gold which had letters on it. The Admiral was angry with them for not buying the gold so that he could see where it had been struck.

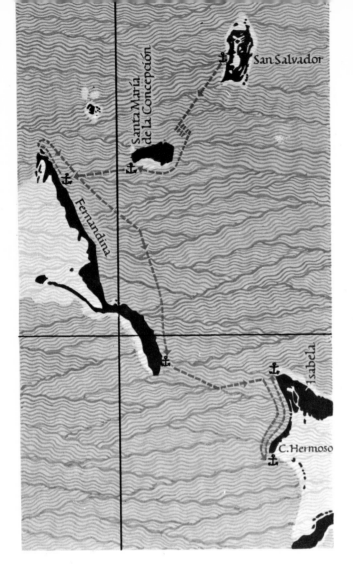

On the map, labels: San Salvador; Santa María de la Concepción; Fernandina; Isabela; C. Hermoso

Only a few of the islands have retained the names given to them by Columbus on his first voyage. San Salvador was long called Watling Island, after a notorious pirate, but now the name San Salvador has begun to appear again on the maps. Santa Maria de la Concepción is now called Rum Cay, Fernandina is called Long Island, and Isabela is called Crooked Island.

Again the sails were hoisted to continue rounding the cape, but the wind died down and then turned against them, blowing from the northwest. They gave up the attempt to circumnavigate Fernandina and sailed before the wind all that evening and night, mostly toward the southwest, parallel with the coast, but during the hours of darkness they sometimes steered to the southeast and east to be certain of keeping a safe distance from land. The night was dark and close with lowering clouds, and after midnight, rain began to fall heavily, lasting until dawn. The next day turned out to be dull, with drizzle and hardly any wind; when the rain began to increase and visibility

became bad, they made an early anchorage near the south cape of Fernandina.

At dawn on October 19, the Admiral sent the *Pinta* to the east-southeast, and the *Niña* to the south-southeast, while he himself took the *Santa María* to the southeast. His intention was that they should sail in those directions until noon and then change course so that they would come together once more, but before they had been under way more than three hours they sighted a new island to the east, and they reached its northernmost point before noon. The men from San Salvador called the island Saomete. The wind was fresh and northerly, so they followed the coast south to find a sheltered anchorage. A narrow sound seemed to separate Saomete from another island, but as the water there was greenish-yellow, a sign of shallows, they sailed on and finally came to anchor to the south of the second island, close to a point which the Admiral called Cabo Hermoso, the Beautiful Cape.

The men from San Salvador again seemed to be trying to indicate gold, and the Admiral understood from their signs that there was a rich king living in the inner part of Saomete. Although he was quite determined to seek contact with this king, he was no longer sure that he correctly understood the words and gestures of the men from San Salvador and resigned himself to spending a long time in search of gold. "I wish to see and discover as much as I can, in order to return to Your Highnesses in April, if it please the Lord. It is true that, if I should find gold or spices in quantity, I shall wait until I have collected as much as I am able. Accordingly I am doing nothing but sailing on until I find them."

They took the boats into the large bay south of Saomete and made a sounding, but they found that it was not deep enough for the ships. On the following day they sailed northward along the same route by which they had come. They sounded the straits between the islands, but, finding that these were also too shallow, continued north in a light breeze. At sunset the caravels moved in to shore and anchored, signaling to the Admiral that the anchorage was good, but he preferred to lie to during the night. When morning came they sailed on and finally achored out of the fresh wind behind a point which they called Cabo del Isleta. They took formal possession of the island in the name of the Sovereigns and called it Isabela, in honor of the Queen.

The inhabitants fled from their sight, but the Admiral gave orders that nothing in their huts was to be touched. He saw many new trees, some in flower and some bearing fruit, and the Journal tells us that he was greatly distressed that he was unable to assess the true value of the trees and plants. Marco Polo had written that there was not a single tree in those regions that did not have a pleasant smell, and this both Columbus and all who were with him were now able to verify. Marco Polo had also said that there

An iguana as it is, and as a 16th-century artist drew it

were many kinds of drugs and spices to be found there, especially aloes and black and white pepper.

As Columbus was unable to decide what was of value or not, he collected flowers and leaves and bark and fruits to take back to Castile, so that those who knew more about such things might examine them. And yet he thought he recognized the aloe (it was, in fact, an agave) and decided to take large quantities of this plant back with him. He writes that the sun was darkened by parrots and other birds and that they sang so beautifully that no one could ever wish to leave that island. He saw a large lizard, an iguana, on the beach of a lagoon, but it scuttled into the water. Some of the men chased it and killed it with spears and removed the skin to take back to the Sovereigns. When the natives saw that nothing had been touched in the deserted huts, some of them eventually plucked up enough courage to approach, and after glass beads and bells had been distributed, they became tolerably good friends.

They remained at Isabela for three days, but they were unable to find any king, and the only gold they saw and managed to buy consisted of a few wretched nose rings. For most of the time they were there the weather was calm but rainy, and they were astonished to find it as warm as it was so late in October, during both the day and night. The Admiral now began to think that he was beginning to understand the men from San Salvador better, and he interpreted certain of their words and gestures as good news. He wrote: "I wish to leave for another much larger island, which I believe must be Cipangu, according to the signs which these Indians whom I have with me make; they call it 'Colba.' They say that there are ships and many very good sailors there. Beyond that island, there is another which they call 'Bofio,' which they say is also very large. The others, which lie between them, we shall see in passing, and according to whether I find a quantity of gold or spices, I will decide what is to be done. But I am still determined to proceed to the mainland and to the city of Quinsay in order to give the letters of Your Highnesses to the Grand Khan, and to request a reply and return with it."

Columbus thought that he was in the East Indies and consequently called the inhabitants *Indios,* Indians. The island of Colba is Cuba, and it seems that he misheard the name at first, since he uses the name Cuba later on. Bofio, or Bohio as he wrote later, was not the name of an island, and Las Casas was the first to correct him on this point: "To call it Bohio was to misunderstand the interpreters, for on all these islands, practically everybody speaks the same language. The word Bohio denotes the houses they live in."

The Admiral's Indian companions had often crossed to Cuba in their canoes, and as they did not seem to have any idea of the draught of the ships, they led the fleet along their usual route. Everything was ready for departure by the morning of October 23, but there was no wind until the following night. The Admiral writes: "They indicated that I should steer west-south-west to get there. I am doing so, for I believe that if the Indians of these islands and those whom I am taking in the ships are correctly indicating by their gestures (for I do not know their language) it must be the Isle of Cipangu, about which marvellous things are said; and indeed, on the globes I have seen, and on the mappemondes, it is shown in this part of the world. I sailed west-south-west until daylight, and at daybreak the wind dropped and it began to rain, which continued all day. I had no wind until noon, after which time a light wind rose and I set all my sail, the mainsail and two bonnets, the foresail, the spritsail, the mizzen, the main topsail, and the boat's sail on the poop. I kept the same course until nightfall, when I had Cape Verde on Fernandina, to the south side of the west part of the island, seven leagues off to my north-west. The wind now blew hard, and I did not know how far it would be to the said island of Cuba, and did not wish to search for it in the night, since all these islands are in very deep water, with no bottom beyond the distance of two lombard shots; and these bottoms are part rock and part sand, so that it is not safe to anchor except in daylight. So I decided to strike all sail except the foresail, and I sailed on under that. Soon the wind became much stronger, and I was very uncertain of my course. And since the clouds were thick and it was raining, I bade them furl the foresail. That night we made no more than two leagues."

The ships made good speed towards the west-south-west and west during the whole of the next day, and in the afternoon a chain of seven or eight islands was sighted. They lay to during the night, and on the next day, October 26, they sailed over an extensive bank of shallows to the south of the islands. The water, usually dark, was now light green, and the men with the sounding lines called out twelve fathoms, then five fathoms, then three and a half; and the lookout in the top shouted that he could see large patches of shallow water. Well before nightfall, they anchored near the islands, which the Admiral called Las Islas de Arena, The Sandy Isles. The Indians now showed them that Cuba lay to the south, only a day and a half's distance in a canoe. When they had sailed for another day with a fresh wind, they saw blue mountains rising above the southern horizon and fired lombards and hoisted flags to celebrate the discovery of Cipangu. Then they lay to for the night.

76

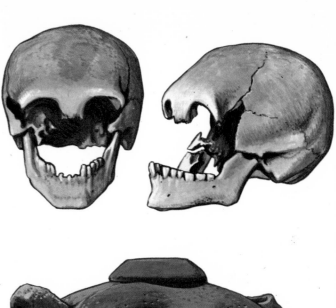

Hitherto, the Indians Columbus had met were Arawak Indians of the Taino culture. Originally from South America, at the time of the Spaniards' arrival they were occupying the Bahamas, Cuba, Española, Jamaica, Puerto Rico, and Trinidad. The broad foreheads which Columbus noted were deliberately produced by compressing the heads of new-born babies so that their foreheads were pushed back. Contemporary skulls show this deliberate deformation. Arawak Indians are still found in Guiana, and from these survivors, from skulls, and from old Taino carvings, it is easy to reconstruct the appearance of Columbus' Indians. They painted themselves with different colors and patterns; the patterns decorating the face of the man to the right are taken from Taino pottery. According to a description from Columbus' second voyage, they painted themselves to keep the mosquitoes away, but the different patterns must certainly have been thought to have a magical function as well.

The mainland

They steered toward the nearest part of the coast, and a bay opened directly in front of them. The boats were sent in to take soundings, and it was found that the bay was the mouth of a river, everywhere deep enough for the ships, and the men in the boats signaled for them to come in. The Admiral and his captains were rowed ashore, and they took possession of this large island, which might well have been Cipangu, on behalf of the Sovereigns, calling it Juana, in honor of the Crown Prince Don Juan.

The Indians who were with them said that the island was so large that they could not round it in a canoe in twenty days, and this fitted in with the Cipangu of the maps. Nor did Columbus expect to find any large island other than Cipangu on that latitude. But on the beach there was nothing but two miserable huts: not a trace of the riches of Cipangu. The natives had run away when the ships sailed in, and there was only one little dog, wandering aimlessly up and down the beach, which did not even bark at them. They saw some nets and lines, fishhooks and harpoons, made of bone. The Admiral gave orders that the natives' belongings were not to be touched, and then they rowed up the river. The trees grew right out into the water, on long roots, and palm trees rose above the party and bowed their heads over the water. The scents

were almost overpowering, and the birds sang so sweetly that the Admiral, at a loss for words to describe the scene, said that he never wanted to leave this wonderful place.

Nevertheless, they weighed anchor the very next day and sailed west to find the city where the king resided. Toward evening, they reached a new anchorage, larger than the previous one; it was an estuary in which three rivers joined. A whole village lay close to the shore, but even though the Admiral sent one of his Indians in the first boat to tell the people that the white men would do them no harm, the villagers fled to the woods. The huts were larger and better made than the ones the Spaniards had seen before, and they found female images and carved wooden masks, but the Admiral did not know whether to take them for ornaments or for idols. According to Marco Polo, the gods on Cipangu had at least four arms each, and the heads of oxen, pigs, and other animals. Columbus saw nothing of any value. Many dogs were running about wildly among the huts, and it was noticed that these did not bark either. They saw the skulls of large animals and thought that the inhabitants kept cattle. The Admiral called this place Rio de Mares.

On the following morning they continued along the coast to the northwest, and the land became more and more low lying as they proceeded. After they had been under way for a few hours, Martín Alonso Pinzón signaled that he had a message for the Admiral, and the *Pinta* came alongside the flagship. Pinzón hailed them and said that the Indians with him had explained that there was a river beyond the next point, and that Cuba lay four days' journey up that river. He therefore believed that Cuba was a city and not an island, and that this coast was not Cipangu at all but a part of the mainland, and that it would soon turn to the north. His Indians had also said that the people of this place were at war with the Grand Khan, whom they called Cami, and they called his country or city Faba or Saba, or some such name.

The Admiral agreed that what Pinzón had said might well be true, but before sailing to the Grand Khan he wanted to reach the river beyond the point and send presents and a letter from the Sovereigns to the king of Cuba.

The wind now began to turn against them, and they beat about the whole night until they had gradually rounded the point. When daylight came they saw the mouth of a river. The Indians made signs for them to sail in, but the lookouts could see from a distance that the river was not deep enough for the ships. The wind freshened, and they noticed that the current, which had hitherto assisted them, was now against them. The Admiral thought that this was a clear indication that they were not far from the point where the coast turned off to the north, and he felt that the wind from the mainland was colder than the other winds. The ships could not make way against both wind and current, and as the sky bore obvious signs of an impending storm, the Admiral decided to turn about. So the ships ran before the wind, and in a few hours they were back at Rio de Mares.

The people of the river were ultimately convinced that the white men meant them no harm, and soon the ships were surrounded by canoes of natives wanting to sell their cotton. Although they were well received and were given small presents, the Admiral had ordered that nothing but gold was to be bought from them, so that it would be clear to them that gold was the only thing the white men wanted. But no gold was forthcoming, not even the small nose rings of the other islands.

The Admiral wrote of the inhabitants: "They are of the same kind and have the same customs as the others. From what I can see they have no religion: hitherto I have neither heard nor seen any of those who are with me saying any prayers, but they do say the *Salve* and the *Ave Maria* with their hands raised, and they make the sign of the cross, as we have taught them to do. Furthermore, they all speak the same language, and they are all friends, and I think all these islands are at war with the Grand Khan, whom they call Cavila, and they call the province Basan. And they all go naked like the others. . . . It is certain that this is the mainland, and that I am near Zaiton and Quinsay, about 100 leagues from either."

The Indians explained that from this place one could reach the king of Cuba by land, and on November 2 the Admiral sent his interpreter, Luis de Torres, and a seaman named Rodrigo de Jerez inland to find out about him. They took one of the Indians from San Salvador, with a man from Rio de Mares as a guide. The Admiral intended them to speak in the name of the Sovereigns if they met the King; they were to tell him that the Admiral of the Ocean had come to establish a friendship and alliance with him and to do him any service he could. They were also to ask the way to the provinces of Mangi and Concha, and to the city of Zaiton. They took samples of several spices, to see if they could find some of the same kind. A few strings of glass beads were to meet the expenses of the journey.

That night was clear, and the Admiral took the altitude of the polestar several times with the quadrant and then worked out the latitude of Rio de Mares. He noted down the result in a private book, and entered 42 degrees in the logbook to confuse anybody who might wish to exploit his discoveries. According to his calculations, they were 1142 leagues west of Ferro, and he wrote once again that he was sure that they had reached the mainland.

One day Martín Alonso Pinzón came to him and said that a Portuguese who sailed with him had found two pieces of bark which he thought was cinnamon, for it smelled like cinnamon. He had seen an Indian carrying two large bundles of this bark, as well as something which looked like nutmeg, but since the Admiral had forbidden all trade he had not ventured to buy any. Juan Quintero, the boatswain of the *Pinta*, thought that he had found some cinnamon trees, but the Admiral looked at them and said that they could not be cinnamon. Later, he showed the Indians some real cinnamon bark, and they nodded and indicated by gestures that there was much of this bark to be had farther on, to the southwest. He showed them some gold and pearls, and they seemed to know where to find these things as well, and he took their gestures to mean that there was plenty of gold to be had on the island of Bohio.

The only thing at Rio de Mares which Columbus seemed to recognize with certainty was mastic. There were some large trees growing there, with leaves and fruit like those of the mastic bush, which grew only on the Greek island of Chios. He remembered that the Genoese made over 50,000 ducats a year out of Greek mastic, and here it was growing in abundance. The trees did not in fact yield more than a few drops of gum, even though he cut the right grooves in the bark, but he thought that this was because of the rain and because it was not the right time of the year; he believed that the trees should be tapped in the spring, just before they were in blossom.

He wrote about a root which the Indians called *mames* and which was similar to the carrot, though it smelled of walnut; and about their cotton, which grew wild on bushes as tall as trees. "I believe that they gather it all the

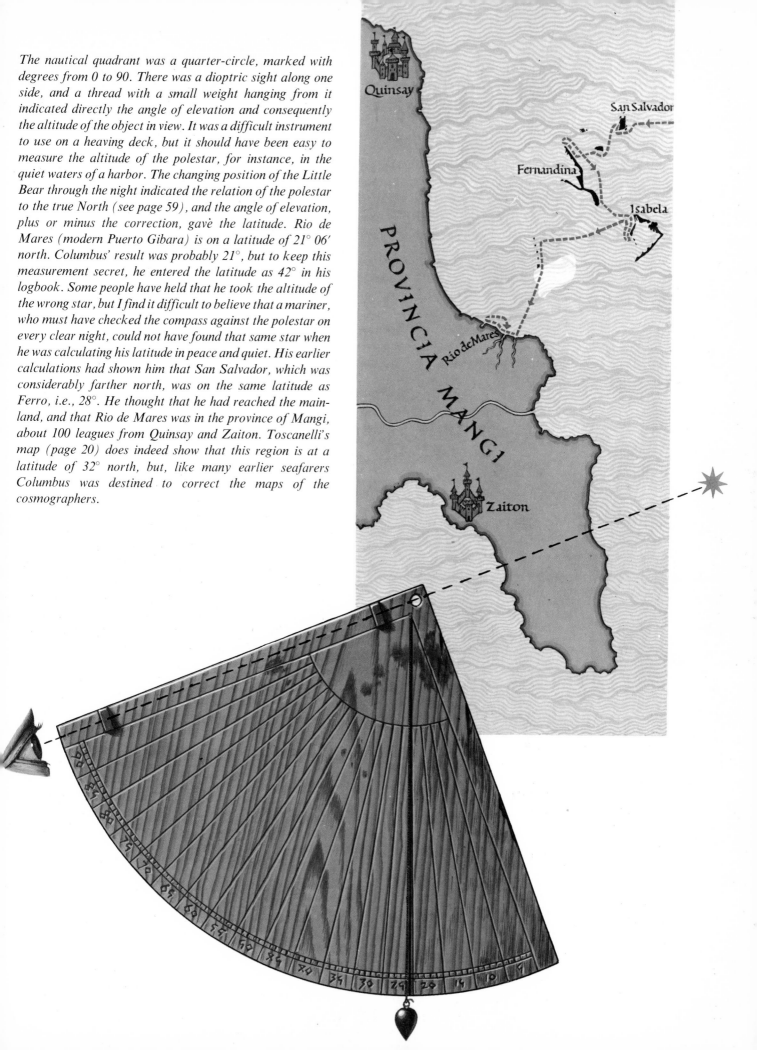

The nautical quadrant was a quarter-circle, marked with degrees from 0 to 90. There was a dioptric sight along one side, and a thread with a small weight hanging from it indicated directly the angle of elevation and consequently the altitude of the object in view. It was a difficult instrument to use on a heaving deck, but it should have been easy to measure the altitude of the polestar, for instance, in the quiet waters of a harbor. The changing position of the Little Bear through the night indicated the relation of the polestar to the true North (see page 59), and the angle of elevation, plus or minus the correction, gave the latitude. Rio de Mares (modern Puerto Gibara) is on a latitude of 21° 06′ north. Columbus' result was probably 21°, but to keep this measurement secret, he entered the latitude as 42° in his logbook. Some people have held that he took the altitude of the wrong star, but I find it difficult to believe that a mariner, who must have checked the compass against the polestar on every clear night, could not have found that same star when he was calculating his latitude in peace and quiet. His earlier calculations had shown him that San Salvador, which was considerably farther north, was on the same latitude as Ferro, i.e., 28°. He thought that he had reached the main-land, and that Rio de Mares was in the province of Mangi, about 100 leagues from Quinsay and Zaiton. Toscanelli's map (page 20) does indeed show that this region is at a latitude of 32° north, but, like many earlier seafarers Columbus was destined to correct the maps of the cosmographers.

year round, for I have seen some open bolls, and others just opening, and some blossoms all on the same tree." He wrote that Rio de Mares was one of the better harbors in the world, and suggested that a fortress should be built there to protect trade, on a high cliff overlooking the entrance.

The messengers were back by November 5. They had gone 12 leagues inland and had reached a village with fifty houses and a thousand inhabitants. The chief men of the village had carried them to a large house and given them chairs to sit on; but the chairs were wooden ones, and the house was roofed with palm leaves, not with gold. Luis de Torres tried to talk to the Indians, as before, in Arabic and Aramaic, but nobody could understand what he said. The Indian from San Salvador then explained to the villagers the way in which the Christian men lived and assured them that these Christians were good men. The villagers then kissed their hands and feet and showed by their gestures that they believed them to have come from heaven. Then they went away, and the women of the village came in, and in their turn kissed their hands and feet and touched their bodies to make sure that they were of flesh and blood.

Columbus' men showed the villagers some cinnamon and pepper and other spices, and from their gestures, and from the interpreters, they learned that plenty of these spices were to be had far to the southeast. But no one had ever heard of Mangi or Concha or Zaiton, or of any city or king whatever, and so they decided to return immediately. More than half the villagers wanted to accompany them so that they could see them fly off to heaven, but they asked to be allowed to go alone, and only one of the village elders and his son escorted them back to Rio de Mares. They had seen many new trees and plants, and large cultivations of *panizo,* and many birds, and they had heard nightingales sing. Apart from dogs which could not bark, they had seen no four-footed animals. Quite often on the way they had passed people who were carrying smoking leaves rolled together, which they would put into their mouths and suck, inhaling the smoke.

The Admiral welcomed the village elder and his son and tried to talk to them through his Indian interpreters. At one stage, he thought of keeping them on board so that he could take them back to Castile, but as the *Santa María* was just then careened for caulking and therefore in no position to defend herself, he did not want to do this by force and risk a fight with the Indians. The man and his son said that they wanted to spend the night ashore; by the next morning they had disappeared.

It is probable that the caravels also were careened at Rio de Mares, for the fleet did not sail until November 12. On the day before they left, the Admiral detained several of the islanders by force, and once well out at sea, he wrote: "Yesterday a canoe with six young men came alongside and five of them came aboard. I gave orders that they should be detained, and I have them with me. Afterwards I sent a boat to a house on the west bank of the river, and they came back with seven women, large and small, and three children. I did this in the knowledge that the [Indian] men would conduct themselves better in Spain if they had women from their own country with them than if they had not. I have often taken men from Guinea to Portugal before, so that they might learn Portuguese, and then they were sent back and people hoped that they might be useful to us in their own country. . . . in fact this never happened. But these, who have their women with them, will find that it is to their advantage to do what they are told, and their women will teach our people their language, which is spoken all over these Indian islands. They all understand each other and go to each other in their canoes, unlike in Guinea, where there are hundreds of languages, so that one man cannot understand another.

"On this night a man came alongside in a canoe, the husband of one of these women and the father of three children, a boy and two girls; he said he wanted to come with us. He begged me earnestly, and now they are all happy together, so I think they must all be related. He is a man of over 45 years of age."

What the Indians had been sucking was rolled-up tobacco leaves, but Columbus had no idea of the virtually worldwide effects which this discovery would have. The Indians grew tobacco, which they called caoba, *and rolled the leaves to make cigars, or ground them to make snuff. The historian Oviedo saw later on how they drew the snuff into their noses through a Y-shaped tube which they called a* tabaco. *He took them to mean that the snuff and the plant it came from were called "tabaco," and it was under that name that the novelty was launched in Europe.*

The root which the Indians called mames *is now known as the sweet potato. The tree which Columbus thought was mastic had no practical use whatever, but the wild cotton was a regular West Indian export for some time. Left: a Cuban parrot on the branch of a cotton tree in bloom*

The ends of the earth

Columbus had not met the king of Cuba, nor had he seen any of the cities which ought to have been along the coast; he had not sailed farther west and north, as the world map suggested, to see the Grand Khan and give him the royal letter; he had not found a single piece of gold in the whole of Juana, and no spices that really were spices; he had not seen one of the thousands of ships which ought to have been sailing between the province of Mangi and the islands.

I suspect that he had his doubts about whether this was the mainland. It had little in common with Marco Polo's description or with the maps. But it lay where it ought to lie, where he had worked out that it ought to lie, and it was not inconceivable that Marco Polo had been exaggerating the wealth of the country and the number of the ships. Plenty of other travelers had done the same. Still, Columbus probably had his doubts. Otherwise, he would not have slipped into the way of so often saying "all these islands," and only occasionally have emphasized that it must be the mainland. In the journal, which was really one long letter to the Sovereigns, there is no hint of disappointment, and he is just as untiring and enthusiastic as ever when he goes on describing the coast and the excellence of its harbors, and suggesting fortresses to protect trade. He is far more the Discoverer than he is the Admiral. Pinzón calls him ruthless and foolhardy, and it is true that he frequently took great risks in sailing too close to land. But he wanted to find out about his viceroyalty and to map it out, and he always kept a careful lookout. In fact, his description of capes and rivers and harbors is so detailed that it has not been difficult to reconstruct his route.

The Indians on Columbus' ship had spoken of a golden island to the east, called Babeque, where the inhabitants collected nuggets of gold on the beaches by firelight in the evenings and then hammered them out into bars. This, at least, was what the Admiral and his men understood that they did, and this was why they continued so doggedly to the east, persuading themselves that it was not the right

time of year to visit the country of the Grand Khan. After no more than one day at sea from Rio de Mares, they thought that they had come to the uttermost end of Juana, and, indeed, of the earth. The Admiral called this spot Cabo de Cuba. They were later to discover that the coast continued a good way to the east. By the third day, wind and currents pressed so hard against them that the *Santa María* made hardly any progress at all, and she was left far behind by the caravels. The Admiral then signaled to them to sail in toward the coast, and before evening they reached a bay which seemed to open out into a sea of innumerable islands to the south.

Here the Admiral records that he thought that the land to the west was the extremity of Juana, and of the earth, and the land to the east was the large island of Bohio. He called these waters the Mar de Nuestra Señora, Our Lady's Sea, and he wrote that all these hundreds of islets were the same as those that were to be seen at the eastern extremity on the maps of the world. He had to modify this opinion the next day, when he discovered that the "sea" was a large circular bay, but he did not change what he had written.

He spent the next five days sailing and rowing in the ship's boat, exploring the Mar de Nuestra Señora, writing exuberantly about these beautiful, lofty islands which looked as if they reached the sky. He saw mastic and aloes and cultivations of *panizo* and *mames*, but no natives, for they all ran away. He saw some Indian rats, two feet long; and one day he noticed a strong smell of musk and hoped to find that rare animal, the musk deer. Even Marco Polo had never seen a musk deer, but if his description was right it was an animal with the hooves and tail of an antelope, four sharp tusks, but no horns. The priceless musk accumulated as a swelling near its navel at the time of the full moon.

His Indians brought up some large snails from the sea, and the sailors fished with nets; one day they caught a fish with a head like a pig, which they salted down as a present for the Sovereigns. They were all ready to continue the voyage by Sunday, November 18, but the Admiral did not want to put to sea on the Lord's Day, so they did not move off until dawn on Monday.

They had noticed that there was nearly always a wind from the land in the early morning, and as the day progressed the winds changed to north and east. They steered north-northwest for two days. They thought they saw an island to the east; this, the Indians gladly assured them, was the golden island of Babeque. The Admiral calculated that they were 12 leagues from Isabela, but since he was afraid that the men from San Salvador would run away if they came close to their own island, he did not want to go there. The wind was blowing from Babeque, and as the flagship could not get closer to that elusive island against

wind and waves and currents, he decided to take the fleet back to the Mar de Nuestra Señora and wait for more favorable weather. But night fell before they got back, and as the wind was strong he thought that the safest thing would be to lie to offshore for the night. The wind dropped before dawn, and they rode the waves for several hours without making any headway until the regular dawn breezes came from the south and they could steer toward the rising sun. Then the wind turned against them again, as inexorably as before.

Without giving any explanation, Martín Alonso Pinzón now sailed away from the *Santa María* and the *Niña*. The *Pinta* was the fastest of the three ships, and it would have been no use to try to catch her in the flagship. She drew slowly away from them in the light breeze, and she might have been quite a long way off before the Admiral realized what Pinzón was doing. He might well have fired a few lombards to attract her attention, but she took no notice, and later on she veered round to the north-northeast. She was still visible, in the moonlight, when the night began, and the Admiral gave orders to reduce sail and light lanterns, so that she might have a chance to find her way back to them. The *Santa María* and the *Niña* drifted slowly south and southwest; when dawn came, the *Pinta* could no longer be seen.

We do not know why Pinzón left the Admiral in this way. There had, it seems, been some disagreement between them at the Canaries, but Columbus does not tell us what it was about. According to Las Casas, Columbus thought that the Indians on board the *Pinta* had promised to take Pinzón to a place where there was a great deal of gold; he adds that it was greed which made him sail away without permission. It is not very likely that Pinzón got any special information from his Indians; it may well be that earlier disagreements, together with the slowness of the flagship, had got on his nerves, and he simply wanted to use his superior speed and be the first to reach Babeque. Perhaps greed was a contributing factor, but it is not edifying to hear Columbus talking about greed, and the only direct reference to this subject which Las Casas quotes from the journal is: "He has also said, and done, many other things to me."

It was only natural for Pinzón to resent and envy this Genoese parvenu, who had done nothing that Pinzón himself could not have done just as well but had ended up as Viceroy of all these islands and countries, and Admiral of the Ocean too. The Journal suggests that Don Cristóbal Colón was a very self-centered leader who very seldom mentioned the work done by his subordinates. We can understand his resentment against Martín Alonso and his ill will toward him after the way he had behaved, but it does not explain why he was equally resentful toward Martín

Alonso's brother, Vincente Yáñez, who was perfectly loyal toward Columbus throughout the voyage.

The *Santa María* and the *Niña* continued south, drifting to the southwest in the light breeze. They thought they saw another island, beyond what they took to be the eastern-most cape, and the Indians said that it was Bohio, where there were cannibals, evil men who ate their prisoners. It was evening before they got close to land and could see that the low island, with its harbor, was one which they had passed ten days ago in heavy weather. The deep harbor was the finest they had seen in the Indies, and large enough to shelter all the ships in Spain. It was the eve of St. Catherine's Day, and the Admiral called the place Puerto de Santa Catalina.

Here he found fir trees, a whole forest of tall, straight fir trees covering the foothills. Las Casas records: "He realized that they could be used to build ships, countless masts, and boards for the best ships in Spain. He saw oaks and strawberry trees, and a good river, with opportunities to build sawmills. . . . At this place he cut a lateen yard and a mast for the mizzen of the Niña. . . . He describes this for the Sovereigns with great enthusiasm, and shows that everything he saw, especially the fir trees, filled him with indescribable joy and happiness. For here one could build as many ships as one wished, since there was an abundance of timber and pitch: all that need be brought here was the tackle for them. And he said that he had not described one hundredth part of all the things which were here, and it seemed to him as if The Lord wanted to show him better things at every step."

They did not stay longer that Sunday in that harbor

The two-foot "Indian rats" Columbus saw were hutias or tree rats. The fish with the head of a pig was a trunk fish; Las Casas says "it was completely covered with shell, very hard, and the only soft places were the tail and the eyes, and on its underbelly was an orifice for the voiding of its waste products."

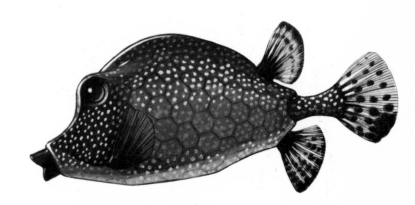

but moved southeast along the steep, forested coast. They noted the positions of rivers, harbors, and capes, and sometimes believed that they had reached the last cape. But the coast went on and on, and the Viceroy's province grew ever larger. On the second day out of Puerto de Santa Catalina they sailed into the mouth of a river, where they saw a village which was larger than any they had yet seen in the Indies. Hundreds of naked men stood on the shore, brandishing spears and shouting at them. But the Admiral's men rowed calmly toward them in the boats, and to avoid alarming them only three men went ashore at first, calling out in the vernacular they had learned that they came in peace. It seemed at first as if the Indians meant to attack them, but all of a sudden they turned and ran into the woods. Nothing of any interest was found in the houses, and about midday they weighed anchor and sailed on.

After half a league's journey, they came to a harbor, round and deep like a bowl. The Admiral could not find words to express what he saw, and recorded that neither he nor a thousand men together could describe this wonderful harbor and the countryside. He wrote of a river with the clearest of waters, of woods like the loveliest gardens, of a boat made of a single tree trunk, as large as a *fusta* of 12 seats.

A fresh east wind kept the ships there for a week, and the crews fished and washed their clothes and made expeditions inland. They saw large cultivated fields and villages and now and then a glimpse of the inhabitants as they ran into hiding. In one of the huts they found a basket with a polished skull in it, and yet another in a second hut.

The Admiral thought that the skulls must be those of the ancestors of the inhabitants.

Once, when the Spaniards rowed into a harbor a quarter-league to the east, they had the luck to make an unexpected contact with the inhabitants. At first the Admiral thought that he had won new friends with his gifts, but an interpreter from San Salvador who was with them thought that the natives meant to attack them and kill them all. He turned pale and made signs to indicate that the party should retire. When he saw that the Admiral did not seem to believe him, he grasped a crossbow, pointed it at the natives, shouting that he could kill them all, even at that distance. As they did not move, he drew a sword and brandished it over his head, whereupon they all ran away. Even so, he was still trembling long after they had disappeared. Later, the Admiral wrote in his journal that ten armed men could put ten thousand Indians to flight.

The bowl-shaped harbor where the *Santa María* and the *Niña* lay weatherbound Columbus called Puerto Santo. He wrote: "I assure Your Highnesses that nowhere under the sun do I think that there can be found lands which are more fertile, more temperate, or more abundant in good and pure water. The rivers are not like those of Guinea, which are all plague-infested. For, praise be to The Lord, not one among all my people has up to the present had as much as a headache, and no one has been in bed from illness, except one old man with gravel, which he has had all his life, and he recovered within two days. And this is true of all three ships. . . . And whereas above I have spoken of a site for a town and a fortress on the Rio

84

de Mares, because of the good harbour and the surroundings, it is certain that what I said is true; yet it cannot be compared with this place, or with the Mar de Nuestra Señora, for here inland there must be large villages and innumerable people and objects of great value, so that I declare that here and in all other places which I have discovered and have hopes of discovering before I return to Castile, all Christendom will find trade, and more especially Spain, to which all this land must be subject. And I say that Your Highnesses must not allow any foreigners, except Catholic Christians, to trade here or to set foot here, for the whole object of the enterprise was that it should be for the increase and glory of the Christian religion, and that no one should come to these parts who was not a good Christian."

They left Puerto Santo on Tuesday, December 4, and sailed in the light breeze along the coast, which now began to turn due east. They saw yet another river, sent a boat to take soundings in its mouth, and entered it on the map, and then came to Cabo Lindo, where the land at last seemed to come to an end. They lay to off the cape during the night, but when morning came they saw that there was yet another cape beyond it. The Admiral did not want to follow the coast any farther, and so he set course for the northeast and the golden island of Babeque. They sailed for a few hours in that direction, but the wind turned against them, and east-southeast was the closest they could keep to their intended course. The haze on the skyline ahead gradually changed into a range of blue mountains and a large island, and they understood that this was Bohio.

The Santa María, *the* Niña, *and their boats on the way in to Puerto de San Nicolao, which was "large enough to contain a thousand carracks."*

The Spanish Island

It seemed, as Columbus had written once before, that it was again the Lord's will to show him something better than anything he had seen thitherto. When he sailed into a large deep harbor at the westernmost cape of Bohio on the day of the feast of St. Nicholas, he found that he had exhausted his vocabulary to describe what he saw, and that this surpassed all that he had seen and described in Juana. Northeast, at its innermost extremity, the harbor narrowed to an arm, where it was deep enough for the largest ship in the world to anchor alongshore with its gunwales against the grass. Here there were groves of low oaks and strawberry trees, but everywhere else the countryside round the harbor was almost treeless and rose in terraces toward the mountains on the east and south. The Spaniards saw only one house, like the houses of Juana, but there were a number of large canoes lying in the shade of the trees, and they deduced that many people lived inland. The Admiral called this harbor Puerto de San Nicolao.

They stayed here for only a day and a night, and then sailed along the coast to the east. The Indians who were with them showed great apprehension and wanted to steer

85

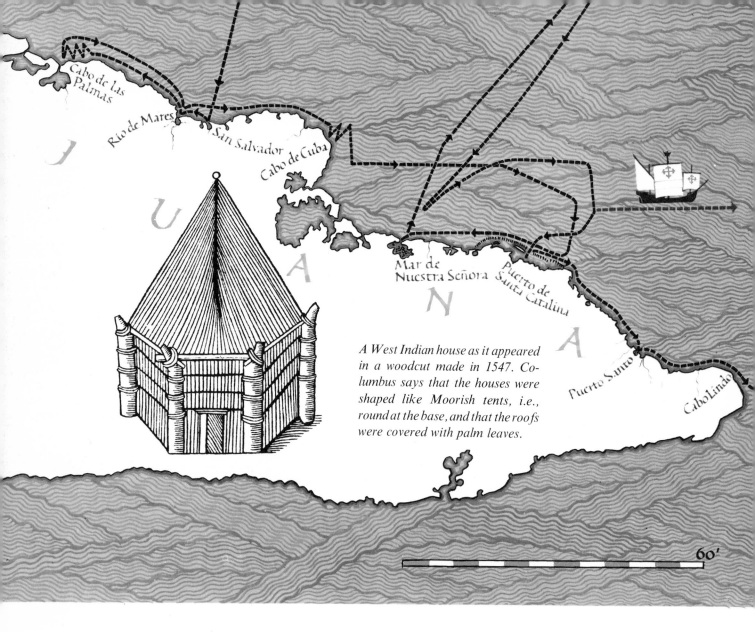

A West Indian house as it appeared in a woodcut made in 1547. Columbus says that the houses were shaped like Moorish tents, i.e., round at the base, and that the roofs were covered with palm leaves.

60'

away from the island, saying that the men of Bohio were cannibals. But the Admiral did not believe them. They said that the island was larger than Cuba, and that it was joined to a large mainland, which they called Caniba or Caribata. The Admiral wrote: "I repeat what I have said earlier: the Caniba are no other than the people of the Grand Khan. They must be very near here, and they have ships, and come and take them prisoner: and since nobody ever comes back, these people believe that they have been eaten. Every day we understand these Indians better, and they us: though they have often mistaken our meaning."

When they had sailed a few leagues east, they noticed that the land became greener, and they saw large cultivated areas, like cornfields, in a valley. They saw bare hills and green dales, and blue mountains farther inland, and they said to each other that this country was like Castile, though more beautiful. But the sky grew dark, threatening

rain and strong winds, so they anchored earlier than usual, in a deep river mouth. As the Admiral was being rowed ashore, a mullet jumped into the boat; this was the first fish he had seen in the Indies which resembled any fish in Spanish waters. Then they found that everything began to remind them of Spain: the fish they caught, the trees, the flowers, and the song of the birds. It was the Eve of the Immaculate Conception, and the Admiral called the harbor Puerto de la Concepción. The island itself he called La Isla Española, The Spanish Island.

They lay there for a whole week, waiting for the rain to stop and the wind to turn. A large round island, which the Admiral called Isla de la Tortuga, Turtle Island, sheltered them from the strong northeast wind, but the harbor was not a good one, and the ships dragged their anchors once or twice in the squalls. One day three seamen came dragging a naked young woman who was

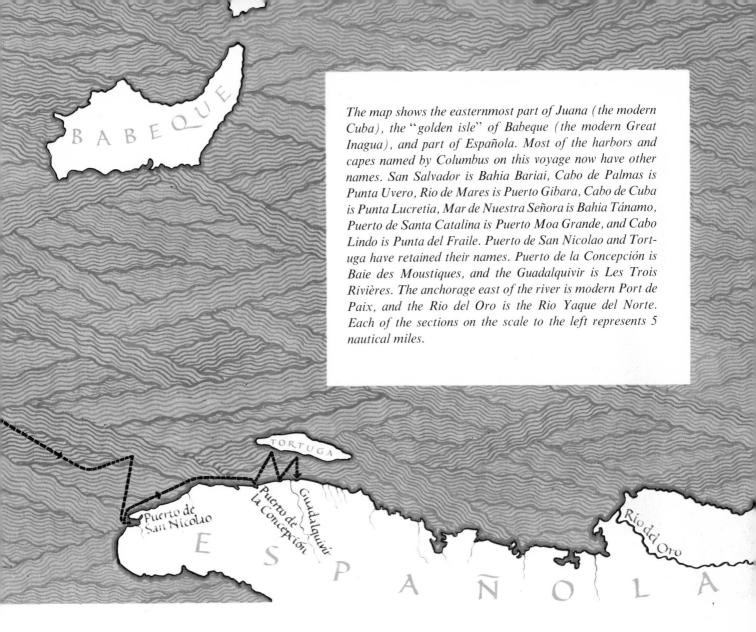

The map shows the easternmost part of Juana (the modern Cuba), the "golden isle" of Babeque (the modern Great Inagua), and part of Española. Most of the harbors and capes named by Columbus on this voyage now have other names. San Salvador is Bahia Bariai, Cabo de Palmas is Punta Uvero, Rio de Mares is Puerto Gibara, Cabo de Cuba is Punta Lucretia, Mar de Nuestra Señora is Bahia Tánamo, Puerto de Santa Catalina is Puerto Moa Grande, and Cabo Lindo is Punta del Fraile. Puerto de San Nicolao and Tortuga have retained their names. Puerto de la Concepción is Baie des Moustiques, and the Guadalquivir is Les Trois Rivières. The anchorage east of the river is modern Port de Paix, and the Rio del Oro is the Rio Yaque del Norte. Each of the sections on the scale to the left represents 5 nautical miles.

struggling wildly. The men had been inland looking for mastic and spices when they had suddenly come across a large body of natives, who immediately took to their heels. But they had managed to capture the woman and bring her back to the Admiral. She was beautiful, and completely naked, though she had a little gold ornament in her nose. The Admiral dressed her in a shirt and decorated her with glass beads and bells and brass rings; and when she had composed herself and talked to the other women on board, she said that she would never want to leave the ship. But the Admiral sent her back under escort.

Next day, he sent nine men to visit her people. They went along the river valley and across into another valley, where they found a village with a thousand huts and three thousand inhabitants. They made friends with the people, and everyone came to them, wanting to place their hands on the Spaniards' heads as a sign of peace. Presents were heaped on them, bread and fruits and cotton and parrots. But no one gave them gold, nor did they see any, except the one ornament in the nose of the woman whom they had captured earlier. When the nine men came back in the evening, they were convinced that the people there were even friendlier and more beautiful than the people on Juana and the islands, and they had seen two young girls with skin as fair as that of Castilian girls. The whole country was much better and more beautiful than Castile, and not even the plains outside Cordova could bear comparison with the green foliage of Española.

Las Casas writes: "Here the Admiral tried to work out the length of the day and night, and from sun to sun it was twenty half-hours by the glass. But he says that there might have been some mistake; perhaps the glasses had not been turned, or perhaps the sand might not have run out [before they were turned]. He says that by the quadrant

It is quite easy to reconstruct a Taino house with the help of contemporary pictures (page 86) and descriptions. There was a tall central post, and a number of shorter posts were driven into the earth all round it, at intervals of 4 or 5 feet. The framework was held together by long beams which met at the center, and shorter beams along the tops of the posts. The roof consisted of slender poles which were tied to the top of the central post and crossed at right angles by reeds or lianas tied together at approximately six-inch intervals. The thatch usually consisted of palm leaves, though Oviedo also mentions long grass or the imposing leaves of the bihao plant (above left). The walls consisted of canes pushed hard into the ground, "as close as the fingers of a hand," with lianas woven through to hold them together. Some of these buildings were large enough to house several hundred people, but the ordinary dwelling houses were probably about 15 feet across, so that hammocks could easily be slung from the center post to the outer posts. Apparently some of the houses had two entrances, one for men and one for women. There was no means of closing these entrances, by shutting a door or otherwise: other people's property was sacrosanct.

The Spaniards had already seen, when they were on Fernandina, that the natives slept in cotton hammocks, and it appears from surviving descriptions that they were of exactly the same type as is used by South and Central American Indians today. White men soon learned to value them in their cramped sleeping quarters at sea, and the Taino word for them, hamaca, was adopted into the Spanish language and has since spread to other languages, including English.

The most important household utensils were calabashes, pots, wooden bowls, and baskets. Bihao-leaf fibers might have been the usual material for basket-making, and Oviedo describes watertight baskets with double sides and whole bihao leaves between them.

The descriptions of Taino settlements, including towns with several thousand houses, say that they were built with no planning at all, except that an open space was left in front of the cacique's house, for public meetings and entertainments. Las Casas makes a point of saying that there were a few exceptions in the province of Higuey on Española, where there were streets crossing in front of the cacique's house.

he found them to be 34 degrees from the equator."

After one unsuccessful attempt, the Spaniards sailed out of Puerto de la Concepción on December 15 to look for the golden island of Babeque. They saw that Tortuga was like the flat country round Cordova, covered with cornfields and villages, but then the wind changed, and for the rest of the day they could get no farther than a river mouth a league and a half from their last harbor. Las Casas writes: "He went in with the boats in order to reach the villages which had been seen by the men whom he had sent out two days before. He ordered a line to be taken ashore, and the sailors hauled the boats a distance of two lombard shots upstream; but they were unable to get farther because of the current. He saw several houses and the large valley where the villages were, and he said that he had never seen anything more beautiful than this river which flowed down the middle of the valley. He also saw people near the mouth of the river, but they all ran away. He goes on to say that these people must be sorely persecuted, since they live in such a state of terror; as soon as they [the Spaniards] came near any place at all, beacon fires burst out all over the district, and this happened more regularly on the islands of Española and Tortuga, which is also a large island, than on any of the other islands they had left behind them. He called the valley Valle del Paraiso [The Valley of Paradise] and the river the Guadalquivir, for he says that it flows as swiftly as the Guadalquivir at Cordova."

They weighed anchor before midnight and managed to sail a league to the northeast in the light breeze from land. Then the east wind came back with relentless force, so that they could make no headway at all. While they were out in the middle of the strait between Española and Tortuga they met a single Indian in a canoe, and although the foam was flying from the tops of the waves, they managed to haul the man and his craft on board without damage to either. After that they yielded to wind and current and allowed themselves to be taken toward the shore, where they anchored close to a newly built village. The Admiral gave the man with the canoe the usual glass beads and bells and then let him paddle himself ashore. It was not long before people began to gather on the beach, and some came out to them in canoes.

At last it seemed as if the Spaniards' labors were to be rewarded. They saw gold. More than they had ever seen in the Indies. Many of the people who came to them had gold in their noses and ears, and they parted with it willingly, without asking for anything in return. While they were in the village, the Spaniards were shown some long, sharp arrows, and the interpreters, no longer afraid of the men of Bohio, explained that the arrows had been shot by the men of Caribata. Two men showed them old

wounds like deep cavities in their limbs, and it was said that the cannibals had bitten away the flesh. But the Admiral did not believe them. A man whom the Indians called Cacique, and whom Columbus took to be the governor of the province, had a flat piece of gold the size of a man's hand, but he would not sell it in one piece; he broke it up and exchanged the bits for glass beads and brass rings. The Admiral asked him and other consequential people about the way to Babeque and its gold, and many of them nodded their heads and pointed vaguely toward the north and east. And one old man explained through an interpreter that there were many islands far to the east which had gold in abundance, and that one of them consisted entirely of gold.

A young man, who was clearly of higher rank than the governor and might have been their king, went aboard the flagship, and of this visit the Admiral wrote the following: "When he came aboard and found that I was eating at the table below the poop, he hurried over and sat down beside me, and he would not let me stand up or go to meet him, but asked me to continue my meal. I thought that he might like to eat of our food, and I immediately ordered things to be brought for him to eat. And when he came in below the poop, he made signs with his hand that all his men should remain outside. They obeyed him with

All the gold which the Spaniards found in the West Indies was melted down, and the only wrought pieces found on Española recently are the two ornaments to the right. The natives did not know how to melt gold, so they beat it into thin sheets which were then cut and hammered into various shapes and patterns. Above, left: a reconstruction based on a small stone ornament found on Española.

the most perfect discipline, and they all sat down on the deck, except two elderly men whom I took to be his counsellors and teachers, who came and sat at his feet. And of the food placed before him, he took only a morsel of each kind to taste, and then sent the rest to his people, and they all ate of it. He did likewise with what he was offered to drink, which he merely raised to his lips and then passed on to the others. All this was done with wonderful dignity and with very few words. . . .

"After the meal was ended, one of his retinue brought a belt, which is like those of Castile in shape but of different workmanship, and this he took and gave to me, and with it two pieces of gold, beautifully wrought but very thin, so I think that it can only be found here in very small quantities; but I am not sure that they are not far from a place where great quantities of it can be found. I saw that a curtain hanging over my bed attracted him, and I gave it to him, together with some fine amber beads which I was wearing round my neck, and some red shoes and a flask of orange-flower water, at which he was wonderfully pleased. . . .

"As it was already late, and he wished to go, I sent him away in the boat with all ceremony, and had many lombards fired. When he had landed, he climbed into his litter and went away with his men, of whom there were more than two hundred. One of his sons was there, carried on the shoulders of a high-ranking official. He gave orders that all the Spaniards in his country should be given food and treated with great respect. A sailor who met him on the way told me later that all the gifts I had given him were carried in his presence by a high dignitary."

The Admiral set up a large cross in the village, in an open space near the shore, "as a sign that Your Highnesses consider this land to be Yours, and chiefly as a token of Jesus Christ Our Lord, and in honour of the Christian Faith." The Indians helped the "men from the sky" to erect the cross, and when everything was ready,

they knelt down with them and raised their hands in adoration. The Admiral did not believe that there were any gold mines on Española and Tortuga; the gold which the people actually possessed must, he thought, have been bought from Babeque. He had been told that Babeque was four days' journey farther on, or in other words about thirty or forty leagues away. If the wind was favorable, they could get there in a day.

But he had other thoughts and plans: "With the few men I have on board I could overrun all these islands without meeting any resistance, for I have seen how they all ran away when only three sailors, with no evil intentions, went ashore where there were crowds of Indians. They carry no arms, they are completely naked, and arrant cowards, so that one thousand of them could not stand up to three; so they are ready to obey orders and to be put to work, to dig the ground and to do anything else that may be necessary. And You may build cities, and teach them to wear clothes, and to adopt our way of life."

Soon after midnight on December 19 they weighed anchor so that they could use the land wind and sail east to Babeque. When day came, they had to struggle against wind and current, but they noted some new capes and gave them names. Beyond the farthest cape a blue mountain rose up, and the Admiral, who thought it lay in the land of the Caribs, called it Monte Caribata. On the evening of December 20 the boats towed the ships past some dark reefs into a great harbor, ten leagues from

The Tainos believed in a supreme deity who lived in the sky: but He was too important to concern Himself with earthly things, and nobody ever prayed to Him for help. There were various zemís, *spiritual beings and ancestral ghosts, who helped people and delivered them from evil, and small images of them were worn round the neck or on the forehead. There were larger effigies of these* zemís *in the houses of the caciques or at special places of worship, and offerings of food and drink were made. In Cuba, Columbus had seen wooden figures of women. He does not describe the images he saw on Española, and most of the wooden figures of that period have been lost. In the decades which followed the discovery of the country, Spanish priests and other zealots systematically destroyed everything that could possibly be taken for an idol, and in Española only a few stone or earthenware figures have been found, usually in remote caves difficult of access. Left: a clay figure which may represent a female* zemí.

90

their anchorage in the strait, and this harbor surpassed their wildest dreams. The Admiral tried to make himself clear: "I have been sailing the seas for 23 years, without leaving them for any time worth speaking of. I have seen all the West and all the East, I have been to Guinea, but never in all those lands have I found such perfect harbours as these are. I have found each one better than the last, so I have always been very careful in my descriptions [of them], and I repeat that what I have written is true, and

Extant 16th-century pictures of West-Indian canoes (top right-hand corner and page 70) are not very satisfactory. Columbus himself says that a large canoe could outdistance a fusta, *i.e., a small galley, and people could not have got up much speed in the tublike craft of the early representations. Paddles, on the other hand, seem to have been drawn correctly; they correspond well enough with the paddle found in the Asphalt Lake in Trinidad (below). I have based my reconstruction of the little craft (above) on the canoes of the Choco Indians and on the knowledge that the Caribs of Dominica still fill their dugout canoes with stones and then pour boiling water into them to force the sides out, thus making them broader than the original trunk from which they were fashioned. While in Cuba, Columbus saw a canoe which was 95* palmos *(66 feet) long and could carry 150 people. The best wood for canoes was the* ceiba, *or silk-cotton tree, but in the entire West Indies today there is not one large enough for such a craft.*

that this harbour surpasses them all, and could contain all the ships in the world; and it is so sheltered that a ship could ride safely on its oldest cables." They came into the harbor on the eve of the feast of St. Thomas, and the Admiral called it Puerto de la Mar de Santo Tomás.

The natives came out to the ships by the thousands, and those who could not get in the canoes swam out. In the canoes they brought calabashes full of water, bread, cotton, and parrots, and they gave it all freely to the men from the sky. "One cannot say that they were ready to give these things because they were of small value, for those who gave pieces of gold gave them in the same way, and just as readily, as those who gave calabashes of water, and it is easy to see when something is given with true readiness and generosity."

Local chiefs came with gifts of gold, and they said that there was more to be found farther east on the island. A large canoe arrived with a message from Guacanagarí, King of Marien, who desired the Admiral to visit him at his residence, which was a few hours farther east. One of the envoys presented Columbus with a belt, which was a gift from the King. Instead of a pouch, the belt had a mask with ears, nose, and tongue of beaten gold. The Admiral could not sail immediately to Guacanagarí because there was no wind, so he sent the boats, with the secretary of the fleet, the interpreter, and some other envoys to explore the waters nearby. They soon returned, and the secretary reported that the royal residence was three leagues beyond Monte Caribata. He added that the island seemed to be larger than Great Britain, and he thought that if they spent Christmas in Guacanagarí's harbor, people would come to see them from all over Española.

91

La Navidad

Everything that happened on December 25, 1492, was recorded by the Admiral and later quoted in full by Fernando Colón in his biography. Let us now read the whole of his thirty-third chapter.

"I continue with the Admiral's account. He relates that on Monday, 24th December, it was very calm, with only light winds, which carried him from the Mar de Santo Tomás to a point about a league beyond Punta Santa [the northeast point of Monte Caribata]. At the end of the first watch, about eleven o'clock, he retired to his cabin, as he had not slept for two days and a night. As it was calm, the helmsman handed over the tiller to a boy, 'which,' says the Admiral, 'I had forbidden throughout the voyage; for my orders were that, regardless of wind, no boy should be entrusted with the tiller. But to tell the truth, I felt quite safe about reefs and shoals, for on Sunday, when I sent my boats to the King, they had gone three and a half leagues east of Punta Santa, and the sailors had explored the entire coast and the reefs along it, which stretch about three leagues east-south-east from Punta Santa, and had charted the course which we must take. And this was something which had not yet been done on the entire voyage.

" 'It pleased The Lord at midnight, when I lay in bed, with the ship becalmed and the sea as still as water in a cup, that they all went to sleep and left the tiller in the hands of a boy. It so happened then that the swell very slowly took the ship on to one of those reefs where the waves break with such a noise that it can be heard more than a league away. When the boy felt the rudder run aground and heard the noise, he cried out. I heard him and got up immediately, and understood what had happened before anyone else did. The ship's master, whose watch this was, came up immediately after, and I ordered him and the other sailors to take the boat, which was in tow, and drop an anchor astern. He and several others entered the boat, and I thought that they were going to carry out my order.

" 'But instead they rowed away, trying to escape in the boat to the caravel, which was half a league off. When I saw that they were running away, and that the tide was on the ebb and that the ship was in danger, I immediately had the mast cut away to lighten her as much as possible and see whether we could get her off the reef. But the water became even shallower; the ship would not move, and then she began to list. Her seams opened, and the water began to come in. Meanwhile, the boat from the caravel had come over to help me, and the men on the *Niña* saw that the men in the boat [from the *Santa Maria*] were simply trying to save their skins and would not let them aboard, and so they had to come back to the ship.

" 'I saw no chance of saving my ship, and to spare the

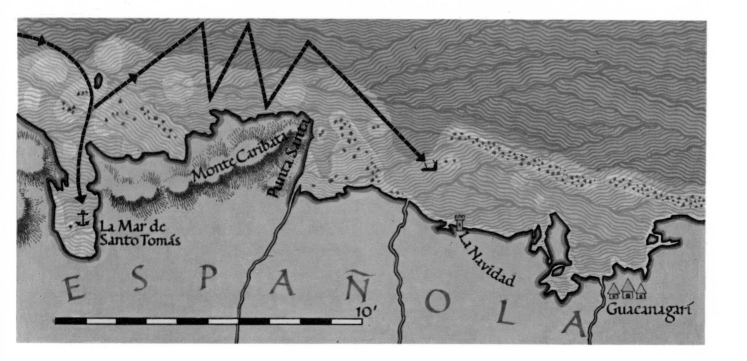

Columbus writes that he had not slept for two days and a night, and we may assume that he and most of his men had been thoroughly enjoying themselves in Puerto de la Mar de Santo Tomás with the open-hearted Indian women. The way through the coral reefs to Cacique Guacanagarí's village was no more difficult than the way into the last harbor they had visited, but it would certainly have been wiser to leave it until daylight. The attempt to pass the blame on to the ship's master, Juan de la Cosa, is not attractive. It must have been almost impossible in the dark to say how far it was to shore, for once past the Monte Caribata and Punta Santa (the modern Cap Haitien), the coast is very flat. The whole stretch of land between La Navidad and Guacanagarí's village is one vast mangrove swamp, and the foothills are some distance inland. Nor is it out of the question that the wind might have risen imperceptibly, so that they reached the dangerous area more quickly than they had expected.

lives of my crew I left her and went with them to the *Niña*, As the wind was coming from land and most of the night was already gone, and as we did not know our way out of those shallows, I lay to with the caravel until daybreak, and then returned to the ship on the reef. But first I sent ashore a boat with Diego de Harana, the chief marshal of the fleet, and Pedro Gutiérrez, Your Highnesses' servant,

to inform the King of what had occurred and to tell him that on my way to visit him—as he had invited me to do on the previous Sunday—I had lost my ship on a reef, one and a half leagues from his city.

" 'When the King heard of our misfortune, he wept and at once sent his people with many large canoes to the ship. So, we all began to unload together, and it was not long before we had cleared the entire deck, of such great service was the King in this matter. Afterwards, he himself, together with his brothers and relatives, kept careful watch aboard and ashore, to see that everything was done correctly. And he frequently sent one of his relatives to me to tell me not to be disheartened, and that he would give me anything he had. I can assure Your Highnesses that the goods would not have been better looked after in Castile, and that not so much as one shoe-lace was missing. He saw to it that all our goods were assembled near the palace, where they remained until two houses, which he gave us to store them in, had been emptied. He set two armed men to guard these goods, both day and night, and he and all the other natives wept as if our misfortune was their own.

" 'They are so friendly, generous and accommodating that I assure Your Highnesses that there can be no better people, and no better country, in the world. They love their neighbours as themselves, and their speech is the sweetest and gentlest in the world, and they always speak with a smile. They go about naked, men and women alike, just as their mothers bore them. But believe me, Your Highnesses, they have very good morals, and the King

93

maintains the most marvellous ceremony, with such dignity that it is a pleasure to see it all. They have excellent memories, and they want to see everything, and when they see a thing they ask what it is and what it is used for.' "

The Admiral was soon consoled for the loss of the *Santa María*. Many Indians came to them, while they were salvaging provisions and equipment from the wreck, and offered them gold in exchange for tinkling hawk's bells, and King Guacanagarí rejoiced at the Admiral's pleasure "and understood that he desired much gold, and indicated by signs that he knew a place nearby where there was gold in abundance, and that he should be of good cheer, and that he would give him as much gold as he wanted."

Guacanagarí gave him gold—though perhaps not as much as Columbus wanted, for his desire was insatiable. He received masks of gold, and a circlet and necklaces and rings of gold. His men obtained much gold by trading, and more of the precious metal was said to be found in a land which the Indians called Cibao. The Admiral now understood Cibao to be a part of Española, that Cibao was the Indians' way of saying Cipangu. That great rich island of Cipangu could be no other than Española. Columbus was now convinced that the cartographers had erred when they drew Cipangu running from north to south, instead of from east to west. This, he thought, was why he had missed Cipangu on his outward voyage. So, just as the Portuguese mariners had corrected the shape of Africa on the earlier maps, Columbus now proceeded to correct the positions of the islands beyond India.

He realized that it had been the Lord's will that the flagship should run aground at this particular spot, so that he should be compelled to found a colony in the land where the people were most friendly. He wrote: "And I assure You that many of my people have asked me to allow them to remain here. I have now given orders for a tower and a fortress to be built, all in the best manner, and a large moat, not that I believe it to be necessary where these people are concerned, for, with the men I have on the ships, I am sure that I could conquer the entire island, which I believe to be larger than Portugal and with more than twice its population. But they go naked and have no weapons and are incorrigible cowards. It is nevertheless proper that this tower should be built, since this place is very far away from Your Highnesses, and they will see the skill and abilities of Your Highnesses' subjects, and therefore serve them with love and fear. And they have timber to build the entire fortress, and supplies of bread and wine for more than a year, and seed for sowing, and the ship's boat, and a caulker, a carpenter, a gunner and a cooper. And many of the natives are very anxious to serve Your Highnesses, and to give me the pleasure of finding the mine where the gold is obtained."

He adds that when he next comes to the colony he hopes to see a barrelful of gold earned by trade, and to find that the settlers have discovered both the gold mine and the spices, so that in three years' time Their Highnesses will be able to equip a crusade to free the Holy Sepulchre. "For I maintained to Your Highnesses that all profits from this enterprise should be devoted to the conquest of Jerusalem, and Your Highnesses smiled and said that such was Your will, and that even without these gains You had the same earnest desire."

On December 27 some Indians came to the *Niña* and told the Admiral that they had seen another ship of the same kind on a river at the end of the island, and he understood that this could only be the *Pinta*. At his request, Guacanagarí immediately sent a canoe to make contact with the caravel, and one of the seamen went with it, carrying a letter to Martín Alonso Pinzón which contained a request to return immediately, since God had been so good to them. The canoe came back five days later without any news of the *Pinta,* but by that time the Admiral had received further intelligence of the caravel, which was now supposed to be riding at anchor in a harbor two days away to the east.

The tower and fortress were built, the moat dug, and the trees and undergrowth round it cleared so that the lombards from the *Santa María* would have an open field of fire. In order that the Indians might have some indication of the strength at the Christians' disposal, the lombards on the *Niña* were aimed at the wreck on the reef, and holes were shot through its sides, and the natives were assured that they need never fear any more attacks from the Caribs. The Admiral called the fortress, and the colony, La Navidad, Christmas, since it was on Christmas morning that the *Santa María* had run aground, and that had been the reason why the colony had been founded. He appointed the marshal, Diego de Harana, commander of the fortress and lieutenant to the Viceroy of the Indies, with Pedro Gutiérrez, officer of the royal household, and Rodrigo de Escobedo, the secretary, as his immediate underlings. Thirty-six volunteers stayed with them; these were the first Spanish settlers in the Indies.

The *Niña* was loaded with wood, water, and food for the long voyage back to Spain. The Admiral recorded that he had not wanted to sail home before he had seen the whole of the country and explored its coasts, but since he had been left with only one ship, he thought it unadvisable to take any further risks and adds that the reason for this unhappy state of affairs was that the *Pinta* had deserted them.

At sunrise on January 4, 1493, he set sail from La Navidad in the *Niña*.

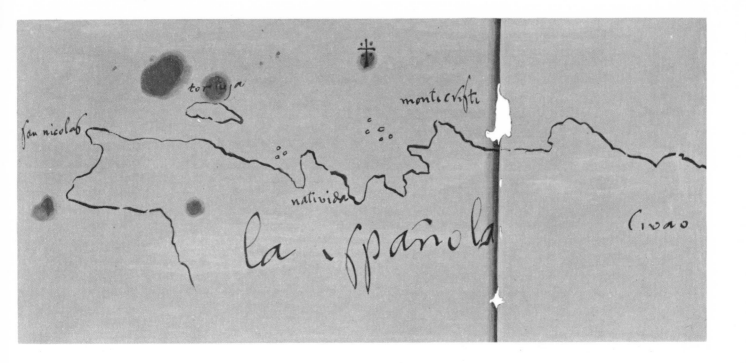

This sketch-map of northwest Española was probably made while Columbus was sailing from La Navidad to the easternmost point of the island. It is the only extant map that is known to have come from his hand, and it is an excellent indication of his draughtsmanship: we may compare it with the same part of the coast on the modern map on page 87.

The first skirmish

Again they had to take up the battle against winds and current all the way up the long northeast coast of Española, and even though the *Niña* was a better sailer than the *Santa María,* it was mostly during the early hours of the morning that they made progress east. On the first day of the voyage they saw a mountain rising like a royal pavilion above the flat country, and the Admiral called it Monte Cristi. The sea was shallow for some distance from land, and they made their way with greater care than ever before, anchoring for the night in 19 fathoms of water about 6 leagues from the mountain. Next day they could only reach a bay a little to the east of the mountain, and the Admiral carefully described his navigation and the dangers of the coast. The wind turned against them and grew strong by the afternoon of the third day, and the lookout, who had been sent up the mast to keep a watch

for shallows, suddenly caught sight of the *Pinta* coming toward them from the east.

The meeting must have been a relief for both the Admiral and Pinzón, and it is unlikely that any harsh words were exchanged. Since it was impossible to anchor at the place where they met, the Admiral gave orders to sail back to the bay at Monte Cristi. The only account of the meeting is the short reference made by Las Casas in the Journal: "Martín Alonso Pinzón came to the caravel *Niña,* where the Admiral was, to excuse himself. He said that they had parted company against his will, and gave reasons for this. But the Admiral says that they were all false, and that his motives for sailing away that night were shamelessness and greed. And the Admiral says that he does not know the reasons for his shameless and disloyal conduct towards him on the voyage, but the Admiral was ready to forget it, so that he should not help Satan in his evil design to do all he could to hinder the voyage, as indeed he had done up to that time."

The meeting, then, was ostensibly a reconciliation, and the Admiral writes that this was no time to think of punishment. Pinzón then gave the information that he had sailed to Babeque, which was a large flat island, southeast of Isabela, but no gold had been found there, and the local Indians had advised him to sail to this same island, which the Admiral called Española. Here he had bought a great quantity of gold, and he had been told of a large island of gold, called Yamaye, south of Juana, and both Yamaye and Española were said to be ten days' distance by canoe from the mainland.

95

The Admiral recorded that Pinzón had kept half the gold for himself and divided the rest among his crew, and he comments on Pinzón's hunger for gold and on his abduction of four men and two young girls from Their Highnesses' island of Española. Later, he clothed Pinzón's captives and sent them ashore, saying that "respect and kindness must be shown to these people, for in this island there is so much gold and good land and spices." Vicente Yáñez might well have offended the Admiral by showing too much pleasure at his brother's return, since for the next few days the journal entries all end with hard words about the Pinzón brothers and their hangers-on.

They remained at Monte Cristi for two days, and during that time they tried to caulk the caravels, which had begun to take in more water than usual. They replenished their stores of fresh water at a river to the west of the mountain, and on the way there the Admiral saw three mermaids who rose in surprise out of the sea and stared at the men in the boat. He says that they were not as beautiful as mermaids usually are in pictures, and adds that he had once before seen a mermaid, off the Malagueta Coast in Guinea. The men went a little way upstream to fill the water butts, and later on they saw the glitter of gold dust in the hoops. In the mouth of the river they found some gold dust, and the obvious name for the river was the Rio del Oro, the River

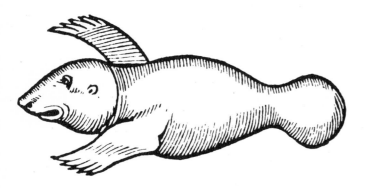

The three ugly mermaids were manatees, closely related to the West African manatee, the mermaid which Columbus had seen in Guinea. The manatee shown here is from a 16th-century woodcut.

of Gold. It seemed to the Admiral that the mine could not be more than twenty leagues away from the river mouth, but he did not want to pan for any more gold there at the moment, for it was not likely to vanish, and it was easy to reach from La Navidad. He says that his only desire now was to sail home with the good news as fast as possible, and then to rid himself of his bad companions. And he stresses that he had always considered them to be a disorderly lot.

On they sailed, usually anchoring for the night, and at times the wind was with them, so that they covered many leagues in a day; and they were amazed at the size of Española. On January 12 they rounded a high cape, which looked like Cape St. Vincent in Portugal, and the Admiral called it Cabo del Enamorado, the Cape of the Enamored. They saw mountains to the south, but they were uncertain whether they were a part of Española or a new island, and they sailed west into what seemed to be a large bay and anchored between a small island and a sandy beach.

Las Casas says: "They sent the boat ashore to a lovely beach to get some *mames* [sweet potatoes] to eat, and they met some men with bows and arrows, and they tried to converse with them and bought two bows and many arrows. They asked one of them to go with them to the caravel to speak with the Admiral, and he did so. It is said that he was very ugly, uglier than any Indian the Admiral had seen. His face was covered with soot, whereas in all other places they use several different colours. His hair was very long, brushed back and tied together at the back of his head with a small net of parrot's feathers. And he was stark naked, like the others.

"The Admiral thought that he must be one of the Caribs, who are man-eaters, and that the bay which he had seen the day before was a strait between two lands, so that this might be a separate island. He asked him about the Caribs, and the Indian pointed to the east, where the Admiral says that he had seen an island the previous day, before he entered the bay. And the Indian told him that there was much gold to be had there, and he pointed to the poop of the caravel [to show] that it [the island] was as big as that, or else that the pieces of gold to be found there were as large as that. . . . The Admiral goes on to say that on all of the islands where he had been there was a great fear of the Carib—on some islands they call them 'Caniba,' but 'Carib' on Española—and that they [the Caribs] must be very enterprising, since they come to all these islands and eat all the people they can capture. He says that he could understand some of his words, and that the Indians in his party could understand more, but they had found some differences of dialect because the lands were so far apart. He gave orders that the Indian should be fed, and he gave him some strips of green and red cloth, and small glass beads, which they value highly, and sent him back to shore and told him to return with some gold, if there was any, which the Admiral thought likely, to judge by certain small ornaments the Indian was wearing.

"When the boat reached the shore, there were about 55 men standing behind the trees, stark naked, with their hair very long, like women's hair in Castile. Behind their heads they wore tufts of feathers, from parrots and other birds, and they all had bows. The Indian went ashore and persuaded the others to put down their bows and arrows, and their staves; these are like very heavy clubs, and they carry them as we carry swords. Then they came up to the boat, and the men in the boat went ashore and began to buy their bows and arrows and the other weapons, for the Admiral had told them to do so. When the Indians had sold two bows they would sell no more, but rather prepared to attack the Christians and seize their persons. They ran to pick up their bows and arrows where they had put them down, and came back with ropes in their hands, to bind the Christians. When the Christians saw them running at them, they were ready, as the Admiral had always warned them to be, and charged upon them; they gave one of the Indians a hard blow on the buttocks and wounded another in the breast with an arrow. When the Indians saw little chance of winning, though the Christians were only seven and they were more than fifty, they broke and fled, and not one remained; one left his bow here, and another left his arrow there. He says the Christians would have killed many of them, had not the pilot, who was with them as their captain, stopped them."

This first clash between Spaniards and Indians did not lead to any serious trouble. The next day a chief came aboard; Columbus gave him some hawk's bells, some ship's biscuit, and some honey, and the chief promised to come back next day with a gold mask in recompense.

The caravel was now leaking badly, and the Admiral complained that the people of Palos had done a bad job of caulking. "But even though the caravels were taking in much water, he put his trust in the Lord Who had led him there, and believed that He in His mercy would bring him safely home, and that His Divine Majesty well knew what trouble he had seen before he could sail away from Castile. None but He had felt any trust in him, for He knew the secrets of his heart, and after God, Their Highnesses; and all others had been against him without reason, and he continues thus: 'And it is through the fault of these men that Your Highnesses' Royal Crown has not had a hundred millions more revenue than it has, for all the seven years that I have been in your service, reckoning from the 20th day of this very month of January, not to count all the increase that would have come from this time forward. But Almighty God will make all things turn out for the best.' These are his words." Columbus means that if his offer had been accepted immediately he could have sailed to the riches of the Indies six years earlier.

The chief who had promised to bring the gold mask did not come; instead, he sent the Admiral his crown. The Spaniards bought a large quantity of strong pepper which the Indians called *axi,* and the Admiral thought that it would be possible to load fifty caravels a year with pepper alone. They also bought some bread and sweet potatoes, and some more bows and arrows, from which the harbor was given its name of Puerto de las Flechas, Port of Arrows. When they had finished trading, the Spaniards kept four Indian youths to take back with them to Castile.

The peppers which the Indians called axi. *We know several different varieties of them today, called chillies or paprikas, according to size and shape.*

The return to Europe

Three hours before dawn on January 16 they sailed with a land wind, intending to make for the island of Carib, which was supposed to lie somewhere to the east or the southeast. But the wind freshened and was ideal for the journey back to Spain. This, together with the fact that the caravels were leaking alarmingly and that the crew seemed to have grown dispirited, made the Admiral decide not to look for any more islands but to sail home instead. They steered northeast, and his object was to sail to the north and northeast on a starboard tack in the winds which had carried them across the ocean until they entered the belt of west winds which would take them due east to Europe.

For almost three-quarters of the voyage the Journal has little more to mention than directions, speeds, and distances covered. There were birds and large quantities of seaweed, and these were duly noted down as on the outward voyage. Over a period of several days the sea about them was teeming with tunnies, and the Admiral thought that that must be the place where all the tunnies came from, including those that appeared off the coasts of Spain later on, to be caught by the fishing fleets which belonged to the Duke of Cadiz. The record for an ordinary day during the first part of the voyage, for January 20, runs in this way: "That night the wind died down, but there were occasional gusts, so that in all he must have made 20 Roman miles to the north-east. After sunrise he must have gone 11 Roman miles to the south-east, and then 36 Roman miles to the north-north-east, which is 9 leagues. Saw countless small tunnies. The air, he says, was very soft and sweet, as in Seville in April and May, and the sea, thanks be to God, is always very calm. Frigate birds and petrels and many other birds appeared."

Many are the thanks he gives to God for the calm seas. A good wind and small waves meant that the caravels leaked less and got home quicker. But the work at the pumps must have been hard, for the ships were suffering badly from shipworm. The *Niña* now proved herself to be the faster of the two ships while beating upwind and sailing on the tack, for the *Pinta's* mizzen mast was weakened by rot, and they could not go under full sail. The Admiral could not help adding that if Martín Alonso Pinzón had been as concerned about obtaining a good mast in the Indies as he had been about filling his ship with gold, they would not have had any of this trouble.

Now and then while making their way northeast on the first part of the voyage they caught fish, and once they ate shark's flesh; the Journal says that the only provisions on board were bread and sweet potatoes. Before they reached the belt of westerly winds, the longest distance they covered in a day was 51 leagues, which is about 163

nautical miles; the average daily distances were no more than 20 to 30 leagues.

By February 1 they were on the thirty-second parallel and had probably come into the first westerly wind. They made 46 leagues and praised God for the good wind and the calm sea. On February 3 the Admiral wrote that the polestar seemed to be as high as at Cape St. Vincent, but that the caravel was rolling so badly that he could not take a reliable measurement with either astrolabe or quadrant. Then the days began to get colder, and the rain more frequent. Once they saw twigs in the water and thought that they could not be far from land. The Admiral was now steering due east.

On February 6 they went farther than they had ever done before in a single day; by the Admiral's reckoning they covered 74 leagues, which is about 274 nautical miles. Since he invariably overestimated the distances covered each day, we may reduce this to about 200 nautical miles, which still puts their average speed at 8.3 knots. That same day, Vicente Yáñez Pinzón and the pilots were convinced that they were close to the Azores. Vicente Yáñez put them directly south of Flores and east of Madeira. Bartolomé Roldán, one of the men who had saved themselves from the gallows by signing on for the voyage at Palos, had begun to lend a hand in the pilots' calculations, and he thought that Fayal or São Jorge lay to the northeast and Porto Santo to the east.

On the following day the pilot, Peralonso Niño, reckoned that the sea between Terçeira and Santa Maria lay due north and that they would go north of Madeira on their present course. The Admiral thought it enough to say that they were 75 leagues south of the parallel of Flores. They saw a new kind of seaweed and convinced each other that this kind grew only in the Azores. Three days later, everyone except the Admiral was sure that they had passed Santa Maria, the easternmost island of the Azores. He himself thought that they were directly south of Flores and were heading east toward Nafe in Africa.

On February 12 the sea grew rough and the wind gradually blew up into a storm and continued to get stronger during the night. The sea became exceptionally rough—the roughest any of them had ever experienced—and the waves crossed and broke against each other, often nearly swamping the ships. They carried only the mainsail without bonnets, "in order to escape from the waves," as the Admiral says. Since sea and wind seemed to be growing continuously worse, they no longer dared to steer their course and decided to run with the storm wherever it might take them. Flares were lit on both ships to maintain contact in the dark, but those on the *Niña* saw the *Pinta's* light get fainter and fainter and then disappear. When morning came there was no sign of the *Pinta*.

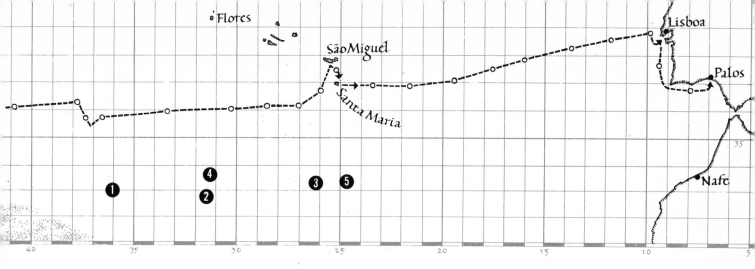

The storm continued and the seas breaking over them grew worse, so they set the foresail and lowered the mainsail. All on board were greatly distressed by now, and the sailors cursed the day they had gone aboard, cursed their own stupidity in allowing the Admiral to cajole them so often into going farther. They took turns at the pumps, and in between turns said their prayers and made solemn vows for their safety. The Admiral suggested that they should draw lots to choose a man to make a pilgrimage to Santa María de Guadelupe in Estremadura if they were saved. They scratched a cross on a bean and put it with several other beans in a cap. The Admiral drew first and got the marked bean. As the storm still showed no signs of abating, they also drew lots to see who should make a pilgrimage to Santa Maria de Loreto in the Papal States; Pedro de Villa, a seaman, drew the marked bean, and the Admiral promised to pay the cost of his journey.

But nothing seemed to appease the fury of the storm. They decided that yet another pilgrim should be sent to keep one night's vigil in Santa Clara de Moguer and to have a mass read there, and as if by miracle the lot again fell on the Admiral. Everybody—the Admiral, his officers, and the men—fell down on their knees and cried out to the Blessed Virgin Mary, loud enough to be heard above the storm, that as soon as they reached land they would all go in a procession, dressed only in their shirts, to a church dedicated to Her if She would only pray for them now, and bring them relief and deliverance.

The Admiral wrote that the thing which worried him most was the thought that everything he had discovered by the grace of God would now be lost to the world, for the Lord wished him to die for his sins. "With my mind in such a whirl, I turned my thoughts to Your Highnesses and endeavoured to find a way by which, if I should die and the ship be lost, You might receive news of my successful voyage, so that the victory I had won would not pass into oblivion. I therefore wrote on parchment, briefly as the situation demanded, about how I had discovered these lands, as I had promised to do, and about the length of the journey and the course, about the excellence of the

The dotted line shows the second half of the journey home, and the rings on it show the position of the ships at sunset each day. The first ring on the left shows where they were on February 6. The numbers indicate where the various navigators of the expedition thought they were. 1. Bartolomé Roldán, February 6. 2. Vicente Yáñez Pinzón, February 6. 3. Peralonso Niño, February 7. 4. Columbus, February 10. 5. The pilots, February 10. For the first half of their journey home see the map on page 67.

country and the customs of its people, and of how I had left Your Highnesses' subjects in command of everything I had discovered. This document, folded and sealed, I addressed to Your Highnesses, with a written promise of 1000 ducats to the person who should deliver it sealed to You. Thus, if it fell into the hands of foreigners, then for the sake of the reward they would not betray to others the information it contained. I sent for a large cask, and after I had wrapped the document in a piece of waxed cloth together with a cake of wax, I placed it in the cask, which I secured with hoops and cast into the sea. All the others thought that it was some kind of votive offering."

After sunset they saw a strip of clear sky to the west, and the storm abated so much that they could set the mainsail and later added a bonnet to it. When the dawn came they saw land to the east-northeast. Some thought that it was Madeira, others that it was Cintra, near Lisbon. The Admiral believed that it was one of the Azores. Then they met a strong head wind, and the swell after the storm was heavy and difficult.

For the whole of that day and the following night they beat through the heaving seas toward that land, which was clearly an island, but by dawn it had vanished behind a bank of dark cloud. They could just make out another island to the north, but they continued to sail in the direction of the first one. After they had sung another *Salve* at sunset, they saw light to leeward and realized that it came from the longed-for island. That night the Admiral rested. He recorded that he had not slept for three days

99

and that his legs were almost paralyzed with cold and damp.

It was only on the following evening, February 17, that they could make out the rocky island clearly, but the cloud ceiling was low and covered the mountains, and no one could say which island it was. They sailed along the line of breakers, seeking an anchorage, before they eventually found what they thought was a suitable place, but the anchor cable gave way immediately, so they hoisted the sails again and lay to until daybreak. When morning came they found a better anchorage and then sent the boat ashore to make contact with the islanders. The shore party were told that it was the Portuguese island of Santa Maria, the easternmost of the Azores, and the people showed them the best place to anchor and said that they had never known anything as bad as the storm which had raged for the past fifteen days.

The Admiral could not help showing his satisfaction at having navigated so accurately, but he admitted that he thought that they had actually sailed past Santa Maria. "He says that he pretended to have sailed further than he had in order to confuse the pilots and the sailors who plotted the course on the chart, so that he might remain master of that route to the Indies."

Three of the shore party failed to return, and in the evening three of the islanders came out to the *Niña* with a message from João de Castanheira, the captain of the island, who said that he would not allow the men to leave him until the following morning, since they were entertaining him with their story of the voyage. But he had given the messengers chickens and fresh bread and other eatables to take out to the *Niña,* and promised to come out to them himself on the following day with more fresh food.

There was a chapel, dedicated to Nossa Senhora do Anjos, not far from the shore, and the Admiral asked the islanders to get a priest from the village to read a mass there. When morning came he sent half the crew ashore to walk to the chapel in procession, dressed only in their shirts, as they had all solemnly vowed to do during the storm. But they did not return either. Columbus began to suspect that the Portuguese had detained them, or that the boat had been smashed to pieces against the rocks, so he weighed anchor and sailed round a point to the landing place to see what had happened.

A group of armed men were standing on the shore, and when they saw the caravel approach they got into a boat and rowed toward her. A man who said he was Captain Castanheira rose and asked the Admiral for safe conduct to come aboard. The Admiral, who by this time had armed his own men, promised him this, but went on to ask him how it came about that his shore party were not in the boat with the captain. The captain grew sus-

picous and kept his distance from the ship. Then the Admiral asked him why he was detaining his men, adding that Portuguese subjects were always well received in Castile. He held up the letters he had from the King and Queen of Castile, and explained that he was their Admiral of the Ocean and Viceroy of the Indies, which now belonged to Their Majesties. He also pointed out that it would be easy for him to sail to Seville with the crew he still had on board, and that the captain and his men would be severely punished for this discourtesy and breach of usage.

The captain replied that he did not recognize any king or queen of Castile, or any letters they might have written, and that the Admiral would soon find out that he was in Portugal. And he commanded the Spaniards in the name of the King to sail into the harbor and give themselves up. But the Admiral told him that he would not leave his ship until he had laid waste the island with fire and sword and taken one hundred Portuguese prisoners and carried them off to Castile. Then he returned to the last anchorage and waited.

But the next day brought a storm. The anchor cables frayed off against the rocky bottom, so they sailed off to find a better harbor to the north at the large island of São Miguel. But the wind became so fierce that they had to lay to throughout that night, and when daylight came and they found that they could not see São Miguel, the Admiral gave orders to return to Santa Maria to see if they could free their men and recover the boat and anchors which had been lost.

Columbus recorded his opinion of the weather and wrote that the European part of the ocean was often visited by severe storms, while the waters of the Indies were always calm and friendly. "In conclusion, the Admiral says that the holy theologians and wise philosophers had been right to say that the Earthly Paradise lay at the uttermost East, for the weather is most temperate there, and so, he says, the lands he has now discovered must be at the uttermost East."

They returned to the anchorage before evening and found that the captain and the islanders had calmed down a little. Two priests and a secretary came out to them in the *Niña*'s boat and asked to see the royal letters. After they had done this they returned to land and immediately set the Spaniards free and sent them back in the boat. The men said that they had been attacked while making their pilgrimage to the chapel, and they were convinced that they would never have escaped if the Portuguese had captured the Admiral as well, because the King of Portugal had given orders to that effect.

On February 24 a southwesterly wind, which would take them home, began to blow, and though it was a Sunday the Admiral gave orders to leave. The *Niña* made good headway to the east on the first three days, but on February 27 the winds became contrary and the sea rough.

While the Niña *lay off Santa Maria, she would certainly have been dressed with flags and pennants, and the castles hung with shields, to impress the people on the island; they would not have been taken down until they were well out to sea again. Columbus had one more storm to fight his way through before he got home to honor and immortality.*

She drifted to the east-northeast in a southerly storm for the remainder of that week, and then on Sunday an ugly squall tore all the sheets to ribbons. They drew lots to see who should make a pilgrimage to Santa María de la Cinta on Huelva, and the lot fell on the Admiral. Everyone promised to fast on bread and water on the first Sunday ashore. They drifted to the northeast with bare poles.

The Journal runs:

Monday, March 4

"Last night they went through so terrible a storm that they thought they were lost, for the seas went over the ship from both sides and the winds seemed to lift her into the air. Water from the sky, and lightning on all sides. It pleased the Lord to help him, and so things went on until the first watch, when the Lord showed him land, and the sailors saw it. Not wanting to get close to the land before he could recognize it, and hoping to see if he could find harbour or anchorage where he could shelter, he set the mainsail, for there was nothing else he could do. With great difficulty he succeeded in steering and keeping out at sea. Thus God preserved them until daybreak, and he says that this was all done with unspeakable labour and anxiety. When dawn came he recognized the coast, with the Cintra mountains, near the Lisbon river, and decided to sail in there, since he could do nothing else. The storm in the town of Casca [Cascais] on the estuary of the river was so terrible that the townsfolk had been praying for them all the morning, and when they had come in everyone came to see them, and to wonder that they had come in safely. At the hour of terce [about 9 *a.m.*] he came to rest at Rastelo in the Lisbon river, where he heard sailors saying that there had never been a winter with such storms, that twenty-five ships had gone down off the coast of Flanders, and that other vessels were still there after waiting for four months without being able to get out. The Admiral promptly wrote to the King of Portugal, whose residence was nine leagues away, and told him that the King and Queen of Castile had told him not to hesitate to go into His Highness' harbours to buy anything he might need, for payment, and he prayed that the King would allow him to go on with his caravel to the city of Lisbon, for fear that thieves might think he had a cargo of gold, and might have plans to attack him while he lay in that almost empty harbour. And he wished the King to know that he had not come from Guinea, but from the Indies.

Tuesday, March 5

"A great ship which belonged to the King of Portugal was also anchored at Rastelo; he says she was the best-equipped ship he had ever seen. That day, the shipmaster, whose name was Bartolomeo Diaz, of Lisbon, came to the caravel in his armed boat, and told the Admiral to come and make his report to the King's officers and to the captain of the said ship. The Admiral replied that he was the Admiral of the Sovereigns of Castile, and that he did not intend to make any report to any such persons, nor to leave his ship, or any other vessel in which he might be, if he were not compelled by main force. The shipmaster then told him to send the master of the caravel. The Admiral answered that neither the master nor anyone else should go, except under compulsion, for if anyone else went in his place it would be the same as if he had gone himself, and the Admirals of the Sovereigns of Castile were accustomed to prefer death to surrender, both for themselves and for their men. The shipmaster now changed his tone and said that if such were the Admiral's decision it should be as he wished, but he asked him to show the letters from the Sovereigns of Castile, if he had them. The Admiral was well pleased to show them, and the shipmaster went straight back to the ship and reported to the captain, whose name was Alvaro Daman. Then the latter came to the caravel in great state, with drums, trumpets and pipes, and talked with the Admiral, declaring himself ready to do anything he might require."

Interlude in Portugal

On his way back across the ocean the Admiral had begun to compose a letter in which he briefly described his discoveries. It was most probably intended for the Sovereigns, but when he arrived safely at Rastelo he addressed it to Luis de Santángel. It seems probable that while Columbus was in Rastelo he made several copies of the letter and sent them to Gabriel Sánchez and other people at the Spanish Court, to make sure that at least one of them would reach its destination. He had long had friends and influential connections in Lisbon, and he now made use of them to get the letter quickly across the border into Castile. Officially, at least, there was peace and friendship between the two kingdoms, but after his experiences at Santa Maria Columbus was on the lookout for traps, and he would feel safer if he knew that the report of his arrival had reached Castile.

The news that the little caravel had returned from a voyage to the Indies spread rapidly through Lisbon, and on the succeeding days the deck of the *Niña* was crowded with visitors who wanted to hear about the voyage and to see and touch the curious Indians. On March 8, Dom Martin de Noronha arrived with a letter from João II which enjoined the Admiral to visit the King, "since the weather does not favour the departure of the caravel." Columbus received the invitation with mixed feelings, and he wrote in the journal that he accepted it only to dispel any suspicion the King might have that he had sailed in forbidden waters.

At that time the plague was raging in Lisbon, and for safety's sake the King had moved to a monastery in Val do Paraiso, nine leagues outside the city. Martin de Noronha had obtained mules to ride to the monastery, and together with several other noblemen he escorted the Admiral, who was accompanied by his pilot, Peralonso Niño, and by two or three Indians. It was a slow journey, in pouring rain, and they did not reach the Court until the evening of March 9.

The Admiral gives us his own assurance that he was well received by the King, who even invited him to sit down in his presence, and expressed his delight that the enterprise had been successful. But he then added that all the newly discovered islands and countries must, by the Treaty of Alcaçovas, belong to him. The Admiral replied that he had never seen or heard of that treaty, but that Their Majesties had given him their orders not to sail to La Mina or any other part of Guinea.

In his *Historia de las Indias* Las Casas says: "While the King was speaking with the Admiral he commanded that a bowl of beans should be placed on a table beside them, and then indicated by signs that one of the Indians who were there should arrange the beans in such a way as to show the many islands in that kingdom which Columbus claimed to have discovered. The Indian immediately showed him Española, Cuba, the Lucayos Islands, and others. The King watched this sullenly, and a short while later brushed the beans away, as if by accident. He then told another Indian to replace the beans, and this one arranged them as quickly, and as readily, as the first Indian had done, and went on to lay out more countries and islands, explaining all the reasons in his own language, which, of course, nobody could understand. And when the King fully realized the extent of the new discoveries, and the wealth they contained, he could not conceal his sorrow at the loss of such invaluable treasures, but beat his breast and cried out in passion: 'O, man of little understanding! Why did you let such an enterprise fall from your hands?'"

The Portuguese chroniclers write that the Admiral was so boastful and supercilious, saying that it was the King's fault for having rejected his propoals in the first place, that the courtiers, when they saw the Admiral so insolent and the King so unhappy, offered to kill Columbus and prevent his taking the news to Castile. But the King would not agree to that.

The Queen, who was staying at a convent near the road to Lisbon, had expressed the wish that the Admiral should pay her a visit and tell her of his discoveries, and on March 11 he took his leave of the King and was escorted to her by Martin de Noronha and other nobles. The next day a royal messenger arrived with the suggestion that Columbus should go by land to Castile, with an official escort, but the Admiral refused, with thanks, and hurried back to the *Niña* at Rastelo. The storm damage had been repaired during the Admiral's absence, and she may well have been given new Portuguese sails and other fittings, all free of charge as King João had directed.

On March 13, at 8 o'clock in the morning, they weighed anchor and sailed out in a light breeze from the north-northwest. The ebb tide helped them past the banks at the south of the harbor entrance, but the sun was setting before they had got far enough to venture to change course to the south. When dawn came they were sailing past Cape St. Vincent, and by the dawn of the third day they were off the river Saltés. They sailed up the river on the tide at noon, with flags and pennants flying, They passed the convent of La Rabida and saw through their tears the houses and church of Palos. They fired a salute with the lombards and anchored. It was Friday, March 15, 1493.

That very evening the *Pinta* also anchored at Palos.

Ferdinand and Isabella on a gold coin

The sun of favor

Martín Alonso Pinzón, who had been separated from the Admiral during the storm on the night of February 13, sailed past the Azores without sighting any of them, and eventually reached Bayona, a Spanish harbor just north of the Portuguese border. From there he dispatched a courier with a letter to the Sovereigns at Barcelona, where they resided during the winter, and offered to come to them and make a report of the discovery. They sent him a brief reply saying that they wished him to come together with his Admiral, so he set sail and steered south to his home port. There is nothing recorded about any last meeting between the Admiral and his overindependent captain; all we are told is that Martín Alonso was already pining away with grief when he arrived home, and he died a few days later.

Although it is not actually mentioned anywhere, we may presume that the crew of the *Niña* now fulfilled the vows which they had made during the storms in the Atlantic. For the Admiral, this involved two short pilgrimages from Palos to the neighboring towns of Huelva and Moguer, and a long journey to Santa María de Guadalupe in the province of Estremadura, which he might have made afterward. We know that within a fortnight of reaching home he made a ceremonial entry into Seville, with some of his men and all of his Indians, and that he publicly

displayed golden ornaments, parrots, dogs which could not bark, and other wonders of the Indies. A week later he received a letter from the Sovereigns, which was addressed to "Don Cristóbal Colón, Our Admiral of the Ocean, Viceroy and Governor of the islands he has discovered in the Indies."

It was a brief acknowledgment that they had received his letter and recognized the great services he had done to God and to themselves, ending with the request that he should come to them in Barcelona as soon as possible. "And since you can see that summer is already come, and you should not make delay in returning to that place, you should inquire if anything can be done in Seville or in other districts to prepare for your next voyage to the land you have discovered. And write to Us at once, through the messenger who is about to leave, so that all may be arranged as well as possible during your absence and that everything may be ready for your next journey."

We do not know what practical steps the Admiral took in Seville, but he immediately wrote a long matter-of-fact letter to the Sovereigns, which shows us that he had already drawn up plans for the first large-scale colonization of the New World. He suggests, among other things, that Española should be colonized by 2,000 voluntary emigrants, who would build and live in three or four towns to be run on Castilian lines. Churches were to be built and priests sent out, not only for the sake of the settlers but also to convert the Indians. No one but the permanent settlers on Española should be allowed to pan or dig for gold, and then only on the express authority of the Governor or other magistrate. All the gold collected was to be melted down into ingots, weighed, and hallmarked, and all unmarked gold found in the possession of the colonists should be confiscated. The Admiral went on to suggest that all trade between Castile and the Indies should pass through Cadiz and one or two ports in Española, and that it should be kept under strict supervision, so that nothing could be held back from the Crown. Since it was only to be expected that most people would sooner look for gold than do other essential work, he suggested that all prospecting should be banned for some part of the year. In his moment of triumph the Admiral made a further suggestion, which he was later to regret bitterly: "Concerning the discovery of new lands, I consider that all who wish to set forth may be allowed to do so." He signed the letter

> .S .
> .S.A.S.
> X M Y
> :Xpo FERENS./

This was the way he signed nearly all letters and documents from that time on. The pyramid of letters never varied, but he often replaced Xpo Ferens, a Graeco-

Latin form of Cristoforo, by *el Almirante* or, occasionally, *Virey,* Viceroy. He set great store by this cipher and specified in his will that his heirs were to use it after him, but he never explained what the letters stood for. Many people have since tried to do so; here are four of the interpretations:

SERVUS
SUM ALTISSIMI SALVATORIS
XRISTE MARIA YESU
I am the servant of the Most Exalted Saviour
Christ, Mary, Jesus

SALVO
SANCTUM ALTISSIMUM SEPULCRUM
XRISTE MARIA YESU
I shall save the Holy, Most High Sepulcher
Christ, Mary, Jesus

SERVIDOR
SUS ALTEZAS SACRAS
XRISTE MARIA YSABEL
The servant of the Most Exalted Majesties
Christ, Mary, Isabella

SUM
SEQUAX AMATOR SERVUS
XRISTI MARIAE YOSEPHI
I am follower, devotee, and servant of
Christ, Mary, Joseph

As indicated in the letter from the Sovereigns, they were extremely eager that the Admiral should get back as quickly as possible to the islands he had discovered: chiefly, of course, to make sure that they would remain under Castilian control. Apart from the Admiral and perhaps one or two of his pilots, no one knew the exact position of the islands, and yet the King of Portugal had maintained from the very beginning that they belonged to him, and the Castilian ambassador in Lisbon wrote a letter saying that the Portuguese were already equipping a fleet to take possession of the islands.

Ferdinand and Isabella immediately instructed their representatives in Rome to get the Spanish-born Pope, Alexander VI, to acknowledge their right to the islands and to any continent that might later be discovered. At the end of March, no more than two weeks after the arrival of the *Niña* in Palos, the letter which the Admiral had sent to Luis de Santángel from Lisbon was printed in Barcelona. Many more copies of it soon appeared, both in Latin and in Italian, and it was not long before the whole of Europe knew that Cristóbal Colón, in the service of Castile, had discovered some hitherto unknown islands

Pope Alexander VI

off the uttermost coast of the Indies. In his letter, the Admiral had not expressly stated that Española was Cipangu, and it is probable that he had his doubts on the matter himself. He said explicitly that Juana might well be an island.

News of the great discovery also spread by letter. The Duke of Medina Celi, who seems to have obtained one of the copies of the Admiral's Lisbon letter, wrote to the Grand Cardinal of Spain as early as March 19 and explained that Cristóbal Colomo had come to Lisbon from the Indies after having discovered everything he had hoped to discover. The most interesting of the correspondents is an Italian author called Petrus Martyr Anglerius, who was employed as a tutor at the Court of Castile. In a letter to a friend in May, 1493, he wrote: "A few days ago, a certain Christophorus Colonus of Genoa returned from the Western Antipodes. He had found difficulty in obtaining three ships from my Sovereigns for the purpose of visiting this province, because they thought that what he told them belonged to the realm of fable." Writing to another person in October of the same year Petrus Martyr said: "A certain Colonus has sailed to the Western Antipodes, and, as he believes, to the very shores of India. I will not deny this, even though the size of the earth's sphere seems to indicate otherwise." In November, Petrus Martyr wrote about "Colonus ille Novi Orbis repertor," Colón, the discoverer of the New World. But let us go back to the middle of April.

Oceanica Classis

The first edition of Columbus' letter was printed in Barcelona in 1493. Only one copy is known to exist: it is preserved in the New York Public Library. A facsimile is reproduced on the endpapers of this book. A Latin version, with woodcut illustrations, was printed in Basle, probably in the same year. Three of those woodcuts are reproduced here. Unfortunately, the ship on the left is not a contemporary picture of the Santa María, but a copy of a woodcut made in 1486. The artist had no idea of the appearance of Columbus' ships; in the picture opposite, where we see Indians running away from a Spanish landing party, he has simply reproduced an earlier picture of a galley. Extreme right: the new "town" of La Navidad.

spices, and of the gold, of which there was such an abundance that the natives gave it away or sold it for glass beads and hawk's bells; of God's mercy and goodness, without which he would never have found the way to these lands of wonder or escaped from the fury of the storms. He showed them his near-naked Indians, who said the *Ave Maria* and crossed themselves. His men brought in cages containing parrots and large Indian rats, and led in small dogs which could not bark. They opened barrels of strange salted fish, and they opened chests containing cotton and aloes and spices and the skins of large lizards. They exhibited bows and arrows and clubs, and the Admiral told them about the man-eating Caribs or cannibals, and about the mermaids off the Monte Cristi, but he assured them that he had not seen any other monsters of the kind which cosmographers believed to live in the islands at the end of the earth. Then he showed them the gold: crowns of gold, large masks decorated with gold, ornaments of beaten gold, nuggets of gold, gold dust. The Sovereigns fell on their knees, and all those present did the same, and thanked the Creator Who had given all these things into their hands. The court singers sang the *Te Deum,* and the records say that all eyes were filled with tears of indescribable joy.

The Sovereigns instructed the entire Court to accompany the Admiral to his quarters. From now on, whenever the King rode out in Barcelona, he invited the Admiral to ride beside him, with the Heir Apparent on his other side; this was a privilege which had never before been granted to anyone who was not of royal blood. At that time, the chief man in the kingdom after the King was the Grand Cardinal, Don Pedro Gonzáles de Mendoza. In this capacity he invited the Admiral to dine with him: he asked him to sit beside him, and gave instructions for all dishes to be tasted before his distinguished guest was

Ferdinand and Isabella had certainly contracted to give Cristóbal Colón great privileges and impressive titles if he had the good fortune to accomplish his objects, and their letter had just shown that they intended to keep their promise. But they realized that it would need more than these titles to transform this needy foreign mariner, at least in the eyes of the Spanish nobility, into the powerful Admiral and Viceroy whom the kingdom now needed for the tricky political question of the Indies. And for that reason they now prepared a reception for him in Barcelona which far surpassed what the Admiral and Viceroy himself had ever dared to expect.

They decorated the city as if for a festival, and when the Admiral and his party approached, they sent their foremost courtiers to meet him. When he entered the throne room the Sovereigns rose to their feet, and as he fell on his knees to kiss their hands they raised him up and ordered a chair to be placed for him. He alone was allowed to sit in their presence.

Then he told his tale: of the voyage, of the islands with their lush vegetation and their naked inhabitants; of the

served. This too was an honor otherwise accorded only to personages of royal blood, and Las Casas, who tells us about these things, adds: "Henceforward he was treated with the pomp and ceremony which the dignity of his position as Admiral demanded."

When the Indians were baptized, the King and Queen and Heir Apparent were the godparents, and the man who was most closely related to the cacique Guacanagarí was given the name of Fernando de Aragon. Another, who in time became the Court favorite, was called and entitled Don Juan de Castilla, and the best of the interpreters, who accompanied the Admiral on many later occasions, was given the name Don Diego Colón.

The Admiral was accorded the privilege and honor of including in his coat-of-arms the castle and lion, the official emblems of Castile and León. He arranged at the same time that his brothers, Bartolomeo and Giacomo, would be ennobled and given the right to call themselves Don. On May 23 he received a gift of 1,000 doubloons, which was equivalent to 335,000 *maravedis,* and on the same day he was granted the 10,000 *maravedis* which the

Sovereigns had promised to the man who first sighted land on the outward voyage.

Certainly there is no proof that Columbus was not the first man to see a glimmer of light which might have come from land on the night they lay off San Salvador. But he wrote with his own hand in the journal that the first man to *sight* land was Rodrigo de Triana on the *Pinta*. It was this man who ought to have had the reward, and who actually expected to get it; it is said that in his disappointment he fled to Morocco and went over to Islam, but this story was probably made up to bring discredit on the Christoferens who wanted to win souls for Christianity.

The Pope's decision reached Barcelona at the end of May. In a Bull dated May 3, 1493, Alexander VI decreed that every island or land that had been discovered or should be discovered by the Sovereigns of Castile and their successors was to belong to them, provided that they did not already belong to any other Christian prince. A Portuguese ambassador came to Barcelona at about the same time and announced that all land to the south and west of the

107

·S.
·S· A ·S·
X M Y
X͞p o FERENS

Canary Islands belonged to the King of Portugal by a Papal Bull of 1481.

Columbus' letter to Santángel was now circulating freely, and contained the statement that the new islands lay 26 degrees north of the equator, and it was common knowledge that the latitude of the Canaries was about 28 degrees. Now, even if the Pope's rather ambiguous Bull had assigned the newly discovered islands to Castile, the Bull of 1481 would still prevent the Admiral from making any discoveries farther south, as he had intended to do. So he suggested that an attempt should be made to induce the Pope to issue another Bull which would assign to Castile all land to the west of a line running from pole to pole 100 leagues west of the Cape Verde Islands. This suggestion was immediately forwarded to the Castilian ambassador in Rome.

At the beginning of June the Admiral took his leave of the Sovereigns and sailed to Seville. Preparations for the great expedition were already being made, and on the suggestion of the Admiral the fleet was equipped at Cadiz. On May 23, Ferdinand and Isabella commissioned Don Juan de Fonseca, Dean of Seville Cathedral, to help the Admiral to collect ships, equipment, and crews, while Juan de Soria, the royal secretary, was to serve as chief inspector and accountant.

Juan de Fonseca, who later became bishop of Badajoz, Palencia, and Burgos successively, was in charge of Spanish overseas interests for more than 30 years. Historians have described him as a scoundrel and as an enemy of Columbus and Magellan and all other independent-minded explorers, but to be called a scoundrel is the common lot of those who have been in conflict with the heroes of history. Las Casas, who has no other good words for Fonseca at all, admits that he was "very capable in the management of the things of this world." This was the sort of man the Sovereigns needed. He was well read, intelligent, shrewd, and a ruthless taskmaster. He and Columbus are commonly said to have been enemies, but in his later correspondence Columbus describes Fonseca as his friend.

This does not mean that there were not many heated exchanges between the touchy, self-important Admiral and the practical, down-to-earth Dean. We know that the Admiral wanted to take with him a number of *continos,* personal bodyguards, a privilege which the new laws of the country allowed to royal persons alone. When Fonseca found that he could not prevent this, he wrote to the Sovereigns on the subject, and they replied: "Concerning the bodyguard which you say the Admiral wishes to take with him, you did right in telling him that he needs none on this voyage, for each and every one of Our men who accompany him must do all that he, in Our name, commands them, and any distinction between his own men and others might lead to great inconveniences. But if he wishes to take men whom he may call his own for his retinue, he may take up to ten esquires of the fifty who are going, and a further twenty of the other thousand persons who are going, and let them be paid like the others."

Juan de Soria, the accountant, also found it difficult to get on with Columbus. A letter from the Sovereigns enjoins him to "honour and respect the Admiral of the Indies, in such a manner as befits his station, and as We desire." Presumably Columbus wanted to make too many decisions for himself and avoid the inconveniences of the royal control, for in a letter to him the Sovereigns say: "You must see to it that he [Soria] signs everything that is paid, since he must account for it to Our inspector-general of taxes." And yet they wrote to Soria at the same time: "We command you to see to it that he departs well satisfied, for it is Our desire and pleasure that this shall be so, and We should be angered if this were not done."

It took much longer than expected to fit out the ships, and the Sovereigns began to worry over the Portuguese claims and wanted the new-found islands to be secured for them as soon as possible. Their first letter exhorting the Admiral to make all haste was written on June 12, and the second, this time addressed to Fonseca as well, was dated July 25. At the beginning of August they sent a letter to Gomez Tello, one of their trusted agents in Cadiz, asking him to do what he could in a discreet way to speed up the work of equipping the fleet. And they wrote to the treasurer of the expedition, and yet again to the Admiral and Fonseca.

Toward the end of summer the new Papal Bull arrived. As the Admiral had proposed, it assigned to Castile all land west of a demarcation line 100 leagues west of the Cape Verde Islands or the Azores. Another Portuguese embassy came to Barcelona at the end of August, and they were shown the Papal decree. They at once declared that their King would never accept such a solution. They asserted that the Portuguese knew of a great country in the south of the ocean which was "very profitable and richer than any other" and that if they agreed to any such

line of demarcation, the Portuguese would be cut off from that country.

The Sovereigns wrote to the Admiral and asked him what he thought about this new country, and they suggested that "the Bull might be improved" so that the country would be secured for Castile. In the same letter, dated September 5, they also asked him to send them the map of the ocean and the new islands, with details of latitudes and courses, as he had promised. And they proposed that a competent astronomer should accompany him on his new voyage, such as his old friend, the priest Antonio de Marchena.

The letter is an indirect proof that the latitudes recorded in the journal are incorrect. The position of the islands, and the way leading to them, were the Admiral's secret, and the Sovereigns might have been afraid that he would never give them the promised information at all; hence

The portrait of Columbus in the Civico Museo Giovio, at Como in Italy. Allegedly it is the lost original in Paolo Giovio's collection, from which the woodcut on page 22 was taken, but it shows a considerably older man, and makes one wonder whether any portraits of Columbus can really be traced back to his lifetime. According to Las Casas Columbus' eyes were bright blue; the eyes in this picture are brown. The superscription, here slightly curtailed, is "CO-LUMBVS LYGUR. NOVI ORBIS REPTOR, Columbus of Liguria, discoverer of a new world." Liguria is the Italian district which includes Genoa.

Left: the coat-of-arms Columbus received from the Sovereigns in May, 1493, with his signature. In January, 1502, he took it upon himself to modify it slightly: for example, the fortress of Castile was put on a red field, as on the royal coat-of-arms. See page 1.

109

their suggestion that he take an astronomer, who could make his own observations and calculations and later communicate them to the Sovereigns. And yet it seems likely that the Admiral dispatched the required information before his departure. This expedition was to consist of seventeen ships and twelve hundred men: it would be quite impossible to keep directions and latitudes secret from so many. His reply to the Sovereigns is lost, but he proably agreed that "the Bull might be improved."

We do not know much about the seventeen vessels. The flagship, which might well have been about 200 tons, was called the *Santa María* like her predecessor; this was the commonest of names among Spanish ships at that time. She was known familiary as the *Maríagalante*. Two other large ships in the fleet were called the *Collina* and *La Gallega*. The *Niña* was to accompany Columbus again, together with eleven other square-rigged caravels. Some of them were probably much smaller than the *Niña* since a contemporary writer says that many of the ships were light shallow-draught vessels, "Cantabrian barques." No one knows what a Cantabrian barque looked like, and so we shall include them among the caravels. Two more small caravels were lateen-rigged.

The owner of the flagship was Antonio Torres, brother to the nurse of the Heir Apparent. He was also master of the ship, and it seems that he was second in command of the expedition, for he later returned to Cadiz as commander of the main part of the fleet. In addition to Spanish sailors, a number of Genoese took part in this expedition, among them the Admiral's brother, Giacomo, who was now known as Don Diego. The Admiral's other brother, Don Bartolomeo, had not yet come back from his travels in England and France. A good many of those on board were soldiers, both cavalry and infantry, and various craftsmen, husbandmen, and farm laborers. The chief surgeon was Diego Alvares Chanca, who wrote a description of the voyage, and the five priests on the expedition were headed by Friar Buil of the Benedictine Order, who had the special responsibility for missionary work among the Indians. Sources say that the number of men who sailed was twelve or fifteen hundred. Over two hundred of these were "gentlemen volunteers" who went at their own expense to look for gold and adventure, and one of them was the Admiral's childhood friend Michele de Cuneo of Savona, who was later to write the liveliest account of the voyage. A young cartographer, Juan de la Cosa, signed on as a seaman. The map which he made of the world in 1500 is the first known map to show all the newly discovered islands.

The owner of the flagship was Antonio Torres, brother No one in Europe had any experience of such large-scale colonization, and it is not surprising that preparations were slow and many mistakes were made. There

were twenty lancers with the fleet, and the Admiral complained afterward about the quality of their horses, and was inclined to suspect that the lancers had lent themselves to some lucrative horse trading just before they left, if indeed Juan de Soria himself was not the guilty party. Enough wine was shipped to last for two years, but the coopers in Cadiz did their work so badly that a great deal of the wine leaked out during the voyage. The voyagers took aboard cattle, donkeys, sheep, goats, pigs, dogs, and cats, together with chickens and salt meat, especially pork. They had grain for sowing, and various kinds of seed, and vine shoots and young sugar canes, to see which grew best in the Indies. In addition to all

of this the fleet was well provided with the thousands of items necessary for sailing, fighting, building, and administration.

On September 26 the Pope issued a new Bull, extending his earlier grant to Castile so that it now embraced all islands and continents that had been discovered or should be discovered by sailing to the west or south, irrespective of whether the territories aforesaid lay to the west, to the south, to the east, or in the Indies. At the same time, he declared that all earlier gifts, promises, and grants concerning these territories made to kings, princes, infantas, and religious or military orders were null and void.

Since it was only too obvious that the reference to the infantas and military orders was aimed at Henry the Navigator and the Portuguese Order of Christ, the Bull aroused considerable indignation in Portugal. New diplomatic negotiations on the sea routes to the Indies were immediately taken in hand, and even Ferdinand and Isabella could see that the Pope had gone too far in his efforts to be accommodating. From then on, he was left out of the negotiations between Portugal and Castile on this question. By that time, the Admiral had sailed away, and he, as well as the Pope, had to be left out of the discussion.

From Cadiz to Navidad

Both Michele de Cuneo, the Admiral's friend, and Dr. Chanca wrote long letters describing the second voyage, and since Columbus' journal has never been found they are invaluable sources of information about what happened on the new islands. They say little about the actual journey across the Atlantic, however; the most detailed description of that is given by Fernando Colón, who possessed a copy of the lost journal. He writes:

"On Wednesday, September 25th, 1493, while my brother and I looked on, the Admiral weighed anchor in the harbour of Cadiz, where the fleet had been assembled, and steered south-west for the Canary Islands, where he intended to take on fresh provisions. They sailed in fair weather, and on September 28th, when they were one hundred leagues from Spain, many small land birds, turtle doves and small birds of other kinds, came to the Admiral's ship. They seemed to be flying to winter in Africa, and probably came from the Azores. He sailed on his course, and on Wednesday, October 2nd, he reached Grand Canary where he anchored. At midnight he left for Gomera, which he reached on Saturday, October 5th. There he busied himself in taking on board all those thing which the fleet needed." Cuneo says that they celebrated his arrival at Gomera with a grand salute and fireworks in honor of the lady who governed the island, "with whom our Lord Admiral had once fallen in love."

Fernando Colón continues: "On Monday, October

7th, the Admiral set his course for the Indies, after having given each of the captains sealed instructions which were only to be opened in the event that the ships became separated from the fleet by stress of weather. The reason for this secrecy was that his instructions showed them how to reach the city of Navidad in Española, and he did not wish anyone else to know that route except in a genuine emergency.

"He sailed with a good wind, and on Thursday, October 24th, having run more than 400 leagues to the west from Gomera, he had not yet met with the seaweed he had found on the first voyage after sailing only 250 leagues. On that day and the two succeeding days the fleet was visited by a swallow, to the astonishment of all. On the Saturday night, in heavy rain and fearful thunder, St. Elmo's fire appeared, with seven lights on the top of the mainsail. The sailors call these lights the body of St. Elmo and sing hymns and say prayers to the Saint, and they are convinced that a storm will not harm a soul when these lights appear. I do not know whether this is true, for I only relate what they have told me, but Pliny said that when Roman mariners saw these lights during a storm at sea they said they were Castor and Pollux. Seneca also mentions it in the first book of his *Natural Questions*.

"I return to my narrative. On the night of Saturday, November 2nd, the Admiral observed a considerable change in the sky and the wind, with dark threatening clouds ahead, which convinced him that they were close to land. So he reduced sail and gave orders that a careful watch should be kept—and this proved to be well-advised, for when dawn came they sighted land to the

west. It proved to be a large mountainous island, which the Admiral called Dominica, since it was discovered on a Sunday morning. Shortly after, he saw another island north-east of Dominica, and another, and yet another further north. Then all the men gathered in the stern to sing the *Salve* and other prayers and hymns, and they gave thanks to God for His grace in allowing them to find land after 22 days at sea from Gomera, a distance which they estimated to be between 750 and 800 leagues.

"As they did not find a suitable place to anchor on the east side of the island of Dominica, they sailed across to another island, which the Admiral called Maríagalante, after his flagship. He went ashore there, and with fitting ceremony he renewed, in the name of Their Catholic Majesties, the possession of all the islands and mainland of the Indies, which he had already done on his first voyage."

Peter Martyr's eyewitness source of the voyage— probably Captain Melchior Maldonado of Seville—says that the distance they had covered was 820 leagues, which is in fact the true distance. The course taken by the fleet was west by south, or one point south of the course followed on the first voyage, and for that reason the ships were able to sail the whole way in good trade winds. Their average speed was 5.2 knots, and Dr. Chanca says that they could have sailed much faster if only the flagship had not been so slow.

The ships stayed at Maríagalante for only a few hours of the night. It seemed to be uninhabited and made its most lasting impression on some of the sailors, who in a heedless moment decided to try a fruit which grew there. No

The fleet off the south coast of Santa Maria de Guadalupe. On the horizon to the far left is the flat island of Maríagalante, and to the right of the ships Dominica. The many small hills on the horizon are the Todos los Santos archipelago.

sooner had it touched their tongues than they felt a searing pain, and Dr. Chanca says that their faces became swollen and that they thought they would go mad with the fiery pain. They had tasted the zanilla apple, from which the Caribs extracted the poison for their arrows.

At daybreak the fleet sailed on toward a large lofty island, which the Admiral called Todos los Santos to commemorate the recent Feast of All Saints. When they got closer, they could make out a waterfall, which seemed to have its source in the clouds, and it sparkled so brightly that many men on the flagship laid bets that it was not water at all but a mass of white rock. A small caravel was sent ahead to reconnoiter. Her captain went ashore where there was a village, and the natives fled from his sight. In the deserted houses he found two large parrots and cotton and five bones scraped clean of flesh. These bones were from the arms and legs of a human being. When he returned and showed what he had found, they realized that this must be the island of the man-eating Caribs. But the Admiral called it Santa Maria de Guadalupe, as he had promised the brethren of the monastery in Estremadura. Late that evening the fleet found a good anchorage on the west coast of the island.

Cuneo writes: "We landed on this island and stayed there about six days. The reason for our long sojourn was

113

that eleven of our men joined together as robbers and went five or six miles into the wilds, where they lost their bearings and could not return, even though all were seamen and looked to the sun: but they could not see it properly because of the dense forest. When the Lord Admiral found that the men did not return and could not be found, he dispatched 200 men in four groups, with trumpets, horns and lanterns, but they still did not find them, and there were times when we were more afraid of losing the 200 than of losing the men whom they were seeking. But it pleased God to guide the 200, now weary and hungry, back to us, and we thought that the eleven had been eaten by the said Caribs, as is their custom. But after five or six days it pleased God that the said eleven, with little hope of finding us, lit a fire on the top of a rock. We saw the fire and understood that they were there, and sent them a boat, and thus were they saved. If it had not been for an old woman, who showed us by signs how we should go, they would have been lost, for we intended to set sail and continue the voyage on the following day.

"On that island we took twelve very beautiful girls, very fat, between 15 and 16 years old, and two boys of the same age. These had been castrated, and we thought that the Caribs had done this to prevent them from having intercourse with the women, or possibly to fatten them for eating purposes. These boys and girls had been captured by the Caribs, and later we sent them to Spain for the King to see."

Dr. Chanca says that they captured more than twenty women who had been held prisoner by the Caribs, and these women told them that all the male children they had borne while in captivity had immediately been eaten by the Caribs and that only the male offspring which the Caribs had by their own women were allowed to live. All boys they managed to catch were castrated at once and then brought up as slaves until they were eaten on some festive occasion. The Spaniards found human bones and skulls in many of the houses, and in one they discovered a stewpot with a human neck in the process of being cooked. And yet those who had been on the first voyage thought that the Caribs were in some ways more civilized than the inhabitants of the other islands, even though they did not appear to possess any gold. Their houses were better built, their weapons very well made, and their cotton was just as skillfully woven as the best Spanish cloth. The expedition managed to capture a number of Carib women as well, and they all had cotton bands round their legs, tied tightly just below the knee and at the ankle so that their calves were swollen. But they did not see many men, and the women explained that the men were out hunting Indians in their canoes.

The Admiral wanted to press on to see the people he had left at Navidad. On November 10 the fleet set sail in a light breeze to the northwest in order to get up into the latitude of Española. They lay to during the night, and on the next day saw another elevated island, smaller than Guadalupe, and the Admiral called it Santa María de Monserrate, after the monastery outside Barcelona, celebrated for its Black Madonna. They sailed on for two days along a chain of islands which were all named after miracle-working madonnas and saints. There were Santa María la Antigua, Santa María la Redonda, San Martin, San Jorge, Santa Anastasia, and San Cristóbal. The Indians who were with them pointed to the west and spoke of an island which they called Ayay, and on the morning of November 14 the fleet anchored off black reefs at an inlet like a river mouth. They had arrived at Ayay, but the Admiral called it Santa Cruz, the Holy Cross.

Michele de Cuneo describes what happened at the island: "On one of the days while we lay at anchor, we saw coming round a point a canoa, that is to say a boat, for that is what they call them in their language, and it was propelled by oars, which gave it the appearance of a well-manned bergantino. On board were three or four Carib men, with two Carib women and two Indian slaves, who had just been castrated, with their wounds still fresh; for thus do the Caribs treat their neighbours on the other islands. And as the flagship's barge was ashore when we saw the canoe approaching, we immediately entered the boat and began to pursue the canoe. As we drew near, the Caribs began to shoot at us with their bows, and half of us would have been hit if it had not been for our shields. But I have to tell you that an arrow came at a sailor with a shield, and it pierced the shield and went three inches into his breast, so that within three days he was dead. We captured the canoe with all the men. One of the Caribs was wounded by a spear thrust, and, thinking that he was dead, we threw him into the water, but we saw that he began to swim at once. We caught him with a grappling iron and hauled him over the side of the ship, where we cut off his head with an axe. We later sent the other Caribs to Spain, together with the slaves.

"While I was in the boat I captured a very beautiful Carib woman, whom the said Lord Admiral gave to me, and when I had taken her to my cabin—she was naked, as was their custom—I was filled with the desire to take my pleasure with her. I wished to satisfy my desire, but she was unwilling, and so treated me with her nails that I wished I had never begun. But—to cut a long story short—I then took a piece of rope and whipped her soundly, and she let forth such incredible screams that you would not have believed your ears. Eventually, we came to such terms, I assure you, that you would have thought she had been brought up in a school for strumpets."

Columbus himself and others who wrote letters and reports say nothing about sexual relationships between

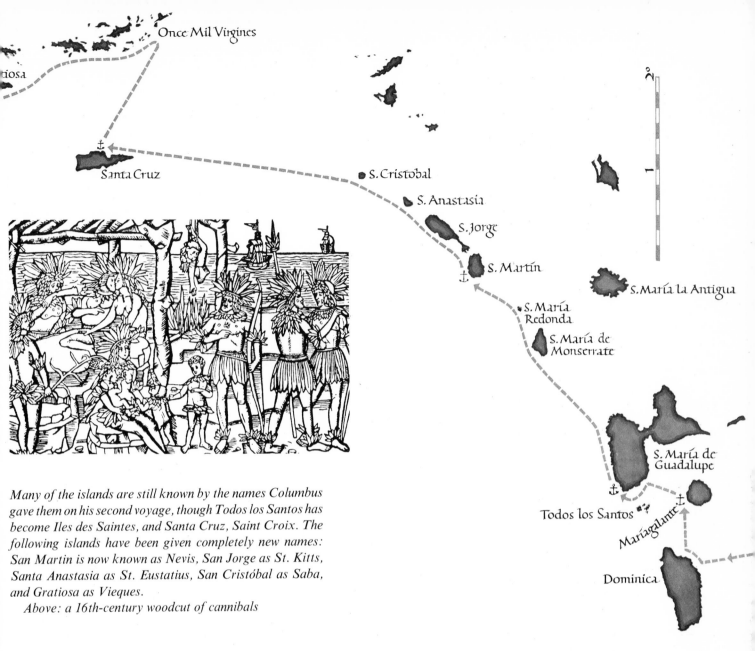

Once Mil Virgines

riosa

Santa Cruz

● S. Cristóbal

S. Anastasia

S. Jorge

⚓ S. Martín

S. María
Redonda

S. María de
Monserrate

S. María la Antigua

S. María de
Guadalupe

⚓

Todos los Santos

Mariagalante ⚓

Dominica

Many of the islands are still known by the names Columbus gave them on his second voyage, though Todos los Santos has become Iles des Saintes, and Santa Cruz, Saint Croix. The following islands have been given completely new names: San Martin is now known as Nevis, San Jorge as St. Kitts, Santa Anastasia as St. Eustatius, San Cristóbal as Saba, and Gratiosa as Vieques.

Above: a 16th-century woodcut of cannibals

members of the expedition and Indian women; it is only the unprejudiced and outspoken Cuneo who dares to speak of his own experiences with them. It is obvious that the sex-starved sailors, on the first voyage and on the later ones alike, must have taken every opportunity to satisfy their hunger, and the "men from the sky" must have had unlimited opportunities. Seldom can they have had to use force as Cuneo did. Most of those who have studied the question are convinced that it was Columbus' men who brought syphilis to Europe from the Indies. It has been shown that a mild form of syphilis was common in those islands before 1492, and nobody has been able to prove that the disease was known in Europe before 1494. Las Casas is convinced that the Spaniards were infected by the Indians, and Oviedo the historian thinks that they caught it on the second voyage. The disease spread throughout Europe like a ghastly epidemic and

reached its culminating point toward the end of the 16th century.

The place where the twenty-five white men in their boat had subdued four Carib men and two women was given the name of Cabo de la Flecha, Arrow Point, by the Admiral, in memory of the sailor who had been shot dead by an arrow. He now wanted to press on with all speed northwest to Española, but a hard wind was blowing from that direction, so he sailed north instead and came across a whole archipelago of small islands, which he called Once Mil Vigines after the eleven thousand virgins with St. Ursula, who, legend has it, were massacred in Cologne by Attila's Huns.

On November 17 the fleet was able to steer west, and on the following day it passed a beautiful green island which was given the name Gratiosa, after the mother of one of the Admiral's friends. For the whole of the next day they ran before a hard wind off the coast of a large island which the Indians called Boriquen and the Admiral named San Juan Bautista, St. John the Baptist. They found a good anchorage on the west coast of the island, and the ships remained there for two days, while fresh water was taken aboard and the men fished; but they made no contact with the natives. And on they sailed, to the west and northwest, passing a small island and eventually reaching a low-lying coast which the Indians said was Española. But neither the Admiral nor any of the men who had sailed with him on the previous voyage could recognize the coast.

It was, in fact, Española, and when the fleet continued along the coast to the northwest the Admiral soon recognized the large Bahia de las Flechas, where they had had a skirmish with some black-painted Indians on the first voyage. On that occasion they had captured four youths and taken them to Castile. One of these youths had returned with them on this second voyage. He had survived the hardships of both journeys, and they sent him ashore here. He was dressed in European clothes, had been christened, and could speak a little Spanish, and he promised to induce his people to live at peace with the good Christians.

The Admiral continued west with all speed, and on November 25 the fleet dropped anchor at Monte Cristi and went on by boat to the Rio del Oro, the large river where the Admiral had found gold dust. On the riverbank they found the remains of two men, one with a rope round his neck and the other with his feet tied together. It was no longer possible to see whether they had been Christians or Indians. On the following day two more bodies were discovered, one of them with traces of a beard. Those who had been on the first voyage knew that the Indians were beardless, and they began to fear that terrible things had happened. The ships sailed on toward Navidad, and as evening approached they came to the reef which protected the large bay. Lombards were fired, but no answering shots came from the fortress.

The Caribs, like the Tainos, had come from South America, and when the Spaniards arrived they were in possession of the Lesser Antilles and Puerto Rico. It is only the faces of their dull-witted descendants, who are now confined to a reservation in Dominica, that enable us to form some picture of the hard, indomitable tribe which struck fear into the Tainos and aroused the respect of the Spaniards and of other Europeans.

116

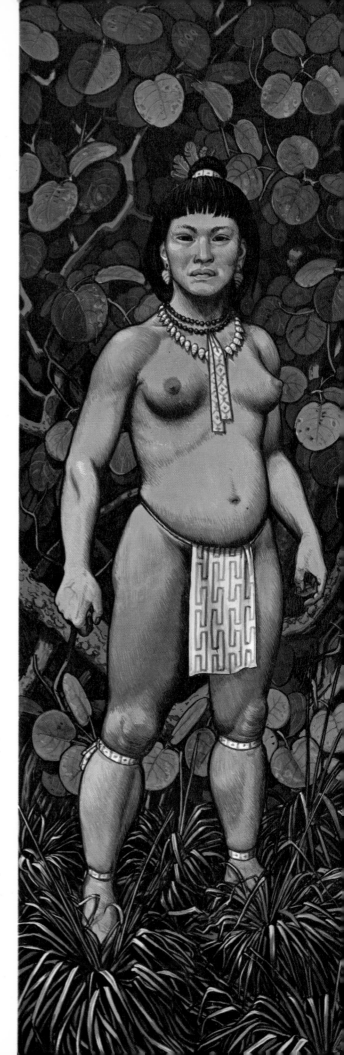

Tragedy in Navidad

The Admiral had long before prophesied that when they reached Navidad the ships would be surrounded by hundreds of canoes and so many friendly Indians that it would be impossible to hold them off. But no canoes came to meet them, and everything was quiet. The ships glided through the dusk toward the black mountain which the Admiral had previously called Monte Caribata, and anchored there.

A canoe arrived after midnight, and from it came voices calling for the Admiral. Six Indians paddled themselves up to the flagship, but they would not come aboard until the Admiral had spoken with them, and they were not reassured until the Admiral had shown them his face by the light of a lantern. One of them was related to Guacanagarí, and they came with greetings from the cacique, bringing with them two gold masks, one for the Admiral and once for Vicente Yáñez Pinzón, who had not come on this voyage. The Admiral questioned them about the Christians at Navidad, but their replies were evasive; first they seemed to say that they were all well, and then that some had died of disease and others had been killed in local quarrels. They also related that the caciques Caonabó and Mayrení had come and attacked Guacanagarí and burned his village and wounded many of his men, so that he now lived in another village farther inland. But he would be coming to visit the Admiral, perhaps on the following day. When the six Indians paddled off in the dark, the Indian interpreters said that they had understood them to say that all the Christians in Navidad were dead. But the Spaniards would not believe them.

When day came the ships sailed in between the reefs and anchored outside Navidad. Not a trace of life was to be seen, and all that the shore party found was the charred remains of palisades and huts and a few scraps of clothing — but not one of the settlers. They waited the whole of that day for Guacanagarí, and many of the men began to think, and to say, it was he who had killed the Christians and set fire to Navidad. The Admiral went ashore on the following day to see the devastation for himself, and then gave orders that the area round the charred fortress should be dug up, since he had told the colonists to bury all the gold they obtained. But they found no gold or anything else of value which had belonged to the colonists.

The Admiral and some of his men rowed to a point where it was hoped that a new town could be built, but the site was too wet. They came across a few huts there which were covered with green mildew, and in them they found several stockings and pieces of cloth and a Moorish mantle which had belonged to the colonists. By the time Columbus returned to what remained of Navidad, a few

Indians had plucked up enough courage to make an appearance and were now trading with the crews. They had also shown them eleven bodies, under the long grass. They had been dead for several months, but the remnants of their clothing showed that they had been Christians. The priests read prayers for their souls, and then they were given a Christian burial.

Fernando Colón probably quotes more or less directly from the Admiral's journal when he writes: "While the Christians were looking for papers or other things left by the dead men, a brother of the cacique Guacanagarí, together with some other Indians, came to speak with the Admiral. They could say a few words in Spanish and knew the names of all the Christians who had been left there. They said that these men had begun to quarrel among themselves as soon as the Admiral had left, and that each one of them had taken as many women and as much gold as he could. As a result, Pedro Gutiérrez and Escobedo had killed one Jácome. Then they had joined forces with nine others and gone away with their women to a country which belonged to a cacique called Caonabó, who was lord of the mines. Caonabó killed them, and a few days later he advanced with a large body of men on Navidad, which was defended only by Diego de Harana and ten other men who had been willing to stay and guard the fortress, for all the others had dispersed to various parts of the island. Caonabó reached the town at night and set fire to the houses in which the Christians lived with their women and caused them to fly in terror into the sea, where eight of them drowned. Three others, whom the Indians could not identify, were killed on land. They also said that Guacanagarí had fought against Caonabó in defence of the Christians, but had been wounded and forced to withdraw."

When Melchior Maldonado sailed out in one of the caravels to find a suitable site for the new town, he met a canoe with two Indians in it, and his pilot, who had been on the first voyage, recognized one of them as a brother of Guacanagarí. This Indian then directed Maldonado and some of his men inland to the village where Guacanagarí was residing, and they spoke with the cacique, who verified the previous reports by telling them that Caonabó and Mayrení had killed the Christians and burned their houses and his own village, and he himself had been wounded in the leg. He received them while lying in his hammock, and his leg was swathed in a bandage. When they left, he gave them a few pieces of gold and said that he hoped that the Admiral would visit him, since he himself found it difficult to move.

The Admiral visited him with all his captains and a large body of men, and they were all dressed in such finery "that they would have created a stir in a capital city." Guacanagarí welcomed them from his hammock. Dr. Chanca writes: "He did not get up, but he made as

JUANA

Tortuga

La Navidad

Rio del Oro

Isabela

MARIEN

MAGUA

CIBAO

MAGUANA

HIGUEY

Puerto de las Flechas

C. San Rafael

XARAGUA

Mona

60'

SAN JUAN BAUTISTA

great a show of courtesy as he could from his bed. With tears in his eyes he expressed great sorrow for the death of the Christians, and he began to speak and to show by signs as best he could how some had died of disease and how others had gone to Caonabó in search of the gold mine and had been killed there. . . . On this occasion he gave the Admiral eight and a half marks of gold [2,125 grams] and five or six hundred cut stones of various colours, and a cap with similar stones, by which they seemed to set great store. . . . I and one of the surgeons of the fleet were present, and the Admiral told Guacanagarí that we had knowledge of human ailments so that he might show us his wound. This he consented to do, and I said that it was necessary to leave the house, if he could, for it was crowded and dark, and we could not see properly. He did as I wished, and I think it was more from timidity than willingness. . . . He told the Admiral that the wound had been made with a *ciba*, that is to say a stone. When we had removed the bandage we examined him. Truth to tell, there was no more wound on that leg than there was on the other, though he pretended that it gave him great pain."

This was enough to persuade most of the Spaniards that Guacanagarí was a false friend, and Friar Buil and others urged that he should at once be taken prisoner and punished. But the Admiral was unwilling to do this and said that he believed what Guacanagarí had told him, and that everyone could see that many of his men had been wounded by Indian weapons. He invited Guacanagarí to the flagship, and honored him, and called him his friend. The horses aboard the ship frightened the cacique and his men, who thought that these animals lived on human flesh, but the Admiral reassured them and showed them that they were quite harmless, and then invited the cacique to eat with him in his cabin.

The ships remained at Navidad for a few more days,

and the Spaniards traded for gold and went on looking for a good harbor and a dry site for the new colony. Early one morning, ten of the captive women managed to swim ashore and escape. Four of them were recaptured, but when the Admiral sent a message to ask Guacanagarí for help to find the others, his village was found to be abandoned.

The Admiral could have established the new settlement at the foot of Monte Caribata, where the harbor was good and the site high and dry, but he was probably much disturbed about the fate of Navidad and might have suspected that his friend Guacanagarí after all was a secret enemy; and he wanted to get closer to "the mines," which were supposed to be farther east, in the country ruled by Caonabó. On December 7 the ships left the anchorage at Navidad and began to press back east, and Dr. Chanca writes that it was a greater labor to sail thirty leagues against the wind than it had been to sail all the way from Castile. Many of the people on board fell ill, cattle and horses died, food was running out, and it was presumably exhaustion and universal discontent that finally determined the Admiral to fix on a place which Dr. Chanca calls "a very good harbour." This was a large bay which, although it gave shelter from the trade winds, was exposed to the north winds of winter. The Admiral himself was very ill, and Fernando Colón points out that the journal contained no entries from December 11, 1493, to March 12, 1494. One source tells us that the fleet reached the new harbor during the week before Christmas. Work was immediately begun on huts for the colonists, and Dr. Chanca tells us that the Admiral was moved ashore on Christmas Day. The Admiral called the new town Isabela, in honor of the Queen. The Indians who were with them assured them that they would not have to go much farther to find the gold.

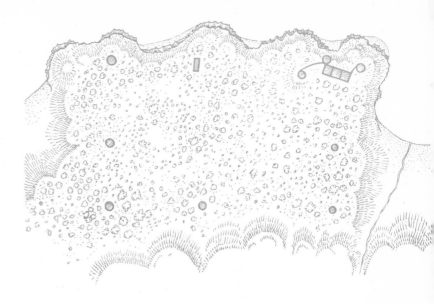

The map on the opposite page shows how the fleet sailed from San Juan Bautista (the modern Puerto Rico) to Navidad and then back to the new settlement of Isabela. When the Spaniards arrived, the island was divided into a number of small kingdoms, each with its cacique. The most important of these chiefs were Guacanagarí, Columbus' friend, in Marien; Guarionex in Magua, Caonabó in Maguana; Mayobanex and Cotubanama in Higuey; and Behéchio in Xaragua.

Not a trace of Isabela is to be seen today except for vague outlines where walls and houses once stood. The map on the right is based on the results of a survey carried out by some U.S. Navy officers in 1891. Even at that date, almost everything was level with the ground, and the sites where traces of towers and stone houses seemed to exist are marked by circles and rectangles.

Isabela

The royal instructions for the second voyage contained the following passage: "The Admiral shall, after the safe arrival of his fleet there, force and compel all those who sail with him, as well as all others who are to go out from here later on, to treat the said Indians very well and lovingly and abstain from doing them any injury, arranging that both peoples converse and associate freely together, the one serving the other to the best of its ability. Moreover, the said Admiral shall graciously present them with those of Their Highnesses' goods which he is carrying for barter, and treat them with great respect, and if any person or persons should maltreat the said Indians in any manner whatever, the said Admiral, as Viceroy and Governor of Their Highnesses, shall punish them severely by virtue of the authority vested in him by Their Majesties for this purpose."

This, then, was the policy, and such was, certainly, the Admiral's original intention. But as it happened, things were very different: Navidad changed everything. Probably Columbus made his first enemies among settlers and soldiers when he refused to take bloody revenge for what most of them clearly regarded as a manifest act of treachery. It was certainly there that he himself began to have his first misgivings about his Indians, so that later on he did not treat them so "very well and lovingly."

No sooner was Isabela established than several hundred of the colonists fell ill. Because of the thin air, said the Admiral. Because of too much work and too little food, said others. There were certainly plenty of causes which contributed to the outbreak. Food was short, and the salted meat in particular had been affected in the heat. The Spaniards bought cassava bread and sweet potatoes

and maize from the Indians of neighboring villages, but at least to begin with, this diet did not suit Spanish digestions. No one specifies what sort of illness it was, but many died of it. It might have been acute diarrhea, fever, or syphilis. This last possibility is rejected even today by the more prudish writers on the subject, but I do not think it completely out of the question that Columbus himself might have contracted the disease. Those who prefer to think of him as the untainted Bearer of Christ may find consolation in the fact that syphilis can be contracted without sexual intercourse. Moreover, many of the colonists might well have been suffering from malaria. Cuneo describes the plague of mosquitoes that beset them and says that the Indians painted their bodies with the red and black juices of certain fruits as a cure for mosquito bite. The Christians soothed their bites by immersing themselves in water.

In its early days the town consisted of a few hundred houses, "as small as our hunting-lodges, and thatched with straw." The river from which the colonists took their drinking water was a lombard shot away, and the Admiral was planning to channel it into the town and hoped to be able to build dams and mills. But most of his laborers were too sick to work, and such of his soldiers as were still in good health generally refused to concern themselves with such menial work. The Admiral was severe with the malcontents and punished them, but Friar Buil, the missionary, took their part, and discontent and enmity were soon universal.

The Admiral had learned enough of the Indians' language to understand that Cibao meant "the rocky land" and had nothing whatever to do with Cipangu. Even so, Cibao was supposed to contain gold, and at the beginning of January he sent Alonso de Hojeda and Ginés de Gorbalán with about 40 men and two Indian guides on an expedition inland. Cuneo, who was one of

119

the party, relates: "And as we drew near to that place called Cibao, in terrible weather, we had to cross another very wild river, so we were afraid that the whole enterprise might end badly and returned to the nearest village to speak with the inhabitants. They told us that there was indeed an abundance of gold in Cibao, and they gave our captains a quantity of gold, including three large pieces—one weighing 9 castellanos, the second 15, and the third 12, though that contained a bit of stone. [Together the three pieces weighed 165 grams.] They brought this gold to the Lord Admiral and told him what I have just related, about what we saw and heard tell of. These were joyful tidings for him as for us all, and we no longer concerned ourselves with spices, but instead directed all our attention to that thrice-blessed gold. And so the Admiral wrote to the King that he soon hoped to be able to give him as much gold as the iron-mines in Biscay gave iron."

Cuneo does not mention that one party, under Gorbalán, penetrated as far as Niti, near Caonabó's headquarters. Dr. Chanca says that the expedition found gold in more than fifty rivers. Since his reports are very accurate descriptions of what he saw and was told, we must presume that Alonso de Hojeda had been telling him some fantastic lies.

The Admiral realized that he could not afford to keep the whole fleet out there, so he decided to send twelve of the vessels home. He kept his flagship *Maríagalante* and *La Gallega* as floating fortresses, and the caravels *Niña, San Juan,* and *Cardera* for later expeditions. Antonio de Torres was put in command of the ships bound for home,

and with him the Admiral sent a long memorandum to be presented to the Sovereigns. He writes that he had instructed Torres to report that he, Columbus, had found everything he had hoped to find and that he would soon be leaving for Cibao to collect gold. He says that everything which had been sown grew vigorously and fast, but that since most of the men had been ill they had not been able to do much work in the fields. He begs them to send him at the earliest opportunity three or four caravels with the most badly needed provisions—especially wine, since their barrels had been poorly made and the wine had leaked out and gone to waste—and sheep, goats, pigs and donkeys, more seed corn, salt meat, salt, muskets, powder and shot, and innumerable other things, among them molasses, which was "the best nourishment in the world and very wholesome." He mentions the best men by name, suggesting better pay or rewards for them, and he asks for permission to recompense such of the "gentlemen volunteers," of whom there were over two hundred, who had been working while others had refused to do so. He begs the Sovereigns henceforth to choose nobody but well-qualified people for various posts in the Indies, so that he will not have incompetent and unwilling subordinates as now. He suggests that Dr. Chanca, who had had a great deal of work with the sick, be given better pay, though not quite as much as the doctor himself asked for. He goes on to say that he has too few interpreters and is therefore sending back many Caribs for instruction, and proposes that plenty of cattle and other necessities should be sent every year to Española; these could then be paid

120

for with shiploads of Carib slaves.

This document has been preserved, with the Royal Secretary's notes on the Sovereigns' decisions about each point. The Admiral was gladly and willingly granted nearly everything he asked for. The only thing to which the Sovereigns were firmly opposed— this is expressed more clearly in a letter— was the transportation of the Caribs.

The twelve ships left for home on February 2, and a report that has come down to us says that the goods unloaded at Cadiz included gold valued at 30,000 ducats (about 230 pounds), a great deal of cinnamon, which, however, was white, like inferior ginger; pepper in pods like beans but not tasting the same as pepper from the East Indies; wood called sandalwood, although it was white; skeins of spun cotton and pieces of cloth woven from the same material; sixty parrots of different varieties and colors; and twenty-six Indians, three of them man-eating cannibals. So most of the Caribs, who might have been treated rather worse than the other Indians, had died on the way.

Not long after Torres had left, the Admiral discovered that the Royal Inspector, Bernal de Pisa, was plotting a mutiny. As Columbus was unwilling to execute one of the King's men, he had him fettered and confined on the flagship, to which all weapons and ammunition from the caravels were also taken. He set some of his most reliable men to guard this floating arsenal, and then left Isabela, on March 12, to explore Cibao with five hundred of his healthiest men.

Michele de Cuneo relates: "We experienced 29 days of

The Indians directed the colonists through a pass in a mountain range and over a plain to the golden land of Cibao. Columbus called the plain the Vega Real, the Royal Plain, and the river running through it the Rio de las Cañas, the River of Canes, not realizing that he had already called the same river the Rio del Oro. Left: the Vega Real, with the mountainous country of Cibao in the background

terrible weather, bad food, and even worse drink; and yet the hunger for gold gave us strength and speed. On the outward and return journey we crossed two very rapid rivers, by swimming, as I mentioned above, and those who could not swim were helped across by two Indians swimming beside them. Out of friendliness and by reason of a few trifles which we gave them, they carried our clothes, weapons, and everything else we had with us across the river on their heads. We arrived at that place which is called Cibao and immediately built a fort of timber in the name of St. Thomas, beyond the power of those Indians to capture. The fort is situated about 27 leagues from our colony. We often fished in the rivers, but nobody ever found as much as a grain of gold. We were therefore highly displeased with the Indians of the region, all of whom had told us that the gold was to be found in the land of King Caonabó, who lived about 2 leagues from our said fort. Many Indians came to look at us while we were in the fort as if we were objects of wonder, some travelling as much as 10 leagues to do so,

121

and they had some of their gold with them. They exchanged it with us, so that we collected gold to the value of about 2,000 castellanos [20 pounds] and also another substance called *tiber* [?]. Not one of us went to see the said King Caonabó, for we had no suitable clothes. They told us that this King commands 50,000 men. Over and above the said trade to a value of 2,000 castellanos, gold to a value of about 1,000 castellanos was bartered for in secret and against the rules and agreement. As you know, Satan first persuades you to sin, and then lets the sin be discovered. Moreover, as long as Spain is Spain, there will never be any lack of informers. The one informed on the other so that nearly all were exposed, and those who were found guilty were soundly flogged, and some had their ears slit, and others their noses, and it was a deplorable sight."

Pedro Margarit was left at Santo Tomás with fifty-six men, many of them laborers; who were to complete the work of building. When the Admiral returned to Isabela with the main force on March 29, he found that many of the sick had died, and that the colonists were on the brink of starvation. Yet he writes optimistically in the journal (according to Fernando Colón) that melons and cucumbers were ripe, and that the wheat was ready for harvesting. Cuneo is more accurate: "The things that grow well are spring melons, cucumbers, pumpkins and radishes. Other things, such as onions, lettuces, other salad plants, and shallots are not successful at all, except parsley, which grows very well. Wheat, chick-peas, and beans usually grow about nine inches in ten days, but then all at once they wilt and dry up. The soil is black and excellent, but they have not yet found the proper season and the right way to sow. The reason is that none of them wish to make their home in these lands." Cuneo was quite right, both about the growth of plants and about the settlers' attitude towards Española.

Two days after his return, the Admiral received a message from Pedro Margarit to the effect that the Indians near the fort were running away, and that Caonabó was expected to attack at any moment. The Admiral immediately sent seventy men with provisions to Santo Tomás. While he had been away, almost nothing had been done to build defenses for the town, and when he tried to make other people work, as well as the craftsmen, there was almost a mutiny. He solved the problem by sending off another expedition—our sources say 16 lancers, 250 crossbowmen, and 100 musketeers—to reconnoiter the island and pacify restless and hostile tribes. This expedition included nearly everybody who was more or less healthy "and who could walk," Las Casas tells us. The only people who remained behind were the craftsmen, the peasants, the sick and the dying, a few doctors, the priests, and the people necessary to man the three

caravels. Alonso de Hojeda, who was ill and weak himself, was told to lead the expedition to Santo Tomás, hand it over to Pedro Margarit, and then get what rest he could as commander of the fort. The Admiral instructed Pedro Margarit to be careful in Española, since the Sovereigns were more concerned to make good Christians out of the Indians than they were to take their treasures from them. Only if the Indians stole things, or proved themselves to be hostile in other ways, were they to be punished. Since Cacique Caonabó was obviously the Christians' chief enemy on the island, Pedro Margarit was ordered to secure his person—not by force of arms but by proffering gifts and promising him safe conduct. But the main object of the expedition was to reconnoiter Española in order to find the gold mines and anything else of value.

Hojeda and the soldiers left Isabela on April 9, and a few days later some of his men returned with three Indian prisoners. The Spaniards explained that some of their party had been swimming across a river, and the Indians who were supposed to have been helping them over had stolen their clothes and their cacique had kept the clothes for himself and refused to give them back. Hojeda had gone straight to the village, cut one Indian's ears off, and taken the cacique prisoner, his brother and nephew as well, and sent them to the Admiral for appropriate punishment.

The Admiral, in desperation, sentenced these three men to death, as proxies for the clothes stealers, but another cacique, who had been of great service to the Admiral, pleaded for them with tears in his eyes, and the sentence was finally revoked. Soon after this, a horseman came to the Admiral and reported that four hundred Indians from the village of the captive cacique had seized five men on their way back from Santo Tomás, but the Indians had been afraid of his horse, and he had been able to free the Christians.

Before long, the Admiral left the problems of Española behind him. From the first, he had wanted to make absolutely certain whether Juana was an island or part of the continent. Now he equipped the three caravels with lombards and falconets and other weapons from the flagship, took on provisions and water, and said farewell to those who were to remain at Isabela. His brother, Don Diego, was put in supreme command, to govern Española together with an advisory council which consisted of Friar Buil, the marshal Pedro Fernández Coronel, Alonso Sánchez de Carvajal, a friend of the Admiral's, and a courtier called Juan de Luxán. Columbus did not think about the instructions he had given to Pedro Margarit, worded in such terms as to give Pedro the impression that he himself was in supreme command of the island. On April 24, after the midday meal, the sails were set, anchors weighed, and the ships headed west in the fresh breeze.

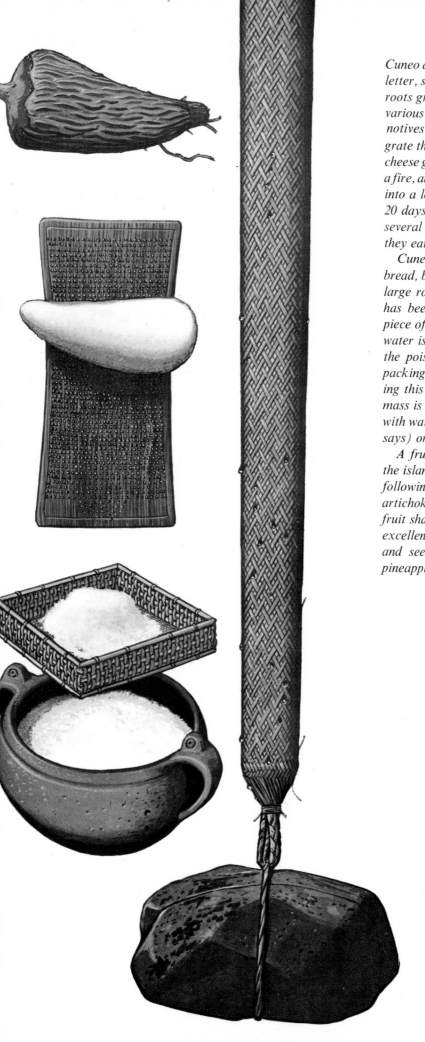

Cuneo describes some edible West Indian plants in his letter, saying among other things: "Many turnip-like roots grow on these islands as well, very large and of various shapes and completely white, from which the natives make bread in the following manner. They grate these roots on certain stones, which are like our cheese graters. Then they set a large slab of stone over a fire, and on top of it the grated root, which they shape into a loaf and treat as bread. It will keep for 15 or 20 days, and these loaves were of great use to us on several occasions. This root is their staple diet, and they eat it raw as well as cooked."

Cuneo is trying to describe the making of cassava bread, but he does not tell us the whole story, for the large roots are extremely poisonous. After the skin has been removed, the roots are rubbed against a piece of wood set with many small sharp stones, and water is added to extract the poison. The water and the poison are forced out of the resulting pulp by packing it into a long sleeve of plaited straw and hanging this up with a heavy weight on the end. The dry mass is then sifted to a fine flour which, when mixed with water, is ready to be eaten, either raw (as Cuneo says) or baked into bread.

A fruit which the Spaniards first came across on the island of Guadalupe is described by Cuneo in the following way: "There are some which are like artichokes but are four times as tall, and they bear a fruit shaped like a pine cone, twice as large, and it is excellent and can be cut with a knife like a turnip and seems to be very wholesome." This was the pineapple.

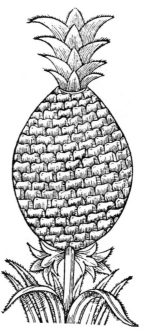

The Queen's Garden

The Admiral was a disappointed man when he left Isabela. The facts no longer corresponded to his dreams, and what was worse, they did not correspond to the reports he was sending back to the Sovereigns. Española was not Cipangu, and gold was not to be found in the quantities described by Marco Polo, nor in the quantities he had hoped to find, nor yet in the quantities reported by Alonso de Hojeda. The Admiral had considered the possibility that Cibao might be Saba, it is true, but he realized that all speculations were worthless if he could not find the riches of Cipangu, Saba, or the Indies to back them up. Nor had the Spaniards yet been able to fulfil the Sovereigns' wishes, and his, to win souls for Christianity. Friar Buil was a very scrupulous man and was unwilling to baptize anyone who had not been taught the elements of the Christian faith. Since the two interpreters were needed elsewhere, the Indians had to go without instruction and baptism.

But the riches must be on the continent, and now the Admiral set sail to prove once and for all that Juana was a part of the continent. After five days at sea, the fleet reached the easternmost point of Juana, and the Admiral went ashore and set up a column with a cross and once more took formal possession of the land, calling the point Cabo de Alfa et Omega, the Cape of the Beginning and End. Bernáldez, the chronicler, writes: "For you must know that this is the end of the continent. The cape at the furthest West is Cabo San Vicente in Portugal. The entire population of the world is gathered between these two capes, so that if one went overland from Cabo San Vicente, it would be possible to go continually east, without crossing any part of the Ocean, until one reached Cabo Alfaeto."

A ships' council was held at the End of the World, and everyone agreed that they should sail on along the south coast of the continent, "for if there was anything of value to be found, it was more likely to be in the south than in the north." That was what Aristotle had said, and that was what the Portuguese had found to be the case in Africa. So the fleet continued along the south coast and discovered two exceptionally good harbors, where some friendly Indians told them that there was plenty of gold to be found, not in their country, it was true, but farther south, on an island called Jamaica.

On May 3 they reached a cape where the coastline

The three caravels which Columbus used to find out whether Juana was an island or a part of the continent were the San Juan, *the* Cardera, *and his favorite, the* Niña. *He commanded the* Niña *himself, with Francisco Niño as pilot and Alonso Medel as master. Juan de la Cosa, the young cartographer, was also on board. The captain of the* San Juan *was Alonso Pérez Roldán, and of the* Cardera *Cristóbal Pérez Niño.*

On the journey west from Cabo Alfa et Omega they came across a fine large harbor, which they called Puerto Grande. Today it is the U.S. Navy Base of Guantánamo Bay. Later they discovered another excellent harbor, with thousands of huts on its shores. Today it is the great Cuban port of Santiago de Cuba.

turned off to the north and the northwest, and here the Admiral decided to leave Juana and sail off to the island of gold. They left in a strong wind which later blew up into a storm, and for considerable periods they had to allow themselves to be carried along in it with bare poles, but on the third day they were able to anchor off Jamaica. While the boats were investigating a harbor which the Admiral called Santa Gloria, so many canoes full of armed natives came out that the Christians thought it wisest to retire to the caravels. They sailed west and reached another port, which was given the name Puerto Bueno, and when more natives came out in canoes and made threatening signs at them, the Spaniards frightened them off with a few blank shots from the lombards. When the shore party landed, the Indians attacked with stones and spears, but the Christians replied with their crossbows, killing a dozen or so, and sent a dog in pursuit of the terrified natives.

The Indians returned on the following day to beg for mercy, bringing cassava bread and water with them as gifts. They were given bells and other trinkets; they were asked about gold and were shown some gold, but none of them seemed to know anything about it. The expedition remained at this spot for four days while the caravels,

which had been damaged in the storm, were repaired; water and firewood were taken aboard, and bread and sweet potatoes were bought. Then the fleet moved on and came to a bay which the Admiral, in an unguarded moment, called the Golfo de Bien Tiempo, the Bay of Fair Weather. By the time they were ready to sail, the wind was blowing hard against them, and so they decided to leave Jamaica and sail back north to Juana. After one day's sailing the caravels were back again at the point which they had left ten days earlier.

The next part of the voyage was one long nightmare, and only the excellent seamanship of the Admiral and his men brought the ships through. To begin with the crews of the three caravels had been hand-picked from among the best sailors available in Spain and then again at Isabela, before Torres had gone home with most of the ships and their crews.

They entered a large shallow archipelago northwest of Cabo de Cruz. Fernando Colón writes: "As he was following the coast, a terrible storm blew up, with thunder and lightning, which together with the many shoals and channels brought him much danger and toil. He had to guard against two dangers which called for conflicting countermeasures: prudence demanded that the sails

125

should be struck in such a storm, while to save himself from running aground he had to sail on. If he had had to sail eight or ten leagues more in this weather, the situation would have become impossible.

"The greatest problem was that the entire sea to the north and north-west was full of innumerable small islands. Some were wooded, but most of them were sandy and could hardly be seen above water. They were about a league in circumference, more or less. The closer they got to Cuba, the loftier and fairer these little islands became. It would have been impossible to give names to them all, and so the Admiral called them collectively El Jardin de la Reina [the Queen's Garden]."

One day they were sailing through a channel when they saw a canoe with some Indians fishing from it; the Indians signaled the fleet to hold off until they had caught their fish. They tied a line round the tail of a remora, a fish with a large sucker on its head, and the remora swam out and attached itself to a turtle. They hauled it in, and it still held on, so that the turtle was caught. When they had caught two large fish in the same way, the Indians paddled their canoe up to the caravels and had no qualms about coming aboard the *Niña*. When they saw the hawk's bells, they were ready to give anything for them — their nets, hooks, calabashes of water, or all together — but the Admiral would keep nothing but the sucker fish. When he asked the Indians about the extent of their country, they explained that Juana stretched out forever to the west and that the sea in the south and west was full of islands.

Everything corresponded so well to the world maps and to Marco Polo's descriptions — everything, that is to say, except the poverty of the people. And none of them had ever heard of the Grand Khan or of the port of Zaiton, which was supposed to be in these parts. Fernando Colón and Bernáldez the chronicler both say that the Admiral had thought of continuing westward round the world until he got back to Spain, but that lack of provisions had decided him against it. Fernando Colón writes: "By this time the Admiral was completely exhausted, both because of the poor food and because, apart from the eight days when he had been seriously ill, he had not taken off his clothes or spent a whole night in bed from the day he left Spain to May 19th, when he set this down in his journal. His trials had been great on other voyages, but on this they were twice as great as ever before."

They came to a larger island and found a deserted village, where they caught, killed, and ate some dogs that could not bark. They had almost no drinking water left, and Cuneo says: "All we had had for twelve days was a cup of water [per man] and a portion of the bread made of the said turnips [cassava bread]....At times, only 8 ounces of bread per man were distributed each day, and

but for the abundance of fish, we would have been in a sorry plight." More than once, the caravels ran aground and on May 23, when they sailed out of the Queen's Garden, it was like waking from a bad dream to find the deep blue sea all round them again.

They made a wide sweep round the last of the islands and then moved in to the mainland to take on fresh water. They found a large village with some friendly natives and were at last able to drink water and eat bread to their heart's content. They were told of a land called Magón, which lay to the west, and the Admiral began to hope that they were at last near the province of Mangi, the fabulously rich province of Mangi. For everyone at this place was poor, and no one knew anything about gold. The fleet pressed on farther to the west and met some more Indians, who told them more about Magón, and said that it was a place where men had tails. When asked about the extent of Juana, the natives said that it took forty months to sail to its end.

They sailed through new islands in a white sea. To their horror, they found it was only two fathoms deep. Cuneo saw quite correctly why the sea was white: the seabed consisted of chalk. They edged their way forward through channels narrower than those in the Queen's Garden and now and then had to warp the caravels over some very shallow banks. Then they came to the mainland again, and one day a sailor who had been hunting in a mangrove swamp reported to the Admiral that he had seen some white men in long white clothes. The Admiral thought that they might perhaps be Prester John's people and sent a party of twenty-five men ashore to establish contact, but they could not find them. On the following day they found tracks of large animals, which they took to be tracks of griffins and lions.

And on they sailed, running aground and hauling themselves off, hungry and thirsty, until they reckoned that they had come 335 leagues from Cabo de Alfa et Omega and the Admiral decided that he would have no more of it. Presumably the crews had had enough, too, but it does not seem that they complained. Probably their endurance, and their loyalty, sprang from the Admiral's own endurance, and his readiness to share in all their hardships. In his letter describing the voyage, Michele de Cuneo has this to say of him: "There has never been a man so noble-hearted and so proficient in the art of navigation as the said Lord Admiral. For while navigating, he could say, just by looking at a cloud or a star at night, what was going to happen, or if bad weather was to come. He kept his share of the watch, and took his turn at the helm, and when a storm had passed, he set the sails while the others slept."

But on June 12, after having sailed 335 leagues along this coast, Columbus found that he had enough. He had found nothing that looked like the province of Mangi, and yet now, as the coast turned south, he still wanted to believe that the land which lay before him was the province of Chiamba, the region that stood farthest east on the maps of the world. He ordered the secretary, Fernando Pérez de Luna, who was also a notary public, to ask every man in the fleet, from the pilots to the ships' boys, if they doubted that this was the mainland. If anyone did, the Admiral was to be told, so that he could prove to them that it must be the continent, as nobody had ever heard of an island more than 335 leagues long.

This notary public was a jack-in-office who was not content to demand that everyone should accept that Juana was part of the continent; he went so far as to threaten that anybody who might change his mind and alter his evidence would be fined 10,000 *maravedis* and have his tongue cut out. Ships' boys and other impecunious people would have a hundred lashes and their tongues cut out. As they all wanted to go home, they all made the required declaration, and he took the names of all those who made it; but the names of the priest who was with them, and of the Admiral's friend, Michele de Cuneo, are not on that list.

They sailed back along roughly the same course by which they had come, through shallow channels and over the white sea. On June 30, the *Niña* went hard aground, but they managed to haul her off. Then they sailed south of the Queen's Garden. Here they met head winds, but after nine days of laborious beating they sighted Cabo de Cruz. It was July 18. There they were struck by such a violent thunderstorm that the caravels were heeled down until their decks were awash. The crews managed to furl the sails and get out their heaviest anchors. Then they pumped, and for a long while they thought they would go under, since they did not seem to be able to pump out as much water as poured in. The Admiral recorded in the log: "May it please God that what is happening to us is for the glory of God, and of Your Highnesses. Were it for my own sake alone, I would no longer endure these torments and dangers, for not a day passes but that we see death staring us in the face."

At last they landed safely at Cabo de Cruz, and the Indians gave them bread and fruit and fish. After four days' rest they were able to go on, but the wind was not favorable for a return to Española, and they set course for Jamaica and sailed in short stages west and south of the island. On August 18, they anchored in a very wide bay which the Admiral called Bahia de la Vaca, Cow Bay. A cacique came out to the *Niña* and had a long conversation with the Admiral about Castile, her Sovereigns, and the Christians. On the following day, while the ships were actually leaving the bay, the cacique paddled up to the *Niña* in a large canoe and came aboard with his wife and

The hunter in the mangrove swamp conceivably might have seen men in long white mantles, but we shall have to ascribe the tracks of lions and griffins to the effects of hunger, disease, and exhaustion. The largest animals on Cuba were the rodents known as hutias. *But the men thought that they were somewhere in the remotest East, and no less an authority than Mandeville said that this was where the terrible griffin dwelt. "And some say that the fore parts of their bodies are like that of an eagle, and the hind parts like that of a lion; and this is certain, for thus were they created. Yet the griffin has a body which is larger than eight lions, and in form it is more imposing than a hundred eagles. He can, to speak truly, fly to his abode with a horse and rider on his back, or a pair of oxen yoked together as they are yoked to the plough, for he has great claws on his feet, as long as the horns of an ox; and the people of those regions make drinking-vessels of them, and of his ribs they make arrows for their bows." Mandeville also says that the trees in the land of the griffins bear wool, as if they were sheep, and that the land of Prester John is only a few days' journey away. "This Priest and Emperor John rules over great lands and many fine cities, and in his kingdom there are many large islands; for this land of India is divided into islands by the great rivers which flow from Paradise. . . . This Priest and Emperor John usually marries the Grand Khan's daughter, and his daughter marries the Grand Khan."*

Wool-bearing trees, men in long white robes, and the tracks of lions and griffins were links in the chain which Columbus forged to convince himself and others. And the Earthly Paradise itself was supposed to be near at hand.

127

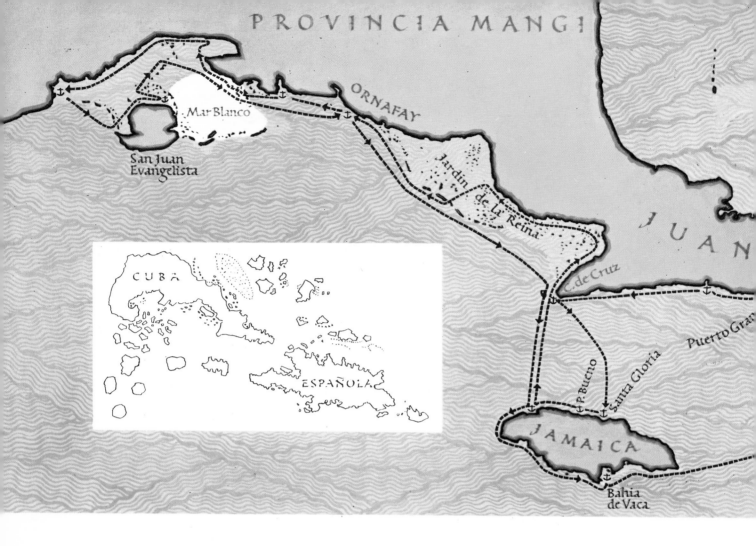

his two daughters, explaining that he wanted the Admiral to take them to the wonderful Kingdom of Castile to serve the Sovereigns. The Admiral explained that it would be a long time before he could return to that country, but he accepted the cacique as a loyal vassal in the name of the Sovereigns and promised to gratify his wish at a later date. They parted on friendly terms, and the caravels went on and passed the eastern tip of Jamaica.

Michele de Cuneo writes: "When we sailed to Española, I was the first to sight land. The Admiral therefore ordered us ashore on a cape where there was an excellent harbour, and he called it Cabo de San Michele Saonese, in my honour, and wrote in his book that he had done so. We sailed on along the coast, finding mountainous shores and good harbours, and we made frequent landings, seeing everywhere innumerable people of the kind to which we were accustomed. And as we sailed along the coast towards our settlement, we found a beautiful island not far offshore, which I was also the first to sight. It was about 25 leagues in circumference, and the Admiral, out of friendship towards me, called it La Bella Saonese [the Fair Savonese. Cuneo, as has been said, was from

Savona]. He gave it to me as a gift, and I took possession of it with the proper words and ceremonies, as the Admiral had done with the other islands in the name of His Majesty the King."

Cuneo does not mention that the Admiral had landed nine men there a few days before to cross the island and tell the people at Isabela that the caravels were safe. Nor does he say anything about the sea monster, perhaps a giant ray, which they saw on the day before they arrived at La Bella Saonese. The general opinion was that the monster presaged a storm, and true enough, a storm blew up.

On September 14 Columbus observed an eclipse of the moon on Cuneo's island. It had been predicted in Regiomontanus' *Ephemerides,* which said that it would be total in Munich at 7:15 *p.m.* According to Abraham Zacuto's *Almanach perpetuum* it was to begin at 5:05 *p.m.* and end at 2:33 *a.m.,* but the last figure is incorrect and should have been 11:33 *p.m.* Columbus tried to calculate his longitude from the local time of the lunar eclipse. Half-hour glasses are not accurate timekeepers,

128

and we do not know how he determined the time and came to the conclusion that the longitudinal difference between Cape St. Vincent and La Bella Saonese corresponded to five and a half hours, i.e., 82° 30′. That result agreed well enough with his earlier estimate, but, in modern terms, it would put the island—the modern Saona— at a longitude of 91° 30′ west, or over 22° west of its true position.

The Admiral had intended to go on to the islands of the Caribs, but when the fleet reached the island of Mona, the plan had to be dropped. Fernando Colón writes: "Henceforward the Admiral made no further daily entries in his book, and he does not say how he returned to Isabela. He only reports that he was very ill, from his exertions, his weakness, and the shortage of food, on the voyage from Mona to San Juan. He had a high fever and a delirium, which deprived him of sight, memory, and all his other faculties. By reason of his sickness, those on board decided to abandon the project of exploring the Carib islands, and they altered course to Isabela, where they arrived five days later, on September 29th."

There is no contemporary map to show Columbus' idea of the archipelago at the End of the Earth, and I have given the islands roughly the outlines that they would have on a modern map, except that the north coast of Cuba turns north, much as Further Asia does on Martellus' map (page 17; see also the maps on pages 21, 79, and 95). On the whole, the discoveries seemed to correspond fairly well to the maps, except that Columbus had found on his first voyage that Cipangu-Española ran east and west, not north and south, and he searched in vain for the city of Zaiton, which ought to have been somewhere to the north or northwest of the Jardin de la Reina. Inset, left: Cuba, Española, and a number of other real and imaginary islands, from Juan de la Cosa's map of the world, 1500. (See also page 157). Juan de la Cosa, like many others, did not believe that Cuba was attached to the continent, though his signature appears on the peculiar document of June 12, 1494. Inset, right: a map of Jamaica from Bordone's Isolario, 1528.

129

Down to earth

In September, 1493, not long after the Admiral had left Cadiz harbor at the head of his large fleet, his brother Bartolomeo was back in Castile after his mission in France. At Seville, he was given a letter in which the Admiral requested him to conduct his two sons to the Court, where he had received a royal promise that they should be employed as pages in the service of Don Juan, the Heir Apparent. Early in 1494, Bartolomeo arrived with his nephews at Valladolid and was well received by the Sovereigns, who also gave him the title that the Admiral had asked for him. When Antonio Torres arrived from Española with his report on the condition of the settlers, and their needs, Don Bartolomeo was immediately dispatched to the Indies, in command of three caravels, loaded with provisions and other necessities. He sailed at the beginning of May, and anchored off Isabela on June 24, 1494.

Three months later, the Admiral, now a very sick man, was in Don Bartolomeo's hands. Together with his brother Don Diego, Don Bartolomeo gave him the best possible care, and we may suppose that for some time they left the Admiral in blissful ignorance of the real state of affairs on Española. Five months passed before the the Admiral was well enough to realize that the island of his dreams had become an inferno, for Indians and Christians alike.

Pedro Margarit's expedition had ended in disaster. The Admiral had assumed that his men would be able to buy their own provisions as they went along, while they explored the island and searched for its treasures. But Spaniards could not live on a handful of maize, cassava, and fruit, and even if they had supplemented their starchy diet with "Indian rats" and large lizards, they were soon reduced to desperate straits by hunger and sickness. Pedro Margarit did not try to control the lust for plunder which his troops were showing; he might well have shared it. Against the express will and command of the Sovereigns, he committed outrages against the Indians, appropriating their goods, their gold, and their women. When the situation was completely out of control, and complaints were trickling back to Isabela, he began to argue with Don Diego on the question of who was in command of the island. In the end, he left the soldiers to look after themselves, and sailed off, with Friar Buil and several other priests, in the caravels which Don Bartolomeo had brought with him.

Technically, of course, Pedro Margarit and the priests well deserved to be branded as deserters. But in his memorandum to the Sovereigns, the Admiral had spoken highly of Margarit, and I can only suppose that the man was temporarily unbalanced through illness. The priests felt that they could not do anything to convert the Indians unless they had some interpreters, and in any case they were soon regarding the absent Admiral as a liar who had misled them about the gold of Española and the alleged peacefulness and amiability of the Indians; so they felt that they could leave the colony with their consciences clear. But one priest, certainly, stayed behind, and the others might have done well to follow his example. Brother Ramón Pane, of the Hieronymite Order, taught himself the local vernacular, and, on the Admiral's suggestion, wrote a report on Indian religious beliefs; but it was not until September, 1496, that he felt he could baptize the first Indians on Española.

We know little of the chaos which must have reigned in the island while the Admiral was away on his search for the rich cities of the continent. A number of Pedro Margarit's solidiers gathered together in Isabela; they might have been sick men hoping to find treatment and comfort from the doctors and priests in the starving settlement. Other small groups went on fighting private campaigns, ravaging and plundering when they met with any resistance. At last, the Indians could stand no more and began to organize reprisals. Some time later, the Admiral discovered that several dozen Spaniards had been waylaid and killed.

In the late autumn of 1494 Antonio Torres arrived from Castile with four caravels, with provisions and other necessities, including women to restore the morale of the settlers. He also carried a letter to the Admiral from the Sovereigns. They thanked him for what he had already accomplished and asked him for more detailed information about the newly discovered islands and the climate, and they told him of the treaty they had signed with the King of Portugal at Tordesillas. They had accepted a demarcation line from the North to the South Pole, but instead of running 100 leagues west of the Cape Verde Islands, as the Admiral had suggested, and the Pope had agreed, it was to run 370 leagues west of them. As they were not sure how this line should be determined in practice, they asked the Admiral to return and advise them. If he himself was not in a position to do so, they added, he could send his brother or anyone else who understood these matters, provided that he was furnished with written instructions, maps, and diagrams.

The Admiral felt unable to return to Castile just then. He was still a sick man. He did not want to tell the Sovereigns to their faces that he had not found any gold, or anything else of any value, on the continent; and he certainly could not have wanted to report that disorder was rife in his viceroyalty. We cannot know what he felt about the white men's conduct in Española, which certainly did not correspond to the Sovereigns' wishes, but in his position he had no alternative but to be loyal to his own men, so he sent a punitive expedition against the men who had dared to attack the Christians. The Spaniards closed in on the Indians with fire and sword, with horses and dogs, and now that the law was on their side, they killed more readily than ever. In the end, they came back to Isabela with 1,600 prisoners, and 550 of the choicest specimens were selected to be sent to Castile as slaves. By contemporary standards, that was legal and correct. They were prisoners taken in battle, and such people could lawfully be enslaved, so the Admiral felt sure that the Sovereigns would have no objection.

Cuneo describes the prisoners thus: "Then it was announced that anyone could take as many as he wished of those that remained; and this was done. And when everybody was satisfied, there were some 400 left, and they were allowed to go wherever they wanted. Among them were many women with infants at the breast. In

order to escape us quickly, and for fear that we might set about catching them again, they left their infants lying on the ground, and ran away....Among those who were captured were a king and two chiefs; it was decided that they were to be shot with arrows on the following day, and accordingly they were put in bonds. But during the night they hit on the idea of gnawing at each other's bonds with their teeth, and this way they worked themselves free and escaped."

Guacanagarí, whose residence was near Isabela, sent two messengers to the Admiral to ask why these things had been done, but the Admiral sent them back to tell Guacanagarí to come in person. Meanwhile, Torres sailed off with the four caravels. The Admiral's brother Don Diego went with him, with instructions to inform the Sovereigns of the Admiral's opinion about the demarcation line. Michele de Cuneo also left Española, and he tells us that two hundred of the Indian slaves died at sea not far from Spain, probably from the cold. More than half of the survivors were seriously ill when they were landed at Cadiz.

The last part of Cuneo's letter tells us that many people remained unconvinced that Juana was a part of the continent. "The Lord Admiral says that he will find Cathay, and on that subject he had a long discussion with an abbot from Lucena, a very learned and wealthy man who had gone to those parts for the mere pleasure of seeing something new. He is a good astronomer and cosmographer, and when he [the Admiral] stated that the aforesaid coast, along which he had sailed 550 leagues, must be the continent by reason of its length, he, the abbot, said no, it was only a very large island. And when we considered the couise we had sailed, most of us were of the same opinion. And this is why the Lord Admiral would not allow him to accompany us to Spain, for if His Majesty the King had asked him his opinion, he would, by his answer, have persuaded the King to abandon the enterprise. And he wants to keep him there until the Lord Adelantado has returned and reported what he has found."

The Admiral had just given the title Adelantado to his brother Bartolomeo. At that time, that title conferred supreme jurisdiction in peace and supreme command in war. Bartolomeo was thus his brother's second-in-command in the Indies, and at the time Cuneo left Isabela he was on the point of setting off with two caravels and a fusta (a small vessel propelled by sails or oars), which had been built in Española. He was under instructions to explore the north part of Juana and push north for five hundred miles along the coast, unless he should have discovered the rich cities of Mangi and Cathay earlier. The Admiral was still convinced that the coast would turn north, as it did on the maps. But the voyage never took place. It was probably the ever loyal Guacanagarí

A stone zemí from Española

who came and told the Admiral that Cacique Guati-guaná had mustered an army on the Vega Real and was planning to drive all the Christians into the sea. Cacique Behechio had killed one of Guacanagarí's wives some time before, and Caonabó had abducted another. Guacanagarí, once so peaceable, now wanted to avenge himself on the more powerful chiefs with the help of the Christians and promised to fight at their side with his men. In his diary of the first voyage, the Admiral had often suggested that he and a handful of men under him could defeat ten thousand Indians and that his crew would be enough to conquer the whole of the island. But that had been only a daydream; he had never really expected that he would have to fight those people "who loved their neighbours as themselves."

He had recovered his health by now, and he marched out at the head of his soldiers in defense of his vice-royalty. He took with him Don Bartolomeo, Alonso de Hojeda, Guacanagarí, and a force composed of two hundred crossbowmen and musketeers, twenty lancers, twenty dogs, and an unknown number of Indians. Ten days after setting out from Isabela, the scouts sent back word that the enemy were just ahead, and the Admiral divided his force into two groups. Fernando Colón writes: "He intended to attack the scattered horde of Indians from different directions, since he believed that the Indians, hearing a great noise from many sides at once, would take fright and break up and flee in panic. And so it fell out. First, the infantry of the two divisions fell upon the hostile Indians and shot them down, with crossbows and muskets; then the cavalry and dogs fell upon them with full force to prevent them from rallying. As a result, the cowardly Indians fled in all directions, hotly pursued by our men, who, with the help of God, soon won complete victory, killing many Indians and capturing others, who were also killed." Fernando Colón says that Guatiguaná's army had 100,000 men, but 10,000 would probably be nearer the truth.

Next, the Admiral wanted to neutralize Caonabó, the ruler of Maguana, who had attacked the settlement of Navidad. Then Alonso de Hojeda, with only ten men under him, went to Caonabó's headquarters and offered him safe conduct to Isabela, to sign a treaty with the Admiral. Caonabó accepted the offer, and after he had provided himself with an armed escort the party set off north across the Vega Real. While they were resting at a river, Alonso de Hojeda took out some brightly polished handcuffs and leg irons and said that the King of Castile was in the habit of wearing them when he rode out on feast days. He suggested that Caonabó should put the royal bracelets on and mount one of the horses. Since Caonabó did not want his escort to see that he was just as badly frightened of the white men's strange animals as most of his subjects were, he allowed them to help him

into the saddle and to put the irons on him. As soon as that was done, his Indians were put to death, and the Christians set off in triumph to Isabela with the valuable prisoner.

Caonabó spent nearly a year in prison at Isabela before he was taken aboard ship and sent to Castile. We are told that he always showed great respect for Hojeda but had no regard for the Admiral, because he had not come in person to capture him.

The Admiral now had no difficulty in restoring peace to Española, though there were still minor skirmishes in various parts of the island. Fernando Colón writes: "He reduced the Indians into such submissiveness and tranquillity that they all promised to pay tribute to Their Catholic Majesties every three months. In Cibao, where the gold mines were, everyone over fourteen years of age was to pay enough gold dust to fill one large hawk's bell; all other persons one *arroba* [25 pounds] of cotton. Whenever an Indian had paid his tribute, he was to be given a token of copper or brass to wear round the neck as a sign that he had paid. Any Indian found without such a token was to be punished."

One day in June, 1495, while the Admiral was preparing to return to Castile with the gold they had collected and the good news that peace had been restored to Española, he saw a thick mist in the sky and a large ring round the sun. Men and animals alike were agitated by this, and that evening at sunset the whole sky turned red as blood. They saw the sea rising far above the high-water marks, and the Indians said that something terrible, which they called *huracán,* was on its way. A strong wind blew up during the night, and it began to rain. By the morning there was a storm coming from the northeast, and everyone was thankful that the ships and the settlement at Isabela were protected from the gale. Then the wind began to rage so loudly that they could not hear each other's voices. The heavens opened and sent torrents of rain down on them, so that the rivers soon broke their banks and swept whole villages away. Giant trees snapped in half or were torn up by the roots, and even on the lee-ward side of the island the sea was whipped to a froth. The caravels at Isabela were blown over on their sides, anchor cables were torn loose, and three of the ships were heeled over so far by the hurricane that they were swamped and sank.

It was as if the Day of Judgment had come, and Las Casas does indeed say that this was God's judgment on the Spaniards for their crimes. Yet the Admiral does not seem to have been conscious of any particular guilt. He had given the Indians a chance to offer their fealty to the Crown of Castile, which had been given by the grace of God, and he had brought them the promise of deliverance from evil and of eternal life. In his victory over these sinful

132

The bell in the church at Isabela, and the strange noise it made, fascinated the natives of Española. The story goes that Alonso de Hojeda managed to induce Caonabó to leave Cibao only by promising to give him the bell as a present.

and unruly multitudes with no more than two hundred sick and poorly armed soldiers he saw only an expression of the will and wonderful mercy of God. However, Las Casas saw things from the Indians' viewpoint.

"When they saw every day how they perished from the inhuman cruelty of the Spaniards, how their people were ridden down by horses, cut to pieces by swords, eaten and torn asunder by dogs, burned alive, and subjected to all kinds of exquisite torture, those of certain provinces, in particular those in the Vega Real, where Guarionex, Maguaná and Caonabó had ruled, decided to resign themselves to their fate and give themselves over into the hands of their enemies without a struggle."

The *Niña* was the only caravel to survive the storm, and so the Admiral ordered his carpenters to set about building a new caravel of the same dimensions as the *Niña*. Other laborers completed the walls and the towers of the settlement, together with the church and Governor's residence, and in the end Isabela was strong enough to withstand an enemy attack. Other fortresses were built in various parts of the island, but the Indians' will to resist was already crushed. Fernando Colón assures us that a Christian could now walk in safety anywhere in the island, and that Indians would even offer to carry him on their backs.

But only a few of the natives of Cibao managed to scrape together their tribute of gold, and the Admiral soon found it necessary to reduce the amount by a half. There were no mines in Española: the gold was panned out of the rivers, or dug out of the silt of old riverbeds. The Indians were not used to hard work, and there was so little gold in the island that it was almost impossible for most of them to pay even half a hawk's bell of gold dust every quarter, and they were savagely punished by the Christian tax collectors. Las Casas writes: "Since violence, provocation, and injustice from the Christians never ceased, some fled to the mountains, and others began to slay the Christians, in return for the wrongs and the torture they had suffered. When that happened, vengeance was immediately taken; the Christians called it punishment, yet not the guilty alone, but all those who lived in a village or a district, were sentenced to execution or torture."

In the gold-producing areas, the fields were deserted. Many of the Indians died of starvation; others poisoned themselves, their wives, and their children to escape from misery and suffering. Fernando Colón is probably quoting the Admiral when he writes: "God wished to punish the Indians and visited them with such great dearth of food and such variety of sickness that He reduced their numbers by two-thirds." Fernando's estimate might have been correct, but the general opinion today is that "only" 100,000 of Española's 300,000 inhabitants died or were killed between 1494 and 1496.

In October, 1495, four caravels arrived from Castile. The Sovereigns had listened to the complaints of Friar Buil and others and were now sending a courtier called Juan Aguado to investigate conditions at the settlement. He reported that nearly everyone at Isabela was either ill or disaffected; anyone who was well enough to do so was inland plundering the country or hunting for gold and slaves. And everyone was longing to go back to Castile.

The new caravel was launched just before the spring of 1496. Her official name was the *Santa Cruz,* but she was always known as the *India.* The *Niña* was thoroughly overhauled and caulked, and by the beginning of March the Admiral was ready to sail for Castile. Don Bartolomeo was to take command in Española and the Indies as Adelantado in his brother's absence, and he was told to choose a site for a new settlement, with a good harbor. The Admiral set sail on March 10, and the Adelantado went with him as far as Puerto Plata, a few leagues to the east, where they thought of establishing the new settlement. But they found the place unsuitable; it was much too far from the gold of Cibao. Don Bartolomeo suggested that the town be built on the River Ozama, in the south of the island. Then the Admiral sailed for home, and the Adelantado went back to Isabela.

Altogether, on the *Niña* and the *India,* there were 225 Christians and 30 Indians, including Caonabó. We do not know how many of them survived the journey to Cadiz, but Caonabó, for one, may be presumed to have died on the way, since nothing more is heard of him. After a month at sea, the two ships put in at Guadalupe to take on food, fuel, and water. Before they could do so, there was a battle with some Carib women, who fought vigorously to defend their village and their property. When that was over, some of the Christians busied them-selves making a large amount of cassava bread, while others went scouting inland. The latter party had the good fortune to capture ten women, including the wife of a cacique. The ships were already overcrowded, and they kept only the cacique's wife and her daughter; the others were set free.

They left Guadalupe on April 20. The Admiral decided to steer a bit farther south than he had done when returning home on his first voyage, in order to avoid the storms of the North Atlantic. They certainly avoided the storms but only at the cost of making it a very lengthy voyage. The Spaniards suffered so much from hunger that many of them were in favor of killing the Indians and eating them, or at least of throwing them overboard so that they should not go on eating the good Christian food. Fifty-three days had to pass before the Admiral could drop anchor at Cadiz, on June 11, 1496.

There he found two caravels under the command of Peralonso Niño, ready to take supplies to Española. Don Diego seems to have sailed back to Española with the ships, but before he left he would have had time to tell his brother the Admiral about the state of opinion at Court.

Joy and sorrow in Castile

"I saw him at Seville on his return, dressed almost like a Franciscan friar," says Las Casas, and reminds us that the Admiral was a fervent admirer of St. Francis. Also Andrés Bernáldez the chronicler, at whose house the Admiral stayed while awaiting the summons to Court, remarked on his unusual clothes, but neither Bernáldez nor Las Casas could see the motives which underlay this outer affectation.

The Admiral was prepared for the worst, that is to say for the royal displeasure, and whatever course things might take, it would be wise to show an outward humility in keeping with the disappointments and disasters on Española. He knew that Friar Buil and others had maligned him, and he suspected that Juan Aguado's report to the Sovereigns would not improve matters. Even though he had the sworn statement of his men that Juana was undoubtedly a part of the mainland, he was aware that many of them were sceptical, and we know from Michele de Cuneo's letter that he was afraid the Sovereigns might abandon the enterprise altogether.

Opposition, and ridicule, Columbus found in plenty, whether among the seamen of Andalusia or among the place hunters at Court. "Some of those Spaniards who went to look for gold came back with faces the colour of gold, though lacking its brightness," writes the historian Oviedo. But by now the Admiral had managed to squeeze a substantial amount of gold out of Cibao. "A necklace of gold links weighing 600 castellanos [2760 grams], which I saw and held in my hands," Bernáldez writes. "Many belts and masks, with inlays of gold in the eyes and ears. And unwrought gold dust, fine, or coarse like peas and beans, some pieces as large as pigeons' eggs," says Fernando Colón.

But it was not the gold which was to convince the Sovereigns, if they really needed convincing. Perhaps they had never fully believed in the golden roofs of Cipangu or in the inexhaustible wealth of the Indies. "For I maintained to Your Highnesses that all profits from this enterprise should be devoted to the conquest of Jerusalem, and Your Highnesses smiled. . . ." Ferdinand and Isabella were realists and could hardly have expected to make any permanent gains unless their own contribution had been a large and wholehearted one, and they had no intention of abandoning their Indian enterprise. The only people who had expected immediate rewards in the form of gold and other treasures had been the Admiral himself and those who went with him, dazzled by the descriptions and promises he had given them. There is nothing to suggest that the Sovereigns expected any immediate return for their investment.

Columbus had promised them such boundless wealth, and he seems often to have suffered agonies of remorse when he could not provide it, but until his dying day he made the most frantic efforts to keep his promises. "May it please God that what is happening to us is for the glory of God and of Your Highnesses. Were it for my own sake alone, I would no longer endure these torments and dangers, for not a day passes but that we see death staring us in the face."

Gold, and plenty of it, would naturally have been a welcome addition to the rather depleted Treasury of Castile. But when we read the Sovereigns' letters and instructions to the Admiral and to others concerned in the administration of the Indian enterprise, we are struck above all by their concern for the welfare of their subjects, including the Indians of Española and the other islands. They were disappointed that their Viceroy and Governor seemed to have had difficulty in maintaining peace and order, but they were far too well used to intrigue and slander to believe the tales of Friar Buil and other such renegades. They had realized that the Admiral, as a foreigner, would have trouble with the Spaniards, and that might have been the reason why, after his first voyage, they had given him more honors and privileges than he himself had asked for. Naturally there must have been many people who envied him from the very beginning; and then there were his unfulfilled promises, his temporary weakness and indecision, his pride and his ill-considered favoring of his brothers, which made him many enemies.

In due time he received a friendly and reassuring letter with instructions to attend at Court. He set off with his retinue, again a small triumphal procession with half-naked Indians and the riches and curiosities of their country. A brother of Caonabó's wore the aforesaid heavy gold chain round his neck, others wore the masks and belts, and still others carried boxes, baskets, and cages containing cotton, spices, red and green parrots, lizards, and other animals.

In Burgos the Admiral once again fell on his knees before Ferdinand and Isabella. He gave them an account of the voyage, was questioned, and gave wise and satisfactory answers. His words might have run in the same way as he later wrote in a letter: "Your Highnesses sent me out a second time, and before long, not by my own powers but by the grace of God, I discovered three hundred and thirty leagues of the continent at the extremity of the East, and seven hundred islands of importance over and above those I discovered on my first voyage, and I sailed round the island of Española, which in its circumference is greater than the whole of Spain and where there are people innumerable, who shall pay tribute. Thereafter came the slander and calumny about the enterprise, which had already begun there, because I had not immediately sent caravels laden with gold, for nobody reckoned how little time there had been, nor thought of the many difficulties I spoke of. Hence, for my sins, or as I rather hope for my salvation, I was held in abhorrence, and all my orders and behests were opposed."

The Admiral describes his meeting with the Sovereigns and his reception at Court: "And I told You of all the nations I had seen, among whom many souls may be saved; and of the services done by the islanders of Española, how they were made to pay tribute, and how they took You as their Sovereigns and Lords. And I brought You abundant evidence of gold, of which there are mines and very great nuggets, and likewise of copper. And I came to You with many kinds of spices, of which it would be wearisome to write, and I told You of the great amounts of brazil wood there, and of innumerable other things.

"All this was of no avail with certain persons who were determined to speak ill of the enterprise, and had already begun to do so. Nor did it avail to speak of the service of God in the salvation of so many souls, nor to say that the glory of Your Highnesses had risen above that of any Prince until this day. . . . And it did not avail to speak of the things which great Princes throughout the world have done to increase their fame, as of Solomon, who sent ships from Jerusalem to the end of the East to visit Mount Sopora [Ophir], in which the ships were engaged for three years, which mountain Your Highnesses today possess in the island of Española; or of Alexander, who sent to examine the government of the island of Taprobane [Ceylon] in India; or of the Emperor Nero, who sent men to discover the sources of the Nile and to find out why its waters increase in the summer, when other rivers are at their lowest; or of many other great things which Princes have done; or to say that such tasks are given to Princes to perform. . . .

"The more I said, the greater were the efforts made to disparage what I had done, to abhor what I had revealed; nor did any consider how fair it seemed throughout the world, and how greatly Your Highnesses are regarded among all Christians for having undertaken this enterprise, so that there was no one, great or small, who did not desire news of it. Your Highnesses answered me, encouraging me and saying that I should feel no concern, since You gave no weight or credit to any who maligned this enterprise to You."

When the Admiral found that the sun of favor again shone over him, he immediately asked for eight caravels. He wanted to send two of them to Española at once with everything the settlers needed, and to take the other six to discover the large country which, if the King of Portugal was right, should lie somewhere in the ocean to the south of the islands. It was also in the south, near the equator, that he expected to find the greatest treasures. Long ago,

Aristotle had written that they were to be found there, and the Admiral himself had just received a letter from one Jaime Ferrer de Blanes, who had spent many years in the East. "I can tell you that in the equatorial regions there are great and valuable goods, such as precious stones, gold, spices, and drugs, and I can tell you this because I have had many conversations on this matter in the Levant, in Alcaire and Domas [Cairo and Damascus], and because I am a jeweller, and for that reason wanted to learn from those people who came to those places from distant lands, from what lands or what provinces they brought the aforesaid goods, and what I could gather from many Indians and Arabs and Ethiopians was that most of those things of value come from a very hot country where the inhabitants are black or brown; and therefore, as I see it, when Your Lordship finds any such people, there will not fail to be an abundance of the said goods; even though Your Lordship knows more on these matters in his sleep than I do when I am awake."

The Sovereigns promised the Admiral that everything would be arranged according to his wishes, but circumstances arose which made him wait a long time for his ships and equipment.

War with France was impending; moreover, the Sovereigns were fully occupied in arranging dynastic marriages for their children. João II of Portugal had died and had been succeeded on the throne by his cousin, Emanuel. The Sovereigns' eldest daughter, Doña Isabel, had been married to João II's son Afonso; she was now a widow, and the new king was begging for her hand in marriage, but she had not yet granted it. Ferdinand and Isabella now came to an agreement with the Emperor Maximilian about their two younger children. Doña Juana was to marry the Emperor's son, Archduke Philip of Hapsburg, who had just inherited the Burgundian throne through his mother, and the Crown Prince Don Juan was to marry the Emperor's daughter Margarita. At the same time an alliance was made with England: their eleven-year-old daughter Doña Catalina, better known to English readers as Catherine of Aragon, was betrothed to Henry VII's son Arthur, Prince of Wales.

All these arrangements cost money, and since it was considered necessary that Doña Juana be escorted to the Archduke in Flanders by a fleet of 130 magnificently equipped vessels, the Admiral could not at the moment be given the eight caravels he had asked for. In due course, the 130 ships returned, with Princess Margarita and her retinue. The Admiral won considerable acclaim, and further strengthened his position with the Sovereigns, by correctly predicting the day on which the fleet bearing the Princess should arrive at the port of Laredo in Astúrias.

On April 3, 1497, the Admiral attended the marriage of Don Juan and Princess Margarita in Burgos, and

Vasco da Gama is often mentioned in the same breath as Columbus, but he was only an instrument, a soldier and commander, chosen from among many others. He had been shown the course he had to take, and his chief pilot, Pero d'Allemquer, was the man who led his fleet in a wide arc across the South Atlantic, so that they could make the best use of the trade winds. This is no disparagement of Vasco da Gama: he might well stand beside the astronauts of today. But not beside Columbus.

twenty days later the Sovereigns at last issued the first instructions about the ships which were to go to Española. In April, 1495, after seeing the reports from Friar Buil, Pedro Margarit, and the other malcontents, which described the conditions on the island and the disaffection of the settlers, the Sovereigns had issued a decree entitling any Castilian to search for gold on Española, provided that he gave the Crown two-thirds of what he found. The Admiral rightly considered that this infringed the privileges he had been given, and he did in fact persuade the Sovereigns to issue a new decree in June, 1497, which revoked the earlier one, but in practice it turned out to be impossible to retract the permission given to the settlers.

On January 23 of the following year, the trusty old *Niña*, in company with the *India*, could at last set sail with food, supplies, and women. During this last period of delay, the Sovereigns had been engrossed with other matters, some joyful and some sad. Doña Isabel, the widow of the Portuguese Crown Prince, had agreed to marry King Emanuel of Portugal on condition that he deported the Jews from his kingdom; many of those whom her parents had expelled from Castile had found refuge there. The wedding was celebrated in the frontier town of

Valencia de Alcántara; and in that town the Sovereigns received the information that Don Juan was at the point of death in Salamanca. After only six months of marriage, the young Princess Margarita was a widow, and Castile had no male heir to the throne.

At this same time the Admiral received news that four Portuguese ships under the command of Vasco da Gama had left Lisbon to sail to the Indies by the long and arduous way round Africa.

Not many volunteers were ready to accompany the Admiral to the Indian islands, those lands of hunger and sickness, and so the Sovereigns had issued an edict, decreeing among other things that "any person of the male sex among Our many subjects and countrymen who up to the time of the publication of this Edict shall have committed any kind of murder or any other crime of whatsoever kind or degree, except heresy, lèse majesté, high treason, treachery, forgery, sodomy, or theft of copper, gold or silver, or of other goods belonging to Us in Our Kingdom, shall go in his own person to Española, and serve there at his own cost in such wise as the Admiral may in Our name command. Those who have incurred sentence of death

137

shall serve for two years, and those who have incurred any lesser sentence, such as the loss of a limb, shall serve for one year, and shall then be free of further punishment."

We may presume that most of the criminals who thus escaped the gallows and other forms of contemporary justice were shipped straight to Española; very few of them could have taken part in the actual voyage of discovery, since the Admiral has no word of complaint against his crew.

The Sovereigns had certainly shown their generosity by signing a whole series of orders for the expedition, including a grant of 1,800,000 *maravedis* for expenses, but by February 17, 1498, the Admiral had received only 350,094 *maravedis*. In the end, the expedition had to be financed by a loan from Doña Isabel's dowry, and by the profits from the sale of the slaves Peralonso Niño had brought back from Española; these had been declared to be lawful prisoners of war and could therefore be legally sold. Las Casas quotes what the Admiral himself had to say about his difficulties: "When I left the Indies, I hoped to get some rest, but I found the difficulties of my task were doubled; there were hindrances and delays in obtaining the means to equip the expedition, there were vexations from the officers of the Crown, there were hindrances and backbiting from persons around Their Highnesses concerning everything that involved the expedition to the Indies; and so it seemed to me that what I had already achieved was not sufficient, and that I must renew my efforts to win further recognition."

We do not know whether Don Juan de Fonseca, now Bishop of Badajoz and still in charge of West Indian affairs, supported the Admiral or not. Las Casas and Fernando Colón assure us that Fonseca was an enemy, but Bernáldez says that the Admiral and Fonseca together paid a visit to his house, and in a letter which the Admiral wrote at a later date he refers to the Bishop in friendly terms. But there were many other officials and contractors in higher and lower positions who could make difficulties for this unpopular foreigner. We do know that on the eve of his departure the Admiral lost his temper with one of Fonseca's insolent subordinates and knocked him down.

He might have felt that predominating circumstances might weaken the Royal favor he was then enjoying, for he persuaded the Sovereigns to reaffirm the rights and privileges they had already granted him; at the same time he obtained a remission of the eighth of the expenses which he was expected to contribute to the supply ships for Española, to cover the three years he had had to spend in idleness in Castile. He had been criticized for making his brother Adelantado without asking permission, but

the Sovereigns now confirmed the appointment. He was also empowered to give plots of land to Castilians living on Española, but he was instructed to see that all brazil wood, gold, and other metals were reserved for the Crown. As an act of princely favor, his two sons, who had been pages to the late Don Juan, were now admitted as pages in the Queen's Household.

As one last precaution, he made his will, covering his titles and privileges, as well as his personal possessions. Everything was to go to his eldest son, Diego, but if Diego should die before Columbus did, the inheritance was to go first to the Admiral's son Fernando; then to his brother Bartolomeo and to his eldest son; and then to his brother Diego and to his eldest son. The heir was to give a fixed percentage of the revenue from the Indies to these relations for the period of their lifetime, and a further sum to the Bank of San Giorgio in Genoa, part of the interest on which was to be used to ease the burden of taxation for the Genoese, and part to maintain a town house in which any member of the Colombo family could live in a style befitting his station. The heir was also required to build a church on Española, dedicated to Santa María de la Concepción, and a hospital, as fine as the hospitals of Castile and Italy. He was also to maintain four theologians to work for the conversion of the Indians of Española. The Admiral was afraid that the Sovereigns might not use the profits of the Indies to equip an army for the liberation of Jerusalem, so he also enjoined the heir to open a separate account with the Bank of San Giorgio, to pay for a Crusade. When this fund was large enough to make an appreciable contribution toward the cost of an army, perhaps the example would be followed by the Sovereigns.

Six ships had been hired for the expedition. Since the *Niña* and the *India* had left some time earlier, the Admiral decided to send three ships straight to Española while he himself sailed farther south with the rest. His flagship on this voyage was called the *Santa María de Guia,* and she was probably a round-bellied ship of the same type as the *Santa María* of the first voyage. Pedro de Terreros, his steward on the first voyage, was now captain of *La Vaqueños,* a 70-ton caravel. Hernan Péres was captain of *El Correo,* probably a considerably smaller caravel. The three other ships were commanded by Alonso Sánchez de Carvajal, who had commanded a vessel on the second voyage, Pedro de Harana, whose sister was the Admiral's mistress, and the Admiral's cousin, Giovanni Colombo, from Genoa. This time the fleet was fitted out in Seville. Toward the end of May, the six ships were sailed down the Guadalquivir to Sanlúcar de Barrameda, where the Admiral went aboard. On May 30 they made for the open sea.

Columbus made his third voyage in the name of the Holy Trinity.

Another World

Castile had been at war with France for the last five months, and as there was a rumor that French privateers off Cape St. Vincent were cutting Spanish communications with the Canaries, the Admiral decided to put in first at the Portuguese island of Porto Santo. He arrived there after eight days at sea, but the inhabitants thought that his ships were the French privateers, and disappeared inland, taking their goods with them. So the fleet went on to Funchal in Madeira, where the Admiral was given a hospitable reception, "for he was well known there and had lived there for some time," as Las Casas puts it. They replenished their stores of fresh water, firewood, and other necessary provisions, and on June 16 continued south, and reached Gomera five days later. As the ships sailed into San Sebastian, three other ships sailed out, and Columbus soon discovered that these were two Frenchmen and a captured Spanish caravel. He dispatched the fastest of his caravels in pursuit, and when the Spaniards on the captured vessel saw that help was on the way, they overpowered the French crew and took her back into port themselves. The Admiral's ships spent only one day at San Sebastian, taking aboard wood, water, and food, "especially cheeses, of which there was an abundance at that place." It was probably out of respect for the French ships that they made such haste to be away.

From here, three caravels made straight for Española, in accordance with the Admiral's orders, which, Las Casas tells us, ran: "He instructed them to sail 850 leagues west by south and told them that they would then be near the island of Dominica. From Dominica they were to steer west-north-west towards the island of San Juan, and then sail to the south of it, as that was the direct course for Isabela Nueva, and when San Juan was behind them they were to sail south of the island of Mona, and thence make for the cape on Española which he called San Raphael. Thence to Saona, which, he says, makes a good harbour on the way to Española. Seven leagues further on there is another island. The distance from the place to Isabela is 25 leagues." This was a clear and accurate description. By "Isabela" the Admiral means Isabela Nueva, New Isabela, the town his brother Don Bartolomeo had founded on the Ozama; Columbus did not know that it had already been given the name Santo Domingo.

139

The instruments used by navigators out on the high seas to measure the altitude of the stars were the quadrant and the astrolabe. The nautical astrolabe was a graduated bronze ring with a dioptric sight on a rotating arm. The quadrant (see page 79) was probably easier to use on a moving deck because it was lighter, and Columbus often explicitly says that he made observations with a quadrant. From the measurements he made on his third voyage, he came to the conclusion that the polestar revolved round the true pole at a distance of approximately 5°, instead of the usual 3° 30'. It is impossible to say whether this was because of his frequent attacks of weak sight, the unsteadiness of the ship, or autosuggestion. Later, he gave a sensational explanation for this phenomenon.

In the name of the Holy Trinity, Columbus left Gomera on June 21, with the *Santa María de Guia, La Vaqueños,* and *El Correo.* First he made for Ferro, the westernmost of the Canaries, and then pressed farther south toward the Cape Verde Islands. His object was to see whether there was any land in the southwest toward the equator, and if so whether it lay east or west of the line of demarcation which by the Treaty of Tordesillas ran from pole to pole 370 leagues west of the Cape Verde Islands.

After six days' sailing the fleet sighted the island of Sal and then passed on to the leper colony on Boavista, where they halted to obtain salt and catch goats. The Admiral was entertained by the governor of the island, who told him that three times a year turtles came to the island in hundreds of thousands and that the lepers used to bathe their sores in the healing blood of these creatures. On June 30, the fleet moved on to the island of São Tiago, where they hoped to get cattle for Española. But they were disappointed, for there were none to be had. The men were now suffering severely from the heat, and some were already showing signs of sickness, so the Admiral decided to sail on. Some of the leading men on the island had assured him that 12 leagues to the west, on the island of Fogo, it was sometimes possible to see an island to the southwest. They added that King João II had been eager to send out expeditions in that direction, and that they had seen canoes from Guinea, loaded with goods and bound for the west.

Las Casas writes: "On Wednesday, July 4th, he gave orders to weigh anchor and set sail from that island of Sant Iago, where, so he says, he had never seen the sun or the stars since the day of his arrival, but the sky was covered with a mist that seemed thick enough to cut with a knife; and the great heat of that place tormented them. He gave orders to set course for the south-west, which is the way from those islands to the south and to the equator, in the name, as he says, of the Holy and Indivisible Trinity. For thus he would come to the latitudes of Sierra Leone and Cabo Sant Ana in Guinea, which lie below the equator. There, in those latitudes, more gold and objects of value can be found. He says that he intended then to sail to the west, if it pleased the Lord, and thence to Española. And on this course he would test the aforementioned theory of King Don João [about an undiscovered country]. He also hoped to check the rumour current among the Indians of Española, to the effect that black men had come to Española from the south and south-east, carrying spears with their points made of a metal called *guanín,* of which metal he had sent a piece to Their Highnesses to be assayed, and it had been found to be made of 18 parts of gold, 6 of silver, and 8 of copper."

When the fleet had sailed 120 leagues to the southwest, they came across seaweed of the same kind as they had seen on the earlier voyages. The Admiral took the altitude of the polestar and noted down that they were on the latitude of 5 degrees north. On July 13 they entered the belt of calms. "So suddenly and unexpectedly did the wind drop and the extreme and unwonted heat strike them that no one would go below decks to see to the casks of wine and water, which burst and snapped their

on the morning of July 31 the Admiral decided to alter course to north by east, in order to reach Dominica or one of the Carib islands. They continued on this course until noon.

"But, merciful as the Divine Majesty has always been towards me, it chanced that a seaman from Huelva, my servant Alonso Pérez, climbed to the top and saw land 15

The three peaks of Trinidad

hoops. The wheat burnt like fire; the salt pork and other meat scorched and went bad. This heat lasted for eight days. The first day was clear, with a sun that scorched them. Then God gave him respite, for the next six days were cloudy and wet."

The description is exaggerated, of course. The Admiral was seriously ill during most of his third voyage—Las Casas mentions gout and insomnia—and his exaggerations, together with his more peculiar statements, should be seen against this background of illness.

The wind seems to have come the next day, since Las Casas' abstract of the diary, and a letter from Columbus to the Sovereigns, both state that seventeen days of favorable winds followed. But in spite of the wind and rain it stayed uncomfortably hot until July 20. Once the calm was over, the Admiral altered his course due west, since he did not dare to go farther south into the windless latitudes, where it might be hotter still. On July 22 they saw large flocks of birds flying northeast and hoped that this was a sure sign that land was near. As time went on, the Admiral calculated that they had come 370 leagues west of the Cape Verde Islands; and they had not sighted any new land on the Portuguese side of the demarcation line. Their supply of drinking water was getting low, and

leagues away to the west, and it appeared in the shape of three rocks or mountains."

The Admiral had already decided that the first new land he discovered on this voyage would be called after the Holy Trinity, and he took it as a miraculous sign from God that the first land sighted took the form of three peaks. As the fleet drew nearer, the three peaks turned into a large island, which Columbus called Trinidad. Toward evening they reached a cape which reminded them of a galley under sail, and they called it the Cabo de la Galera. They thought that they saw a good harbor to the west of the cape, but it turned out to be too shallow, and they continued west all that night in the light breeze with little sail along the south coast of Trinidad, and in the bright moonlight they saw that the woods came right down to the water, and wonderful scents came out to them from land.

When dawn came they saw smoke and tilled fields, and after sailing for a further five leagues they found a bay and dropped anchor. They took water from a river and bathed. They saw footprints and fishing tackle, goat

141

tracks, aloes, and palms. Everything was incredibly beautiful, and they gave thanks to the Holy Trinity. To the south they could make out another island, lying very low like a shadow on the horizon, and they estimated it as at least twenty leagues long. The Admiral called it Isla Sancta.

As far as we know, this was the first time any Europeans ever saw the South American continent. Isla Sancta was probably what is known today as the Punta Bombeador in the great delta of the Orinoco.

We may speculate freely about João II's "knowledge" of a large continent in the western ocean. It might have been only one of those misty islands in the southwest which could sometimes be seen from Fogo, the same sort of island which the inhabitants of São Tiago had discussed with Columbus. Some home-bound mariner from Guinea might have been carried far off his course and caught a glimpse of the South American coast and reported it in Lisbon. But if João II had been so sure, why hadn't he sent people to take possession in his name? I am more inclined to think that the King of Portugal simply wanted to secure an adequate amount of the ocean for his own kingdom, partly on the off-chance of finding some undiscovered islands, but perhaps mainly because Portugal needed most of the South Atlantic for the projected course round the Cape of Good Hope.

Columbus had certainly observed the prevailing winds on his earlier voyages to Guinea, and he had probably drawn bolder and more accurate deductions about the pattern and the extent of the trade winds, and the westerlies, than had occurred to his Portuguese instructors. Perhaps, too, it had been the knowledge of his voyage to the West Indies that had opened the eyes of the Portuguese pilots to the possibility that they might make better use of these winds for their voyages to the Cape of Good Hope. However, for that they needed plenty of room to maneuver in the ocean; in fact, they needed the whole sea to the east of the demarcation line agreed upon in the Treaty of Tordesillas.

Hitherto, they had battled their way down the west coast of Africa in their lateen-rigged caravels, more often than not *against* the wind. When Vasco da Gama set out with his square-rigged ships, quite a different course was set. From the Cape Verde Islands, they sailed as far southeast as they could with the northeast trade winds. Once through the calm belt, they sailed cross-wind to the southwest and south in the southeast trade winds until approximately 35 degrees south, where they entered the belt of the westerlies and could run straight to the southern extremity of Africa. This involved a long detour but took considerably less time than the old route into the teeth of the wind.

When Cabral followed this course with his large fleet in 1500, he swung so far west into the Atlantic that he discovered a new part of South America, the region which was later known as Brazil. And that part did actually lie on the Portuguese side of the demarcation line. Historians are still discussing whether this was a pure coincidence or whether he had deliberately taken a more westerly course on the King's instructions in order to rediscover and annex a country with which the Portuguese were already acquainted.

The anchorage did not protect the Admiral and his fleet from the wind, and so they spent only one day there and then sailed on west until the sea narrowed to a strait, where yellowish waters churned in turmoil. They came to the end of an island, a low-lying cape which the Admiral called Punta del Arenal, Sandy Point, and after rounding it they found calmer waters on the lee side, and they dropped anchor.

Twenty-four Indians came out toward them in a large canoe, and shouts were exchanged, but nobody could understand what the Indians were saying. After some unsuccessful attempts to entice the Indians aboard by showing them a brass chamber pot and other bright objects, the Admiral ordered the ship's boys to play the tabor and strike up a dance on the poop. The Indians probably took this to be a war dance, for they began to shoot arrows at the flagship. The dance was broken off, and the Spaniards replied with a volley from their crossbows. Thereupon the Indians paddled off, and nothing more was seen of any natives on Trinidad.

The Admiral had noticed that they were all well built young men, with paler coloring than the natives on Española; he had expected to find darkskinned men in the land of gold, close to the equator. He also recorded that the climate was mild, so much so that it felt almost chilly in the mornings, though the sun was in Leo. Time and time again he recorded in his diary how he had noticed on all his voyages across the ocean that the air became cooler after he had gone a hundred leagues west of the Azores. It was not only the air that was different; the sky and the sea had also improved. Here at Trinidad the sea was not salt anymore; it was almost drinkable. He also noted that the westward current in the strait between Trinidad and Isla Sancta was faster than the Guadalquivir at Seville, and the difference between high-tide and low-tide levels was so great that carracks could be caulked without being careened. Day and night he heard the sea roaring in the strait as if great ocean waves were breaking on the shore.

He writes: "And very late that night, when I was on deck, I heard a terrible roaring, which came towards the ship from the south....And I saw the sea rise from east to west, like a hill as high as the ship, and advance slowly towards me. And on its crest was a wave which roared

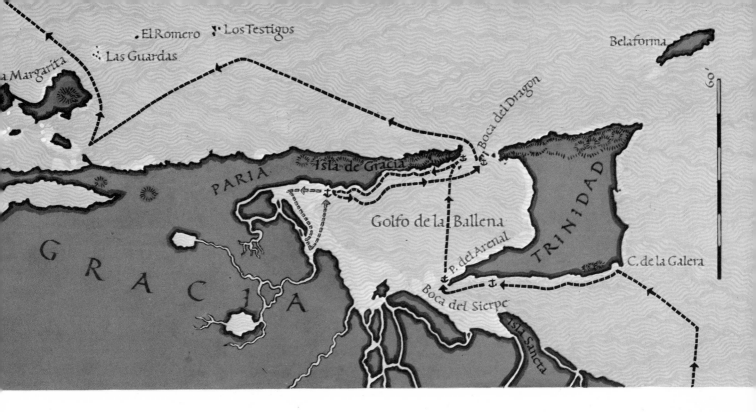

along with a very great noise. . . . I remember to this very day the fear I had that the wave would smash the ship when it reached her, but it passed on and went into the strait, where it went for a long distance." To this place the Admiral gave the name Boca del Sierpe, the Serpent's Mouth.

On the following morning, which was August 4, they sailed north toward a mountainous island which the Admiral had already christened Isla de Gracia, and soon they sighted other islands, smaller but just as high in the water, rising from the sea between this island and the northern part of Trinidad. Isla de Gracia stretched far to the west, farther than they could see in the damp mist which had come up, and when they reached its eastern-most cape in the evening they saw that the woods came right down to the waterline, as they did on Trinidad, and deduced that this part of the world must be free from storms. They anchored for the night and noted that there were strong currents here too, and they heard the sea roaring as loudly as in the Boca del Sierpe.

The Admiral writes: "I had not yet conversed with any people from these lands, which I greatly desired to do, and so I sailed west along the coast, and the further I went the fresher and more wholesome became the waters of the sea. When I had sailed a great distance, I came to a place where the land seemed to be cultivated. I anchored and sent the boats ashore. My men found that people had been there recently, and that the whole mountain was swarming with monkeys. They came back, and I thought that as the country here was mountainous there might be flatter land to the west, which was presumably inhabited.

This map shows the course taken by the expedition from the time it discovered Trinidad to the time it left Margarita for Santo Domingo. The whole area south and southwest of Trinidad consists of the Orinoco delta. The great wave which swept past the anchorage at Punta del Arenal was probably caused by a submarine volcanic eruption. The Golfo de la Ballena was so called because they had seen a whale there; it is now known as the Gulf of Paria, from the Paria Peninsula, which Columbus first took to be an island and called Isla Gracia. Later, he extended the name Gracia to cover the whole of this south continent. The red dotted line indicates the approximate course taken by El Correo *when reconnoitering the mouths of the rivers now known as the Rio Grande and the Rio San Juan. The island of Belaforma, which they sighted on the northeastern horizon, is the modern Tobago. The white patches south of Margarita represent the rich pearl fisheries which Columbus knew by repute but was never able to visit personally. Only the principal anchorages are shown.*

"I gave orders to weigh anchor and set off along the coast to the end of this mountainous stretch, and there I anchored in the mouth of a river. And immediately many people came, and they told me that they called this land Paria, and that it was more populous further west. I took four of them, and then went further west, and when I had sailed eight leagues, I found, beyond a point which I called the Punta del Aguja [Needle Point],

143

a country which was the loveliest in all the world, and very populous....

"Some of the natives came out to the ship at once in their canoes and asked me, on behalf of their king, to go ashore. And when they saw that I was not inclined to do that, they came out in hordes to the ship, and many of them wore pieces of gold on their breasts, and some had pearls round their arms. I rejoiced greatly when I saw these things, and spared no effort to find out where they obtained them, and they told me that they got them there, and in a land further north. I had wished to remain there, but the supplies I had with me, corn and wine and meat for the people here [on Española], were beginning to go bad; and I had carried them so far, and with such great labour. Accordingly, I sought only to bring them to safety, without delaying on any account.

"I endeavoured to obtain some of those pearls, and sent the boats ashore....They told me that no sooner had the boats reached the shore than two chiefs with all the people came towards them, and they think that they were father and son. And they guided them to a very large house, with sloping roofs and not round, like a tent, as the others are [on Española]....They set out bread and many kinds of fruit and various kinds of wine, both white and red, but not made from grapes....Both sides were sorry that they could not understand one another, they because they wished to ask about our country, and our men because we wished to learn something about theirs. And when they had been given a meal there in the house of the older man, the younger man took them to his own house and invited them to another meal of the same kind, and then they went to the boats and came back to the ship.

"I weighed anchor at once and made all speed to save the supplies, which I had brought with such labour and which were now going bad; and also to restore my own health. For my eyes were sore from lack of sleep, and even though I had gone thirty-three days without sleep and was blind for some time on the voyage which I had made to discover the continent, my eyes were not then so sore and did not bleed or give me such great discomfort as now."

They went further west, but the sea became shallow, and low-lying islands began to appear to the west and south. The Admiral sent the shallow-draught *El Correo* to reconnoiter the coast and the waters, and when she came back her captain reported that he had entered four bays whose waters were clear and fresh, and it was assumed that these bays were in fact estuaries. They had not been able to find a way out to the north. The Admiral would not believe that this was the mouth of a large river, "for he knew that neither the Ganges, the Euphrates, nor the Nile carried so much fresh water. What puzzled him was that he could not see a land which was large enough to contain the sources of such large rivers, unless,

he says, it was a continent. These are his words," Las Casas tells us.

This is where Columbus began to suspect the true extent of his discovery. But he was seriously ill. His mental processes were rather hazy, and his diary, as abridged by Las Casas, frequently bursts into violent denunciatons of "enemies" and "doubters" in Castile and complains bitterly about all the difficulties he had been forced to overcome. He also wrote at this time: "Your Highnesses have also gained these immense territories, which amount to *Another World,* in which Christendom will take great joy, and our Holy Faith will in time wax mightily. I say this in all honour, and because I wish Your Highnesses to be the greatest rulers in the world, I mean rulers of it all."

This is the first time Columbus mentions "another world" *(que son otro mundo),* and he means a world unknown to Ptolemy, Marco Polo, and all cosmographers and mapmakers past and present. He does not yet venture to regard it as an undiscovered continent, but he can see the islands, and he feels that they may well be large and wealthy ones.

They did not find any pearl oysters in that bay, though the Admiral called it the Golfo de las Perlas, and so they sailed back to the strait between Isla de Gracia and Trinidad. They found a good harbor on the westernmost island in the strait and spent the night there at anchor, and on August 13 they succeeded, with considerable difficulty, in sailing through the strong currents of the strait, which they called the Boca del Dragon, the Dragon's Mouth. They set course to the west and sailed north of Isla de Gracia in order to reach the northwest part of the island, where they had heard there were pearls to be found.

By now, the Admiral's eyes were bleeding more severely than ever, and he was almost blind for long periods at a time. Unable to keep a lookout himself, and unwilling to trust the discretion of others, he gave orders to hold a course well out from the coast. An island was just visible to the far north, and as it was the Feast of the Assumption of the Blessed Virgin, they called the island Asunción. To the northwest they saw a group of small islands, and they called them Los Testigos, The Witnesses. When the Admiral was told that they had sighted a large island rising high to the west, he decided that it should be called Margarita, after the widowed princess who had been Don Juan's consort for six months. Then they made for land, in the direction of Margarita and Isla de Gracia.

Las Casas writes: "The preceding day, Monday, and this day, Tuesday, the Admiral seems to have sailed some 30 or at most 40 leagues from the Boca del Dragon, although there is no record to that effect, since he was so

ill at the time: indeed, he expresses his sorrow that he did not write everything down, as he should have done. He observed that the land stretched further and seemed more level and more beautiful towards the west. . . . So he concluded that so extensive a land was not an island but a continent, and, as if addressing Their Majesties, he says: 'I have come to believe that this is a vast continent, hitherto unknown. I am greatly supported in this view by the great river and by the fresh water of the sea, and I am also supported by Esdras, who in Book 4, Chapter 6, says that six parts of the world consist of dry land, and one part of water. . . . And now the truth appears, and before long will appear in still greater measure. And if this is a continent, it is a wonderful thing, and all men of learning will agree, since so great a river flows from it that it makes the sea fresh for 48 leagues from shore.' These are his words."

In the end, the Admiral's illness, and his anxiety about the decomposing food supplies he was carrying, made him abandon his search for pearls, and his attempts to discover the true extent of the new continent. He could not have known that he was practically on top of the valuable pearl fisheries on August 15 when he gave orders to set course for Española.

Las Casas says of the people of Paria: " They would give nothing for beads, but they gave everything they had for hawk's bells, they did not want anything else. Brass they valued highly. Here the Admiral says that when anything from Castile was put into their hands, the Indians would hold it to their noses to see what it smelt like. They brought with them two or three kinds of parrots, he says, especially the very large long-tailed ones that are also found on the island of Guada-lupe. They brought cotton fabrics, elaborately embroidered and woven in colours, like those which come from the rivers of Sierra Leone in Guinea."

It was probably the brass bells, more than any-thing else, that the Indians kept smelling at; pre-sumably they wanted to see if they contained any copper, which was far more sought-after than gold in that part of the world. Las Casas says that the natives had "golden eyes" round their necks. These were probably gold discs, imported from the west, embossed with eye-shaped figures. The Spaniards saw some horseshoe collars, also, but Columbus was not inter-ested in these, as they did not seem to contain much gold. They were in fact made of guanín, an alloy of gold, silver, and copper, but the Spaniards had not yet recognized its full value.

The Earthly Paradise

The thoughts which occupied Columbus after he had come to the conclusion that Isla de Gracia, the Isle of Grace, was in reality a continent, are most clearly reflected in the letter which he wrote to the Sovereigns from Española. I have already quoted certain passages from it in the last two chapters. What follows is taken from the latter part of the letter.

"No sooner had I reached this line [100 leagues west of the Azores] than the temperature became cool, and the further I went the cooler it was; but I did not find the stars to be consistent with this observation. When night fell, I found the Pole Star had an altitude of 5°, with the Guards [the two outermost stars of the Little Bear] at the head. Later, at midnight, I found that the Star had an altitude of 10°, and at dawn of 15°, with the Guards at the feet. The sea was smooth, as it should be, but I saw no seaweed. I wondered greatly at these movements of the Pole Star, and so I spent many nights taking careful measurements of its altitude with the quadrant. But I always found that the plumb line cut the same point [on the scale]. I regard this as something new, and it may well be that we are to believe from this that the sky undergoes great change in this small area.

"I have always read that the world, both land and water, is spherical, as the studies of Ptolemy and the writings of all other authorities on this subject have demonstrated and proved, as also do the eclipses of the moon, and other experiments which have been made from east to west, and the elevation of the Pole Star from north to south. But now, as I have already said, I have seen this inconsistency. [Columbus means that he had observed how the polestar described a wider circle round the true pole as he sailed west near the equator than it did at home.] I am therefore forced to conclude this about the world: I have found that its shape is not that of a true sphere, as scholars have told us, but more like that of a pear, which is completely round except towards the stalk, where it protudes considerably; or that it is like a round ball, with a protuberance on one side, like a woman's breast; and the part where the stalk would be is the highest and the nearest to the sky, and it is situated in the Ocean below the Equator, at the end of the East, by which I mean the point at which the countries and islands of the East come to an end.

"In support of this, I may appeal to all the above-mentioned arguments concerning the line from north to south 100 leagues west of the Azores. For when one sails west across this line, the ships gradually rise towards the sky and thus enjoy milder weather; and the compass needles deviated a point on account of this mildness. The further and higher we went the greater was the deviation of the needle to the north-west. This elevation causes the change in the circle described by the Pole Star and the Guards. The closer one comes to the equator, the higher one gets, and the greater will be the deviation of the said stars and their courses. . . .

"Holy Scripture testifies that the Lord created the Earthly Paradise, and planted in it the Tree of Life, and that a fountain issued from it, which is the source of the four chief rivers of the world; namely, the Ganges in India, the Tigris and the Euphrates, which cut through a mountain range and form Mesopotamia and flow thence into Persia, and the Nile, which rises in Ethiopia and flows out into the sea at Alexandria. I do not find, and have never found, any Latin or Greek work which gives the precise terrestrial position of the Earthly Paradise, nor have I seen it marked, by any reliable authority, on any map of the world. Some place it at the source of the Nile in Ethiopia, but others have visited all those countries without finding any evidence of it in the coolness of the air or in their proximity to the sky, by which it might be understood that it was there. . . . Some pagan writers tried to show by argument that it was in the Fortunate Islands, which are the Canaries, &c. St. Isidore, Bede, Strabo, the master of *Historia Scholastica,* St. Ambrose, Duns Scotus, and all reliable theologians are agreed that the Earthly Paradise is in the East, &c. . . . I do not think that the Earthly Paradise is shaped like a rugged mountain, as the descriptions have told us, but that it is at the summit, where I have said that the point of the pear is situated, and that, when it is approached from a distance, there is a gradual ascent towards it. . . .

"I return to my discussion of the land of Gracia and of the river and lake I found there, which latter is so large that it could more correctly be called a sea than a lake, for a lake is a place where there is water, and if it is large it is called a sea, as we speak of the Sea of Galilee and the Dead Sea. I say that if this river does not come from the Earthly Paradise, then it must come from an immense land in the south, about which we as yet know nothing. But I am quite convinced in my own mind that the Earthly Paradise is where I have said, and I rely on the arguments and authorities I have cited above."

Columbus was already a sick man when he took the altitude of the polestar on his journey across the Atlantic, and perhaps he would not have attached so much importance to the surprising results of his calculations if he had not later come to believe that they bore out his theory of a pear-shaped earth. The whole of his argument was, of course, nonsensical, and had he been in good health he would probably have been more inclined to accept the alternative suggestion of "a vast land to the south, of which we as yet know nothing."

We do not have any contemporary criticism of his theory about the Earthly Paradise. All that Las Casas wrote was that he did not believe it personally, though he found it "neither absurd nor unreasonable." In his biography, Fernando Colón says nothing about either the pear-shaped earth or the Earthly Paradise, but this is obviously because he wanted people to forget about his father's grosser errors and eccentricities. However, Amerigo Vespucci later wrote about South America: "If there is an Earthly Paradise in this world, then it cannot be far from these southern lands."

This was roughly how Columbus pictured the position of the Indies and the Earthly Paradise in relation to Europe. Comparison with the maps on pages 17, 20, and 29 will show that he now supposed the ocean to be even narrower than before. I have drawn the map on the longitudinal measurements which were taken at Saona in 1494 (see page 129). The grey dotted line indicates where the land and sea began *to rise toward the Earthly Paradise. It was quite in accordance with contemporary thinking that the rivers of Paradise could flow for long distances underground, pass beneath the ocean, and then reemerge suddenly as the Indus, the Euphrates, the Tigris, and the Nile. Each of the marked sections on the equator, the tropics, and the polar circles represents ten degrees.*

The course they set from Margarita is shown by the blue line. Their actual course, as modified by the currents, is shown in brown. The coasts and the islands which Columbus did not yet know are shaded in darker blue. Right: the Santa María de Guia, La Vaque-ños, *and* El Correo *off Alto Velo, an island 450 feet high, shown on the map as a small dot immediately southwest of Madama Beata.*

Chaos in the viceroyalty

Columbus was an excellent seaman, and one of the foremost navigators of his age, so much is clear from contemporary evidence. But when he and his son Fernando tell us that on all his voyages he was the one and only reliable navigator, we must reserve our judgment. It is very likely that even his illness did not stop him from trying to check the calculations of his pilots and the decisions of his captains, but this does not mean that many of his closest associates were not very well qualified for their tasks. Once he had blazed a trail across the ocean, many other men took caravels from Spain to Española, and it was not long before it became clear that he was not the only person who could make discoveries in western seas.

Nevertheless, it was a considerable achievement when, on the third voyage, after a long journey over uncharted seas, and the exploration of an unknown country, the Admiral and his men could reckon their position so exactly that they could plot an accurate course from Margarita to the new settlement of Santo Domingo on Española. They steered northwest by north, and with the normal drift this would have taken them almost directly into the harbor. A routine measurement of the polestar on August 16 showed that the compasses had suddenly deviated $1\frac{1}{2}$ to 2 points west, and the pilots corrected the compass roses accordingly.

On August 19 the mountains of Española appeared on the distant horizon, and immediately ahead of them the Spaniards could see an island emerging from the coastal mist. Las Casas says: "It was a small island, which he called Madama Beata, with an even smaller one beside it, on which there was a mountain that, when seen from a distance, resembled a sail, and he called the latter island Alto Velo. He took Beata for an island called Sancta Chaterina, which he had discovered when he sailed along this south coast on his way back from the island of Cuba, and thought it was 25 leagues from the port of Santo Domingo.... He was perturbed to find that he had come so far to leeward, but he says that this should not be thought exceptional, since they had lain to during the nights for fear of being carried ashore or running aground [the nights were dark, as there was a new moon], or, alternatively, the strong currents flowing west towards the continent must have carried the ships

148

to leeward without their knowledge."

The Admiral's conjecture about the currents was quite justified, but contemporary mariners had no means of allowing for such factors.

To sail to Santo Domingo would have meant a difficult journey against the wind, and the Admiral decided to anchor in the strait between Madama Beata and Española, and to send some Indians overland with a message for his brother the Adelantado. Six Indians came out to his ship, and when he saw that one of them was carrying a Spanish weapon, a crossbow with its appurtenances, he suspected that another and greater tragedy had been enacted than at Navidad.

Accordingly, they started to beat to the northwest, and they were soon met by a caravel coming downwind. It turned out that the Adelantado had seen three caravels sailing west past Santo Domingo and had come out to find them and show them the way to the settlement. The Admiral realized that these must have been the three supply ships he had sent on from Gomera, and in their anxiety to keep well out to sea they had overshot their objective. Hoping that the caravels would find their way back, the Admiral and the Adelantado beat their way forward and anchored in the mouth of the Ozama on August 31.

The news that Don Bartolomeo had for his brother was extremely discouraging. Many of the settlers had died, mainly of illness and privation, and over a hundred and sixty of the survivors appeared to be suffering from the illness later known as syphilis. Juan Aguado's investigations, and his comments, had given a widespread impression that the Admiral was out of favor and would not be coming back to his island. In the summer of 1496, Peralonso Niño had arrived with supply ships and reported that the Admiral had reached Cadiz safely, but then more than a year and a half passed before any more supplies or information arrived from Castile.

Meanwhile, the Spaniards had started to build their new settlement on the Ozama, and were, relatively speaking, at peace with the Indians, but when the food began to run out and there was no news from home, the settlers began to act in a way which menaced the Adelantado, whom they saw as a foreign-born slave driver, and his completely inoffensive brother Don Diego. While the Adelantado was away in the southwest, trying to collect taxes from the Indians of Xaragua, Francisco Roldán, the *alcalde mayor* or burgomaster of the settlement, and several other malcontents made an attempt to launch a caravel beached at Isabela, meaning to sail her home to Castile. Don Diego, who was in command of the settlement in the absence of the Adelantado, tried to dissuade Roldán from leaving, but when they took no notice of him he sent word to his brother in Xaragua. The Adelantado promptly came back and prevented Roldán from going any further with his plans.

This led to an open revolt, and under Roldán's instigation the rebels marched to the Vega Real and struck up an alliance with Marque, the local cacique, promising to release the Indians from taxation and forced labor in

149

return for their help in overthrowing the Adelantado. They were hoping to take the strong fortress of Concepción de la Vega, a road station between Isabela and Santo Domingo, but Miguel Ballester, the officer in charge, heard about their plans and got a message through to the Adelantado, who hastened to his rescue.

Thereupon, Roldán and his men went back to Isabela and took all the weapons and provisions they could lay their hands on, while Don Diego and a few of his servants locked themselves up in a tower. Next, the rebels made an alliance with Guarionex, who had once been a very powerful cacique, and prepared a new attack on Concepción. It was now the end of February, 1498, and the *Niña* and the *India* had just arrived with their supplies, and brought the news that the Admiral was once again in favor at Court, and that the Sovereigns had confirmed Don Bartolomeo's appointment as Adelantado. At this news, the rebels resigned themselves and withdrew to Xaragua. Guarionex, fearing reprisals, retired to the Samaná peninsula, but the Adelantado went after him with a handful of reliable men, took stern measures against his subjects, set fire to the villages in his province, and finally managed to secure his person. By the time the Admiral reached Española, the resourceful Adelantado had the situation under control.

Roldán and his rebels might well have given in at this point, but the three supply ships that had missed Santo Domingo happened to drop anchor at a harbor in Xaragua, nor far from the rebel headquarters. Their captains naturally did not know anything about the rebellion, and they let most of their exhausted crews go ashore. Many, perhaps most, of them were convicts who were going to work out their sentences at Española, and practically the whole party went over to the rebel side. In time, the small number who had remained on board managed to get the ships back to Santo Domingo, but Roldán's force was appreciably strengthened, and once more he began to march on Concepción de la Vega.

In October, 1498, the Admiral sent his flagship and *El Correo* back to Castile with a cargo of Indian slaves, brazil wood, cotton, a little gold, and a few sample pearls from Paria. He also sent the Sovereigns a report of the disorder on Española and a request for priests and a judge, a scholarly and experienced man who could dispense their "royal justice." He also asked for new settlers and suggested that fifty or sixty should be sent out with every fleet of ships. But like the long report on his voyage and the discovery of the Earthly Paradise, all these communications suggested confusion if not megalomania, and it was not very surprising that the Sovereigns from that time on lost faith in their viceroy and governor.

He ended his description of the voyage with the following words: " And now, while You receive information about the lands which I have recently discovered, and where I am convinced the Earthly Paradise is situated, the Adelantado will sail out with three ships, well equipped, to that region and explore it further. . . . Meanwhile, I send Your Highnesses this document and the drawing of the land [i.e., a map], to enable you to decide what is to be done, of which you will instruct me, and with the assistance of the Holy Trinity I shall fulfil your instructions with all diligence, so that Your Highnesses will be served and find pleasure therein. Thanks be to God."

Like the other projected voyage to Mangi and Cathay in the northwest, the Adelantado's journey to the Earthly Paradise in the south was never made. In fact, the Admiral's indefatigable brother never did lead an expedition of discovery on his own.

With the Adelantado in command, the rebellion might still have been suppressed, but the Admiral had again assumed full responsibility and showed himself totally unable to cope with the complexities of the situation. He might have shrunk from the consequences of shedding Spanish blood; he might have felt that the loyalists were all too few. Instead of forcing Roldán into submission in the name of the Sovereigns, he began to negotiate with him, and in time this led to humiliating concessions. A written agreement, dated November 21, 1498, contains the following clauses, among others: the Admiral was to send Roldán two fully equipped caravels, so that he and his men could go back to Castile; he would pay the rebels' wages until the day they left Española; and he would inform the Sovereigns, in writing, that the returning emigrants had served him well, so that they would be paid any wages still outstanding.

But it was found that many of the rebels were unwilling to leave Española, particularly those who had come there to work for two years as an alternative to the gallows. It was a long time before the caravels were ready, and they did not reach Xaragua until April 1499. This gave the rebels a pretext to break their agreement with the Admiral. After new negotiations, Roldán promised that the rebels would return to their allegiance provided that fifteen of them were allowed to go home with the first ship from Castile; and the others were given land and houses in lieu of the pay promised by the earlier agreement. The Admiral was to make a public announcement that all the trouble had been caused by the misrepresentation of a few wicked men; and he was to reinstate Roldán as *alcalde mayor* of Española.

Fernando Colón writes: "The Admiral was eager to put an end to this wretched business, which had dragged on for two years, for he saw that the number and obstinacy of his enemies were increasing, and that many of his own

Bartolomeo Colón, who founded Santo Domingo, called it after his father, Domenico Colombo the weaver. When Columbus arrived at the settlement in 1498, it consisted of no more than a few towers and a dozen or so houses and huts. No picture of Santo Domingo in its early years has come down to us; this drawing is copied from an engraving made in 1589.

men were conspiring to form groups of their own and go off as Roldán had done. So he decided to sign whatever they put before him, and he issued two orders, the one appointing Roldán alcalde mayor for life, and the other agreeing to the four demands set out above."

The Admiral was a sick man, and for the moment he had had quite enough of the Indies and their troubles. His only desire was to go back to Castile with the Adelantado. "For he knew that if the latter remained behind as Governor, it would be difficult to forget old quarrels," Fernando Colón tells us. The Admiral wanted peace and quiet at any price, and he realized that there were limits to the amount of humiliation the indomitable Adelantado would accept. While they were preparing for their departure, news arrived from Xaragua that a fleet under Alonso de Hojeda had anchored at the harbor of Brazil on September 15.

Hojeda, who had gone back to Castile with Peralonso Niño, had seen the map of Trinidad, Paria, and the land of the Earthly Paradise which Columbus had sent to the Sovereigns. It also showed the pearl fisheries, and this

enabled Hojeda to persuade Fonseca to approve a permit for an expedition to those regions. He then equipped a fleet, and followed in the Admiral's wake. His companions included Juan de la Cosa, a seaman and apprentice pilot on the Admiral's second voyage who was later to achieve fame as a cartographer, and Amerigo Vespucci, a Florentine who afterward wrote a description of the voyage. A false date was appended to this description, either by Vespucci himself or by the printer, and it was on account of this that the new continent in the south was called after his first name.

Hojeda and his men reached Trinidad, continued west to Margarita, and discovered the rich pearl fisheries of Cubagua, where they struck a profitable bargain with the natives. Then they sailed on, discovered a chain of new islands off the mainland, and finally came to a large bay, where they saw a village built on piles out over the water. This they called Venezuela, Little Venice. After they had sailed a few leagues farther west, they turned north and reached Brazil on Española, where they began to cut down brazil trees and hunt the Indians.

Brazil wood, like gold, was Crown property, and the Admiral had every reason to intervene. Roldán offered to capture the rebellious Hojeda, but after a few skirmishes, during which they snatched hostages from one another, Hojeda grew tired of the game. He sailed off to the islands north of Española, loaded his caravels with slaves, and went safely back to Castile.

Hojeda was not the only man who had been granted a license to sail to the newly discovered countries. He was closely followed by Peralonso Niño, who went straight back home with pearls from Cubagua and gold from the land to the south. At about the same time, Vicente Yáñez Pinzón, who had commanded the *Niña* on Columbus' first voyage, was given command of four caravels and sailed so far southwest that they crossed the equator and made their first landfall at the modern Cabo São Roque, where the coast of Brazil turns south. From there he coasted along to the northwest, discovered the mouth of the Amazon, and eventually reached the Gulf of Paria and Santo Domingo. "This gave rise to consternation and suspicion, but he did no harm," says the Admiral in a letter. It is probable that the fifteen rebels whom Columbus had promised to send home at the first opportunity took a chance to go back to Castile with Pinzón.

But Columbus himself could not sail home. Peace was by no means yet restored on Española. Although Roldán, in his own interest, lent the Admiral his support, there were rivalry and dissatisfaction among the old rebels, and when they saw the Admiral's lack of self-confidence they tried to extort other concessions from him by further outbreaks. Even the Indians took up arms, and chaos seemed to have come again. Fernando Colón quotes one of the Admiral's effusions: "The day after Christmas, 1499, after everyone had left me, I was attacked by Indians and ill-disposed Christians, and was placed in such an extremity that I had to flee for my life in a small caravel. Then the good Lord helped me, saying: 'O man of a little faith, fear not, for I am with thee.' And He scattered my enemies and showed me how I might fulfil my vows. Unhappy sinner that I am, to have to place all my trust in the things of this world."

On August 23, 1500, while the Adelantado was suppressing a local rising in Xaragua, and the Admiral was suppressing another at Concepción de la Vega, a fleet of Castilian ships sailed into the Oxama estuary. It was commanded by Francisco de Bobadilla, Comendador of the Order of Calatrava, who had been sent by the Sovereigns to dispense their "royal justice." With him he had a decree which showed that he had been appointed governor of the islands and mainland of the Indies, and he carried a letter addressed to the Admiral which ran:

"Don Cristóbal Colón, Our Admiral of the Ocean.

"We have sent the Comendador Francisco de Bobadilla, the bearer of this letter, to say certain things to you on Our behalf. We desire you to place your full trust in him and pay him all respect, and to act accordingly."

Bobadilla did not leave Castile before July, 1500, by which time Alonso de Hojeda, and the fifteen rebels who went with him, had brought even more alarming news about the Admiral's incompetence, which had certainly lost nothing in the telling. Fernando Colón, who was page to the Queen at that time, together with his brother, tells us how the ex-colonists called after them, as they walked through the streets of Granada in July, 1500: "There go the sons of the Admiral of the Mosquitoes, of the man who discovered the lands of vanity and fraud, the cemetery of Castilian noblemen."

The sight that met Bobadilla's eyes when he landed at Santo Domingo seemed to confirm everything he had heard. Seven Spaniards were dangling from a gibbet, and Don Diego, who was in command of the settlement in his brother's absence, told him that these men were rebels, and that five more were to be hanged the next day. Bobadilla made some rapid inquiries, and on the following day he made his first move. Don Diego, who refused to hand over the five men under sentence of death without the Admiral's permission, was put under arrest. The new governor installed himself in the Admiral's house and impounded all his papers and other possessions. He sent orders to Concepción de la Vega that the Admiral was to return to Santo Domingo immediately. The Admiral came back and was promptly put in irons and kept under arrest.

When the Adelantado heard news of this, he wanted to free his brothers by force of arms, but the Admiral sent him a message ordering him to obey Bobadilla, who seemed to be acting on the royal instructions. No sooner had the Adelantado reached Santo Domingo than he too was put in irons. When he had heard the complaints of the original rebels and everyone else who was dissatisfied with the way things had been run by this family of aliens, Bobadilla decided to send Columbus and his brother home to Castile in irons to stand trial.

During his imprisonment in Santo Domingo, the Admiral wrote a long letter to Doña Juana de Torres, the sister of his friend Antonio de Torres, who had taken the main part of the fleet back to Castile after the Admiral's second voyage to the Indies. She had been nurse to the Crown Prince Don Juan, and after his death she had become an intimate of the Queen. This may explain why the Admiral wrote to her, for he knew that his words would be bound to reach the Queen's ears. Since the greater part of the letter deals with events that have already been described, I shall quote only a few short passages which throw a certain light on the Admiral's thoughts and feelings.

"Of the new heaven and the new earth which the Lord made, and of which St. John writes in the Apocalypse, as the Lord told of it through the mouth of Isaiah, He made me the messenger, and He showed me the way. None would believe me, but to my Lady the Queen He gave the gift of understanding, and of great courage, and made her the heiress of all, as His dear and best loved daughter. And I went to take possession of all in Her Royal Name....

"Things have come to such a pass that there is none so vile as dare not insult me....If I had stolen the Indies, or the lands near them of which we are now speaking, from the Altar of St. Peter, and given them to the Moors, no greater enmity could have been shown me in Spain. Who would believe such a thing of a country where there has always been such magnanimity?

"If it were honourable towards my Queen, I would gladly rid myself of the whole business. But the support of the Lord God and of Her Highness gave me the will to persevere, and in order to lighten the grief which Death had brought upon her [the death of Don Juan], I made a new voyage, to a new heaven and a new earth, which up till then had lain hidden; and if these, like the rest of the Indies, are not regarded there, I do not wonder at it, for they were brought to light by my exertions. The Holy Spirit inspired St. Peter, and the other Holy Apostles with him, and they all wrestled mightily here below, and great were their toil and their weariness; but in the end, they gained the victory over all...."

"In Spain, they judge me as if I had been a governor in Sicily, or in some well-ordered city or town, where laws can be kept to the letter, without risking total disaster. I feel that this is completely unjust. I should be judged as a captain who has gone from Spain to the Indies, to conquer a numerous and warlike nation, whose customs and beliefs are entirely different from ours, who live in the highlands and among the mountains, with no abiding habitations, where, by the Grace of God, I have brought a new world into the dominions of Our Sovereigns the King and Queen of Spain, whereby Spain, which was once held to be poor, is now the wealthiest of countries."

This fine portrait, perhaps by Ridolfo Ghirlandaio of Florence, is said to represent Columbus embittered and prematurely aged.

Prophecies

At the beginning of October, 1500, the Admiral was taken aboard the caravel *La Gorda* and transported to Castile to be tried and sentenced together with his brothers. "As soon as they had put to sea, the captain, who had learnt of Bobadilla's hardness of heart, offered to free him of his chains, but this the Admiral refused. He had been put in irons in the name of the Sovereigns, he said, and he would wear them until they gave orders for them to be removed; for he was determined to keep those fetters as a token of how well he had been rewarded for his many services. And this he did, for I always saw them in his bedchamber; and he wanted them to be buried with his bones," Fernando Colón writes.

The Admiral and his brothers were landed at Cadiz on November 20, and when the people saw them in chains, their taunts and jeers were soon replaced by honest indignation over the unjust way they were being treated. The chains were even more effective than a brown Franciscan habit. The Admiral managed at once to get a letter off to the Court, which was then in Granada. Even the Sovereigns were shocked at the news that their Admiral of the Ocean had been sent home in chains, and they gave immediate orders to set the brothers free, sending them 2,000 ducats so that they should be able to present themselves at Court in a dignified manner.

The scene at Granada on December 17, when the Admiral and his brother were received by the Sovereigns, was pathetic. The Admiral fell on his knees and cried. The Adelantado presumably fell on his knees too, but he did not allow himself to be intimidated by Royalty. He said quite openly that he had been injured and despoiled in their service and went on to demand the rewards that he had been promised for his services. He certainly affirmed his readiness to serve them in the future but added that he could manage without their help. Oviedo the historian describes the meeting thus: "The Admiral went to kiss the hands of the King and Queen, and, weeping, gave his excuses as best he could. And when they had listened to him, they comforted him with great gentleness and spoke such words as composed him to some degree. And since his services had been so great, though somewhat erratic, the princely gratitude of Their Royal Highnesses could not allow the Admiral to be wrongfully used, and accordingly they gave immediate instruction that all the revenues and privileges which had been taken from him at the time of his arrest be now restored to him. But they gave no promise that he would be reinstated as Governor."

The Admiral now expected that everything would be as it had been before, that he would be reinstated as

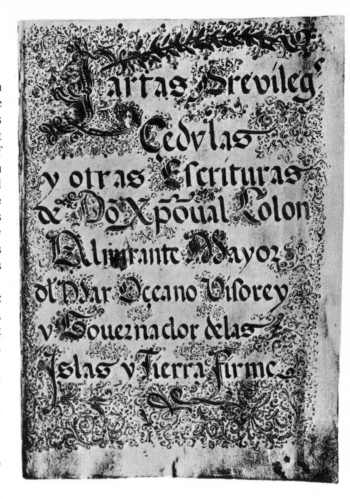

The title page of The Book of Privileges, *from the copy in the Palazzo Municipale, Genoa*

Viceroy and Governor, but the months went by, and his inquiries and petitions were met with evasive answers. He heard news from the Indies, which he himself had now begun to call the West Indies, to distinguish them from the Indies which Vasco da Gama had discovered when he sailed south and east. A Portuguese explorer called Cabral had crossed the ocean and found land in the southwest, probably a part of the same continent which the Admiral had discovered and Vicente Yáñez Pinzón had explored. Another Portuguese explorer, Gaspar Corte-Real, had found land in the northwest of the ocean, and word came from England that a Giovanni Caboto of Genoa, a fellow-townsman of the Admiral, had discovered land in the west while in the service of Henry VII.

One of the Admiral's close friends during that period was Don Gaspar Gorricio, a Franciscan friar from the monastery of Las Cuevas in Seville, and with his help Columbus drew up various memoranda concerning his titles and privileges. Eventually, they brought together copies of forty-four documents dealing with these matters under the title of *The Book of Privileges,* of which four copies were made. One was kept at Las Cuevas in Seville, one was given to the Admiral's son Diego, and the two others were sent to the bank of San Giorgio in Genoa. The Admiral thought that this guaranteed him against injustice and against the possible forgetfulness of the Sovereigns.

It appears from a letter which the Admiral wrote to Friar Gorricio on May 24, 1501, that the Sovereigns' 15-year-old daughter Catherine had left to marry the Prince of Wales, and that there would probably be time to look into his affairs. He continues: "My Lady the Queen sent me word that it would gratify her if I reconciled myself with the Lord Bishop [Fonseca], and that Her Highness would mediate if there were any disagreement. He has gone to Flanders, but before he left he came and visited me."

The Admiral seems to have resented Fonseca's action in authorizing Hojeda and others to make voyages to the Indies without the Admiral's consent, but the wording of the letter does not indicate any great animosity. The The Admiral had forgotten that in 1493 he had sent a letter to the Sovereigns containing the words: "Concerning the discovery of the new lands, I consider that all who wish to set forth may be allowed to do so."

The Admiral also began to write the *Libro de las Profecías,* the Book of Prophecies, at about that time. In the introduction, which takes the form of a letter to the Sovereigns and was intended to explain why he wanted to recapture the Holy Sepulchre for the Holy Church, he begins by describing his experiences as a mariner, and tells how God gave him sufficient understanding of astrology, geometry, and arithmetic, and of how he had learned to "draw the sphere, and upon it the cities, rivers and mountains, the islands and the harbours, all in their proper places." He describes how with God's help he had learned the way to the Indies, and of how he had been encouraged by the testimonies and the prophecies of the Old and New Testaments, and by the twenty-three Epistles of the Holy Apostles, to carry out his plan, in spite of disagreement from most men of learning, and mockery and opposition from the whole Court.

He goes on to say that he learned to forget all his earlier knowledge and experience and to put his whole trust in Holy Scripture and in certain prophecies of holy men. "It is possible that Your Highnesses and any others who know me, and who might come to see this document, may privately or publicly find fault with me on various grounds, and say that I am not a man of learning, and call me a half-crazed mariner, a mere layman, &c. I answer in the words of St. Matthew: 'I thank thee, O Father, Lord of heaven and earth, because thou hast hid these things from the wise and prudent, and hast revealed them unto babes.' "

He cites St. Augustine and Pierre d'Ailly in his support and maintains that the world will come to an end 7,000 years after the Creation. King Alfonso the Wise had calculated that the age of the world at the birth of Christ was 5,343 years and 318 days, and this, with the 1,501 years which had passed since then, would bring the age of the world to almost 6,845 years, which left 155 years before the end of all things. The Saviour had promised that all holy prophecies should come to pass before all things be fulfilled, and the signs showed that the Lord was hastening their fulfilment. The proof was that the Word had been preached in so many new countries in so short a time.

"I will speak of one [prophecy], because it is connected with my enterprise, and it gives me peace and bestows contentment upon me whenever I think of it....I have already said that neither reason nor mathematics nor maps of the world were of any help to me, that I should fulfil the enterprise of the Indies. But the words of Isaiah were completely fulfilled, and this is what I wish to write here, that it may be firmly set in Your Highnesses' minds, and that You may rejoice over the other undertaking, as I shall say what the aforesaid holy men said concerning that enterprise: if You have faith, You may be very confident of victory."

The introduction was never finished, and the appended collection of Biblical and other quotation can hardly have been completed either, and we may therefore presume that the *Book of Prophecies* was never presented to the Sovereigns. In a letter to Friar Gorricio, the Admiral mentions that he hoped to put the prophecies into verse later on, but this project can hardly have been realized. The intention behind the book was to represent himself as chosen by God to take Christianity to the ends of the earth, and to persuade the Sovereigns to risk everything, as he was prepared to do, to liberate the Holy Sepulchre from the infidels. "The Abbot Joachim of Calabria said that he who was to rebuild the Sepulchre on Mt. Zion would come from Spain."

His main sources of prophecy about his own activities were from Isaiah. "Listen, O isles, unto me; and hearken, ye people, from afar; The Lord hath called me from the womb; from the bowels of my mother hath he made mention of my name....I will also give thee for a light to the Gentiles, that thou mayest be my salvation unto the end of the earth....Surely the isles shall wait for me, and the ships of Tarshish first, to bring thy sons from far, their silver and their gold with them....For, behold, I create new heavens and a new earth: and the former shall not be remembered, nor come into mind."

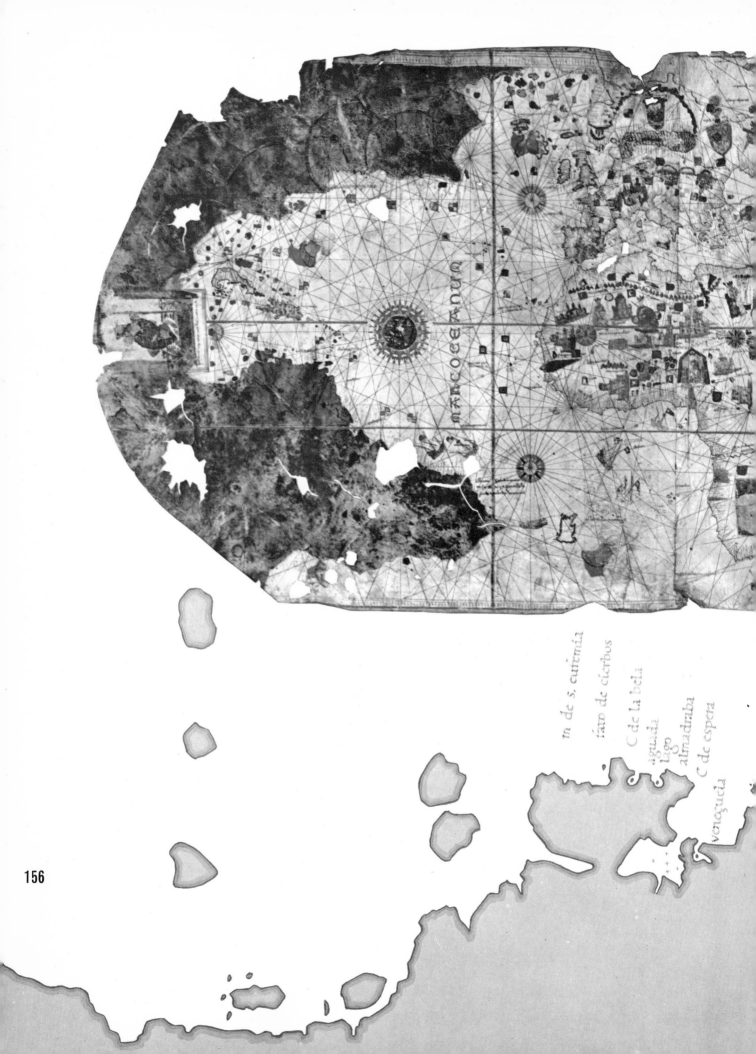

mn de s. eufemia
faro de ciervos

C de la bela
aguada
lago
almadraba
C de espera
veneçuela

156

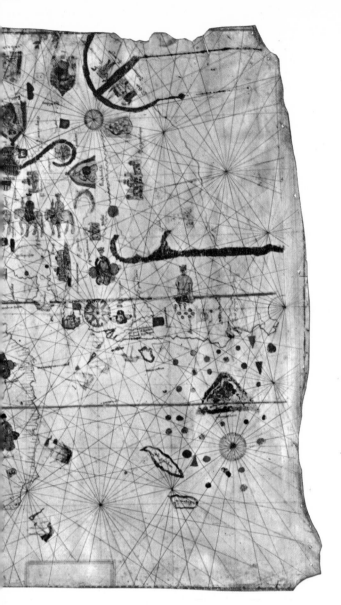

This is Juan de la Cosa's celebrated map of the world, which he made at Puerto de la Santa María in 1500. It is preserved in the Museo Naval, Madrid.

The section which particularly concerns us is the left-hand side, showing the newly discovered islands and coasts of what was thought to be the Indies. Many scholars are of the opinion that at least parts of the map were drawn after 1500, on the ground that it shows certain coasts which had not been discovered by that year. Cuba does not seem to have been circumnavigated before 1509, though Michele de Cuneo's letter tells us that many of Columbus' company believed that Cuba was an island, clearly because the natives had told them so. (See the map on page 128, where a part of Juan de la Cosa's map is inset.)

The enlargement below the map represents the coast west of Trinidad. Although the unmarked part west of m de s. eufemia is very similar to the actual coastline, I am inclined to believe that the cartographer, who was a pilot on Hojeda's expedition to the Pearl Coast in 1499, noted that the coastline eased off to the southwest and drew a reasonable approximation. The large islands he drew there do not show any firsthand knowledge of the region. Juan de la Cosa sailed on an expedition with Rodrigo de Bastidas in October, 1500, and on that voyage he did in fact discover this particular stretch of coast, but they did not return to Castile until two years later. (See the modern map on page 166.) Note that Española, Jamaica, and Cuba are put north of the Tropic of Cancer. Obviously, Juan de la Cosa did not believe that to be their position, nor did anyone else in Spain who had been there; the map was perhaps intended to be shown to foreign visitors, and secrets were secrets.

Far southeast of Trinidad, off the cape now known as Cabo São Roque, we can see the words: "esto cauo se descubrio en ano de mil y CCCC XCIX por castilla syende descobridor vicent ians," or "This cape was discovered for Castile in 1499; the discoverer was Vicente Yáñez [Pinzón]." The Portuguese explorer Cabral is generally credited with the discovery of Brazil, but evidently Vicente Yáñez Pinzón must have explored a considerable stretch of the Brazilian coast the year before Cabral set out. The cartographer shows a large island to the east of the easternmost part of the continent and says in a note that it was discovered for Portugal, thus implying that Cabral had discovered an island, rather than any part of the new southern continent.

Juan de la Cosa drew also the North American discoveries of English and Portuguese explorers, but he ran his demarcation line north and south through the Azores, hoping to suggest that all the new lands in the west really belonged to Castile. In fact, the Treaty of Tordesillas made the demarcation line run 370 leagues west of the Cape Verde Islands.

157

In September, 1501, the Sovereigns appointed Don Nicolás de Ovando Governor and Chief Justice of the islands and mainland of the Indies, and in the same month they confirmed in writing that all the property which Bobadilla had taken from the Admiral would be restored to him, and that he would, as before, receive his tolls of one-eighth and one-tenth of the Indian trade. Alonso Sánchez de Carvajal was appointed to look after the Admiral's interests on Española.

The Admiral must have been relieved to hear that Bobadilla was no longer Governor and that Ovando was not made Viceroy. The Sovereigns said nothing explicit about his own titles, but they still referred to him as "Our Admiral of the Ocean." He felt that he had been unjustly treated, and indeed he spent the rest of his life seeking restitution, but there are indications that when the Sovereigns made their decision they also hinted that his repeated petitions were becoming irksome. A long rambling letter he wrote five months later about the art of navigation, containing a reminder of his accurate forecast of the date on which the Princess and her fleet should arrive back from Flanders, begins with the words: "I would wish to be an occasion of pleasure and contentment to Your Highnesses, and not of trouble and distaste."

On February 13, 1502, Ovando set sail for Española with thirty ships. By then, Columbus had already begun to prepare for another voyage of discovery. On February 26 he wrote to the Sovereigns and asked them for the necessary instructions and documents, and for particular concessions. This letter is lost, but its contents can be reconstructed from the Sovereigns' reply.

The Admiral wanted to sail to Española first and then west to the continent, down its eastern and southern coasts past the province of Chimba, past the long peninsula with Cattigara, until he reached India, the Land of Spices, to which Vasco da Gama had set out on his second journey sixteen days earlier. As Columbus expected to enter the Portuguese sphere of interest, he suggested to the Sovereigns that King Emanuel should be informed of the expedition, so that there would be no trouble if he met Portuguese ships. He wanted to take his son Don Fernando with him and asked whether his salary as a page could temporarily be paid to his elder son Don Diego. He asked for two Arab interpreters, since it had been found that the natives of the Portuguese Indies knew Arabic. He suggested that the crews should be given a fixed percentage of the profits from the voyage, since this would make recruiting easier. He suggested that ten thousand silver coins be struck, since silver was said to be in great demand in the Portuguese Indies. He asked for an extra large allowance of powder and guns, and, in conclusion, he asked them to reinstate him as Viceroy

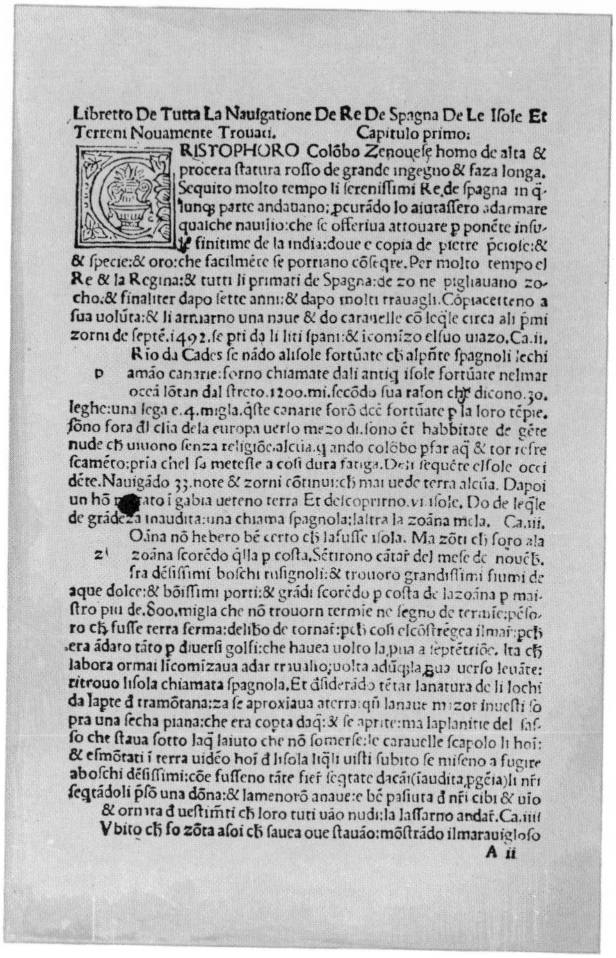

Libretto De Tutta La Nauigatione De Re De Spagna De Le Iſole Et Terreni Nouamente Trouati. Capitulo primo:

CRISTOPHORO Colõbo Zenoueſe homo de alta & procera ſtatura roſſo de grande ingegno & faza longa. Sequito molto tempo li ſereniſſimi Re de ſpagna in q̃lunq; parte andauano; pcurãdo lo aiutaſſero adarmare qualche nauilio: che ſe offeriua attrouare p ponẽte inſule finitime de la india: doue e copia de pietre pcioſe: & ſpecie: & oro: che facilmẽte ſe porriano cõſeqre. Per molto tempo el Re & la Regina: & tutti li primati de Spagna: de zo ne pigliauano zocho: & finaliter dapo ſette anni: & dapo molti trauagli. Cõpiacetteno a ſua uolũta: & li armarno una naue & do carauelle cõ leq̃le circa ali pmi zorni de ſeptẽ. 1492. ſe pti da li liti ſpani: & icomizo el ſuo uiazo. Ca. ii.

Partio da Cades ſe nãdo ali ſole fortũate ch̃ alpñte ſpagnoli lechiamão canarie: forno chiamate dali antiq iſole fortũate nelmar occã lõtan dal ſtreto. 1200. mi. ſecõdo ſua raſon ch̃ dicono. 30. leghe: una lega e. 4. migla. q̃ſte canarie forõ dcẽ fortũate p la loro tẽpie. ſono fora dl clia dela europa uerſo mezo di. ſono ẽt habbitate de gẽte nude ch̃ uiuono ſenza religiõe alcũa. q̃ando colõbo pſar aq̃ & tor refreſcamẽto: pria chel ſa meteſſe a coſi dura fatiga. Dẽti ſequẽte el ſole occidẽte. Nauigãdo 33. note & zorni cõtinui: ch̃ mai uede terra alcũa. Dapoi un hõ [illegible]ato i gabia ueteno terra. Et delcoprirno. vi. iſole. Do de leq̃le de grãdeza inaudita: una chiama ſpagnola; laltra la zoãna mela. Ca. iii.

Zoãna nõ hebero bẽ certo ch̃ la fuſſe iſola. Ma zõti ch̃ foro ala zoãna ſcorẽdo q̃lla p coſta. Sẽtirono cãtar del meſe de noueb. fra dẽſiſſimi boſchi ruſignoli: & trouoro grandiſſimi fiumi de aque dolce: & bõiſſimi porti: & grãdi ſcorẽdo p coſta de lazoãna p maiſtro piu de. 800. migla che nõ trouorn termie ne ſegno de termie: pẽſoro ch̃ fuſſe terra ferma: delibò de tornar: pch̃ coſi elcõſtrẽgea il mar: pch̃ era ãdato tãto p diuerſi golfi: che hauea uolto la pua a ſeptẽtriõe. Ita ch̃ labora ormai licomizaua adar trauaiio; uolta adũq; la gua uerſo leuãte: ritrouo liſola chiamata ſpagnola. Et dſiderãdo tẽtar lanatura de li lochi da lapte d tramõtana: za ſe aproxiaua aterra: qñ lanaue mazor inueſti ſopra una ſecha piana: che era copta daq̃: & ſe aprite: ma laplanitie del ſaſſo che ſtaua ſotto laq̃ laiuto che nõ ſomerſe: le carauelle ſcapolo li hoi: & eſmõtati i terra uidẽo hoi d liſola liq̃li uiſti ſubito ſe miſeno a fugire a boſchi dẽſiſſimi: cõe fuſſeno tãte fier ſeqtate dacãi (iaudita pgẽia) li nři ſeqtãdoli pſõ una dõna: & lamenorõ anaue: e bẽ paſiuta d nři cibi & uio & ornata d ueſtimti ch̃ loro tuti uão nudi: la laſſarno andar. Ca. iiii

Vbito ch̃ fo zõta aſoi ch̃ ſauea oue ſtauão: mõſtrãdo il marauiglioſo

A ii

The first printed book about Columbus, containing 29 pages of text. A secretary at the Venetian Embassy in Castile borrowed Peter Martyr's descriptions of Columbus' voyages in 1501. He translated them into Italian and sent the translation to a friend in Venice, where they were printed in 1504. The book is known as the Libretto, *after the first word on the first page. Only one copy is known to exist, and that is now in the Biblioteca Marciana at Venice.*

and Governor of the islands and mainland of the Indies, and to arrange before his departure that the original agreement concerning the inheritance of these offices by his sons and brothers should be confirmed.

The Sovereigns replied promptly, and drew up the necessary royal instructions for the expedition at the same time. Meanwhile, they told him that he was not to land on Española, ostensibly because there was no time to spare, but in fact, of course, because they were afraid that the Admiral's arrival at Santo Domingo would immediately spark off another rebellion. This suggests that they had not officially deprived him of the viceroyalty. Only on the way back, if the situation required it—supposing, of course, that he did not circumnavigate the earth—was it their wish that he should put in at Santo Domingo.

The King of Portugal had already been officially informed about the expedition, and with Columbus' instructions they enclosed a letter to be presented to Vasco da Gama, or to any other Portuguese captain he might meet in the Indies. It ran thus:

"We, the King and Queen of Castile, León, Aragon, Sicily, Granada, &c., &c., send greetings to you.... Captain under Our Son, the Most Serene King of Portugal. We inform you that We are dispatching Admiral Don Cristóbal Colón, the bearer of this letter, with certain ships on the course they are accustomed to follow, and he is to sail to the West. And, since We have learnt that Our Son, the said King of Portugal, is sending you with certain ships to the East, and since by good chance you may meet at sea, We have instructed the said Admiral Don Cristóbal Colón that, should you meet, you are to treat one another as friends, and as the captains and subjects of Kings who are bound together by so much kinship, love and affection. Wherefore We beseech you to do likewise on your part."

They accepted the various ·suggestions about Fernando's salary, the Arab-speaking interpreters, and the powder and guns, but the crews' wages were to be paid as before, and the issue of silver coinage was to be postponed until the next voyage, by which time more would be known about the circumstances and the requirements in those parts of the Indies.

"Concerning the other matters set forth in your memorials and letters touching yourself, your sons, and your brothers, no decision can be made on these questions until We have established a permanent residence in some place, since, as you see, We are on Our travels, and you are about to depart, and if you were to await Our answer, the voyage which you are preparing would never begin. Accordingly, since you have everything ready that you need for your voyage, you are to depart immediately with no delay whatever, and leave your son to see to the matters dealt with in the said memorials. And you may rest assured that We were deeply grieved by your imprisonment, as you have already discovered and as all men well know. For as soon as We had intelligence of it, We gave orders for your release, and you know that We have at all times required that you should be treated with deference, and now We are even more eager to show you honour and favour, and the favours We have vouchsafed to you shall be fulfilled in their entirety, according to the form and tenor of Our privileges which you enjoy, with no exceptions or reservations whatever. And you and your sons shall enjoy them, as is just. And if it be

necessary to confirm them anew, then We shall confirm them, and We shall ordain that your son shall remain in full possession thereof, and We intend to honour and favour you in other matters likewise, and We shall take care of your sons and brothers, as is just. All this will be possible if you set off with speed, and leave the responsibility in the hands of your son, even as We have said. And so We pray you not to delay your departure.

At Valencia de la Torre, March 14th, 1502
I the King   I the Queen."

Without reading between the lines, we can see that the Sovereigns were sighing with relief to see the last of their Admiral, and that they were practically running him out of the country. They even resorted to blackmail, suggesting that if he did not sail immediately the expedition would not be sent at all.

Apparently, some royal clearance had been given before the actual instructions were drawn up, for by March 16 a large number of the officers and men had already been signed on and given six months' pay in advance. Four caravels were hired, and on April 3 they left Seville to be caulked farther downstream under the Adelantado's supervision. They were equipped and loaded in Sanlúcar de Barrameda and Cadiz, and set out on the voyage on May 9.

Alonso de Morales, the Treasurer of Castile, had forced upon Columbus the company of his mistress' brothers, Francisco and Diego de Porras; Francisco by royal command, was entrusted with the care of all valuables obtained on the voyage, and he was also made captain of one of the ships. We do not know what intrigue prevented the Adelantado from being given command of a ship; together with the Admiral and his son Fernando, he drew no pay. A surviving letter makes it clear that he did not wish to go at all but allowed himself to be persuaded by the Admiral.

Complete lists of the crews and their salaries have been preserved. The names of the most important members of the expedition were:

The flagship La Capitana, caravel of 70 tons
Admiral of the Ocean, Don Cristóbal Colón
Diego Tristán, captain
Ambrosyo Sánchez, master
Juan Sánchez, chief pilot of the fleet
Antón Donato, quartermaster
Master Bernal, surgeon
Don Fernando Colón
Also four "escuderos" (serving gentlemen, presumably trained soldiers), one cooper, one caulker, one carpenter, two master-gunners, two trumpeters, fourteen seamen, and nineteen ship's boys; making 51 in all.

The caravel Santiago de Palos, called the Bermuda, of 60 tons

> Francisco de Porras, captain
> Diego de Porras, chief clerk and accountant of
>   the fleet
> Francisco Bermúdes, master
> Pedro Gómes, quartermaster
> Don Bartolomeo Colón
> Diego Méndez, serving-gentleman
> Also five serving gentlemen, one master-gunner,
> one cooper, one caulker, one carpenter, eleven
> seamen, and fourteen ship's boys; making 40 in
> all.

The caravel La Gallego, of 60 tons

> Pedro de Terreros, captain
> Juan Quintero, master
> Alonso Ramón, quartermaster
> Also one serving gentleman, nine seamen, thirteen
> ship's boys, and a page; making 27 in all.

The caravel Viscaýno, of 50 tons

> Bartolomeo Fieschi, captain
> Juan Pérez, master
> Martín de Fuenterabía, quartermaster
> Pedro de Ledesma, pilot on seaman's pay
> Friar Alixandre, priest
> Also three serving gentlemen, seven seamen, nine
> ship's boys, and one page; making 25 in all.

Diego Tristán, the captain of the flagship, had accompanied the Admiral on his second voyage as a serving gentleman; Pedro de Terreros, the captain of the *Gallego*, served as the Admiral's major domo ashore; and Bartolomeo Fieschi, the captain of the *Viscaýno*, came from Genoa and had known the Admiral since childhood. There were six other men from Genoa on the voyage. Only one man is expressly entered as a pilot, and we must assume that some of those who signed on as seamen served as pilots, as on the previous expeditions. The number of ship's boys was unusually large, 55 in all, as against 41 seamen. This may mean that there had been some difficulty in finding experienced sailors, or that someone wanted to save public money, for a ship's boy was paid 666 *maravedis* a month, compared to a seaman, who was paid 1,000 a month. The captains and the pilot were paid 4,000 *maravedis* a month, the masters 2,000, and the quartermasters 1,500; the coopers 1,500, the carpenters 1,200; and the caulkers, the master-gunners, the trumpeters, the serving gentlemen, and the priest were paid at the seamen's rate of 1,000 *maravedis* a month.

In the early years of the 16th century, we may be sure, there were no maps which showed all the new discoveries with any degree of accuracy. The new colonial powers treated all such matters as a State secret. In Portugal, it was held to be high treason, a capital offense, to give any foreigner or other unauthorized person a map of the African coast or the route to the Indies, or even to let him see it. But contemporary letters tell us that spies were trying hard to learn the results of the latest ocean voyages.

A remarkable document is the map drawn in Portugal in 1501–2, generally known as the Cantino map. Alberto Cantino, the Duke of Ferrara's ambassador in Lisbon, persuaded a Portuguese cartographer to draw him a map of the world with details of contemporary discoveries, including the data from Vasco da Gama's latest voyage, for the sum of 12 ducats, a very large fee for a map at that time.

The details of this large map cannot all be shown in small-scale reproduction, and the copy of it reproduced here (above, right) is considerably simplified. There are no degrees on the original map, and it is difficult to assess the distances, but we see at a glance that the draughtsman had reduced the length of the south coast of Asia to some approximation to reality. For the first time we are shown the East African coast and the Indian peninsula in a form we can recognize. Ptolemy's only legacy is the wildly exaggerated protraction of the southeast Asian peninsula. The cartographer is less certain of himself in the west. He has not heard of the North American discoveries made by John Cabot in the service of the English Crown, and Gaspar Corte-Real's discovery of Labrador is only indicated by an island to the southwest of Greenland. In accordance with the official Spanish practice, Cuba and Española are shown north of the Tropic of Cancer, and Cuba is given the name Yssabella. Columbus' description of Cuba as part of the mainland confused the cartographer, and he put in the far west a rectangular country, which might be regarded as the extremity of Asia, yet it does not fit the Asia he has drawn in the east. The Pearl Coast south of the islands is obviously copied from a stolen Spanish map.

We may assume that Columbus possessed a globe (reconstruction, right) and marked his own discoveries, and those of other people, on it. But as far as concerned the Indies beyond Juana (Cuba), he had to rely on earlier authorities, and perhaps chiefly on Martellus. Columbus had underestimated the distance to the Indies by sea, and in consequence he had to exaggerate the size of the continent, but even if his world was considerably smaller than that of other experts, he must have realized that his projected circumnavigation of the globe would take an immensely long time. From Cadiz to Española, and on past the Chiamba peninsula and home round the Cape of Good Hope would have been at least five times the distance from Cadiz to Española.

Circulus articus   Parte de assia   Circulus articus

Oceanus
occidetalis

Tierra del Rey de portugall

Este he ou mar que parte castellas portugall

Las antilhas del Rey de castella

Tropicus cauri

Linha equinocialis

Oceanus orientalis

Circulus capricorni

Oceanus yndias
meridionalis

Pollus antarticus

Pollus antarticus

cathaia

china

provincia manegi

fuana

chidia

occeanus indicus
orientalis

india orientalis

provincia
chianba

ganges fluu.

sinus
magnus

provincia
moabar

sinus
gangetic

aurea
cuersonso

catigara

taprobana

ᴀARZILLAᴀ

The Province of Chiamba

As the Admiral was preparing to sail, news reached him that the Moors were laying siege to the Portuguese fortress of Arzila in Morocco. He decided to go to the assistance of the Portuguese, but on May 9, when he had intended to set sail, the wind suddenly changed, and he had to wait two more days at the mouth of Cadiz harbor. When he actually dropped anchor at Arzila on May 13, the Moors had already gone away, and all he could do was to send the Adelantado, the captains, and his thirteen-year-old son Fernando on a formal visit to the defenders of the fortress.

This time he did not put in at Gomera; he stopped at Maspalomas on Grand Canary to take on wood and water and sailed away on May 25. The fleet passed Ferro on the following day, and then altered course to west by south, the usual route for Española. On the second voyage, this route had taken the fleet to Dominica, but this time, after twenty-one days at sea, they arrived slightly farther south, at the Caribbean island of Matininó. There they took on wood and water, washed their clothes, and after a brief investigation sailed past the islands southwest of Dominica to Santa Cruz and San Juan, and thence to Española, where they dropped anchor off Santo Domingo on June 29.

The Admiral had good reason to put in at Española in spite of the Sovereigns' injunctions. The *Santiago* had been found to be a bad sailer, and in a fresh wind she heeled over so much that her decks were almost under water, so the Admiral wanted to buy or hire another ship. He did not go ashore himself but sent his major domo, Pedro de Terreros, the captain of *La Gallego,* to try to get another ship from the governor and at the same time to warn him that, by all appearances, a hurricane was

blowing up. There was a fleet of twenty-eight ships in the Ozama estuary, ready to leave for Castile with a varied cargo which included gold and slaves, and it was in their company that Bobadilla, his commission now terminated, was going to sail home. Nicolás de Ovando explained that there was no ship available for the Admiral and refused the Admiral permission to enter the estuary. Unperturbed by Terreros' hurricane warning, he ordered the large fleet of homeward-bound ships to depart.

While at Santo Domingo, Terreros probably met Rodrigo de Bastidas, who had sailed out with Fonseca's permission a year earlier, and sailed past the limits reached by Alonso de Hojeda to discover a further stretch of coastline which turned southwest beyond the Bay of Venezuela. Juan de la Cosa, the cartographer, had gone with him, and Terreros was given a sketch-map of the new discoveries.

The Admiral then led his ships some miles to the west and took shelter from the approaching hurricane in the mouth of a river. The hurricane came in great gusts from the north, northwest, and west, straining the anchor cables until the ships began to drag. All except the flagship were driven out to sea. *La Gallego* lost one of her boats, and they all lost a great deal of equipment. Fernando Colón writes: "The caravel Bermuda [*Santiago*] was in even greater distress, for water swept over her decks from stem to stern as she ran out to sea, showing that the Admiral had been quite right in wanting to exchange her for another. And everyone was sure that, next to God, the Adelantado, the Admiral's brother, had saved her by his skill and courage; for, as we have said above, there was no man living more expert in sailing than he. And so, after all the ships except the Admiral's had taken great punishment, it pleased God to bring them together on the following Sunday in the Harbour of Azua, on the south side of Española, where they all recounted their own misfortunes, and decided that the Adelantado's good fortune came from his good seamanship, because he had steered away from land, and that the Admiral had avoided the danger because he had kept close to land, since as a wise astrologer he had known from what quarter the danger would come."

The hurricane struck the homeward-bound fleet with terrific force. Only four of the twenty-eight ships were saved, and over five hundred people were drowned or smashed to death on the shores of Española, including the ex-governor Bobadilla, Roldán the mutineer, Cacique Guarionex, and the commander of the fleet, Antonio de Torres, the Admiral's friend. It is said that 200,000 *castellanos* (2,000 pounds) of gold went down at the same time. Three sorely battered ships managed to limp back to Santo Domingo, and only one small caravel, which had been hired by Alonso Sánchez de Carvajal to take 4,000 *castellanos* (405 pounds) of the Admiral's gold, was able to sail straight home to Castile. We need not be surprised that the Admiral's enemies maintained that he had raised the hurricane by sorcery, while his friends spoke of Divine justice.

After repairs had been made and the men had rested for a few days in Azua, the Admiral's four caravels continued to the southwest, passing Madama Beata and Alto Velo, and dropped anchor in the harbor of Brazil, in Xaragua, since there were signs of another storm. They set out again on July 14 but the wind gradually dropped, and they drifted toward some flat islands southeast of Jamaica. Then a light breeze rose, and they sailed due west for four days, during which they saw the blue outline of Jamaica in the north. Then a rising wind made them alter course to the northwest and north, and on July 24 they reached a flat island which the Admiral thought he recognized as one of the islands in the Queen's Garden. Diego de Porras, who wrote a brief official report of the voyage, says that the ships were "more damaged than they had supposed," and they might have careened and caulked one of them there, since they stayed until July 26. But they might only have been waiting for wind, and the Admiral knew that the local winds were unreliable at that time of year. A good wind came at last, and they sailed south by west for three days, until they saw some islands on the horizon. They made for the nearest one, and anchored, and to the south they could see a long coast with blue mountains.

Fernando Colón says: "After we had reached the island of Bonacca, the Admiral told his brother, the Adelantado Don Bartolomeo Colón, to go ashore with two boats, and there they found people like those of the other islands, though their foreheads were not so broad ....While the Adelantado was ashore on that island trying to discover its secret, there came by chance a canoe as long as a galley and eight feet wide, made of a single tree trunk and shaped like the others....Amidships it had a hut of palm leaves, not unlike those on the Venetian gondolas, which sheltered all within it, so that neither rain nor storm could harm them. Within this hut were the children, the women, and their baggage and articles of trade. There were twenty-five men aboard, but they offered no resistance when our boats took them prisoner.

"Our men brought the canoe to the side of the ship, where the Admiral gave thanks to God for showing him all the produce of the country, all together and with no trouble or danger to our people. He gave instructions to take aboard all the things which seemed to him to be the most beautiful and of the greatest value, such as some large blankets and sleeveless cotton tunics, embroidered and coloured in various patterns, some small cloths of the same kind as the Indians use to cover their genitals, and the shawls which the women in the canoe wrapped about

them, like the Moorish women in Granada. And long wooden swords, with grooves on each side, where the edge of the blade should be, with sharp flints which cut like steel, lashed into them with tarred twine; and axes to cut wood, like the stone axes used by the other Indians, but made of good copper. They had bells of the same metal, and crucibles to melt it. They had roots and corn, of the same kind as those eaten on Española, and a kind of wine, made of maize, which tasted like English beer."

The Admiral paid for everything he took, and then allowed the Indians to continue in their canoe. The only person he detained was an old man, to employ as interpreter and contact man on the remainder of the voyage. This man did not speak the same language as the Indians on Española, but the Spaniards understood him to say that there was a large rich country called Maian to the west, and "Maian" could easily be interpreted as "Mangi." But the Admiral's objective on this voyage was not Mangi; he wanted to go farther south, along the coast of the continent, past the province of Chiamba, and then southwest until he reached the Indian Sea and found the gold and jewels of Taprobane and the spices of Maabar, as the maps of the world showed him. Once he had done that, it would be no great distance before he reached the Cape of Good Hope and could sail up past Guinea to Castile and thus complete his circumnavigation of the world.

Fernando Colón says that the large canoe came from a land in the west, near Mexico, but modern historians do not think that such large vessels were made in the Yucatan Peninsula; they think it must have come from Honduras in the south. I do not see why the canoe could not have been trading between Bonacca and the mainland to the west. The "Land of Maian" was clearly the Maya kingdom, which included Honduras. Bright sleeveless tunics and colorful blankets are still made in that district. I do not know whether any copper bells of that period are still in existence: the illustration is based on a gold bell found in Costa Rica.

It has often been said, on Fernando's authority, that on the fourth voyage Columbus was looking for a strait which would lead to a sea on the other side. But Fernando's biography was written years after the event, when it was common knowledge that a narrow isthmus separated the Atlantic from the Pacific. There is no reason to suppose that before Columbus began his fourth voyage he saw the new-found continent, his own New World, as anything more than a single country, a gigantic island hitherto unknown, or that he doubted that Asia had roughly the same shape as was shown on the best contemporary maps. So he was not looking for a strait, but for a cape, the southernmost cape of the long peninsula which formed the eastern limit of the Indian Sea.

It proved to be a long and arduous task to sail east, against head winds and storms, before the coast finally turned south. The Admiral himself wrote: "I had the wind, and a terrible current, against me all the way. I struggled against them for sixty days, and yet I made no more than 70 leagues. I did not once enter a harbour during this period, nor could I have done. The fury of the heavens gave me no rest. Rain, thunder, and lightning never ceased, and it seemed as if the end of the world were at hand."

In actual fact, this particular journey took only thirty-eight days. The Admiral is not an accurate authority for this voyage. His health was now so bad that he was unable to move for considerable periods, and he probably never went ashore himself. So that he could keep an eye on what was going on, he had a small cabin built for him on the poop deck. Porras describes the journey from Bonacca in this way: "The Admiral found a harbour which he called Puerto de Caxinas. Thence he began to sail along the coast, but the winds were against him and he made slow progress. He never drew away from the coast during the daytime, and he anchored close inshore for the night. The coast is very forbidding, or so it appeared because of the great rain and many storms from the skies. And so he pressed on, always within sight of land, in the same way as those who sail from Cape St. Vincent to Cape Finisterre never let the coast from their sight. Fifteen leagues beyond that point he took possession of a large river which comes from the highlands and is called the Rio de la Posesion. From there on the land was very flat and the people very savage, with few goods or chattels. Near the end of that flat stretch is a cape, which was the most difficult ever seen to pass. And he called it the Cabo Gracias á Dios," the Cape of Thanks Be to God: thanks because this part of the voyage was over at last, and thanks because the coast was turning south.

Then they ran before the wind for two days and covered almost as much distance as they had covered with the wind against them in the last thirty-eight days. They

After leaving Bonacca, they first sailed south to the mainland and stayed there for a few days behind a cape which the Admiral called the Punta de Caxinas. Fernando Colón writes:" The Indians on the Punta de Caxinas were clothed like those in the canoe, in coloured shirts and loincloths. They also wore thick padded cotton corslets, which gave adequate protection against Indian arrows and even withstood several blows from our swords."

Earthenware figures of the kind shown above appeared during the second peak of Maya culture, several centuries before the arrival of the Spaniards; nevertheless, we can recognize them from Fernando Colón's description of the native warriors' loincloths and padded corslets. The disc in front of the chest, and the large ear plates, were in fact made of beaten gold.

sighted the mouth of a large river, and anchored there to take on fresh water. While they were doing this, one of the boats capsized in the breakers, and two seamen were drowned. The Admiral called it the Río de los Desastros, the River of Disasters. They sailed on for eight days, observing that the coast became higher and that mountains began to appear inland, and here the coast began to turn southeast. On September 25 they anchored at a beautiful island which the Admiral called La Huerta, The Garden; the Indians they met called it Quirivi.

Fernando Colón writes: "This small island is hardly a league from an Indian village [on the mainland] called Cariai, near a large river. Crowds of people gathered there from neighbouring districts, many of them with bows and arrows, and others with small spears of palm wood, black as pitch and hard as a bone, which were tipped with certain bones of animals or with sharp fish bones. Still others were armed with wooden swords or large clubs. They had assembled to show us that they were prepared to defend their country. The men wore their hair in plaits which were wound round their heads. The women wore their hair short, like ours.

"When they realized that we came in peace, they were very ready to exchange their possessions for ours; and theirs consisted of weapons, cotton mantles, the afore-mentioned cotton shirts, and eagles made of *guanín,* a very inferior gold, which they wear about their necks as we wear an Agnus Dei or other adornments. They carried all these things to us by swimming out to the boats, for the Christians did not land on that day or the next. And the Admiral would not allow anything to be taken from them, lest they should take us for men who coveted their goods. Indeed, he ordered us to give them many of our possess-ions. The result was that the less we showed ourselves to be interested in trade, the more eagerly they sought it, and they made various signs from land, holding up their blankets like flags and inviting us to go ashore. At last, seeing that nobody came, they took all the things which had been given to them, and left them well tied together at the place where our boats had first landed, without keeping a single thing; and this was where our men found them when they landed on the following Wednesday.

"The Indians thought that the reason must be that the Christians did not trust them, and they sent a man of venerable appearance out to the ships, holding a flag on a pole, and accompanied by two small girls, the one aged about eight, and the other about fourteen. He lifted them into his boat and made signs that the Christians might go ashore in safety. Upon this invitation, the Christians went ashore to draw water, and the Indians took care not to move or to do anything that might alarm them; when they saw them going back to the ships, they made signs, urging them to take the girls, who were wearing *guanín* necklaces. As the old man seemed to wish it, we took the girls aboard.

Many " eagles," made of gold as well as guanín, *have been discovered in Veragua, the largest of them more than 6 inches in height.*

"In so doing, those people showed more discretion than we had yet seen, and the girls showed great courage, for although the Christians were complete strangers to them in appearance, customs, and race, they gave no sign of distress or fear, but always appeared to be happy and contented. And the Admiral treated them well in return. He gave them food and clothing, and then gave orders for them to be put ashore at a place where there were fifty men. And the old man who had come with them received them back with great joy."

They stayed there for eleven days, repairing the ships, for these were already badly worm-eaten and were leaking alarmingly. When they found that the Indians along this part of the mainland did not understand the language of the neighboring tribes, the Admiral gave orders that two men from Cariai were to be kept as guides and inter-preters. Their kinsmen thought that the Spaniards were holding them for ransom, and so they came out to the ships with ornaments of *guanín,* small wild boars, and other presents, and this time the Admiral kept the presents and gave them some hawk's bells and other objects in exchange. But he did not hand over the inter-preters.

In a letter to the Sovereigns he describes an occurrence which amused everybody: "I had at the time two wild boars which would have frightened an Irish wolfhound. One of our crossbowmen had brought down an animal which looked like a monkey, but was much bigger and had a face like a man. The bolt had gone through it from chest to tail, and as it was so fierce, the man cut off one of its arms and one of its legs. When the boar saw the monkey its bristles stood up on end, and it ran away. When I saw

165

CUBA

JUANA

San Juan
Evangelista

Jardin de la Reina

Las Tortugas

Santa Gloria

JAMAICA

MAIAN

I. de las Pozas

Bonacca

P. de Caxinas

MAIAN

Costa de las Orejas

C. Gracias á Dios

PROVINCIA CHIAMBA

Rio de los
Desastros

La Huerta

Cariaí

Aburema

Cativa

Mumbreo

VERAGUA

CIGUARE

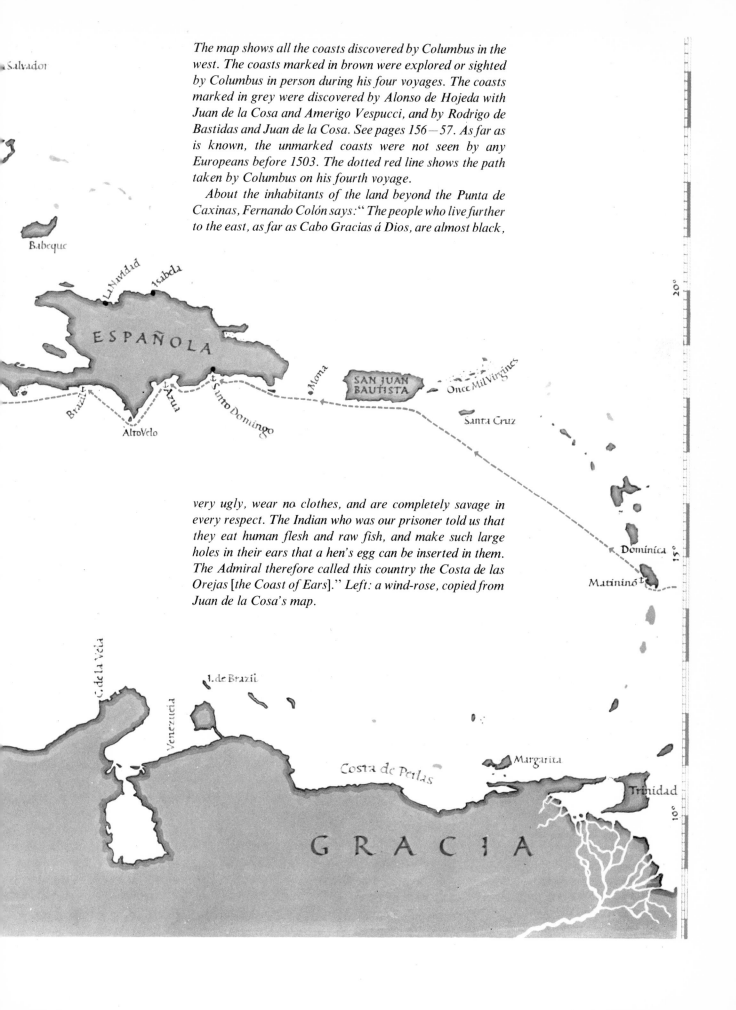

The map shows all the coasts discovered by Columbus in the west. The coasts marked in brown were explored or sighted by Columbus in person during his four voyages. The coasts marked in grey were discovered by Alonso de Hojeda with Juan de la Cosa and Amerigo Vespucci, and by Rodrigo de Bastidas and Juan de la Cosa. See pages 156—57. As far as is known, the unmarked coasts were not seen by any Europeans before 1503. The dotted red line shows the path taken by Columbus on his fourth voyage.

About the inhabitants of the land beyond the Punta de Caxinas, Fernando Colón says:" The people who live further to the east, as far as Cabo Gracias á Dios, are almost black,

very ugly, wear no clothes, and are completely savage in every respect. The Indian who was our prisoner told us that they eat human flesh and raw fish, and make such large holes in their ears that a hen's egg can be inserted in them. The Admiral therefore called this country the Costa de las Orejas [the Coast of Ears]." Left: a wind-rose, copied from Juan de la Cosa's map.

Salvador

Babeque

LNavidad

Isabela

ESPAÑOLA

Brazil

Azua

AltoVelo

Santo Domingo

Mona

SAN JUAN BAUTISTA

Once Mil Virgines

Santa Cruz

Dominica

Matininó

20°

15°

10°

C. de la Vela

Venezuela

I. de Brazil

Costa de Perlas

Margarita

Trinidad

GRACIA

that, I told them to throw the *begare*, as they called the monkey, in front of the boar. It was more dead than alive, and was still transfixed by the bolt, but when it came near the boar it twisted its tail round the boar's snout and held it tight, and caught its head with its one arm, as a man does to an enemy. This unusual and enjoyable entertainment inspired me to write this."

At dawn on October 5 they again set sail and continued the voyage with a good wind, and before evening they had passed through a narrow channel into a bay where there were many islands. The Indians called this bay Cerebaru. Here, at last, they found real gold, of the right color, and in exchange for three hawk's bells they obtained a "golden mirror" weighing ten ducats (35 grams). But the natives were not interested in Spanish goods, and after two chiefs had been forced aboard, to give some local information which the interpreters might convey to the Admiral, the party moved on southwest, through an extremely narrow strait into a large lagoon known as Aburema. There they stayed till October 17, exploring the country and mending the leaky caravels, and heard tell of the golden land of Veragua, and of Ciguare, on the other side of the high mountain range.

The Admiral writes: "The people go naked, and wear golden mirrors round their necks. But they will not sell them, or give them in exchange. They gave me the names of many places on the coast, where they said that gold could be found, and mines. The last name was Veragua, which is about 25 leagues off. . . . Everywhere I have been, I have found that everything I have been told has been the truth, and this convinced me that the same will be the case in the Province of Ciguare as well, which they tell me lies nine days' journey overland to the west. There, they say, can gold be found in unlimited quantities. . . . In all that I say, all the inhabitants of these places are in agreement, and they tell me so much, that I would be happy to believe a tenth of it. They also know of pepper. In Ciguare the people are accustomed to trade in fairs and markets, so these people said, and they described for me their customs and the way they do barter. Further, they say that their ships carry guns, bows and arrows, swords and shields, that the people wear clothes, and that there are horses in their country. They are said to be warlike, wear rich clothing, and live in fine houses. They also told me that the sea surrounds Ciguare, and that the River Ganges is a ten days' journey from there. It seems that

these lands lie in relation to Veragua as Tortosa to Fuenterrabia, or Pisa to Venice."

Columbus meant that Veragua is situated on one sea, and Ciguare on another, as Tortosa is on the Mediterranean coast and Fuenterrabia on the Atlantic, or as Pisa is on the Ligurian Sea and Venice on the Adriatic. He understood that he had reached a place where the long peninsula was narrowest, with only nine days' journey across the mountains to the Indian Sea. Ciguare was obviously the same as Chiamba. His Indian "interpreters," whose Spanish vocabulary cannot have been extensive, nodded cheerfully whenever he asked them any questions, and so he peopled the province of Ciguare-Chiamba with the inhabitants he expected would be found there: richly appareled townsfolk who traded in bazaars and sailed the seas in ships which carried guns. His maps showed him that the Ganges was a good ten days' sail from Chiamba, and the Indians confirmed this, with their usual nod of the head. Unfortunately, the maps were not entirely reliable: the long peninsula turned southeast and east, instead of southwest and west.

After the four caravels had left the river Cativa, they had to go through two long months of toil in the face of terrible storms.

Gold in Veragua

On they sailed, anchoring at night where they could, or lying to offshore. There were no more villages along the coast, but the sight of smoke inland told them that the river valleys were inhabited. The natives here were a suspicious lot, always ready to fight, but courage and perseverance often won their confidence and induced them to part with their coveted golden mirrors. Near a river called the Cativa they came across the remains of a house which appeared to have been built of stone and

169

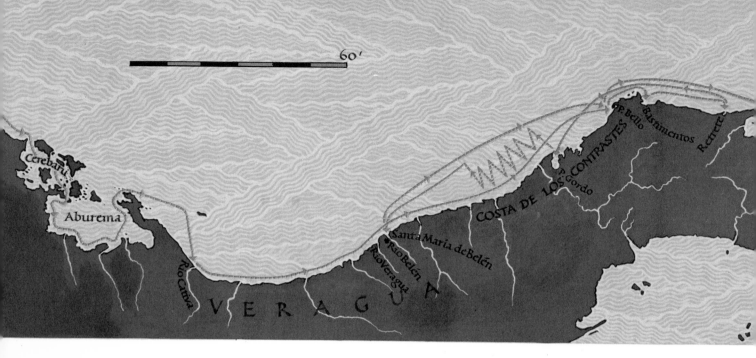

plaster. They thought it must be very old, and broke away pieces of it to take home with them. Then the wind became too strong for them to anchor along the open roadstead, and so they had to continue east and northeast past Veragua and the wealth of gold that was supposed to be there. And the coast ran on northeast.

The Admiral writes: "On the vigil of St. Simon and St. Jude [October 27] I ran before the wind, being unable to make headway against it. I sheltered for ten days from the great violence of the sea and sky in a harbour [Puerto Bello], and there I determined not to go back to the mines, which I regarded to be already ours. It was raining when I set out to continue my voyage. I reached the harbour of Bastimentos, which I entered against my better judgement. The storm and the great current kept me there for fourteen days. And then I went on again, but without good weather. I had made no more than 15 leagues when a raging wind and current drove me back. On the way back to the harbour from which I had come, I discovered El Retrete, which I entered with great danger and difficulty to take shelter; and everything was worn out, ships and men alike.

"There I had to stay for many days, on account of the cruel weather, and when I thought that it was easing up, I found that it had only just begun. There I altered my plans and decided to go back to the mines in order that we should have something to do while waiting for the weather to improve enough for us to continue the voyage. But when I had gone 4 leagues [to the west], the storm returned and so exhausted me that I did not know what to do. My old wound opened, and for nine days I saw myself lost, without hope of life.

"Eyes never saw the sea so high, so vicious, or foaming so wildly. The wind would neither allow us to go forward nor to take shelter behind any headland. I had to keep out in the sea that had turned to blood, and was seething like a cauldron on the high fire. Never did the skies appear more dreadful, for they blazed like a furnace for a whole day and night, and the lightning came in such great flashes that I wondered every moment whether it had destroyed my masts and sails; and the flashes struck with such terrible fury that we thought that the ships would be consumed. And all that time water came down from heaven without ceasing; I cannot call it rain, for it was as if there had been a second Deluge. The men were so exhausted that they longed for death to release them from their miseries. The ships had twice already lost their boats, anchors, and rigging, and they lay with bare masts at the mercy of the elements.

"When it pleased the Lord, I returned to Puerto Gordo, where I made the best repairs I could. Then I set out again for Veragua, but winds and currents were still against me for that journey, though I was prepared to continue. I approached the place where I had been before, but I was again faced by contrary winds and currents. And yet again I went in to anchor in a harbour, for in such danger off a wild coast I did not dare to await the opposition of Saturn with Mars, for that usually means storms and heavy weather. This was on Christmas Day, at the hour of Mass.

"I made my way back to the point from which I had so laboriously set out, and with the New Year I resumed my struggle. But although the weather was fair for my voyage, the ships were no longer seaworthy, and the crews were

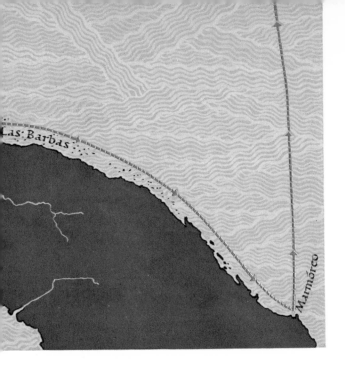

This map shows the route taken by the caravels from Cerebaru and Aburema (the modern Bahia de Almirante and Bahia de Chiriqui) past Veragua to Puerto Bello and Retrete (the modern Puerto Escribanos), and thence back to Puerto Gorda (the modern Colón at the mouth of the Panama Canal) and Rio Belén. Finally, east again, by way of Puerto Bello, to Cabo Marmóreo, probably the modern Cabo Tiburon on the Panama-Colombia frontier, and then north, in the hope of reaching Española.

mortally sick and exhausted. I reached Veragua on the day of the Epiphany, completely dispirited. There the Lord gave me a river and a safe harbour, although the harbour mouth was only 10 palmos deep. [A Spanish *palmo* equals 8¼ inches; a Genoese *palmo* equals 9¾ inches.] I entered there with difficulty, and next day the storm returned. If I had been outside then, I would not have been able to sail in, because of the sandbank.

"It rained without ceasing until February 14th and I was quite unable to go ashore to improve my situation. Just when I believed myself safe, on January 24th, the river suddenly rose violently to a great height, and this sundered my cables and moorings and almost swept my ships away. Indeed, they were in greater danger than ever before. But the Lord came to my assistance, as He has always done. I do not know whether any other man has suffered such torment.

"On February 6th, in the rain, I sent seventy men into the interior, and 5 leagues from the shore they found many mines. The Indians who were with them led them up a very high hill. They showed them the country all round, as far as the eye could see, and said that there was gold everywhere, and that the mines extended west for a journey of 20 days. They gave the names of the towns and the villages, and pointed to where they were to be found in greater or lesser numbers. I learnt later that Quibian [the local cacique], who had supplied these Indians, had told them to show us some distant mines which belonged to another man, his enemy, whereas within his own territory a man could collect a child's weight in gold within ten days, whenever he wished. I have with me some Indians, servants of his, who will confirm this. The boats could go all the way to his village. My brother came back with the party, all of them with gold which they had collected in the four hours they had spent there. The quantity is great considering that none of them had ever seen any gold-mines before, and very few of them had seen any gold [i.e., in its natural state]. Most of them were seamen, and almost all with the rank of ship's boys."

When the Admiral speaks of mines, he means open goldfields. Fernando Colón tells us that they rooted for gold under the trees with their bare hands. Diego de Porras says that they found two or three *castellanos* (9—14 grams), without using tools. He must have meant two or three *castellanos* each, otherwise no one would have been much impressed.

Columbus' narrative is certainly obscure and confused, but it is unlikely that his own impressions were much clearer. Fernando Colón gives us more details and writes quite calmly about harbors and skirmishes with the Indians, as one can if one is writing several decades after the event. "And apart from all these different dangers, there was another, no less dangerous and astonishing: a waterspout, which on Tuesday, December 13th, passed between the ships; and if we had not broken it by reciting from the Gospel according to St. John, it would surely have drowned those whom it struck. For it sucks up water into the clouds in a column which is thicker than a water butt, and twists it about like a whirlwind."

One day the ships were surrounded by sharks, and the men began to catch them to supplement their rations. "Some of the crew saw them as a bad omen, and others as poor food, but everyone ate of their flesh, for we were short of provisions, having been eight months at sea and having consumed all the meat and all the [dried] fish that we had carried from Spain. And what with the heat and the dampness from the sea, the biscuit had become so full of worms that, God help me, I saw many men wait until nightfall before eating their porridge [of soaked biscuit], so that they would not see the worms."

Columbus called this troublesome stretch of coast La Costa de los Contrastes, and it was here that he definitely gave up his plans to sail to the end of the peninsula and round into the Indian Sea. He was a defeated man. He and his men might have regained their strength and their courage, but the ships were by now almost unserviceable.

The River Belén, in which they had cast anchor, was barely a league from the River Veragua, at the very heart of the gold-producing region. Investigation showed that it was the deepest river in the district, and the Admiral decided to found a colony and build a settlement, to be called Santa María de Belén. The Adelantado was to stay there with eighty men, and they cleared a headland on the west bank of the river and began to build log cabins and thatch them with palm leaves. In March, when a dozen or so cabins had been put up and the Admiral was preparing to sail back to Castile, the river fell so much that the caravels could not cross the sandbank at the river mouth. Earlier they had prayed to God for fine weather; now they found themselves praying for rain, and plenty of it, to raise the water level.

The Indians in Veragua were disturbed by the arrival of their new neighbors, and the Admiral learned through his loyal interpreters that Cacique Quibian was planning to set fire to the settlement and massacre the Christians. So Columbus decided to capture him and send him to Castile, in order to "punish him, to set an example, and to frighten his neighbours." Under the joint leadership of the Adelantado and Diego Méndez, one of the Admiral's servants, an attack was made on Quibian's village. The cacique was taken prisoner, together with many of his subordinate chieftains, with their wives and children. But he managed to escape while they were taking him down-river, and the others ended up in the hold of the flagship without him. The spoils from Quibian's village comprised "golden mirrors, eagles, small golden cylinders which they string round their arms and legs, and braided gold which they wear on their heads like crowns, about 300 ducats' worth."

Then it pleased God to send enough rain to make the river rise, and during a few calm days the Spaniards managed to tow out three of the ships, almost empty. La Gallego, the most seriously worm-eaten and weather-beaten of them all, was left to the settlers, as a stronghold and supply base. The ships dropped anchor a good way out from shore, and then food and fresh water and equipment were laboriously taken out to them in the boats. On April 6, when all the boats but one were up in the river, a powerful wind blew up suddenly and they could no longer get through the breakers. The Admiral was afraid that the cables might give and the ships be driven ashore, and then he suddenly heard shots and cries and realized that the Indians had begun an attack. He heard sounds of fighting for three hours, and then dead silence. That evening, he saw bodies floating down the river, with carrion crows cawing round them. Most of his men were ashore. The breakers were too fierce for anyone to get in or out.

"I was outside and all alone on this very dangerous coast, with a high fever and greatly exhausted. There was no hope of rescue. In this state, I climbed in pain to the highest point of the ship and called, in tears and trembling, to Your Highnesses' mighty men of war, in all the four corners of the earth, for succour, but none of them answered me. At length, groaning with exhaustion, I fell asleep, and I heard a most merciful voice saying: 'O fool, so slow to believe and to serve thy God, the God of all! What more did He do for Moses or for His servant David? He has had thee in His care from thy mother's womb. When He saw thee a grown man, He caused thy name to resound most greatly over the earth. He gave thee the Indies, which are so rich a part of the world, and thou hast divided them according to thy desire. He gave thee the keys to the gates of the Ocean, which were held with such great chains. Thou wast obeyed in many lands, and thou hast won a mighty name among Christians. What more did He do for the people of Israel when He led them out of Egypt, or for David, that shepherd boy whom He made a king in Jewry. Turn thyself to Him, and acknowledge thy sins. His mercy is infinite. Thine old age shall not prevent thee from achieving great things, for many and vast are His domains. Abraham was more than a hundred years old when he begat Isaac; and Sarah, was she a girl? Thou criest for help, with doubt in thy heart. Ask thyself who has afflicted thee so grievously and so often: God or the world? The privileges and covenants which God giveth are not taken back by Him. Nor does He say to them that have served Him that He meant it otherwise, or that it should be taken in another sense; nor does He inflict torments to show His power. Whatever He promises He fulfils with increase; for such are His ways. Thus have I told thee what thy Creator has done for thee, and for all men. He has now revealed to me some of those rewards which await thee for the many toils and dangers which thou hast endured in the service of others.'

"I heard all this as if in a trance, but I could find no reply to give to so sure a message, and all I could do was to weep over my transgressions. Whoever it was that had spoken, ended by saying: 'Fear not, but have faith. All

these tribulations are written upon tablets of marble, and there is reason for them.' "

Some of Quibian's sons and subordinates escaped from the flagship during the night. Although several seamen were sleeping on the hatch, some of the prisoners managed to force it open, and then rush to the side of the ship and leap overboard. But these were a minority, and it was discovered next morning that the others had hanged themselves. In their cramped quarters under hatches, the Indians had had to raise their knees to their chins before they could swing clear.

The wind showed no signs of abating for the next few days, and when they could detect no sight or sound of life ashore, a small party rowed toward the land in the one remaining boat. When they reached the breakers, Pedro de Ledesma, the pilot, jumped off and managed to swim into the river. He found the settlers on the right bank, behind a barricade which consisted mainly of barrels, holding the enemy off with two bronze falconets. Seven of them had fallen during Quibian's first attack, and Captain Diego Tristán and three others had been killed while rowing up the river to get water. The Adelantado and many others were wounded. Everyone begged to be allowed to return to Castile with the Admiral.

Ledesma managed to swim back to the boat and was rowed out to the Admiral to give a report. On April 14 the weather improved, and within two days, under the supervision of Diego Méndez, the stores, the water butts with their precious contents, the arms, and the men were carried out to the flagship in the one remaining boat and a few canoes lashed together. On April 16, 1502, the Admiral sailed from Rio Belén with *La Capitana,* the *Santiago,* and the *Viscaýno.*

La Capitana *and the* Santiago *among
the Las Barbas islands*

Stranded on Jamaica

If Fernando Colón is to be believed, the Admiral and his
brother were the only people who realized that they would
have to sail a good way east along the coast before they
could turn north and reach Española with the northeast
trade winds; the pilots all supposed that Santo Domingo
was due north of the Rio Belén. I do not accept Fernando's
evidence. He is far too ready to emphasize his father's
brilliance at the expense of others. Diego de Porras, describing the Costa de los Contrastes, says that some of the
seamen (pilots?) connected it on their charts with the land
"which Hojeda and Bastidas had discovered, that is to
say, the Pearl Coast."

Now, on an expedition like this one, every ship must
have carried its own general chart of all the newly discovered coasts in the West Indies. Later, Porras expressly
says: "The seamen no longer had any charts, for the
Admiral had taken them all." This must have happened
on the way home, but then the Admiral and his brother
were each virtually in command of a caravel of his own,
and it was no longer necessary for the others to know
exactly which course they were following, or in the
brothers' interests to disclose such information. In his
letter to the Sovereigns, Columbus says: "Let them [the
pilots] speak out, if they know where Veragua lies. I will
warrant that they can say no more than that they visited
certain lands that were rich in gold, and they may take
their oaths on that. But they have no notion of the way
there." Of course, that is nonsense. He wanted the Sovereigns to suppose that he was the only man who held the
keys to the gold; but later on many people sailed to Veragua without any difficulty at all.

So they profited from the varying winds along the coast
and slowly pressed on, in their leaky ships, to the north-
west and north. They had to leave the *Viscayno* to sink at
Puerto Bello, and the three crews totaling 130 men had
to crowd on to *La Capitana* and the *Santiago*. They passed
a group of small islands which the Admiral called Las
Barbas, the Moustaches, and eventually came to a headland where the cliffs were streaked with pale veins, and

174

this he called Marmóreo, Cape Marble. The coast had already begun to turn to the southeast, and they might have hoped that they were reaching the end of it, but the Admiral altered course to the north on May 1, in the faint hope of being able to reach Española.

On May 10, they sighted two low-lying islands, and the water round them was so full of turtles that it looked as if there were large sandbanks there; so they called them Las Tortugas, the Turtle Islands. Three days later, they reached the Queen's Garden, proof that they had been carried far west of Española by the wind and currents. Everybody was exhausted from hunger and work at the pumps, and they anchored here to rest. A strong wind blew up during the night, and drove the Santiago into the flagship, damaging them both. A week was spent making repairs and fishing. Then they beat against the wind for a whole month, and got no farther than Macaca in the southernmost part of Juana. The Admiral made one more attempt to force his way east for a few days in the vain hope of reaching Española, but although the pumps were kept going day and night, and the men were bailing with pots and ladles, the water kept rising in the holds, and eventually he decided to run downwind to Jamaica.

They reached Puerto Bueno on June 23, but since there was no river there, they continued on the following day to Santa Gloria, a sheltered harbor behind some black reefs. At high tide on June 25 they steered the fast-sinking caravels to the beach in close formation and then propped

them up. There was no more sailing, and the ships were now a fortified camp. Gradually, palm-leaf shelters began to appear on the decks and the castles. Provisions were quickly running out, and the Admiral sent Diego Méndez and several others to bargain with the Indians for cassava bread, or for anything else that was eatable.

At Santa Gloria, the Admiral finished the letter to the Sovereigns which he had begun on Dominica and continued at the Rio Belén. We have seen considerable excerpts from it already. It ended with the words:

"The Genoese, the Venetians, and all other peoples who have pearls, precious stones, and other things of value carry them to the ends of the world to trade with them and turn them into gold. Gold is a most excellent thing; he who possesses gold may do all that he wishes in this world, and may also lead souls into Paradise. The lords in these lands, in the country of Veragua, when they die, I am told that their gold is buried with them.

"On one voyage alone, 674 quintals of gold were carried to Solomon, apart from that which was brought him by the merchants and the mariners, and the tribute which was paid in Arabia. From that gold he made two hundred spears and three hundred shields, and the covering above his throne he overlaid with tablets of gold, adorned with precious stones. . . . Josephus says that all that gold came from the Aurea. If that is so, I declare that

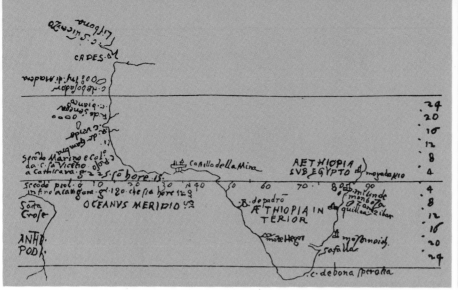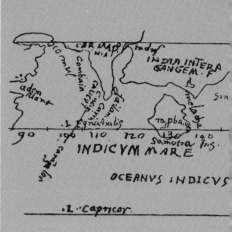

the mines in the Aurea are one and the same, and are joined to those of Veragua, which, as I have said, extend twenty days' journey to the west, and are half way between the Pole and the Equator. [According to Ptolemy, the Aurea Chersonesus lay between the equator and 10 degrees north. Veragua is approximately 9 degrees north.] Solomon bought all that gold, and You may order it to be collected here if You wish. In his testament, David left Solomon three thousand quintals of gold from the Indies, towards the cost of the Temple buildings, and according to Josephus it came from these same countries. Jerusalem and Mount Zion are to be rebuilt by the hands of a Christian, for God says so through the mouth of His Prophet in the fourteenth psalm. The Abbot Joachim has said that he who rebuilds it must come from Spain.... Who will offer himself for that work? If the Lord God takes me back to Spain, I promise, in His name, that I will lead him thither.

"The people who came with me have endured great danger and sore labour. I beg Your Highnesses to give orders that they may be paid immediately, for they are poor, and that every man may be rewarded according to his rank, for I warrant that they bring the best news that has ever reached Spain....

"I believe that Your Highnesses will remember that I wished to give orders to build a new kind of ship. But time was too short for that to be done, and I had foreseen the things that came to pass. [He had probably suggested the building of light sailing ships which could if necessary be propelled by oars.] I set greater store by that trade, and those mines, and that harbour, and that domain, than by anything else which had been won in the Indies. This is no child, to be left in the care of a step-mother. I cannot think of Española, Paria, and the other countries without tears coming to my eyes.... They are exhausted, and even

if they are not dead, their sickness is incurable or very severe. Let him who brought them to this state supply the remedy, if he can or if he knows of any. They [Bobadilla and Ovando] are all masters of destruction.

"I was twenty-eight years old when I entered Your service, and now there is not a hair on my head that is not white, and my body is sick and exhausted. Everything my brothers and I possessed has been taken from us and sold, even the very clothes on my back, without hearing or trial. It must be believed that this was not done on Your royal command. The restitution of my honour and my possessions, and the punishment of those who took them from me, who robbed me of my pearls and infringed the privileges of my Admiralty, will magnify Your royal honour....

"I now pray for Your Highnesses' pardon. I am ruined, as I have said. Hitherto I have wept for others: now may Heaven pity me, and may the Earth weep for me. Of worldly goods I have not a *blanca* to give in charity; and I have moved away from the practices of religion in the Indies. Alone, desolate, sick, in daily expectation of death, surrounded by a million savages full of cruelty, and hostile to us, and deprived of the Holy Sacraments of the Holy Church, my soul will pass into oblivion if it departs from the body while I am here. Weep for me, O men of charity, truth, and justice. I did not set out on this voyage to gain honour or wealth; this is certain; for by that time the hope of such things had died within me. I came to Your Highnesses with honest purpose and true zeal, and I do not lie. I humbly pray Your Highnesses that, if it please God to guide me from this place, You will help me to go to Rome and on further pilgrimages. May the Holy Trinity protect and prolong Your lives and Your high estate.

Written in the Indies, on the island of Jamaica, on July 7th, 1503."

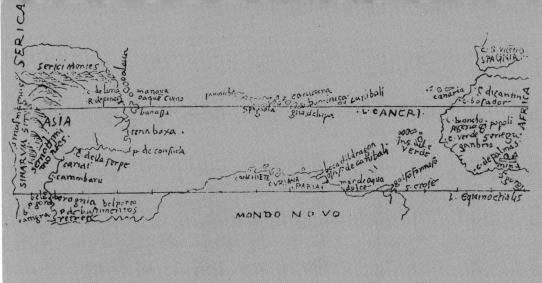

In the 1520s Alessandro Zorzi of Venice compiled the *Alberico, an anthology of exploration, which includes an Italian translation of Columbus' letter to the Sovereigns from Jamaica. Its marginalia include the three maps printed above, which were once thought to be the work of Bartolomeo Colón. Modern authorities prefer to believe that Zorzi himself copied them from sketches enclosed in a letter from the former Adelantado. It has been suggested that they represent Columbus' mental picture of the world after his fourth voyage.*

The map on the extreme left has a latitudinal scale, and on all of them the equator is divided into sections of ten degrees. The right-hand sketch would supposedly show the world known to Columbus from personal experience, but we cannot recognize it as such. Juana (i.e., Cuba) is missing, and the distance across the sea is quite different from Columbus' estimate. Here, the distance from the Canaries to the westernmost point of Española is about 57°, and to Veragua 115°.

Columbus' letter to the Sovereigns contains the following information, in addition to passages already quoted: "What I know is that in the year ninety-four I sailed 24 degrees west to the end of the ninth hour.... Ptolemy thought that he had corrected Marinus' errors, but it is now clear that Marinus' reckoning is very near the truth. Ptolemy placed Cattigara 12 lines [180°] beyond his westernmost point, which he placed at 2° beyond Cape St. Vincent, in Portugal. Marinus allows 15 lines [225°] for the inhabited world and its limits."

Translators and interpreters have often misunderstood his first sentence. "The end of the ninth hour," when the globe is divided into 24 hours, lies 120° west of the zero meridian, which in Columbus' time passed through the Canaries. When he says that he sailed "24 degrees," he means 24° west of Cabo Alfa et Omega, so that he explored 24° of the mainland. The "335 leagues" in the description of that grueling journey correspond, on Columbus' grid, to 24° at the equator; this would place Cabo Alfa et Omega 94° from the Canaries. Columbus and his brother must both have realized that the westernmost point on Española and the easternmost point on Cuba must have been approximately on the same meridian, but the above map puts Española 37° farther east. From the reports of the second voyage, we can see that the distances covered at sea could be calculated with almost complete accuracy. Columbus' degrees were so much shorter than other peoples'; his distances, when expressed in degrees, were always too large, and his astronomical calculations of longitude agreed remarkably well with his estimates of distance covered. But it is surprising that the distance from the Canaries to Española on the above map corresponds almost exactly to the true distance, since, to the best of our knowledge, European scholars also used "short" equatorial degrees in their calculations.

At official hearings, long after Columbus' death, Bartolomeo Colón explained that he and his brother had both been convinced that Veragua was connected to the new-found continent in the south. The map agrees there, and if we turn the page 90° to the left, we can recognize in the far west the coastline Columbus discovered on his fourth voyage. (cf. pages 166, 170.) So we may well believe that Bartolomeo Colón sent Zorzi a sketch-map of the newly discovered coastline, adding that it was probably connected to the southern continent, and that Cattigara and the Sinus Magnus were a nine days' journey beyond Veragua. Zorzi was responsible for everything else, for the wrong orientation of the map, for the copying of the southern continent from other sources, and for the position of Española at a point suggested by different data.

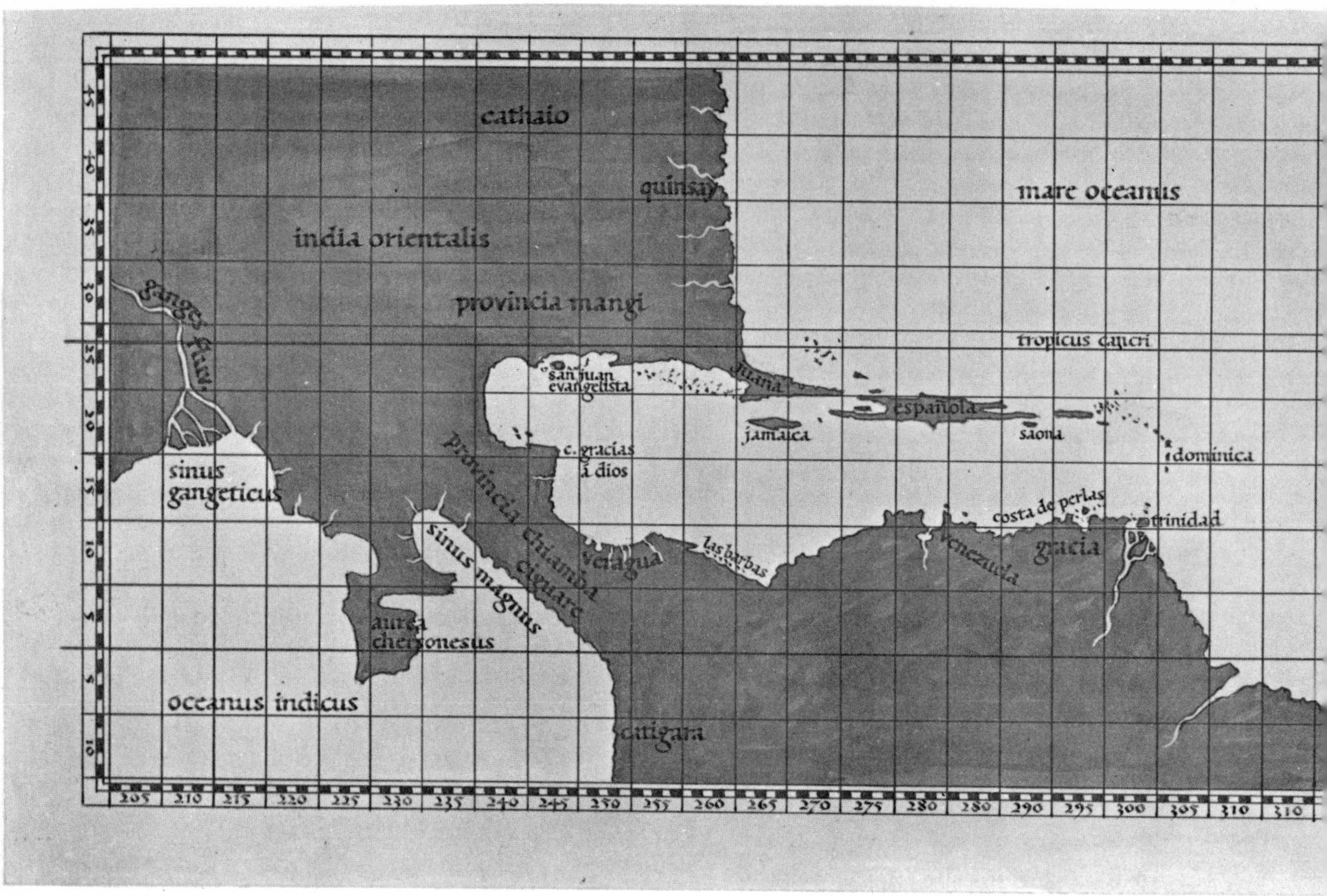

cathaio

quinsay

mare oceanus

india orientalis

provincia mangi

tropicus cancri

san juan
evangelista

iuana

españiola

ganges fluu.

jamaica

saona

dominica

sinus
gangeticus

c. gracias
à dios

provincia chiamba

veragua

costa de perlas

trinidad

sinus magnus

las barbas

venezuela

gracia

aurea
chersonesus

oceanus indicus

catigara

205 210 215 220 225 230 235 240 245 250 255 260 265 270 275 280 285 290 295 300 305 310 315

I have tried to make a map based on Columbus' official communications about his new discoveries, with reference to their extent, their relative positions, and their distance from Europe. I have drawn it on Toscanelli's projection, with the zero meridian running through the Canaries, and the degrees of longitude ascending in order of magnitude to the east.

There are several more or less definite points from which we can start. Fernando Colón says that the distance from Gomera to Dominica on the second voyage was estimated at 750—800 leagues. If we say 800, and measure off that distance on a globe after converting it to Columbus' equatorial degrees, each of which were 56 miles, or roughly 14 leagues, we will find Dominica at a longitude of 301°. I assume that the latitudes of the different islands and coasts were more or less correctly known. Columbus calculated that Saona was on a longitude of 287° 30' during the eclipse of September 14, 1494. In the letter describing the first voyage he says that Española is 188 leagues long; he was referring here to the north coast, which is considerably shorter than the south coast. The letter he wrote from Jamaica gives the position of Cuba (cf. the quotation on page 177), and during a lunar eclipse at Jamaica he was able to calculate that Santa Gloria was 108° 45' west of Cadiz, which puts the harbor at about 264°.

A map of the Caribbean and its islands based on these figures and on Juan de la Cosa's description of the Pearl Coast, together with the parts of Zorzi's maps which might have been drawn by Bartolomeo Colón, is far too elongated, and Española is flattened almost beyond recognition. Yet the strange thing is that both calculations of longitude made from Columbus' astronomical observations, although completely off the mark, do in fact put Saona and Jamaica in their right places in Columbus' world. This has quite convinced me that Columbus chose his figures to fit his preconceived ideas, and that the results of both observations were pure falsifications. If he had drawn an accurate map of the area, he would have seen that the proportions were all wrong. Later cartographers, who had access to his calculations of longitude, did indeed have difficulty in getting the picture to fit: Waldseemüller, for example, who drew his map (page 186) in 1507, puts a part of Cuba north of the Tropic of Cancer and the Pearl Coast 4° north of the equator.

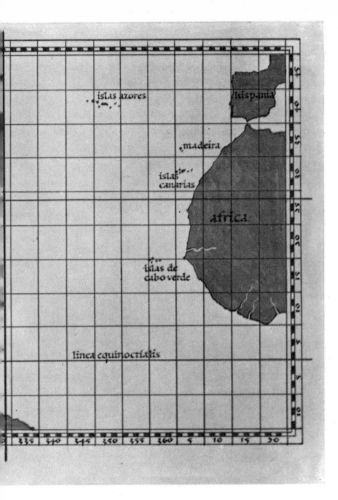

It may well be that even when Columbus was aglow with the success of his first voyage, the experts were beginning to question the length of his equatorial degrees, and that this induced him to make all possible efforts later on to prove that he had sailed farther west than was really the case. When he asserts that he sailed 335 leagues beyond the Cabo Alfa et Omega, he is doubling the true distance. On his fourth voyage, he might occasionally have wondered whether he had really reached the province of Chiamba; that may explain why he wanted to persuade himself, as well as the Sovereigns, that even the great Ptolemy had been wrong about the extent of the known world, and that Marinus of Tyre had come nearest the truth.

We do not know where Columbus wanted to put Cattigara, but the isthmus which separated him from the ocean on the other side was, according to the natives of Veragua, a nine days' journey across. On Zorzi's maps it is about 10° wide. We do not know if he shared Juan de la Cosa's view, that the English and Portuguese discoveries to the northwest were a part of Asia, or whether he thought that they were simply islands.

Since it was generally known that there was no gold to be found on Jamaica, the Admiral could not depend on the chance that any ships would come there, and so he had to get word of his predicament to Española and ask for help. Diego Méndez, the Admiral's servant, who had now become captain of the flagship after Diego Tristán's death, and Bartolomeo Fieschi, the former captain of the *Viscaýno*, volunteered to try to sail across to Española.

They selected two medium-sized canoes and fitted them with washboards in the bow and stern, and with false keels and sails. The Admiral gave them his letter to the Sovereigns, together with letters to Ovando, to his son Diego, and to Friar Gorricio, and then the two captains went off to the easternmost point of Jamaica with mixed crews of Christians and Indians. While they were waiting for winds that would take them to Española, they were attacked by natives and eventually had to go back to Santa Gloria to ask for an escort. The Adelantado marched on the cape with seventy men, and at the end of July, Méndez and Fieschi set off, paddling and sailing their canoes in fair weather. If they reached Española in safety, Fieschi was to come back to Jamaica immediately and report their arrival.

The Admiral, who had learned from bitter experience what could happen if the sailors were allowed to move among the Indians as they pleased, kept strict discipline and allowed no one to go ashore without permission. By means of an organized system of barter, they obtained food from the Indians, chiefly cassava bread and maize, but also including large Indian rats and lizards, which were now considered delicacies. Over a hundred men were crowded in the huts on the decks, forecastles and poops, and some forty of them were suffering greatly from fever and undernourishment. This went on for month after month, and there was no sign of Fieschi. The result was inevitable.

Long inactivity, overcrowding, and suspense led to hysteria and then to open mutiny. The ringleaders were Francisco and Diego de Porras, those two brothers whom Columbus had accepted under compulsion; Fernando Colón says that they swore that the Admiral did not want to go back to Castile and was keeping them all there to die with him. On January 2, all hell broke loose. There were shouts of "Kill the Admiral and his men!" and "To Castile, to Castile!" The Admiral tried to rise from his sickbed to meet them, but his servants stopped him. They also disarmed the furious Adelantado and managed to convince the mutineers that bloodshed could only harm them all and was sure to be severely avenged by the Sovereigns.

The mutineers then left the ships and began to fit out some canoes to cross to Española, and many others who saw them doing so went over to their side for fear of being

179

left behind. Only twenty men in good health, in addition to those too sick to move, stayed with the Admiral. The mutineers made three attempts to sail to Española, but each time they were driven back by wind and currents, and so they began to wander about the island, living in the Indian villages and ravaging and plundering to satisfy their needs.

The mutineers once gone, the Admiral's men were able to restore some degree of order on the ships and gradually nurse the sick back to health. But the Indians, realizing that the white men had been weakened by discord, and already having more beads and bells and red caps than they needed, soon announced that they did not intend to sell them any more food.

When the Admiral had considered this new development for a few days, he found that God once again had miraculously come to his aid, for he read in Abraham Zacuto's *Almanach Perpetuum* that there would be a total eclipse of the moon in three days. He allowed the hostile Indians to be told that he was going to pray to his God to punish them by putting out the light of the moon. On the crucial evening, hundreds of the natives gathered on the beach near the ships, most of them sceptical and derisive.

But when the moon rose, part of it was already obscured. As its blood-red face grew smaller and smaller, panic spread among the Indians, and before long they were crying out that they would do anything the Admiral asked them to if he would only persuade his God to restore the moon to them. Their wish was granted, of course, but not before they had been told that the Admiral was saying his prayers; and the light gradually came back. From then on, the white men had no difficulty in buying food.

While all this was going on, Columbus made use of the eclipse to try to determine his longitude. He wrote in his *Libro da la Profecias:* "On Thursday, February 29th, 1504, when I was on the island of Jamaica in the Indies, at the port called Santa Gloria, which is almost in the centre of the north coast of the island, there was an eclipse of the Moon, and as it began before sunset I could observe only the end of it, when the light of the Moon had just begun to return; and it must have been two and a half hours after sunset, five half-hour glasses to be precise. The difference in time between the centre of Jamaica in the Indies and the Isle of Cadiz in Spain is seven hours and fifteen minutes; so that the Sun sets seven hours and

fifteen minutes earlier there than on Jamaica—see the *Almanac*. In the harbour at Santa Gloria on Jamaica the altitude of the Pole Star was 18 degrees, with the Guards at the arm."

The latitude of Santa Gloria is 18° 27', and the result shows that Columbus could calculate his latitude correctly even when he was seriously ill. We do not know how time was measured with the half-hour glass, but his calculations were wildly off the mark for the longitude. Seven hours and fifteen minutes are equivalent to a longitude of 108° 45', which would put Jamaica in the Pacific, off the west coast of Mexico.

Eight months after Méndez and Fieschi had left for Española, several of the men who had remained loyal to the Admiral began to grow weary of waiting and planned another mutiny. Then, toward the end of March, a small caravel from Española cast anchor in Santa Gloria. The captain came over in the boat with greetings from Ovando to the Admiral, and with the gift of a cask of wine and a flitch of bacon. He also brought a letter from Méndez. He said that he had to sail back to Española immediately, but his ship was too small to take anyone else with him. He left that same evening.

Fernando Colón writes: "The truth was that the Comendador [Don Nicolás de Ovando] was afraid that if the Admiral returned to Castile Their Catholic Majesties would restore him to his office and relieve the Comendador of the governorship. He therefore did not want to help the Admiral to reach Española, and sent the small caravel to ascertain his circumstances and to see whether he could destroy him. The Admiral knew this from a letter which Diego Méndez had sent with the caravel, in which he described his journey and what happened afterward. This is the story.

"When Diego Méndez and Fieschi left Jamaica the weather was fair. They sailed until the evening of the first day, urging the Indians to maintain a good speed with those paddles they use as oars. Since the heat was oppressive, the Indians refreshed themselves from time to time by swimming in the sea. And so they steered over calm waters, and by sunset they had lost sight of land. When night came, half the Indians were set to paddle, while they were watched by as many Christians, in case of treachery. They paddled all that night without respite, and by dawn they were utterly spent. Each captain urged his men on, and sometimes took a turn at the paddles himself; and after the rowers had eaten a little to regain their strength, they took up work again. And they saw nothing but sea and sky.

"It may be said that it was with them as with Tantalus, who had water so close to his lips and yet could not quench his thirst. Our men suffered greatly on account of the folly of the Indians, for in the great heat of the previous day and during the night they had drunk all the water, without thought of future needs. As the sun rose in the sky, the heat and their thirst grew in intensity, so that by noon they were completely exhausted. Fortunately, each of the captains had a small keg of water with him, from which they now dispensed a few drops of water to the Indians, to sustain them until the cool of the evening. They encouraged them with the hope that they would soon be sighting Navassa, which is eight leagues from Española. The Indians were not only utterly exhausted, from the lack of water and the labour of two days' paddling, but also thoroughly disheartened and convinced that they had lost their way, for by their reckoning they had paddled twenty leagues and should have sighted Navassa already.

"It was their exhaustion and faintness which deceived them: neither a boat nor a canoe can make more than ten leagues in a day and a night against the currents which run between Jamaica and Española; but when one is under a great strain one's efforts are always thought to be greater than they really are. That night one Indian died of thirst, and they had to throw him into the sea, and with others stretched out on the bottom of the canoe they were so weak and dejected that they could hardly make any progress at all. Yet on they pushed, rinsing their mouths with sea water to refresh themselves, which was the comfort given the Lord when he said 'I thirst.' And thus they continued until nightfall of the second day.

"But since they were the messengers of him whom God wished to save, He so ordained that when the moon rose Diego Méndez saw a small island covering its lower half, like an eclipse. At that hour he could not have sighted that island in any other way, since it was a very small one. Méndez joyfully pointed it out to the others, and by giving them a little water from the keg he so strengthened them that by morning they had paddled up to the small island, which is called Navassa.

"They found it to be of hard rock, and about half a league in circumference. They landed as best they could, and gave thanks to God for His mercy; and since the island was without trees and springs, they climbed from cliff to cliff, collecting water in calabashes, and they found such large amounts of it that they could fill their stomachs

as well as their vessels. Though they were warned not to drink too much, several Indians drank their fill and died, and others were in sore distress. Overjoyed at having Española in sight, they rested that day until evening, refreshing themselves and eating food they caught on the shore and cooked with the aid of a flint and steel Diego Méndez had brought with him. Fearing bad weather, they were anxious to complete their journey, and at sunset, in the cool of the evening, they set off in the direction of Cabo San Miguel, the nearest point on Española, where they arrived on the following morning, which was the fourth day since their departure. There they rested for two days.

"Bartolomeo Fieschi, a nobleman and a man of honour, wanted to go back with his canoe, as the Admiral had commanded. But the crew, who were Indians and seamen, were so exhausted and sick from their labours, and from drinking sea-water, that none of them would go with him. They thought that God had delivered them from the belly of the whale, and that their three days and nights corresponded to the days of the prophet Jonah. Diego Méndez had already set off at great speed along the coast of Española in his canoe, although suffering from a quartan ague [malaria] which he had contracted from all his hardships afloat and ashore. Later, he landed and went with his men over mountains and along some wretched tracks to Xaragua, a province in western Española, where the Governor was at that time. The Governor showed pleasure at his arrival, but he was very slow to help him, for the aforementioned reasons. By great persistence, Diego Méndez at last obtained the Governor's permission to sail to Santo Domingo, and, with the means which the Admiral had there, to buy and fit out a ship. When the ship was ready, which was at the end of May, 1504, he sent it to Jamaica; he himself went home to Spain, as the Admiral had instructed him to do, to give an account of the results of his voyage to the Catholic Sovereigns."

When the Admiral heard that help was on the way, he sent a message to the mutineers, offering them a general amnesty if they would return to the ships in peace. But Francisco de Porras began to make conditions. If two ships came, he wanted one for himself and his men; and if only one ship came, then a half of it was to be reserved for them. Since they had hardly any clothes or other possessions, he also demanded that the Admiral should divide all the equipment and goods on the ships equally among them all.

The Admiral refused to agree to any of those conditions. When the mutineers assembled in a village not far from Santa Gloria in obvious preparation for an attack, he sent the Adelantado with fifty armed men to offer them peace or a war. They chose war, and lost. Francisco de Porras was captured, Juan Sánchez, the chief pilot, was killed, and Juan Barba, the master-gunner, was wounded so badly that he died a few days later. Pedro de Ledesma, the pilot who had swum through the breakers into the Rio Belén, had received several severe sword cuts and fallen over a cliff, and everyone expected him to die; but he recovered. The other mutineers ran away. The Adelantado wanted to follow them, but he was held back by his men, who, so Fernando Colón tells us, said that "it was right to punish, but not too severely; for if he killed many of them, the Indians, who were watching impartially for the outcome, with weapons in hand, might attack the victors."

Pedro de Terreros, who had accompanied the Admiral on all his voyages to the Indies, first as major domo, and on the last two in command of a ship, was wounded by a spear and died on the flagship on May 29, twelve days after the battle. The Adelantado had been slightly wounded in the hand. These were the only casualties among the loyalists.

The mutineers now sent a message to the Admiral asking him to grant them an unconditional amnesty, and he agreed to do so, with the exception of Francisco de Porras, who was put in irons. Since the ships were already overcrowded, he sent a man to take charge of the mutineers while they wandered about the island, bargaining for food with the inhabitants as best they could. This went on until the end of June, when word was sent that a caravel had reached Santa Gloria.

This was the vessel which Méndez had hired and equipped. The hundred or so castaways crowded themselves aboard the caravel, and on June 28th she was able to leave Jamaica. They had spent a year and five days on the island. The voyage was slow, against wind and currents, and after stopping at Brazil and Madama Beata, they finally reached Santo Domingo, on August 13.

"The Governor received the Admiral very hospitably, and gave him accommodation at his house; but this was like the kiss of a scorpion, for at the same time he released Porras, the ringleader of the mutineers, and proposed to punish those who had been responsible for his imprisonment. He also wished to pronounce judgement in other matters, which were the sole concern of the Catholic Sovereigns, who had appointed the Admiral to be their Captain-General of the fleet," Fernando Colón tells us.

They hired another ship at Santo Domingo, and the Admiral went aboard with Fernando and the Adelantado and twenty-two of the old loyalists. Others were to have sailed home in the caravel which had brought them from Jamaica, but many of them chose to remain on Española, perhaps because they were inclined to trust Ovando's protection more than the Admiral's pardon. Fernando Colón describes the voyage home: "We set sail on September 12th and had gone two leagues out to sea beyond the river mouth when the ship's mainmast split right down to the deck, and the Admiral sent her back to shore. We on our ship continued on our way to Castile. After having enjoyed fair weather for about a third of the journey, we were struck one day by such a terrible storm that the ship was in great danger. And on the next day, which was Saturday, October 9th, when the weather had improved and we felt relieved, our mainmast broke in four parts. But the courage of the Adelantado and the ingenuity of the Admiral saved us, in spite of the fact that the Admiral was unable to leave his bed, for they made a temporary mast out of a yard, and reinforced it in the middle with boards from the forecastle and poop, which we took to pieces. Then, in another storm, our foremast broke, but it pleased God to let us sail in that condition for 700 leagues, until we reached the port of Sanlúcar de Barrameda. From there we went on to Seville, where the Admiral found some relief after his many hardships and exertions."

The moment of truth

After the Admiral had been taken ashore, he wrote his customary letter to the Sovereigns, who were in residence at Medina del Campo, and then awaited the customary summons to the Court to give an account of his voyage. But the situation at Court had changed. Queen Isabella was lying on her deathbed.

It is generally said that she died of sorrow and exhaustion after overexerting herself on behalf of her subjects. It is unlikely that she actually died of sorrow and overwork, but she had certainly had more than her full share of both. A year after the death of the Crown Prince Don Juan, she had lost her daughter, the Queen of Portu-

gal, who had died in childbed after having borne a son. The child was proclaimed heir to the thrones of Portugal, Castile, and Aragon, and would thus have united the kingdoms of the Iberian Peninsula, but he died before he was two years old. Then Doña Juana, who was married to the Archduke Philip, was proclaimed heir apparent in Castile, but in June, 1504, she was reported to be showing signs of insanity. In her will, Queen Isabella specified that King Ferdinand was to be sole ruler over Castile if Doña Juana was absent or otherwise incapable of governing the country. Isabella died on November.26, 1504, at the age of 53.

On November 28, before he had heard about the Queen's death, the Admiral wrote to his son Diego, who was looking after his interests at Court: "Although I am greatly distressed by my sickness, I am preparing for my departure [to Court] every day. It would make me extremely happy to receive a letter from Their Highnesses, and I wish that you could arrange it. I also wish Their Highnesses to arrange for the payment of the emoluments to those poor people who have suffered infinite privations and who have brought them such great news."

On December 1 he wrote: "I have heard nothing from you since I received your letter of November 15. I wish you would write more often. I wish that I could receive a letter from you hourly. You must realize that there is no one else to whom I can turn. Many couriers come each day, and the abundant news is so contrary to what my soul desires that my hair stands on end. May it please the Holy Trinity that our Lady the Queen is restored to health, that she can settle what is already under discussion. . . . I think that I should make a fair copy of the part of Their Highnesses' letter to me where they say that they will fulfil their promises to me, and will place you in possession of everything. This copy should be given to them with a letter which informs them that I am ill; that it is at present impossible for me to go and kiss their royal feet and hands; that the Indies are being lost and are on fire in a thousand places; that I am neither receiving nor have received anything of the revenues from the said Indies; that no one dares to accept or demand anything for me there; and that I am living upon borrowed money. The money I received there I used in bringing the people who went with me back to their homes, for it would have been a great weight upon my conscience to have abandoned them there. . . . Take good care of your brother. He has a good disposition, and is no longer a boy. Ten brothers would not be too many for you. Nowhere have I found better friends than my brothers. We must strive to obtain the government of the Indies, and then to adjust the revenues. . . . Today is Monday. I will try to persuade your uncle and your brother to leave tomorrow. Remember to write to me often, and tell Diego Méndez to write at length."

News of the Queen's death reached Seville on December 3. "I am much astonished not to have received a letter from you or from anyone else, and this astonishment is shared by all who know me. Everyone here receives letters, and I who have greater reason to expect them get none. Attend to this most assiduously. . . . Our first duty is to commend the soul of our Lady the Queen to God, with affection and great devotion. Her life was always Catholic and Holy, and she was always prepared to act in the service of God, and we may therefore believe that she is now received into His Glory, beyond the demands of this rough and painful world. Our next duty is to be alert and apply ourselves in the service of our Lord the King, and to exert ourselves in keeping him from discomposure. . . . Consider the proverb which says that when the head aches, so does the whole body ache."

And he continued in this vein with letter upon letter containing instructions, describing his misgivings about developments in the Indies, recounting his own financial difficulties, and adding constant reminders that his men had still not been paid. He also asked Diego to ascertain whether the Queen had mentioned him in her will. He wanted to pay a visit to the Court, but he was too ill to ride, and so he borrowed a magnificent hearse from the cathedral in which to make the journey. Time and again he was on the point of setting out, but the wintry weather put him off.

His financial situation was good, since he had more than sufficient ready money as well as credit, and so his complaints must be seen in relation to his expectations, which had, understandably, been far greater. He put up a stout fight for his tolls of one-eighth and one-tenth of the Indian trade, and he wrote to Diego: "I swear, and this is meant for your eyes alone, that the loss I am suffering, according to the rights guaranteed to me by Their Highnesses, amounts to ten million a year, and it can never be paid back."

He heard a rumor that three bishops were to be sent to the Indies, and he hoped that his case would be heard before they were appointed. He was probably hoping that his brother Diego, who had taken Holy Orders, would be given a bishopric. He wrote to the Bank of San Giorgio in Genoa and asked why he had received no reply to the letter he had written before his last voyage. He wrote to the Pope about developments in the Indies and perhaps once more about his plans for a Crusade. Toward the end of December he felt rather better, and he asked Diego to get the King's permission for him to ride to the Court on a mule.

As there had been some difficulty in finding enough horses for the war against Granada, the Sovereigns had decreed that nobody, except women and the clergy, should be allowed to ride a mule, and as a result the number of mounts in the kingdom had increased. In any case, the Admiral was given the required license without any difficulty, but he was not yet capable of riding.

On February 3, he was visited by Amerigo Vespucci, the Florentine explorer who had sailed to Trinidad and the Pearl Coast with Hojeda and later sailed south along the coast of the new continent in the service of Portugal. On February 5 the Admiral wrote to Diego: "I have spoken with Amerigo Vespucci, the bearer of this letter. He is going to Court, where he has been summoned in connection with points of navigation. He has always been anxious to please me. He is a very honourable man. Fortune has been against him, as against so many others."

Vespucci had offered to see what he could do for the Admiral at Court, but there was not much that could be done for the moment.

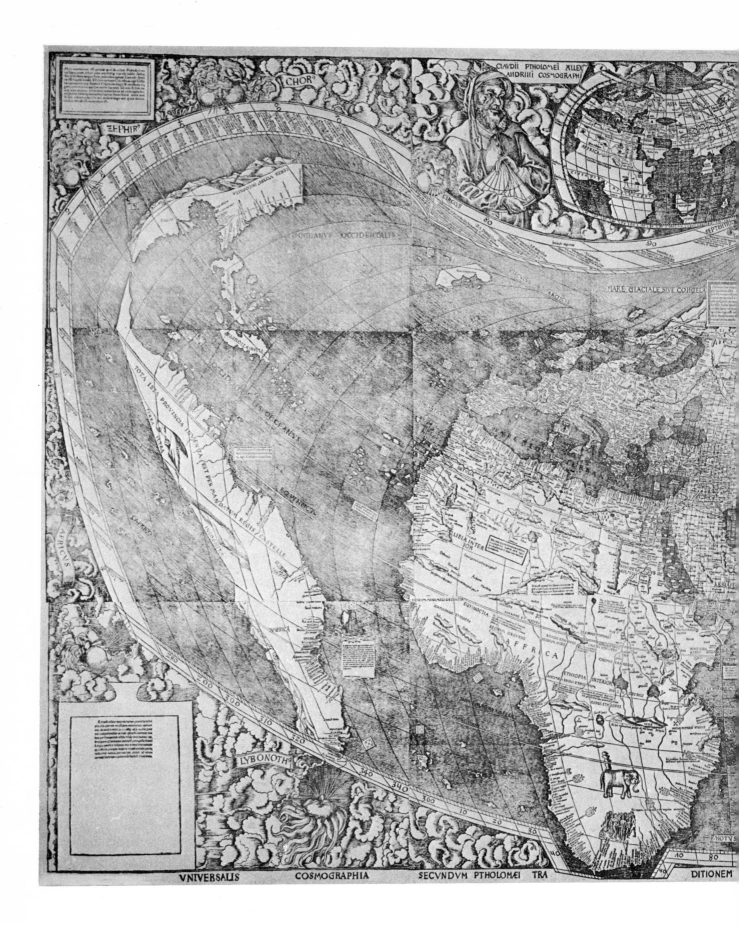

Martin Waldseemüller's map of the world, 1507. For a description, see page 188.

Duke René II of Lorraine had a circle of scholars about him in the town of Saint-Dié, chiefly to engage in scientific and cosmographical research. One of their number was Martin Waldseemüller. Their projects included the publication of a map of the world according to Ptolemy, but when news arrived about Amerigo Vespucci's letter describing the New World in the west, Waldseemüller laid Ptolemy aside and drew a map of the world which was destined to arouse the keenest interest.

Although he payed impartial homage to Ptolemy and Vespucci, whose portraits stand together at the top of his map, he might have done better to make some acknowledgment of Henricus Martellus, from whose map Waldseemüller's Old World is almost exactly copied (cf. page 16); evidently, news of Portuguese voyages to the Indies, and their contributions to geographical knowledge, had not reached Saint-Dié. The map was printed in 1507 from wood blocks on twelve sheets, which, when fitted together, measure 49 by 91 inches.

In the West, Waldseemüller was bolder and more accurate than anyone before him. He completely separated the New World from the Old. As a precaution, he presented two different versions. On the large map, the new continent is divided by a strait. On the small map to the right above it (shown in greater detail on this page), it is one continuous land mass. As far as we know, Florida was not discovered until 1515, by Juan Ponce de León. But the peninsula to

the west of Isabella (Cuba), and the district beyond it, are so similar to Florida, Yucatán, and Honduras that the matter seems to be open to doubt. However, the greater part of Waldseemüller's "North America" is exactly like the corresponding part of the Cantino map (page 161), and the names along the coast correspond closely. This cape is marked Cabo do fim do abrill (Cape of the end of April) on the Cantino map and Caput doffim de abril on Waldseemüller's map, and has similar names on other contemporary maps. It seems most likely that it has nothing to do with Florida but is simply Columbus' Cabo Alfa et Omega, which he discovered on April 29, 1494. If Waldseemüller had actually seen the Cantino map, his picture of the Indian peninsula should have been far better, and it seems probably that both cartographers were using the same Spanish source. Cuba appears under the name of Isabella because Columbus' letter, which had circulated widely, contains the information that the Admiral sailed from the island of Isabela to a land which he called Juana and which he believed was a part of the continent. Little further information leaked out from Spain, and some of what did was misleading, so that foreign cosmographers often drew the wrong conclusions from it.

Spanish secretiveness, rather than Amerigo's letter, may explain how it came about that just above the Tropic of Capricorn Waldseemüller marked the new continent with the word America.

In May, 1505, the Admiral made a weary journey on muleback to Segovia, where the King was residing. He was graciously given an audience, and after hearing his petition, the King suggested that an arbitrator should be appointed to settle the question of his privileges. The Admiral proposed his old friend Diego de Deza, who was now Archbishop of Seville, and the King agreed.

By now there was nobody in Spain, with the possible exception of the sons and brothers of the Admiral, who could see any reason why this elderly invalid should be reinstated as Governor of the Indies. In the eyes of the Sovereigns and other responsible authorities, he had already forfeited his right to that office in 1495, when his inefficiency had turned Española into an inferno, for natives and Christians alike, and the letters he had written on his last two voyages had made many people at Court begin to question his sanity. Nor was Diego de Deza, who had once helped him to obtain three caravels from the Sovereigns, able to come to any other conclusion than that the Admiral's rights of property and revenue from the Indies should be decided by skilled lawyers, and that the questions of the governorship should be left open or be entrusted to the King to decide.

The Admiral wrote to the Archbishop: "As it seems that His Highness is unwilling to fulfil what he has promised on his word of honour over with his hand and seal, together with that of the Queen—may she rest in the glory of the Saints—I believe that I would be beating the air if I, a common man, were to strive against him, and that, since I have done everything I can, it would be best to leave matters in the hands of the Lord God. Who had always been merciful and helpful towards me."

The King never expressly removed the Admiral from office, but he did suggest that the governorship of the Indies might be exchanged for a profitable tenancy in Castile. The Admiral indignantly rejected this offer.

In October the Court moved to Salamanca, and in April to Valladolid. The Admiral and those closest to him followed after, but the King had no time to spare for them. Ferdinand, who did not find it amusing to have to share the throne with his unbalanced daughter and her Hapsburg husband, was hoping for a marriage to a niece of Louis XII of France, which might provide him with a male heir to the throne. News of this alliance reached Flanders, and the Archduke and his wife hurried off to Castile in order to protect their own interests.

It was to them the Admiral now turned, in one last attempt to obtain justice. Too weak to travel, he sent the Adelantado to them with a letter.

"I am certain that Your Highnesses will believe that I have never before wished more eagerly to be sound in body than when I heard that Your Highnesses were on the way here by sea, so that I might have been able to come and serve You, and to offer You the use of my experience and knowledge as a sailor. It is the Lord's will, and I therefore humbly pray Your Highnesses to count me as one of Your vassals and servants, and to be assured that, although this sickness is for the moment tormenting me unmercifully, I will still be able to serve You in such a manner as no man has yet seen."

But the Admiral was not destined to serve anyone any longer. His strength left him quickly. On May 19 he was just strong enough to sign his will. Fernando Colón says: "In great pain from his gout, full of sorrow over the possessions which had been taken from him, and beset by other troubles, he gave up his soul to God on Ascension Day, that is to say upon the 20th of May, 1506, in Valladolid, after having devoutly received all the Sacraments of the Church and spoken these last words: 'Father, into Thy hands I commend my spirit.'"

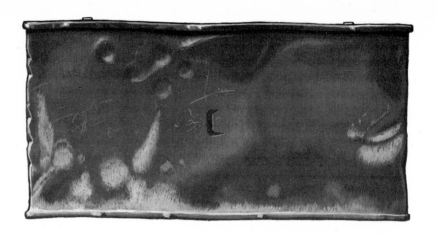

Columbus was buried in Valladolid, but in 1509 his son Don Diego transferred the body to the monastery of Las Cuevas in Seville. Don Diego died in 1526, and in 1541 his widow, Dona Maria de Colón y Toledo, Vicereine of the Indies, took his remains and those of Columbus to Española, where they were interred in the Cathedral at Santo Domingo. In 1795, Spain had to surrender Española to France, and Columbus' remains, or what were taken for them, were removed to Cuba and laid to rest in Havana Cathedral. But in 1877, when the Cathedral at Santo Domingo was undergoing repair, a small vault was discovered, containing a lead box, seventeen inches long, which bore the initials C C A. The underside of the lid was inscribed Illtre u Esdo Varon Don Cristoval Colon (Illustre y Esclarecido Varon Don Cristóbal Colón, i.e., The Illustri-

ous and Excellent man, Don Cristóbal Colón). In the box were a few fragments of bone and dust, together with a small lead ball, and a thin silver plate, inscribed U"a p"te de los rtos del pmer Alte D Cristoval Colon Des (Ultima parte de los restos del primer Almirante, Don Cristóbal Colón Descubridor, i.e., The last part of the remains of the first Admiral, Don Cristóbal Colón, the Discoverer). Spanish opinion refused to recognize these as the remains of Columbus, and when Cuba achieved independence in 1898, the remains in Havana Cathedral, which were still regarded as genuine, were removed to Seville, where they now lie in the Cathedral, in a stately sarcophagus. The evidence seems to indicate that Don Diego is the man whose remains are now honored in Seville and that the first Admiral still lies at rest in the Cathedral at Santo Domingo.

Conclusion

The object of this book has been to give a picture of Columbus' life, his abilities, his thoughts, and his theories, and the deeds which he and his contemporaries performed. It is not a complete picture; there can never be a complete picture. The more we learn about the thoughts, words, and deeds of humanity's giants and pygmies, the less do we find it possible to fit all the details into a coherent picture. Unless, of course, we want to simplify and vulgarize history into a tale of heroes and villains.

One of the many fascinating problems about Columbus is that he, a hero of history, possessed so many essentially unheroic attributes. The less edifying qualities of great men have always been inviting targets for the unskilled marksman, and Columbus has not been exempt. Mudslinging historians have represented him as a charlatan, a foreign immigrant, a Jew, an impostor who stole other men's ideas, a canting humbug, a hopelessly incompetent navigator, a pious fraud, a blood-sucking murderer, a man who had no idea where he touched land, and worst of all, a man who did not even discover America.

Other people have been anxious to see him as their countryman, as the greatest mariner and navigator in history, as the true Bearer of Christ, worthy enough to be numbered among the saints.

I have gone into the question of his nationality in sufficient detail. The question of whether his piety was true or false no one can decide conclusively. Personally, I think it was deep and sincere. People of today may object to the way he showed it, but he was a man of the Middle Ages. It is generally said that he introduced the the Modern Age, but historical epochs have fluid boundaries. The question of his character must remain open. We can see from his letters that he yearned for gold and power, that he seldom forgot or forgave an injury, and that in his last years he was a sniveling old fogy. But we also find that he was a visionary and a prophet, that he was inexhaustibly energetic and almost unbelievably brave, burning with curiosity, and ever active in his friends' interests.

The idea of sailing to the west in order to reach the Orient was an old one, and Columbus never suggested that he had been the first to think of it. His theories about the size of the earth, and the measurements he made to check them, were wildly incorrect, with a strong tinge of wishful thinking, but they did come to serve as a foundation for his enterprise. His one revolutionary innovation was his route across the ocean, out with the trade winds, and home with the westerlies. I think it not only possible but probable that he had heard of the Norse voyages to Markland and Vinland, and about the Danish expedition to Labrador in 1476; but the knowledge of such "islands" in the North Atlantic had no bearing on his plans to sail to the Indies. The question as to which Europeans first set foot in America has little or no relevance to the story of Columbus and it is by no means answered by some finds in Newfoundland and by a few words on a map. Columbus was certainly not the first, but his discovery was the first to lead to any practical results.

It is often asserted that he was convinced until the very end, and against all better-informed opinion, that he had reached India, and did not realize that he had discovered a new world. It is true that he thought that Cuba was the easternmost cape of Asia, and that Honduras, Nicaragua, and Costa Rica were the provinces of Mangi and Chiamba. His views on Cuba soon met with opposition, but few indeed among his contemporaries were those who doubted that North and Central America were parts of Asia. Most European scholars had a better idea about the size of the earth than Columbus, but none of them could know for certain how far the continent extended to the east. It is true that Peter Martyr Anglerius soon began to suspect that Columbus had discovered a new continent, but there is nothing to show that such a view was widely held at first.

Columbus was the first European to land on the shores of South America, and a few days after he had done so he was prepared to call it *Another World,* a yet unknown continent. This was all the more remarkable since he took it as the site of the Earthly Paradise. Two years after Columbus' death, Martin Waldseemüller drew his map of the world with the newly discovered countries completely separate from Asia. And it is on the large continent to the south that we first meet the name America. At the same time, Waldseemüller published a book called *Cosmographiae Introductio,* in which he suggests that the southern continent should be called Americus' Land, or America, after Americus Vespucius (Amerigo Vespucci), who had discovered it. As we have already seen, a misdated letter describing Vespucci's voyage with Hojeda to the Pearl Coast and Trinidad had been printed and was in circulation. This, together with a mistaken entry on a map, led to the new continent being known as America, after a man who explored only what others had discovered, rather than as Columbia. In later years, Waldseemüller became aware of his mistake and tried to correct it, but by that time the name America had won general acceptance. For a long time it was applied only to the southern part of the continent. When Waldseemüller drew a new map of the world in 1516, he was rather more

191

cautious and presented the countries lying north of the new continent as a part of Asia, and cartographers followed his example for several more decades.

Columbus' skill as a mariner and navigator has often been called in question. His extraordinarily brilliant seamanship is not often questioned today, and I am inclined to think that it has been sometimes overrated to the disadvantage of contemporary mariners. It has been said that in dead reckoning he had no peer, but that his stellar reckonings were hopelessly inadequate, and the last statement is usually supported by the records of latitude which he entered in his diaries. I have already indicated that these were all intentionally falsified. I do not believe that anyone could have found his way back to a given point on the other side of the ocean time and again so unerringly by dead reckoning alone. On the other hand, any experienced sailor can tell the height of the polestar above the horizon, and thus his approximate latitude with his hand alone. Although Columbus was a "man of little learning," he must have been better read and better informed than most contemporary mariners, and there is no reason to believe that he was inferior to the best pilots of his day.

As a colonial governor he was a complete failure. He was inconsistent in his treatment of Spaniards and Indians alike, sometimes lax, and sometimes severe, and the fact that he was a jumped-up foreigner who showed an excessive favoritism toward his brothers made things harder for him. In the lengthy dispute about his privileges and his deposition from office, I think I would have taken the side of the Sovereigns. It is true that they had promised him that he should be governor for life, but in their country's interest they could not let the colony perish under the direction of the two extremely unpopular brothers from Genoa. It was not easy for them to break their word, and that they had originally intended to keep their promise is shown by his reception in Barcelona after his first voyage. Then the enterprise grew into something greater and more complicated than had been foreseen either by Columbus or by the Sovereigns, and the Admiral of the Ocean did not come up to the requirements of a governor and viceroy.

Yet it seems that Ovando's appointment as governor was only a temporary measure. His severity toward the settlers, and his virtual extermination of the natives of Española aroused bitter hatreds, but he did bring order of a kind out of chaos. In 1509 the King gave the governorship of the Indies to Columbus' son Don Diego, who had inherited his father's title of Admiral of the Ocean. Don Diego's son, Don Luis, inherited the titles and governorship in his turn, but from the very first he was a disappointment, and finally his mother had the sense to agree, on his behalf, with a suggestion of the King's that he should exchange the heritage of Columbus for a dukedom in Veragua.

Fernando Colón says that the Admiral died full of sorrow and disappointment. We do not know whether his sorrow arose exclusively from the bad faith and ingratitude of the King. He had not found what he had set out to find: no Cipangu, none of the rich cities of the Grand Khan, no route round the long peninsula to the spices of India. Most people would have been glad to accept the Castilian tenancy that the King had offered him. Most people, indeed would have settled down long ago, instead of driving themselves to death in stormy seas along fever-ridden coasts. But Columbus was not like most people. He was God's chosen vessel, chosen to loose the bonds of the ocean, to bear Christ across the waters, and to free Jerusalem from the Infidel. It is no easy matter to serve such a vessel or to win his approval. If all his men had been like the Adelantado, or Diego Méndez, of Peralonso Niño, or Vicente Yáñez Pinzón, or Michele de Cuneo, or Bartolomeo Fieschi, or Pedro de Terreros, he might perhaps have been a good viceroy and governor. But then he would hardly have found the way to the Earthly Paradise.

1451 Birth of Isabella, future Queen of Castile, at Madrigal, April 22. Birth of Cristoforo Colombo at Genoa, between August 25 and October 31.

1470—75 Columbus lives with his parents, going to sea in the summer. He is known to have sailed to Chios at least once.

1476—79 Columbus in Lisbon, earning his living as a mapmaker and perhaps as a commercial agent. He also visits England, Madeira, and Genoa.

1479 Columbus in Lisbon. Marries Felipa Moniz de Perestrello. Stays briefly on the islands of Madeira and Porto Santo.

1480—81 Birth of the Idea. Correspondence with Toscanelli. Birth of Columbus' son Diego on Porto Santo. Death of Felipa, probably in childbirth. Spain declares war on Granada.

1482—84 Columbus makes at least two voyages to Guinea. Plan presented to John II of Portugal and rejected by a Royal Commission. Columbus leaves for Spain with his son.

1484—85 Columbus in the household of the Duke of Medina Celi, from whom he tries to obtain financial backing for his plan.

1486 January 20 Columbus arrives in Cordova.
May Plan presented to Ferdinand and Isabella. A commission appointed to investigate it.

1488 January Columbus writes to John II of Portugal, again offering him his services but asking for a safe conduct in Portugal, where he fears to meet his creditors.
March 20 Reply received from John II with invitation and guarantee of safe conduct.
August 15 Columbus' son Fernando born in Cordova, to Columbus' mistress, Beatriz Enriques de Harana.
December Arrival in Lisbon of Bartolomeu Diaz, after rounding the Cape of Good Hope.

1490 Columbus' plan rejected by the Talavera Commission. Columbus' brother Bartolomeo tries to win support in England and France.

1492 January 2 Granada capitulates.
March 30 All unconverted Jews expelled from Spain.

1492 April 17 Columbus' first agreement with Ferdinand and Isabella.
May 12 Columbus goes to Palos.
August 2 The last Jews leave Spain.
August 3 The *Santa María,* the *Pinta,* and the *Niña* sail from Palos.
August 12 The *Santa María* and the *Niña* anchor at Gomera.
August 25 The *Santa María* and the *Niña* rejoin the *Pinta* at Gando on Grand Canary.
September 1 The three ships sail for Gomera.
September 6 Departure from Gomera. The voyage across the ocean begins. Course due west.
October 7 Course altered to west-southwest.
October 11 A light is seen two hours before midnight.
October 12 San Salvador sighted at dawn. Later, Columbus lands and takes possession for Spain.
October 15 The ships sail on to Santa María de la Concepción (Rum Cay).
October 16 To Fernandina (Long Island).
October 19 To Isabela (Crooked Island).
October 26 Anchors dropped at Las Islas de Arena (Little Ragged Island).
October 28 Anchors dropped in a harbor on Cuba, later called San Salvador (Bahia Bariai). Columbus thinks he has reached Cipangu, but calls the country Juana.
October 29 They sail farther west to Rio de Mares (Puerto Gibara).
October 30—31 They sail on, and meet with head winds near modern Puerto Padre. The belief spreads that this coast is part of the continent. They return to Rio de Mares.
November 12 They set off east for the Golden Isle of Babeque.
November 14—16 The ships lie at Mar de Nuestra Señora (Bahía Tánamo).
November 22 The *Pinta* sails away from the others and makes for Babeque (Great Inagua).
November 24—26 The *Santa María* and the *Niña* at Puerto Santa Catalina (Puerto Cayo Moa).
November 27—December 4 At Puerto Santo (Baracoa).
December 6 At Puerto de San Nicolao (in the modern Haiti).
December 7—14 At Puerto de la Concepción (Baie des Moustiques).
December 15 Off the River Guadalquivir (Les Trois Rivières).
December 16—18 Off the coast, near the modern Port de Paix. Quantities of gold obtained.

1492 December 20—24 At La Mar de Santo Tomás (Baie de l'Acul).

December 24 The *Santa Maria* runs aground and founders off the modern Cap Haitien.

December 26 Fortress of La Navidad founded, on the site of the modern Limonade Bord-de-Mer.

1493 January 4 Columbus leaves La Navidad in the *Niña*.

January 6 The *Pinta* rejoins the *Niña* off Monte Cristi (in the modern Dominican Republic).

January 11—16 At Puerto de las Flechas (Bahia de Samaná). The first fighting with the Indians.

January 16 The Spaniards begin the voyage home.

February 13 The *Pinta* and the *Niña* are separated by a storm.

February 15 They sight the island of Santa Maria.

February 17—24 At Santa Maria.

March 4 The *Niña* anchors in Rastelo, the outer harbor of Lisbon. Columbus dispatches a letter to the Sovereigns describing the results of his first voyage.

March 9 Columbus visits King John II at Val do Paraiso.

March 13 The *Niña* leaves Lisbon.

March 15 The *Niña* drops anchor at Palos. The *Pinta* arrives a few hours later.

April Columbus' letter printed in Barcelona soon after April 1. On or before April 30, he is officially received there by the Sovereigns.

May 28 Confirmation of Columbus' privileges.

September 25 Columbus sets out on his second voyage to the West Indies, sailing from Cadiz with 17 ships.

October 2 The fleet arrives at Grand Canary.

October 5 The fleet reaches Gomera.

October 7 Atlantic crossing begins.

November 3 Dominica sighted. Anchors dropped at Mariagalante.

November 4—10 At Guadalupe.

November 11 They pass S. Maria de Monserrate, S. Maria la Antigua, S. Maria Redonda, and anchor for the night at San Martin (Nevis).

November 12 They pass S. Jorge (St. Kitts), S. Anastasia (St. Eustatius), and S. Cristóbal (Saba).

November 14 At Santa Cruz. Skirmish with some Caribs.

November 16 They sight the Once Mil Virgines (Virgin Islands), which some of the vessels explore.

November 20—22 At San Juan Bautista (Puerto Rico).

November 23 The fleet anchors in the Bahia de las Flechas, Española.

1493 November 26 At Monte Cristi. Two bodies discovered, probably Spanish.

November 27 The fleet anchors off La Navidad, to find that the garrison has been massacred.

December 7 The fleet leaves La Navidad and sails east against the wind.

1494 January 2 Anchors dropped in a bay where Columbus founds the settlement of Isabela, in what is now the territory of the Dominican Republic.

January 6—20 Hojeda and Gorbalán explore Cibao.

February 2 Antonio de Torres leaves for Spain with 12 vessels.

March 12—29 Columbus explores Cibao and builds the fort of Santo Tomás.

April 24 Columbus sails west with the caravels *Niña, San Juan,* and *Cardera.*

April 29 They go ashore at Cabo Alfa et Omega (Cabo Maysi, Cuba).

April 30 In Puerto Grande (Bahía Guantanamo).

May 1 In harbor, at the site of the modern Santiago de Cuba.

May 3 At Cabo Cruz. Thence south toward Jamaica.

May 5 Jamaica sighted. Anchors dropped in Santa Gloria (St. Ann's Bay). A skirmish with the Indians.

May 6—9 In Puerto Bueno (Rio Bueno).

May 9—13 In the Golfo de Bien Tiempo (Montego Bay).

May 14 The ships enter the Jardin de la Reina (Laberinto de Doce Leguas, off the south coast of Cuba).

May 23 Out into the open sea.

May 30 They enter the Mar Blanco (Golfo de Batabanó).

June 12 The fleet anchors in the modern Bahía Cortés. The crews sign a statement that they believe Juana (Cuba) to be a part of the continent.

June 13 Beginning of the long eastward journey upwind.

July 18 At Cabo de Cruz, southwestern extremity of Cuba.

July 19—August 8 The fleet sails south to Jamaica, round its westernmost point, and continues along its south coast.

August 8 In the Bahia de la Vaca (Portland Bight), Jamaica.

August 20 At Cabo de San Michele Saonese (Cape Tiburon), Española.

September 14—24 At Saona. Eclipse of the moon, during which Columbus tries to determine his longitude.

September 25 The fleet passes the island of Mona.

195

1494 Columbus serously ill and in coma. Decision made to return to Isabela.
September 29 Anchors dropped at Isabela.

1495 **March 28** Columbus wins battle against Guatiguaná on the Vega Real.
June Hurricane. Three ships lost in harbor at Isabela.
October Arrival at Isabela of Juan Aguado, the Royal Inspector.

1496 **March 10** Columbus leaves for Spain with the *Niña* and a newly built ship called the *India*.
April 10—19 At Guadalupe.
April 20 Homeward journey begins.
June 11 The *Niña* and the *India* anchor at Cadiz.

1497 **May** Giovanni Caboto (John Cabot) leaves Bristol for the west. He reaches Labrador, and arrives back at Bristol at the end of July.
July 8 Vasco da Gama leaves Lisbon with four ships, intending to sail round the Cape of Good Hope to India. Columbus stays at Court for some time but spends most of the year at the monastery of Las Cuevas, Seville.

1498 **January 23** The *Niña* and the *India* leave for Española with supplies.
April John Cabot sets out on his second voyage and explores much of the eastern coast of North America.
May 30 The third voyage begins. Columbus sets out from Sanlúcar de Barrameda with six caravels.
June 7 Anchors dropped at Porto Santo.
June 10—16 At Funchal, Madeira.
June 19 Arrival at Gomera.
June 21 Three caravels set out on the direct route for Española; Columbus leaves for the Cape Verde Islands with the *Santa María de Guia, La Vaqueños,* and *El Correo*.
June 27—July 3 At the Cape Verde Islands.
July 4 Departure from São Tiago. Course southwest.
July 31 Trinidad sighted.
August 1 American mainland sighted for the first time, at the modern Punta Bombeador.
August 2 Through the Boca del Sierpe to the Punta de Arenal (Icacos Point), Trinidad.
August 4 A high wave in the Serpent's Mouth. Evening: anchors dropped at the easternmost point of Isla Gracia (Paria Peninsula).
August 5—10 West along the south coast of Isla Gracia.

1498 **August 11** *El Correo* investigates rivermouths to the south.
August 12 At El Caracol (Chacachacare) in the Boca del Dragon.
August 13 Out through the Dragon's Mouth. Belaforma (Tobago) and Asunción (Grenada) sighted. Columbus almost blind.
August 14 Columbus' fleet passes Margarita. Columbus begins to realize that he has discovered "another world," i.e., a new continent, and speculates about the Earthly Paradise.
August 19 Nearing the south coast of Española, they pass Alto Velo.
August 20—22 At Madama Beata (now Isla Beata).
August 31 Anchors dropped in the mouth of the Ozama, near the newly founded settlement of Santo Domingo.
October 18 The *Santa María de Guia* and *El Correo* sail for Spain with Columbus' report on the newfound world and its geographical position.

1499 **June** Alonso de Hojeda sails from Castile, together with Juan de la Cosa and Amerigo Vespucci. They discover the Pearl Coast west of Margarita and sail west as far as Cabo de la Vela.
September 9 Vasco da Gama in Lisbon, having sailed successfully to India. Columbus, faced with mutiny in the settlement on Española, comes to terms with Roldán, the leader of the mutineers, by the end of the month. Toward the end of the year Vicente Yañez Pinzón sails from Palos and discovers the coast of Brazil. He sails north of Cabo São Roque, explores the coast, and discovers the Amazon.

1500 **March 9** Pedro Alvares Cabral leaves Lisbon for the Indies. Discovers by accident a part of Brazil and calls it Terra de Santa Cruz.
May Gaspar Corte-Real sails from Lisbon and explores the coast of Newfoundland.
August 23 Francisco de Bobadilla arrives at Santo Domingo and places Columbus and his brothers under arrest.
October Soon after October 1, the caravel *La Gorda* leaves Española, with Columbus in irons, and reaches Cadiz before October 31. Meanwhile Rodrigo de Bastidas leaves with Juan de la Cosa and sails along the coast from the Pearl Coast as far as the modern Gulf of Darien.
December 12 Ferdinand and Isabella hear of Columbus' arrest and send orders for his release.
December 17 Columbus and his brothers received by Ferdinand and Isabella at Granada.

1501 Amerigo Vespucci sets out in the Portuguese service and sails along the coasts of Brazil and Argentina.
September 3 Nicolás de Ovando appointed governor of the West Indies.

1502 **February 10** Vasco da Gama leaves Lisbon on his second voyage to India.
February 13 Ovando sails from Cadiz.
May 9 Columbus sails from Cadiz on his fourth voyage with the caravels *La Capitana,* the *Santiago, La Gallego,* and the *Viscayno.*
May 13 Fleet off Arzila, Morocco.
May 24 Fleet at Maspalomas, Grand Canary.
May 25 Fleet leaves Grand Canary. Course west by south.
June 15 Anchors dropped at Matininó (Martinique).
June 29 Fleet off Santo Domingo. Permission to enter harbor refused.
June 30 Hurricane.
July 3 The ships rejoin in Azua (Puerto Viejo de Azua), Española.
July 14 Fleet leaves Brazil harbor (modern Jacmel, Haiti).
July 17 Fleet at Los Poros (Morant Cays, a small island southeast of Jamaica).
July 24—27 At an island in the Jardin de la Reina (perhaps the modern Cayo Largo).
July 30 At Bonacca.
August 1—7 At the Punta Caxinas (Cabo Honduras, in the modern Honduras).
August 8—September 14 Fleet sailing upwind to the east.
September 14 Cabo Gracias a Diós rounded.
September 16 They anchor in the Rio de los Desastres (the Rio Grande or Bluefields in the modern Nicaragua).
September 25—October 4 At La Huerta (Puerto Limón in the modern Costa Rica).
October 5 In Cerebaru (Bahia Almirante in the modern Panama).
October 6—16 In Aburema (Laguna Chiriqui).
October 17 Off Cativa (Rio Chererequi).
November 2—9 At Puerto Bello.
November 10—25 At Puerto de Bastimentos (Nombre de Dios).
November 26—December 5 At Retrete (Puerto Escribanos).
December 5 Back at Puerto Bello.
December 6—17 Fleet at sea, through heavy storms.
December 17—20 In Puerto Gordo (Bahia Manzanilla, at the modern Colón, in the mouth of the Panama Canal).

1502 **December 20—25** More heavy storms.
December 25—31 Back in Puerto Gordo.

1503 **January 1—3** In Puerto Gordo.
January 6 Anchors dropped off the Rio Belén.
January 9—10 Fleet enters the Rio Belén.
February Exploration of Veragua. Columbus founds the settlement of Santa Maria de Belén.
April 6 Fighting with Indians in Belén. Cacique Quibian captured.
April 16 Departure from Belén. *La Gallego* is left in the river.
April 23 In Puerto Bello. The *Viscayno* is left there.
May 1 At Cabo Marmóreo (Cabo Tiburón, Colombia). Course set north for Española.
May 10 They pass Las Tortugas (Little Cayman and Cayman Brac).
May 13—20 At an island in the Jardin de la Reina.
June 20 Anchors dropped on south coast of Cuba, east of Cabo de Cruz, probably on the site of the modern Puerto Pilón.
June 25 *La Capitana* and the *Santiago* are beached at Santa Gloria (St. Ann's Bay), Jamaica.
July 7 Columbus completes his letter to Ferdinand and Isabella.
July 17 Diego Méndez and Bartolomeo Fieschi leave for Española, in native canoes.

1504 **January 2** Mutiny on Española, led by Francisco and Diego de Porras.
February 29 Total eclipse of the moon, exploited by Columbus to impress the natives and to determine his longitude.
May 17 Mutiny suppressed.
June 29 Columbus and his party rescued by a caravel which had been hired by Méndez.
August 13 They reach Santo Domingo.
September 12 Columbus sails from Santo Domingo.
November 7 Anchors dropped at Sanlúcar de Barrameda near Cadiz.
November 26 Queen Isabella dies.

1505 **May** Columbus rides to the Court at Segovia on a mule.
October Columbus follows the Court to Salamanca and refuses Ferdinand's offer of a dependency in Spain in exchange for his viceroyalty in the Indies.

1506 **April** Columbus follows the Court to Valladolid and sends his brother Bartolomeo to negotiate with Queen Juana.
May 20 Death of Columbus at Valladolid.

Sources, illustrations

All the illustrations other than those listed below are the original work of the author. Figures in bold type indicate pages.

4. Copied from a detail in Juan de la Cosa's *Mapa Mundi,* 1500, MS, Museo Naval, Madrid. **11.** Ptolemy, copied from a relief by Giotto and Andrea Pisano in the Campanile in Florence. **12.** The Emperor Augustus, miniature in the Bibliothèque Nationale, Paris. Macrobius' map, from a manuscript of Isidore of Seville, University Library, Leyden. **13.** The O—T map is from the manuscript of Beatus, Bibliothèque Nationale, Paris. **14.** Simplified adaptation of a map in Ptolemy's *Cosmographia,* Ulm, 1486. **15.** Detail from Hanns Rüst's map of the world, Nuremberg, *c.* 1495. **16.** Henricus Martellus' map of the world, MS, *c.* 1490, Yale University Library, New Haven. **19.** Adapted from a mural by Giorgio Vasari, Palazzo Vecchio, Florence. **22.** Woodcut by Tobias Stimmer in Jovius' *Elogia Virorum Bellica Virtute Illustrium,* Basle, 1575. **30.** Drawing by Columbus in Pierre d'Ailly's *Imago Mundi,* Biblioteca Columbina, Seville. **32.** Copied from an original by an unknown artist, Windsor Castle. **33.** Copied from an original by Bartolomé Bermejo (?), Museo del Prado, Madrid. **36.** Ferdinand and Isabella. Woodcut in Ludolphus of Sachsen's *Vita Christi Cartuxano,* Alcala de Henares, 1502. **37.** Adapted from a fifteenth-century marble sculpture, Victoria and Albert Museum, London. **54.** Detail from a woodcut in the *Libra de las Dones* by Cardinal Ximenes, Barcelona, 1496. **62.** Section of a map by Jacme Bertran, 1482, MS, Archivio di Stato, Florence. **70.** Woodcut from Girolamo Benzoni's *La Historia del Mondo Nuevo,* Venice, 1563. **75.** Woodcut from Gonzalo de Oviedo's *La Historia General de las Indias,* Salamanca, 1547. **76—77.** Taino artifacts. Museo Nacional, Santo Domingo. **81.** Man smoking. Detail from a woodcut in Thevet's *Singularitez,* Paris, 1558. Nosepipe. From a woodcut in Oviedo's *La Hystoria General,* Salamanca, 1547. **90.** Taino figurine, Museo Nacional, Santo Domingo. **91.** Woodcut from Oviedo's *La Hystoria General,* Salamanca, 1547. **95.** Drawing by Columbus, January, 1493, Duke of Alba's Archive, Madrid. **96.** Woodcut from Oviedo's *La Hystoria General,* Salamanca, 1547. **104.** Gold coin, 4 *excellentes,* minted in 1474—1516, $1\frac{3}{16}$ inches in diameter. **105.** Bronze medallion, Bibliothèque Nationale, Paris. **106—7.** Woodcuts from the printed version of Columbus' letter, Basle, 1493. **109.** Portrait by an unknown artist, Civico Museo Giovio, Como. **115.** Woodcut, 1505. **123.** Woodcut from Oviedo's *La Hystoria General,* Salamanca, 1547. **127.** Woodcut from Sebastian Münster's *Cosmographey,* Basle, 1598. **128.** Simplified copy of Juan de la Cosa's *Mapa Mundi,* 1500, MS, Museo Naval, Madrid. **129.** Woodcut from Benedetto Bordone's *Isolario,* Venice, 1528. **131.** Taino figure, Museo Nacional, Santo Domingo. **134.** Woodcut from the *Epistola Albericij, De Nouo Mundo,* Rostock, 1505. **137.** Copy from a drawing in the MS of Pedro Barreto de Rezense's *Brieve Tratado ou Epilogo dos Vizos-Reys de India,* Bibliothèque Nationale, Paris. **151.** Copy of a plan in W. Bigge's *A Summarie and True Discourse of Sir Frances Drakes West Indian Voyage,* London, 1589. **153.** Portrait by Ridolfo Ghirlandaio (?), d. 1561, Museo Navale, Pegli. **154.** MS, Palazzo Municipale, Genoa. **156.** Juan de la Cosa's *Mapa Mundi,* 1500, MS, Museo Naval, Madrid. **158.** Title page of Angelo Trevigiano's *Libretto,* Venice, 1504, Biblioteca Marciana, Venice. **161.** Simplified adaptation of the Cantino map, 1502, MS, Biblioteca Estense, Modena. **162.** Engraving from Braun and Hogenberg's *Civitates Orbis Terrarum,* 1572—1618. **164, 165, 173.** From the Robert Woods Bliss Collection, National Gallery of Art, Washington. **176—77.** Facsimile reproduction from G. E. Nunn's *The Geographical Conceptions of Columbus,* New York, 1924. **184.** Fragment of a fifteenth-century marble sarcophagus, Museo Marés, Barcelona. **186—88.** Martin Waldseemüller's *Universalis Cosmographia,* Saint-Dié, Strasbourg, 1507. **190.** From drawings in John Boyd Thatcher's *Christopher Columbus,* New York, 1903.

Bibliography

Aeneas Sylvius (Pope Pius II), Historia Rerum ubique Gestarum, Venice, 1477. Columbus' personal copy, containing transcriptions of the Toscanelli letters, and marginal notes, in the Biblioteca Columbina, Seville.

d'Ailly, Pierre, Ymago Mundi, Louvain, 1480 (1483?). Columbus' own copy, with marginal notes, in the Biblioteca Columbina, Seville.

Albertus Magnus, Opera (ed. Jammy), Lyon, 1651.

Almagia, Roberto, Amerigo Vespucci, Rome, 1926;
—I primi esploratori dell' America, Rome, 1937;
—Recenti scritti su Colombo, *Archivio di Storia della Scienza,* Vol. II, 1926;
—Una carta attribuita a Cristoforo Colombo, *Rendiconti dell' Accademia dei Lincei,* June, 1925.

Altolaguirre, Angel, Colón Español?, Madrid, 1923;
—Cristóbal Colón y Pablo del Pozo Toscanelli, Madrid, 1903;
—Llegada de Cristóbal Colón à Portugal, *Boletin de la R. Academia de la Historia,* Vol. XXI, Madrid, 1892.

Anderson, R., America Not Discovered by Columbus, Chicago, 1891.

Anderson, R. C., Italian Naval Architecture about 1445, *Mariners' Mirror,* Vol. XI.

de Artiñano, G., La Arquitectura Naval Española, Madrid, 1920.

Assereto, Ugo, La data di nascita di Cr. Colombo, Spezia, 1904.

Babcock, W. H., Antilia and the Antilles, *Geographical Review,* Vol. IX, 1920;
—Legendary Islands of the Atlantic, New York, 1922.

Bacon, Roger, Opus Majus (ed. Bridges), Oxford, 1897.

de Barros, João, Da Asia, Venice, 1551.

Beazley, Sir Raymond, The Dawn of Modern Geography, 3 vols., Oxford, 1897—1906.

Beltran y Rozpide, Ricardo, Cristóbal Colón Genoves?, Madrid, 1925.

Bensaude, Joaquim, Histoire de la science nautique portugaise à l'époque des grandes découvertes. Collection de documents publiés par ordre du Ministère de l'Instruction Publique de la République Portugaise, 1914—1919, Vol. I: Regimento do astrolabio e do quadrante: tractato da sphera do mundo, Munich, 1914;
—L'astronomie nautique au Portugal à l'époque des grandes découvertes, Berne, 1912.

Berger, Hugo, Die geographischen Fragmente des Eratosthenes, Leipzig, 1880.

Bernáldez, Andres, Historia de los Reyes católicos D. Fernando y Da. Isabel, Biblioteca de Autores Españoles, Vol. LXX, Madrid, 1878.

Blake, John William, Europeans in West Africa, 1450—1560, Hakluyt Society, Glasgow, 1942.

Bove, Salvador, Le beat R. Lull é lo descubrimient des Amériques, *Revisita Luliana,* Barcelona, 1902.

Brebner, John, The Explorers of North America, 1492—1806, London, 1933.

Brøgger, A. W., Vinlandsferderne, Oslo, 1937.

Buron, Edmond (ed. and trans.), The Imago Mundi of Pierre d'Ailly, with Columbus' notes, Paris, 1930.

Caddeo, R. (ed.), Historie della vita e dei fatti di Cristoforo Colombo per D. Fernando Colombo suo figlio, Milan, 1930.

Calzada, Rafael, La patria de Colón, Buenos Aires, 1920.

Capistrano de Abreu, João, O Descobrimento do Brasil pelos Portugueses, Rio de Janeiro, 1929.

Caraci, Giuseppe, The Reputed Inclusion of Florida in the Oldest Nautical Maps of the New World, *Imago Mundi,* Vol. XV;
The Vespuccian Problems — What Point Have They Reached?, *Imago Mundi,* Vol. XVIII.

Carnabià, Romulo, La carta de navegar atribuida a Toscanelli, Buenos Aires, 1932.
—La patria de Cristóbal Colón, Buenos Aires, 1923.

Charcot, G. B., Christophe Colomb vu par un marin, Paris, 1928.

Colmiero, Manuel, Informe de la R. Academia de la Historia al gobierno de S.M. sobre el supuesto hallazgo de los verdaderos restos de Cristóbal Colón en la iglesia catedral de Santo Domingo, Madrid, 1879.

Colón, Fernando, Historia del S. D. Fernando Colombo, Nella quale s'ha particulare e vera relatione dell' Ammiraglio D. Cristoforo Colombo, suo padre, Nuovamente di lingua spanuola tradotte nell'Italiana dal S. Alfonso Ulloa, Venice, 1571.

Cortesão, Armando, Cartografia e cartografos portugueses dos seculos XV e XVI, Lisbon, 1935;
—The Nautical Chart of 1424; Coimbra, 1954.

Cortesão, A. & A. Teixeira De Mota, Portugaliae monumenta cartographica, 5 vols., Lisbon, 1960.

Cortesão, Jaime, The National Secret of the Portuguese Discoveries of the Fifteenth Century, London, n. d.;
—The Pre-Columbian Discovery of America, *Geographical Journal,* Vol. 39, 1937.

Crichton-Mitchell, A., The Discovery of the Magnetic Declination, *Terrestrial Magnetism and Atmospheric Electricity,* September, 1937.

Destombes, Marcel (ed.), Mappemondes A. D. 1200—1500, Amsterdam, 1964.

Dockstader, Frederick J., Indian Art in Middle America, Milan, 1964.

Dourster, Horace, Dictionnaire universel des poids et mesures anciens et modernes, Antwerp, 1840.

van Driel, A., Tonnage Measurement, a Historical and Critical Essay, The Hague, 1925.

Duff, Charles, The Truth about Columbus, New York, 1936.

Duro, Cesáreo Fernández, Colón y Pinzón, Madrid, 1883;
—Pinzón en el descubrimiento de las Indias, Madrid, 1892.

Fischer, Josef & Franz von Wieser, Die älteste Karte mit dem Namen Amerika von 1507 und die Carta marina von 1516, Innsbruck, 1903.

Fontoura da Costa, A., A marinharia dos descobrimentos, Lisbon, 1933.

Garcia de la Riega, D. Celso, Colón español, su origin e su patria, Madrid, 1914.

Genova, Citta di, Cristoforo Colombo, documenti & prove della sua appartenenza a Genova, Bergamo, 1931.

Gould, Alice B., Nueva lista documentada de los tripulantes de Colón en 1492, *Boletin de la Real Academia de la Historia*, Vols. 85—88, 90, 92, 110, 111.

Greenlee, William Brooks (ed.), The Voyage of Pedro Alvares Cabral to Brazil and India from Contemporary Documents and Narratives, Hakluyt Society, Oxford, 1938.

Guillén y Tato, J. F., La carabela Santa María, Madrid, 1927;
—La parla marinera en el Diario del primer viaje de Cristóbal Colón, Madrid, 1951.

Harrisse, Henry, Christophe Colomb, Paris, 1884;
—Christophe Colomb devant l'histoire, Paris, 1892;
—Christopher Columbus and the Bank of St. George, New York, 1888;
—Don Fernando Colón, historiador de su padre, Seville, 1871;
—Fernand Colomb, sa vie, ses oeuvres, Paris, 1872;
—Jean et Sebastien Cabot, Paris, 1872;
—Les sépultures de Christophe Colomb, Paris, 1879;
—Letters of Christopher Columbus describing his first voyage to the Western Hemisphere, New York, 1865;
—The Discovery of North America, London—Paris, 1892.

Hellman, Gustav, Die Anfänge der magnetischen Beobachtungen, *Zeitschrift der Gesellschaft für Erdkunde*, Berlin, 1897.

Helps, Arthur, The Life of Las Casas, the Apostle of the Indies, London, 1868;
—The Spanish Conquest of America, 4 vols., London, 1855—61.

Hennig, Richard, Atlantische Fabelinseln und Entdeckung von Amerika, *Historische Zeitschrift*, 1936;
—Columbus und seine Tat, Bremen, 1940;
—Die These einer vorcolombischen portugiesischen Geheimkenntnis von Amerika, *Historische Vierteljahrschrift*, Vol. XXX, 1936;
—Terrae Incognitae, 4 vols., Leyden, 1936—39.

Hughes, Luigi, La lettera di Paolo di Pozzo Toscanelli a Fernam Martins, Casale Monferrato, 1902;
—L'opera scientifica de Christoforo Colombo, Turin, 1892.

Ingstad, Helge, Västervägen till Vinland, Stockholm, 1965.

Irving, Washington, A History of the Life and Voyages of Christopher Columbus, 4 vols., London, 1828.

Jacob, Ernst Gerhard, Christoph Colombus, Bordbuch, Briefe, Berichte, Dokumente, Eschwege, 1956.

Jane, Cecil (ed.), Select Documents Illustrating the Four Voyages of Columbus, 2 vols., Hakluyt Society, London, 1932, 1933.

Jayne, K. G., Vasco da Gama and His Successors, London, 1910.

Jones, Gwyn, The Norse Atlantic Saga, Worcester, 1964.

Kahle, Paul, Die verschollene Columbus-Karte von 1488, Berlin, 1933.

Keen, Benjamin (ed. and trans.), The Life of the Admiral Christopher Columbus by His Son Ferdinand, New Jersey, 1959.

Keuning, J., The History of Geographical Map Projections until 1600, *Imago Mundi*, Vol. XII.

Kimble, George H. T., Geography in the Middle Ages, London, 1938.

Kretschmer, Konrad, Atlas zur "Entdeckung Amerikas," Berlin, 1892.
—Die Entdeckung Amerikas in ihrer Bedeutung für die Geschichte des Weltbildes, Berlin, 1892.

Landström, Björn, The Ship, Weert, 1961;
—The Quest for India, Stockholm, 1964.

Larsen, Sofus, Nordamerikas opdagelse 20 aar for Columbus, *Geografisk Tidskrift*, Copenhagen, 1925.

de Las Casas, Bartolomé, Historia de las Indias, Colección de documentos ineditos para historia de España, Vols. 62—66, Madrid, 1875—76;
—El Libro de la Primera Navegación, MS, Biblioteca Nacional, Madrid.

Lehmann, Henri, L'Art précolombien, Paris, 1960.

Letts, M. (ed.), Mandeville's Travels, Texts and Translations, 2 vols., Hakluyt Society, London, 1953;
—Sir John Mandeville, the Man and His Book, London, 1949.

Levillier, R., New Light on Vespucci's Third Voyage, *Imago Mundi*, Vol. XI.

de Lollis, Cesare, Cristoforo Colombo nella legenda e nella storia, Milan, 1892;
—Qui a découvert l'Amérique?, *Revue des Revues*, Paris, January 1898.

Lothrop, S. K., W. F. Foshag & Joy Mahler, Robert Woods Bliss Collection, Pre-Columbian Art, Basle and Aylesbury, 1959.

Lovén, Sven, Origins of the Tainan Culture, West Indies, Gothenburg, 1935.

Lullus, Raimundus, Questiones per Artem Demonstrativam, Lyon, 1491.

de Madariaga, Salvador, Christopher Columbus, Norwich, 1949.

Magnaghi, Alberto, La storia della scoperta d'America, Turin, 1937;
—Precursori di Colombo?, Rome, 1935;
—Questioni Colombiane, Naples, 1939;
—Sui presunti errori attribuiti a Colombo nella determinazione delle latitudini, *Bolletino della R. Societa Geografica Italiana*, Vols. IX—XII, 1928.

Mangones, Edmond & Louis Maximilien, L'Art précolombien d'Haiti, Port-au-Prince, 1941.

Markham, Sir Clements, The Journal of Christopher Columbus and Documents Relating to the Voyages of John Cabot and Gaspar Cortereal, Hakluyt Society, London, 1893;
—The Letters of Amerigo Vespucci, Hakluyt Society, London, 1874.

Menéndez Pidal, Ramón, La Lengua de Cristóbal Colón, Buenos Aires, 1942.

Morison, Samuel Eliot, Admiral of the Ocean Sea, 2 vols., Boston, 1942;
—Journals and Other Documents on the Life and Voyages of Christopher Columbus, New York, 1963.

Morison, Samuel Eliot & Mauricio Obregón, The Caribbean as Columbus Saw It, Boston, 1964.

Moule, A. C. & Paul Pelliot (ed. and trans.), Marco Polo: The Description of the World, 2 vols., London, 1938.

Nance, R. Morton, The Ship of the Renaissance, *Mariners' Mirror*, Vol. XLI.

de Navarrete, Martín Fernández, Colección de los viajes y descubrimientos que hicieron por mar los Españoles, Madrid, 1825—37.

Nordenskiöld, A. E., Periplus, Stockholm, 1897.

Nowell, Charles E., The Discovery of Brazil—Accidental or Intentional?, *Hispanic-American Historical Review*, Vol. XVI, 1936.

Nunn, George E., Marinus of Tyre's Place in the Columbus Concepts, *Imago Mundi*, Vol. II;
—The Geographical Conceptions of Columbus, New York, 1924;
—The Mappemonde of Juan de la Cosa, New York, 1934;
—The Three Maplets Attributed to Bartholomew Columbus, *Imago Mundi*, Vol. IX.

de Oviedo y Valdés, Gonzalo Fernández, Historia general de las Indias, Salamanca, 1547.

Palacio, Garcia, Instrucción Náutica, Mexico, 1587.

Parry, J. H., The Age of Reconnaissance, London, 1963.

Payne, Edward John, History of the New World Called America, Oxford, 1892.

Peres, Damião, Historia dos descobrimentos Portugueses, Oporto, 1943.

Peretti, Christophe Colomb, Français, Corse et Calvais, Paris, 1888.

Peter Martyr Anglerius, De Orbe Novo (ed. F. A. MacNutt), New York, 1912.

Pleitos de Colon, Colección de documentos inéditos para la historia de España, Series II, Vols. 7 and 8, Madrid, 1875.

Prescott, William H., History of the Reign of Ferdinand and Isabella the Catholic, Liverpool, 1962.

Prestage, Edgar, The Portuguese Pioneers, London, 1933.

Raccolta di documenti e studi pubblicati dalla R. Commissione Columbiana pel quarto centenario dalla scoperta dell' America, 15 vols., Rome, 1892—96.

Ravenstein, E. G., Martin Behaim, His Life and His Globe, London, 1908;
—The Journal of the First Voyage of Vasco da Gama, 1497—1499, Hakluyt Society, London, 1898.

Ricart, José Gudiol, Pintura gótica, *Ars Hispaniae,* Vol. IX, Madrid, 1955.

Roma Machado de Faria e Maia, Carlos, Prioridade dos portugueses no descobrimento da America do Norte e ilhas de America Central, Lisbon, 1931.

de la Roncière, Charles, La Carte de Christophe Colomb, Paris, 1924.

Roukema, E., A Discovery of Yucatan prior to 1503, *Imago Mundi,* Vol. XIII;
—Brazil in the Cantino Map, *Imago Mundi,* Vol. XVII;
—Some Remarks on the La Cosa Map, *Imago Mundi,* Vol. XIV;
—The Mythical "First Voyage" of the Soderini Letter, *Imago Mundi,* Vol. XVI.

Ruge, Sophus, Columbus, Berlin, 1902;
—Die Entdeckungsgeschichte der Neuen Welt, Hamburgische Festschrift zur Erinnerung an die Entdeckung Amerikas, Hamburg, 1892;
—Die Weltanschauung des Columbus, Dresden, 1876.

Salembier, Louis, Pierre d'Ailly and the Discovery of America, *Historical Records and Studies,* Vol. VII, 1924.

Sanchez, Prudencio Otero, España, patria de Colón, Madrid, 1922.

Sanz, Carlos, Carta marina de 1516, Madrid, n.d.;
—(ed.) Diario de Colón, Madrid, 1962;
—La carta de Colón 15 febrero—14 marzo 1493, Madrid, 1961;
—Mapa universal de 1507, Madrid, n.d.

Skelton, R. A., Explorers' Maps, London, 1958.

Stanley, Henry E. J., The Three Voyages of Vasco da Gama and His Viceroyalty, Hakluyt Society, London, 1869.

Stevens, B. F., Christopher Columbus, His Own Book of Privileges, London, 1893.

Sumien, N., La correspondance du savant florentin Paolo di Pozzo Toscanelli avec Christophe Colomb, Paris, 1927.

Sølver, Carl V., Imago Mundi, skitser fra de store opdagelsers tid, Odense, 1951.

Thacher, John Boyd, Christopher Columbus, His life, his work, his remains as revealed by original printed and manuscript records together with an essay on Peter Martyr of Anghera and Bartolomé de las Casas, the first historians of America, 6 vols., New York, 1903—4.

Thomson, J. Oliver, History of Ancient Geography, Cambridge, 1948.

Ulloa, Luis, El predescubrimiento hispano-catalano de America en 1477, Paris, 1928;
—Noves proves de la catalanitat de Colón, Paris, 1927.

Unger, E., From the Cosmos Picture to the World Map, *Imago Mundi,* Vol. II.

Uzielli, Gustavo, Paolo del Pozzo Toscanelli, iniziatore della scoperta, Florence, 1892.

de Vaudrey-Heathcote, N. H., Christopher Columbus and the Discovery of Magnetic Variation, *Science Progress,* No. 105, London, 1932.

Vignaud, Henri, Études critiques sur la vie de Christophe Colomb avant ses découvertes, Paris, 1905;
—Histoire critique de la grande enterprise de Christophe Colomb, Paris, 1911;
—Le vrai Christophe Colomb et la legende, Paris, 1921;
—La lettre et la carte de Toscanelli, Paris, 1901;
—The real birth-date of Christopher Columbus 1451, London, 1903;
—Toscanelli and Columbus, London, 1902.

Wagner, Henry R., Marco Polo's Narrative Becomes Propaganda to Inspire Colón, *Imago Mundi,* VI.

Wagner, Hermann, Die Reproduktion der Toscanelli-Karte vom Jahre 1474, *Göttingischen Gelehrten Nachrichten,* No. 3, 1894.

Waters, D. W., The Art of Navigation in England in Elizabethan and Early Stuart Times, London, 1958.

Williamson, James A., The Cabot Voyages and Bristol Discovery under Henry VII, Hakluyt Society, Glasgow, 1962;
—The Early Falsifications of Western Indian Latitudes, *Geographical Journal,* March, 1930.

Winsor, Justin (ed.), Narrative and Critical History of America, 8 vols., Boston, 1884—89.

Winter, Heinrich, Die Erkenntnis der magnetischen Missweisung und ihr Einfluss auf die Kartographie, Extraits des Comptes Rendus du Congrès International de Géographie, Amsterdam, 1938;
—Die katalanische Nao von 1450, Magdeburg, 1956;
—The Origin of the Sea Chart, *Imago Mundi,* Vol. XIII.

Zechlin, Egmont, Das Problem der vorcolombischen Entdeckung Amerikas, *Historische Zeitschrift,* 1935;
—Maritime Weltgeschichte, Rendsburg, 1947.

Index

202

204

205

DESIGN BY BJÖRN LANDSTRÖM

MAP LETTERING BY OLOF LANDSTRÖM

TRANSLATED FROM THE SWEDISH BY MICHAEL PHILLIPS AND HUGH W. STUBBS

PRODUCED BY INTERNATIONAL BOOK PRODUCTION, STOCKHOLM

SET WITH 10-PT. TIMES NEW ROMAN TYPE BY

LYCKES FILMSATS AB, GOTHENBURG

PRINTED AND BOUND BY ESSELTE AB, STOCKHOLM

LMB "INDIA" MATT-COATED PAPER FROM

LESSEBO AB, LESSEBO, SWEDEN

PRINTED IN SWEDEN

se y puedo dezir y todas las tengo por de sus altezas qual dellas pueden disponer como y tan co plidamente como delos Reynos de castilla en esta española en el lugar mas conuenible y mejor comarca para las minas del oro y de todo trato asi dela tierra firme de aqua como de aquella dealla del gran can adonde hauria grand trato e ganancia he tomado possession de vna villa gran de ala qual puse nombre la villa de nauidad: y en ella he fecho fuerza y fortaleza que ya a estas horas estara del todo acabada y he dexado en ella gente que abasta para semejante fecho con armas y artellarias e vituallas por mas de vn año y fusta y maestro dela mar en todas artes para fazer otras y grande amistad con el Rey de aquella tierra en tanto grado que se preciaua de me llamar y e tener por hermano e haũ que le mudase la voluntad a hofender esta gente el ni los suyos no saben que sean armas y andan desnudos como ya he dicho son los mas temerosos que ay en el mundo asi que solamente la gente que alla queda es para destroir toda aquella tierra y es ysla sin peligro de sus personas sabiendose regir en todas estas islas me parece que todos los ombres sean contentos con vna muger i a su maioral o Rey dan fasta veynte. las mugeres me parece que trabajan mas que los ombres ni he podido entender si tienen bienes propios que me parecio ver que aquello que vno tenia todos hazian parte en especial delas cosas comederas en estas islas fasta aqui no he hallado ombres mo… …antes es toda gente de muy lindo acatamiento ni son neg… …orredios y no se crian adonde ay i peto demasiado delos… …grand fuerça puesto que es di distinta dela liña i qui n… …ay montañas grandes: ay tenia a fuerça el frio este yu… …ne con la ayuda delas viandas comen con especias mu… …ostruos no he hallado ni noticia saluo de vna ysla… …yndias que es poblada de vna gente que tienen en tod… …omen carne vmana estos tienen muchas canaus con las… …y toman quanto pueden ellos no son mas disformes… …traer los cabellos largos como mugeres y vsan arco… …con vn palillo al cabo por defecto de fierro que no tienen… …de demasiado grado couardes mas yo no los tengo… …aquellos que trata con las mugeres de matremonio que es la… …islas que se falla enla qual no ay hombre ninguno: ellas no… …omo los sobre dichos de cañas y se arman y cobigan con… …ysla me seguran mayor que la española en que las p… …o si cuento y destas y delas otras traigo comigo… …o solamente que sea fecho este viage que fue asi de co… …o quanto ouieren menester con muy poquita ayuda… …ó quanto sus altezas mandaran cargar y almastica q… …no se ha fallado saluo en grecia en la ysla de xio y… …quanto mandaran cargar y esclauos quantos mand… …uer fallado ruybaruo y canela e otras mil cosas… …que yo alla dexo porque yo no me he detenido ni… …de nauegar solamente en la villa de nauidad en… …a verdad mucho mas ficiera si los nauios me sir… …y eterno dios nuestro señor el qual da a todos… …que parecen imposibles: y esta señaladamente fue la vna por q… …o exemplo todo va por coniectura sin allegar de vista saluo comprendiendo a tanto que los oyentes los mas escuchauan e juzgauan mas por fabla que por poca… dello asi que pues nuestro Redemtor dio esta victoria A nuestros Illustrisimos rey e reyna… reynos famosos de… alta cosa A donde toda

180